MARCO  POLO

ICELAND

www.marco-polo.com

Sightseeing Highlights

The list of sights is long, but what are the highlights on Iceland? Does Reykjavík have to be seen? Is a trip into the interior worthwhile? Can you see all the important sights by following the Ring Road around Iceland? To make the decision easier for you we've put together everything here that you should not miss under any circumstances.

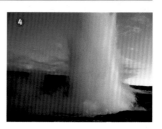

❸ ✶✶ Þingvellir
One of the world's oldest parliaments met here. Þingvellir has been on the UNESCO world heritage list since 2004.
page 303

❹ ✶✶ Haukadalur
Iceland's best known geothermal region. Strokkur geyser sends up its fountain of water every few minutes.
page 158

❶ ✶✶ Reykjavík
The country's best museums are located in Iceland's capital. Reykjavík's nightlife is legendary.
page 220

❺ ✶✶ Gullfoss
The »Golden Fall« is one of the most impressive waterfalls on Iceland.
page 157

❷ ✶✶ Blue Lagoon
Total wellness on Reykjanes Peninsula. A bath in the midst of volcanoes is a must on every trip to Iceland.
page 216

❻ ✶✶ Hekla
Changing landscape. The regular eruptions of the active volcano Hekla see to it that appearances change.
page 166

Do You Feel Like ...

... Iceland just the way you want it? Maybe these suggestions will help; they will make you run hot or cold.

FIRE

WATER

ICE

WHALES

VIKINGS

MUSIC

Perlan in Reykjavík: hot water tanks can't look better than this

A restful place under Iceland's open sky at Jökulsárlón

Romantic: on the Golden Circle between Þingvellir and Laugarvatn

PRACTICAL INFORMATION

PRICE CATEGORIES
Restaurants
(main dish without a drink)
££££ = over 4000 ISK
£££ = 3000 – 4000 ISK
££ = 2000 – 3000 ISK
£ = up to 2000 ISK
Hotels (double room)
££££ = over 35 000 ISK
£££ = 22 000 – 35 000 ISK
££ = 12 000 – 22 000 ISK
£ = up to 12 000 ISK
Note
Billable service telephone numbers are marked with an asterisk: *0180…

BACKGROUND

Information about the largest volcanic island in the world, the country and its people, economy and politics, society and everyday life

Facts

Nature and Environment

What are pseudo craters, solfataras and fumaroles? How does a geyser work? Are the Iceland glaciers shrinking too? What is so special about the Icelandic horse? Does Iceland have an army? Who settled this island in the North Atlantic? When did the country become independent?

Iceland is a very young island, which only emerged from the sea 20 million years ago. The island owes its existence to a **hot spot**, where magma rises continuously from the bowels of the earth; its centre is assumed to lie under the Vatnajökull, the largest glacier in Europe. Forming part of the Mid-Atlantic Ridge, Iceland is one of the few sections that peak out of the sea. The ridge runs from the southwest to the northeast across the island, a geologically highly active strip some 50km/31 miles wide, with numerous volcanoes, hot springs and high-temperature areas.

Island geology

According to the theory of plate tectonics, the earth's surface consists of several plates, floating on the underlying liquid magma. On the plates' edges, the Earth's crust is particularly thin – and here in Iceland, two tectonic plates drift apart. Depending on the direction of the plates' movement, along the boundaries mountain ranges rise up, earthquakes or volcanic eruptions happen, or the earth's crust is restructured. Along the Mid-Atlantic Ridge, the North American and the Eurasian continental plates drift apart by about two centimetres each year, with rising magma constantly filling up the gap created.

Split island

That Iceland is an island split in two can clearly be seen along the **Almannagjá Gorge at Þingvellir**, which scores the landscape for several kilometres. Steep, craggy walls of dark basalt, along with narrow gorges and trenches characterize this dramatic landscape. Geology doesn't get more vivid than here at the interface of two continental plates, where visitors can stand with one leg in Europe and the other in America.

PICTURE-PERFECT VOLCANOES

On Iceland, traces of volcanism are everywhere. Thirty still active volcanoes constantly change the island's surface as well as its geo-

Fjaðrárgljúfur: the impressive gorge is two million years old. It was created by the river Fjarðra near Kirkjubæjarklaustur.

logical make-up. How active the Icelandic volcanoes have been over the past 500 years is demonstrated by the fact that around a third of the lava worldwide was produced by volcanoes on Iceland. It comes as no surprise then that the island consists nearly exclusively of basalt rock, tuff (rock composed of volcanic ash) and lava.

Types of volcano Iceland features practically all the different types of volcano. The shape a volcano has depends on many factors, such as the amount and temperature of the lava or the number of eruptions. Generally, scientists distinguish between fissure volcanoes and central volcanoes. With fissure volcanoes, the lava extrudes along a cleft which can be kilometres long and can also result in smaller craters that may sometimes merge into one. During the eruption on the Westman Islands (the small archipelago south of Iceland) in 1973, such a cleft opened up; the »fire canyon« of Eldgjá and the Laki volcanic fissure also fall into this category.

Alongside fissure volcanoes, Iceland also has many central volcanoes, divided into various subgroups. The most common are stratovolcanoes, also called composite volcanoes, which can be recognized by their high, perfectly formed, relatively steep cones. These volcanic cones usually only form over the course of several eruptions. Not all volcanoes in Iceland appear as such at first glance, as some lie hidden below glaciers. Examples of **stratovolcanoes** are Snæfellsjökull, Eyjafjallajökull, Öræfajökull and the highest mountain in Iceland, Hvannadalshnúkur.

Shield volcanoes and table mountains Shield volcanoes have very flat slopes, which is why they can sometimes be difficult to recognise as volcanoes. Formed by eruptions that brought up thin liquid lava but little ash, this otherwise fairly rare type is quite common in Iceland where some 20 shield volcanoes formed following the last Ice Age.

Skjaldbreiður at Þingvellir is a typical shield volcano, and in fact gave this type of volcano its name. Also of volcanic origin are slag cones, ash cones, maars and table mountains. The latter emerged during the last Ice Age, when the volcanoes erupted under a carapace of ice. Good examples of this kind of table volcano are Bláfjall, Búrfell, Þórisjökull and one of the most beautiful mountains in Iceland, Herðubreið.

Pseudo craters Impressive examples of so-called pseudo craters can be found at **Mývatn** and on a lava stream north of **Mýrdalsjökull**. Strictly speaking, pseudo craters are not volcanoes, as they have no vent through which the lava could extrude. They were formed by lava streams flowing over moist ground or flat lakes. Due to the heat, the water evaporated explosively, blasting away the lava lying above and leaving a crater that can easily be mistaken for a volcano.

POST-VOLCANIC PHENOMENA

At many places in Iceland, columns of steam rise up, hot mud caul-   Spectacular
drons simmer and bubble away, or warm springs and rivers force   landscape
their way to the surface. All of these are signs of the post-volcanic
activities that occur when moulten magma cools down inside the
earth, releasing gases and vapours. Penetrating upwards through
cracks and fissures to the earth's surface, these create spectacular
landscapes.

Solfataras count amongst the most beautiful and colourful manifesta-   Solfataras
tions of post-volcanism. Particularly impressive examples can be
seen in high-temperature areas, such as the **Námafjall** near the Mývatn. Solfataras occur when groundwater beneath the earth's surface
heats up to the point of evaporating.
The steam, mixed with the gases of the magma, emerges through
cracks onto the surface. At the point of escape, with the steam mixture reaching temperatures of 100 °C – 250 °C (212 °F – 482 °F), sulphur is deposited around the vent, glowing in all shades of yellow and
orange.

Fumaroles are also openings that allow gases to rise to the surface. As   Fumaroles
opposed to the solfataras, fumaroles are usually situated directly in
or on a volcano crater. The extruding gases, mainly water vapour, are
very hot and fortified with acids. When the gas rises up to the surface
it cools down, at which point **iron or sulphur compounds** crystal-
lize near the vent, colouring the surrounding lava yellow, orange or
red.

What is interesting looking at the distribution of hot springs is that   Hot springs
they tend to occur in places where there hasn't been volcanic activity
for a long time. They are particularly common in plains, valleys and
fjords. Even if the volcanoes in those areas have long been extinguished, there is enough residual heat to warm the groundwater that
penetrates the cracks. At depths of up to 2,000m/6,560ft, the water
heats up through contact with the hot rocks and enters a circuit that
may last for thousands of years, at the end of which it emerges onto
the surface again. Hot springs are rich in minerals, containing common salt, sodium sulphate, calcium, iron, fluoride and boron, but
also dissolved gases such as oxygen and nitrogen. Some of the approximately 600 thermal springs, such as the **Blue Lagoon** or the
one in **Landmannalaugar**, are well-known tourist attractions, while
others are used to heat flats, swimming pools and hothouses. Anyone
who has taken a dip in a hot pool on a cold, rainy day in the middle
of nowhere, will know just how enjoyable these side effects of post-
volcanic activity are.

Formed by Elemental Forces

Fire-spewing volcanoes, eternal ice. Harsh winds sweep across unforgiving landscapes, dark clouds promise rain. Here, nature is still nature in the raw sense of the word: pure, sometimes threatening, rarely soothing with colourful flowers or lush, green grass. Welcome to Iceland, to a country where the elemental forces of nature have created landscapes of breathtaking beauty!

Visitors arriving at Keflavík airport and heading for Reykjavík are confronted straightaway with Iceland's volcanic past as, up to the suburbs of the capital, the road leads through a barren lava field. Seeming bleak and hostile in gloomy weather, just a few rays of sun are enough to transform it into a fascinating fairy-tale landscape. However, this is only a taster of the many varied forms of volcanic phenomena awaiting visitors. Those arriving by ship in Seyðisfjörður, on the island's east coast, see Iceland's second face, characterized by ice but no less impressive. The colourful houses of Seyðisfjörður lie on a deeply-cut fjord, framed by steep hills with

Glowing summits: volcano Hekla shows its true face

numerous layers of basalt and volcanic slag. While East Iceland cannot deny its volcanic origin either, the times when fire and lava shaped this landscape lie further back in the past. Here, the glaciers of the last Ice Age were the shaping forces of the landscape, carving deep gashes into the coastline and creating picture-book fjords.

Breathtaking and...

Whether arriving at Keflavík or Seyðisfjörður, be sure to leave enough time to explore – Iceland is not a country that can be »done« in a hurry. If nothing else, the roads demand a leisurely pace, with the traveller forced to slow down by the dirt tracks and narrow strips of tarmac that wend their way around dozens of fjords like unravelling balls of wool. This is just as well, as the panoramas going by outside the car window are often breathtaking. Hardly any other country on earth is as varied as Iceland, which in geological terms is still young and constantly changing – sometimes even highly dramatic – with violent volcanic eruptions or glacier-bursts. In the numerous high-temperature areas, when geysers aren't spouting jets of water high into the sky, there is a constant bubbling, steaming and hissing. Seething mud-pots and water holes, yellow and ochre-coloured steam fountains and sinter deposits form surreal lunar landscapes. Liparite mountains in flamboyant colours, dark ash cones, bizarre volcanoes, pseudo craters and, again and again, lava fields – some black, barren and menacing,

others covered by thick green carpets of moss – characterize large parts of the island. Alongside the volcanoes, the glaciers are the main attraction, as the most imposing of them, Vatnajökull, is by itself larger than all the glaciers of the European mainland put together. From its mighty plateau, icy tongues move down the valley, forming massive abysses, caves and lagoons, with bizarrely eroded icebergs often swimming on top.

... Unexpectedly Pleasant

However, Iceland also has a surprisingly pretty face that is unexpected in an island this far north. The narrow coastal strip and some valleys surprise with lush green meadows, where countless sheep graze. Or take the Mývatn, in reality a geologically restless area shaped by volcanoes, but which, with its islands, bays and headlands, seems like a green oasis. Although the summer sun, even in northern Iceland, still disappears for a few minutes below the horizon – the »real« midnight sun only shines on the small island of Grímsey – there are several weeks where it never really gets dark. For the locals this »light shower« is the long-awaited compensation for the long dark winter months. And for visitors from more southern regions, the light-filled Nordic summer nights work almost like a drug. In this period, day and night meld into one, and those who have enjoyed the stillness of the night and the often fantastic light ambiences of the midnight sun will never forget the experience.

FIRE SLUMBERING UNDER THE ICE

The largest glacier in Europe

For glaciologists Iceland is paradise, as some 11 % of the country is covered by glaciers. In **Vatnajökull** Iceland boasts the largest glacier in Europe. Under its icy coat, up to 1,000 m/3,280ft thick, lies a ragged highland landscape, responsible for the formation of crevasses – some of them huge – on its surface. Vatnajökull's southern flank bears the largest valley glacier, Breiðamerkurjökull, 18km/11 miles long. Looking at such glacier tongues shows that glaciers are no static chunks of ice but always in movement. Like a stream of huge ice blocks, the **glacier tongues** push valleywards in slow motion, powered by gravity. Some tongues only advance a few centimetres per day, others manage to push forwards a few metres. This constant draining results in countless fissures on the surface seemingly running in all directions with no guiding principle. These movements create enormous tensions inside the glaciers, to the point where the ice splits, opening up crevasses of up to 30m/100ft in depth. Deeper inside the glacier, the ice is exposed to such enormous pressure that it changes shape elastically without rupturing in the way of the more brittle surface ice.

Icebergs on Jökulsárlón, Iceland's largest glacier lake

The Icelandic glaciers are no relics of the last Ice Age, but were formed in the cold spell some 2,500 years ago, reaching their largest extent between the 14th and 19th centuries. In recent years, the Vatnajökull, in line with many other glaciers in Iceland and the rest of Europe, has shrunk. Below the glacier, the active volcano of **Grímsvötn** last erupted in 2004. An earlier eruption, in 1996, was so forceful that two to three cubic kilometres/0.5 to 0.7 cubic miles of ice melted, subsequently pouring as a mighty glacier run into the Skeiðarársandur plain, pulling along huge blocks of ice and destroying roads and bridges. When **Eyjafjallajökull** erupted in April 2011 smaller glacier runs also occurred. This cause the glacier lake Lónið to be filled up with sediments and to disappear.

No relics of the last ice age

LIVING WITH DISASTER

Since the settlement of Iceland, its people have lived with the certainty that natural disaster can strike at any time. In the past, volcanic eruptions, earthquakes and disastrous glacier runs have caused destruction, massive economic damage and claimed human lives too. The history of Iceland reads like a succession of catastrophes: In 934 the **Eldgjá fire fissure** opens, expelling large quantities of lava. In 1104 **Hekla** erupted, a volcano that to this day has made its presence felt a further 168 times. In 1783, the eruption of the **Laki fissure** led to the worst catastrophe since the settlement of the island. In the aftermath of the eruption, around 10,000 Icelanders died. In 1947 Hekla erupted massively. In 1963, underwater eruptions off the southern coast resulted in the emergence of a new island: **Surtsey**. In 1973, on the island of **Heimaey**, a fissure 1.6 km/one mile in length suddenly opened, shooting out fountains of lava. This eruption on the Westman Islands resulted in massive damage, leading to the temporary evacuation of the population. After a volcanic eruption under the Vatnajökull in 1996, parts of the glacier melted, leading to a mighty glacier run destroying parts of the ring road. On March 20, 2010 **Eyjafjallajökull** (»island mountain glacier«) erupted and caused headlines worldwide for the next weeks. While the damage on Iceland is limited, only one road bridge was destroyed, the hot lava's contact with the glacier ice caused gigantic clouds of ash that brought air traffic to a standstill in Europe in April. Since then volcanologists fear that the neighbouring volcano Katla will erupt, which in the past has often happened within a few years of an Eyjafjallajökull eruption. Hekla, located about 50km/30mi away, is also overdue; since 1970 it has erupted every 10 years without fail, the last time being in 2000. In Grimsvötn below the ice cap of Vatnajökull experts believe that things are building up to a dangerous level.

Seething under ice

ICELAND'S FLORA

Only little colour

Compared with Central Europe, the vegetation of Iceland is extremely sparse. The forests that have been created through reforestation are still limited. The vegetation consists mainly of mosses covering many lava fields, and meadows, mostly found in the plains and along the coast. Otherwise, dwarf shrubs, the stunted Arctic downy birch, heather and lingonberries flourish. Plants fare better along warm springs and brooks, as shown by the often lush green vegetation. The landscape is given spots of colour by herbs such as Arctic thyme, cotton grass, cranesbill, angelica, yarrow, dandelion, marsh marigold, marsh violet and stemless bladder campion.

Exploited nature

Before the long Ice Ages of the Tertiary Period, when a much milder climate reigned on the island in the North Atlantic, large stretches of land were covered in dense deciduous and mixed woodlands. There were oak, beech, bald cypress and elm, as well as the North American **sequoia**, as evidenced by brown coal deposits and fossilised leaves. Still, even after the last Ice Age and before settlement by humankind, Iceland must have looked completely different. The old texts report that the island was wooded from the mountains to the sea. Estimates say that at the time around half of the lowlands was covered in woods. However, the early settlers soon set about decimating the forest. Wood was needed for the construction of houses and ships, for heating and to smelt bog ore. Whatever young shoots remained were gobbled up by sheep, which the settlers had brought with them. Due to the harsh Arctic conditions, the delicate vegetation was never able to recover from this **exploitation**, and so the island's current appearance is also a product of 1,000 years of settlement history.

Decimated plant life

Not only did the last Ice Age decisively shape the landscape of Iceland, today's flora and fauna is also a result of this cold spell. With the ice many plant species disappeared, and due to the country's isolation, its harsh climate and volcanic activities, after the warming-up and melting of the ice sheet relatively few species managed to settle anew. Although there might be some **5,000 different species of plants and fungi** growing on Iceland today, only 440 are higher-order flowering plants, and of those some only came to Iceland with human help.

Apart from a few endemic species, all Icelandic plants can also be encountered in Norway and the British Isles. The fact that the island still appears green in many places is due to the lava surfaces covered in moss, as basalt lava, full of nutrients, offers an ideal soil for dense carpets of moss and lichen. However, Rhyolitic and obsidian lava do not support vegetation.

ICELAND'S FAUNA

The wildlife of Iceland cannot boast much variety of species either. Before the arrival of the first settlers, the **Arctic fox** was the only mammal on the island. The only creatures sharing its huge territory were those that reached the remote island more or less by chance, usually by air or sea. There would have been the occasional insects and birds, and perhaps the odd **polar bear** would drift by on an ice floe, but none ever decided to stay. Humans brought **sheep and horses** and, as stowaways probably, **mice and rats** too. In 1771, a few **reindeer** were introduced from Norway, in order to enrich the Icelanders' diet. The animals bred well, and today there are still around 3,000 of them living in the wild in the east and northeast, but without ever becoming a significant economic factor as in Lapland. A few mink managed to break out of fur farms and have since been decimating the bird population.

Visiting polar bears

The first settlers also brought the first horses to Iceland. Due to the island's isolated position in the North Atlantic, these **original Icelandic horses** have hardly changed over the past 1,000 years. In order to preserve this unique breed, in 982 the Alþing enacted a law prohibiting the import of animals. This import ban is still in place today, and even an Icelandic horse born and bred on the island that has been abroad is not allowed to return. As a result, Icelandic horses are the purest bred in the world. The animals are excellently adapted to the hard conditions, being small, muscular, sure-footed and with a lot of stamina, and having a dense fur that turns shaggy in winter. For many centuries, they were the only means of transportation on the difficult terrain of the island. Their distinctive characteristic, known as the fourth gait or the **tölt**, makes riding very comfortable. Unlike with the trot, the rider is not lifted from the saddle, as a horse doing the tölt always keeps one or two alternating legs on the ground. Icelandic horses that can do the tölt as well as walk, trot and gallop are called »**four-gaiters**«, while those that on top of this can also do the **skeið**, or »flying pace«, are known as »**five-gaiters**«.

Icelandic horses

Unlike the land mammals, the bird population is numerous and varied. Visitors might encounter snow grouse, falcons, oystercatchers, golden plovers, snow buntings, redwings, godwits, Arctic terns and, at the Mývatn in particular, many different species of duck. One of the most impressive natural spectacles in Iceland is provided by the **bird rocks** on the coast, each year hosting millions of breeding sea birds. The rocks operate by a strict hierarchy where each species has its allocated space: near the water breed the black guillemots, shags and kittiwakes; above them nest the fulmars, common guillemots, razorbills and **northern gannets**. The top storeys are occupied by

Organized chaos on the bird rocks

Puffins are typical for the northern hemisphere

the **puffins**, which are already endangered due to the effects of climate change. All of them fear the predatory skua.

Fish, whales and seals In the inland waters there are no purely freshwater fish – here too the level of biodiversity is low. In some rivers however, there is a substantial quantity of salmon, trout, Arctic char, eels and sticklebacks. In the coastal waters, some **300 species of fish** find good living conditions; of those, cod, herring and capelin are of the most economic value. Other fish caught are plaice, halibut, haddock, turbot, hake and redfish. The coastal waters also harbour common seals and other types of seal, as well as several species of whale. On whale-watching safaris, which mainly depart from the Snæfellsnes peninsula and from Húsavík, visitors stand a good chance of seeing orcas, harbour porpoises, minke whales, humpback whales or fin whales. With a bit of luck, one of the extremely rare blue whales might even make an off-shore appearance.

Whaling Whaling for research purposes has been allowed in Iceland since 2003; commercial whaling within certain boundaries has been allowed again since 2006. Whale watching operators subsequently registered a collapse of bookings by 90 %. In this way, Iceland's insistence on whale hunting might seriously endanger whale tourism and thus an important economic factor. The WDCS whale and dolphin protection organization even goes as far as to claim that in Iceland whale hunting and whale tourism cannot coexist, as in the past minke whales were hunted near tourist boats. It has to be said that the Icelanders' stubborn refusal to give up old traditions is counterproductive economically, as today's commercial whaling has **no economic importance** any longer, and this situation is not going to change in the foreseeable future. The controversy surrounding Iceland whaling continues to be a factor in the negotiations on Iceland's membership in the European Union.

People · Politics · Economy

The Icelanders are the direct descendants of the Vikings from Norway that settled the island in the North Atlantic. There is, however, also a dash of Celtic blood from Great Britain and Ireland flowing in the veins of today's Icelanders.

Icelandic society is considered homogenous, with a low percentage of foreigners due to a restrictive immigration policy. Sometimes it even seems as if everybody is related, which perhaps makes it less surprising that many Icelanders dedicate themselves with great patience and enthusiasm to **genealogical research**, and that everybody can trace back their lineage for many generations. Icelanders address each other by first names, as was already the case during the time of the Viking settlement – only that today a lot more people live in Iceland than in those days, which makes it hard work to look somebody up in Reykjavík's telephone directory, which is arranged by first names. For Icelanders, the first name is more important than the last name, which, following Old Germanic tradition, is formed by adding a »-son« to the first name of the father, with sons, and a »-dóttir« in the case of daughters. Thus, Einar Jónsson is called Einar and is the son of Jón, while Guðrún Egilsdóttir, listed in the telephone directory under Guðrún, is the daughter of Egil.

Restrictive immigration policy

FROM POORHOUSE TO WELFARE STATE

For a long time, Iceland was one of the poorest countries in Europe. It was only in the 20th century that a rapid change took place – from a backward agrarian country to a modern welfare state. While agriculture was never particularly productive due to the small amount of available land and the short vegetation period, 100 years ago half of the population still lived on individual farms along the coast. Today, they are fewer than 10 %. The economic and social development of Iceland after the Second World War was shaped by the so-called **Reconstruction government**, consisting of a coalition of the bourgeois-conservative Independence Party, the Social Democratic Party and the People's Unity – Socialist party. The prime goal was to boost the economy and to improve living conditions for the population. The biggest investment went into the **fisheries and fish-processing companies**. Thus, the country soon had one of the largest and most modern fishing fleets in the world. At one stage over 90 % of the country's exports came from this sector of the economy. Today, the main fish caught are still cod, herring, redfish, haddock and halibut.

No prosperity without fish

MARCO POLO INSIGHT

Location:
In the **North Atlantic**, about 1,000 km (600 mi) west of the Norwegian coast and about 300 km (180 mi) east of Greenland

22° 36' 20" west longitude

European North Sea

Iceland
■ *Reykjavík*

63° 59' 06" north latitude

Area
103,000sq km/40,000sq mi
of this 23% with vegetation, 63% desert/barren/lava, 3% lakes, 11% glaciers. Claimed fishing waters: 758,000sq km2/293,000sq mi

Atlantic Ocean

1863km/1157mi

Population: 325,000
Life expectancy:
Women 83.2 years
Men 80 years

Population density:
3 per sq km/8 per sq mi
(UK: 255/662)

London

©BAEDEKER

▶ Religion

80% of the population belongs to the state Lutheran church

▶ Language

Icelandic, which is still very similar to Old Norse

▶ Government

Form of government:
Republic of Iceland (since June 17, 1944)
(Lýðveldið Ísland)
Administrative structure:
8 regions, 122 rural communities
Prime minister:
Sigmundur Davíð Gunnlaugsson
President:
Ólafur Ragnar Grímsson
Parlament:
Alþing with 63 members, elected every four years
Capital: Reykjavík
(120,000 residents, metropolitan area about 200,000)

▶ Flag

The flag has existed in this form since 1915. The blue background stands for the Atlantic Ocean and the sky over Iceland. The colour red in the cross stands for the fire of the volcanoes, the white colour is for the ice. The cross also shows the connection to the other Scandinavian countries.

▶ Iceland extreme

Highest peak :
Hvannadalshnúkur (2110m/6922ft)
Largest lake: Þingvallavatn
(83 sq km/32 sq mi)
Longest river: Þjórsá (230km/138mi)
Coast line: 4970km/2982mi
Largest glacier:
Vatnajökull (about 8300sq km/3200sq m

▶ Economy

Gross domestic product 2013:
£8.4 bil.
(UK: £1517 bil.)

GDP per capita 2013:
£33,638
(UK: £23,158)

Unemployment rate (2013):
4,6 %

Inflation rate (2013): 3,1 %

▶ Economic structure

**Financial services,
real estate:** 17 %

Industry: 20 %

Trade, service: 12 %

**Transport, storage,
communication:** 8 %

Fishing, fish processing: 7 %

Construction: 4 %

Others: 32 %

▶ Climate in Reykjavík

Average temperatures

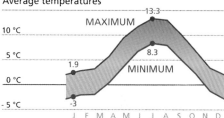

MAXIMUM
13.3
10 °C
5 °C
1.9   8.3
0 °C   MINIMUM
-5 °C   -3
J F M A M J J A S O N D

Precipitation

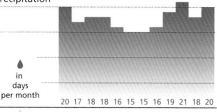

in
days
per month

20 17 18 18 16 15 15 16 19 21 18 20

in
hours
a day

1 2 4 5 6 6 6 5 4 2 1 0

J F M A M J J A S O N D

▶Foreign trade

Import: 583 bil. ISK (£3 bil.)   Export: 610 bil. ISK (£3.1 bil.)

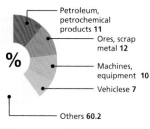

%

Petroleum,
petrochemical
products **11**

Ores, scrap
metal **12**

Machines,
equipment **10**

Vehiclese **7**

Others **60.2**

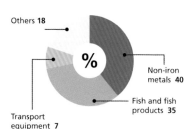

Others **18**

%

Non-iron
metals **40**

Fish and fish
products **35**

Transport
equipment **7**

The most important trading partners

▶ Import

Norway
Germany
Sweden
USA

missing percentages: Other 60%

▶ Export

Netherlands
UK
Germany
USA

missing percentages: Other 40%   Data basis: 2013

With the revenue from the fisheries, Iceland finances much of its basic commodities, food, fuel and machinery imports. Since the 1960s, in order to somewhat reduce dependence on the fish sector, some energy-intensive industries have been established with foreign help.

Enroute to the 21st century Between the mid-1990s and the financial-services meltdown in 2008, Iceland's economy was stable. After a few years of strong economic growth, the new millennium saw a short-term slowdown, but until 2008 Iceland ranked among the countries with the highest per-capita income in the world. But Iceland having to spend a lot of money on importing most goods – excluding fish, energy and some cost-intensive agricultural products – will also probably remain an issue for a while. **Today, tourism is the largest source of income**. At around 275 billion Icelandic króna it passed fishing and the fishing industry for the first time in 2013 with 15.4% of the gross domestic product. After the collapse of banking in 2008 and the nosedive of Iceland's currency, Iceland has become an affordable tourist venue. The number of foreign tourists grew at a double-digit rate in recent years and in 2013 it reached a new record of 807,000 guests.

Crisis years Iceland was hit hard by the financial crisis in 2008. The national debt grew beyond measure, the Iceland króna lost its value, unemployment approached 10%. In fall of 2008 Iceland **faced bankruptcy**. Strong public protests ensued, which blamed the politicians and bankers for the critical economic situation. The liberal-conservative government had to step down. The early parliamentary elections in April 2009 led to a clear move to the left. Jóhanna Sigurðardóttir became the new prime minister. She led a coalition of social democratic and left-green parties and sought for EU membership. The now effective regulation of Iceland's banks as well as international financial support led to a hesitant recovery in the Icelandic economy from fall 2009.

After the **eruption of Eyjafjallajökull** in spring 2010 it was feared that the economy would collapse again, but this never happened. Instead tourism experienced a heretofore unknown upswing In other areas the economy recovered more quickly than expected.

Smelting aluminium One thing is still available in Iceland in abundance, even after the financial crisis: energy. The country's energy needs are covered almost completely by **hydro-power** and **geothermics**. The **low electricity costs** are attracting more and more large industrial projects into the country. Take **aluminium production**, for example: about 40% of the production cost is from the high consumption of energy. This makes shipping the raw materials from Australia and Brazil to Iceland worthwhile. By now there are several large aluminium plants in Iceland. New power plants and dams need to be built to produce energy for these plants. But since the completion of Kárahnjúkar Dam in the east of Iceland (2006) at the latest there have been protests against this.

POLITICS AND PARTIES

According to the constitution, the head of state is the president, elected directly by the people for a term of four years. In 1980, when **Vigdís Finnbogadóttir** became the first woman to take on the office of president, she was also the first woman worldwide to have been elected head of state. Reelected three times, she held office until 1996, when she renounced a further candidature. Her successor was Ólafur Ragnar Grímsson. The government consists of the prime minister and ten ministers. The parliament (Alþing) is elected every four years in eight electoral districts and consists of 63 members.

The first woman to lead the country

The party-political landscape is dominated by the left-liberal Progressive Party, the conservative-liberal Independence Party, the Social Democratic Party and the Socialist People's Alliance. Since the founding of the Republic in 1944 no party has been able to govern alone – coalition governments have always had to be formed. The long-term coalitions of Conservatives and Social Democrats (1959 – 1971) led to domestic stability, while in the following years the coalitions changed more frequently.

Parties

The parliamentary elections in April 2013 were won by Bjarni Benediktsson, the top conservative candidate, who was against EU membership. But president Grimmson nominated the leader of the liberal party Sigmundur Davíð Gunnlaugsson instead of Benediktsson for prime minister and head of a coalition government. Benediktsson became minister for finances and economy. Nevertheless it's astonishing that the conservatives, who only a few years earlier were blamed for the fact that Iceland almost went bankrupt, are already back at the rudder in Iceland.

Elections 2013

Membership of NATO and strong links with the US since the Second World War are the most important pillars of Icelandic foreign policy. In NATO, the country plays an important role as a strategic outpost in the North Atlantic zone. Following an agreement signed in 1951, the US maintained a somewhat controversial air base in Keflavík, which they gave up however in 2006.

Icelandic foreign policy

Welcome to Everyday Life

Where and how do you meet »real« Icelanders? – Here are a few tips.

IN A PRACTICUM ON AN ICELAND HORSE FARM

Many tourists who come to Iceland want to ride horses. No wonder then that Iceland's horse farms are always looking for help. Anyone who is interested should be good with horses and people and sit well in the saddle. Family contact is guaranteed. It's worth sending an email to the farm. More information is available e.g. online at www.herridarholl.is/praktikum.htm and www.polarhestar.is/d/team.html.

These and other jobs can also be found via *Employment agency Ninukot, Síðumúli 13, Reykjavík, Tel. 5612700, www.ninukot.is*

VOLUNTEER IN THE WHALE MUSEUM HÚSAVÍK

Insider Tip

Helping out on whaling trips, in the museum, tour guiding: volunteers in the whale museum have lots to do. While the work itself doesn't pay, they'll help you find a job to support yourself while volunteering. *www.whalemuseum.is/museum/volunteer-program*

LANGUAGE COURSE

Several universities offer courses and whole degrees in Icelandic. Everything from a language course between semesters to a complete BA course on language and culture is available.
www.studyiniceland.is

PLAY FOOTBALL

Football is fun even if you don't win. Icelanders know this since they hardly ever make it to international tournaments. But one Icelandic football club is known far beyond the shores of the island, the football club UMF Stjarnan. While it hardly ever scores a goal, when it does the team surprises its fans with funny skits and dances, which have made it all the way to You-tube and gained Stjarnan fans all over the world..
Find dates for football games here:
www.ksi.is

SHEEP DRIVE

Taking part in a traditional sheep drive in Iceland is an unforgettable experience. This is right in Icelandic life and part of old traditions. Anyone who can't ride a horse waits in the valley until the sheep arrive. Riders can accompany the farmers into the mountains to drive the sheep together. But this isn't easy! The terrain is in parts very difficult – and in all kinds of weather. But you'll only experience the high feelings of the Icelandic farmers when the sheep flow down the mountain into the valley.
Infos at
www.lythorse.com

History

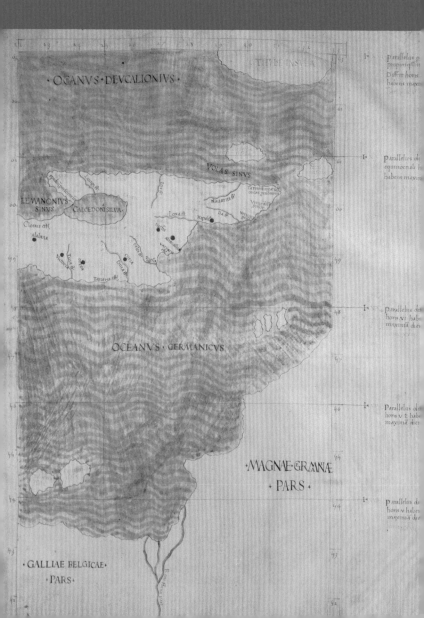

An Island is Discovered

From the discovery to the settlement of the North Atlantic island, from the free state to Norwegian and Danish rule, from the Reformation to independence – Iceland's history is closely linked to developments on the (north) European mainland.

THE FIRST IMMIGRANTS

1st century AD	Tacitus writes about »Thule«.
from the 6th century onwards	Irish monks on Iceland?
from the 8th century onwards	Vikings approach the island.

Iceland was the last country in Europe to be discovered and settled; no other country in the »Old World« has such a recent history. There was no prehistoric phase. The **opening up of the North Atlantic** was more of a slow island-hopping. Some 4,000 years passed between the time when the first traces of settlement on the Scottish Orkney Islands can be documented – c3500 BC – to the first contact of Europeans with Iceland. The most famous dwellers of the North Atlantic, the **Norsemen**, better known under their epithet of **Vikings**, also did not establish themselves in the region overnight. Starting in the early 7th century, they proceeded gradually via the Shetland and the Faroe Islands to Iceland, reaching Greenland around 980 and 20 years later even North America. Their discoveries were more guided by chance than systematic search. Mighty storms blew their ships off course, allowing the people on board to step onto new shores. Where the Iceland ferry Norröna today plies its course with twin engines, 21 knots of speed and the help of satellite navigation, the people of the settlement period in the 9th and 10th century came up against the **borders of the known world** – to be precise, they feared falling off the edge of the earth.

Island-hopping across four millennia

Rome's best-known chronicler, **Tacitus**, described the visit of a Roman fleet in around 83/84 AD to the waters north of the British Isles, the southern part of which was at the time under Roman rule: »ac simul incognitas ad id tempus insulas, quas Orcadas vocant, invenit domuitque, dispecta est et Thule ...– At the same time, it [the fleet] found islands that were at the time still unknown, called Orcades, and pacified them. Far in the distance, Thule was spotted ...« Here,

Romans on Iceland?

Historic map based on the writings of Pytheas: Is his »Ultima Thule« (northern edge of the world) today's Iceland?

Daring Fellows

Overpopulation and lack of resources in Scandinavia, the desire to enter new markets and the worthwhile service as warrior brought the Norsemen to leave their homeland and explore new lands. But Vikings were not only feared pirates but also excellent shipbuilders and clever traders. In Iceland they established the world's first parliament, the Althing (Alþingi), in Þingvéllir, where the first signs of democracy can be seen.

Foldable mast with square sail

40–80 crew

Bow extended stem with dragon's head decoration

Steering rudder

Mast

Sea chest

GREENLAND

ICELAND

from 860 on

FAROE IS around 800

around 982

NORTH AMERICA

around 1000

▶ **Discovery of America**
Eric the Red founded the first Viking settlement on Greenland in 985. His son Leif discovered Vinland (Newfoundland) around 1000, so he was in America half a millennium before Columbus.

▶ **Settling Iceland**
Around 874 Ingólfur Arnason was the first to settle permanently in south-east Iceland. He later named a small bay »smoke bay« -- Reykjavik.

©BAEDEKER

79

Stern

Bow

Steering rudder

▶ **Knorr**
The knorr was a freight and trading ship that the Vikings used on their journeys of conquest. It did not offer protection for cargo or crew.

Typical clinker building style

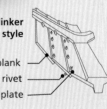

plank

rivet

plate

812

82

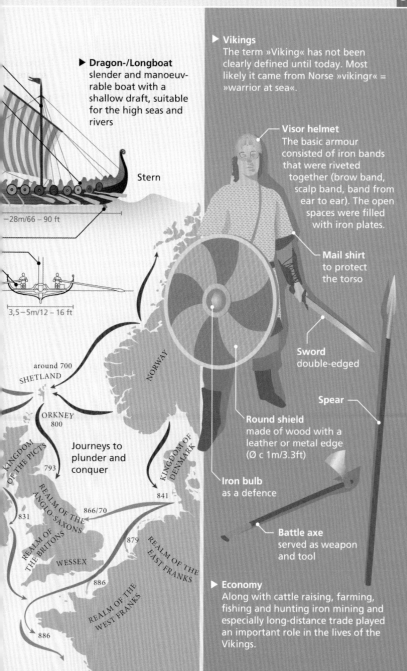

▶ **Dragon-/Longboat**
slender and manoeuvrable boat with a shallow draft, suitable for the high seas and rivers

Stern

−28m/66 – 90 ft

3,5−5m/12 – 16 ft

around 700
SHETLAND

ORKNEY
800

KINGDOM OF THE PICTS

Journeys to plunder and conquer

793

NORWAY

KINGDOM OF DENMARK

REALM OF THE ANGLO-SAXONS

831

866/70

REALM OF THE BRITONS

841

879

REALM OF THE EAST FRANKS

WESSEX

886

886

REALM OF THE WEST FRANKS

▶ **Vikings**
The term »Viking« has not been clearly defined until today. Most likely it came from Norse »vikingr« = »warrior at sea«.

Visor helmet
The basic armour consisted of iron bands that were riveted together (brow band, scalp band, band from ear to ear). The open spaces were filled with iron plates.

Mail shirt
to protect the torso

Sword
double-edged

Spear

Round shield
made of wood with a leather or metal edge (Ø c 1m/3.3ft)

Iron bulb
as a defence

Battle axe
served as weapon and tool

▶ **Economy**
Along with cattle raising, farming, fishing and hunting iron mining and especially long-distance trade played an important role in the lives of the Vikings.

Tacitus used the name of Thule for the »most northern«. He was undoubtedly familiar with the writings of **Pytheas of Marseille**, who in the 4th century BC had made a journey into northern territories and whose notes circulated amongst geographers and explorers far into the Middle Ages, but only came down to us in the form of quotes of varying authenticity from other authors.

The writings of Pytheas Pytheas gave the northernmost country that he found the name of **Ultima Thule**. He even described the midnight sun, although doubt has been cast on whether he saw it with his own eyes. According to current research, Pytheas probably reached central Norway around Trondheim or the northern end of the Gulf of Bothnia, but under no circumstances Iceland, as his Thule is a country with inhabitants. Since Pytheas, the name has been haunting the literature of the discoveries and is always picked up again when a name is needed for the absolute northernmost point in the known world of an era. In this way, Iceland became the »Thule« of the European Middle Ages; today an American air base in northeast Greenland bears this name.

Irish monks looking for solitude Apart from the writings of Pytheas and those that copy from him, it took until the 9th century for North Atlantic discoveries to be mentioned in literature. Around 825, the Irish **monk and geographer Dicuil**, teaching in France, wrote down what he had heard from colleagues on their travels at the end of the 8th century in the direction of the Faroe Islands and Iceland, without having taken part in them himself. His *De mensura Orbis terrae* tells of encounters of godfearing Irishmen with Norsemen on the Faroe Islands: »As early as a hundred years ago, the desire for the hermit's life led a few Irish monks to the many islands in the northern part of the British sea, which can be reached, provided the winds are favourable, in two days from the British Isles. The islands, uninhabited and nameless since the creation of the world have now, following the appearance of Nordic pirates, been abandoned again by the hermits«. Dicuil's writings showed furthermore that the monks visited Iceland, spending a summer there and even sailing on, »a day's voyage north, until they found the sea frozen over«.

Brendan's Voyage According to legend, a **monk named Brendan, and other friars** from the Emerald Isle, cross the Northern Seas with small hide boats, or »currachs«, in the daredevil search for solitude. Doubts about whether Brendan, a monk born in Kerry in Ireland in 484 – and who is credited with descriptions of geysers and »burning mountains« – really did reach Iceland, emerge from the long period of time between the alleged voyage in the early 5th century and its recording in the 9th century, when Iceland had already been discovered and these phenomena known. Today, many historians assume that the explorer

Brendan is a composite figure who was invested with the dates of birth and death of a real man of the church. This figure then served as a canvas onto which true reports were projected, as well as legends and sagas about seafarers that are circulating in the Celtic world.

DOCUMENTED HISTORY

12th century	Ari Þorgilsson writes the Íslendingabók.
around 870	Harald Finehair gains power over all Norway.
from 870 onwards	The permanent settlement of Iceland begins.

A more reliable documented account of the history of Iceland and the whole North Atlantic was provided by Nordic settlers. In the early 12th century Ari Þorgilsson – one of the few historians of medieval Iceland known by name – wrote the Book of the Icelanders, the **Íslendingabók**, with the benefit of some 200 years of hindsight. As opposed to the sagas this work can lay claim to historical fact. Ari also confirmed the words of his Irish colleague Dicuil: the first Nordic »Icelanders« encountered Christians whom they called »Papar«. Modern archaeology has proven however over the past decades that there were Nordic settlers on Iceland before the settlement documented in writing, and that they too lived alongside the Papar. However, the official story of Iceland, which also governs the national celebrations, continues to follow the Book of the Icelanders chronicle of Ari Þorgilsson, as well as the **Landnámabók**, the book by an unknown historian telling the story of the island's settlement.

Ari Þorgilsson

In the early 870s, **Harald I Hårfagre**, Harald Finehair, established autocratic rule in Norway and put an end to the oligarchic system of petty kingdoms, in which chieftains, farming large estates, ruled in their districts in the manner of small kings. Those who refused to pledge allegiance to the new central power leave their homeland and head for new shores. The Shetland and Orkney Islands, the Hebrides and Ireland could not serve as places of refuge for long, as according to the understanding of the time all these areas belonged to **Harald Finehair's Norway**, and soon after the subjugation of the Norwegian heartlands he asserted his claim to power here too, placing loyal men in important positions.

Political upheaval

This is what Snorri Sturluson, of whom more in due course, wrote in his **Heimskringla**– a work on the Norwegian kings – of Harald Finehair's military expedition: »First he reached the Shetlands and killed all the Vikings there that had not taken flight in time. Then he sailed to the Orkneys and cleansed them too of all Vikings. Finally he took his army on to the Hebrides and slew many Vikings ... Then he

Harald's tour of the Western Isles

battled in Scotland ... When he arrived on the Isle of Man, the story of all the battles that he had fought had already preceded him. Everybody fled to the interior of Scotland, and the Isle of Man was deserted.« The consequences of Harald's Western Iceland tour turn out to be the same as in the mother country: whoever did not want to accept the new balance of power had to flee.

Slaves as the first permanent settlers

Fortunately, we have the tales of the voyages of two men. On their way to the Faroe Islands, strong winds blew a certain **Naddoður**– as well as a **Garðar Svavarsson**– off course, while looking for a country that his mother, blessed with a psychic gift, had described to him. Both arrive at Iceland's coast. Naddoður landed in the area of the eastern fjords, but soon set sail for the Faroe Islands. By circumnavigating Iceland, Garðar found out that the country he has discovered is an island, subsequently spending a winter in the north, the site of today's town of Húsavík. After their return, both report on this new country that Naddoður called Snæland, Snowland, and Garðar, with the utmost modesty, Garðarshólmur. All these details of Iceland's settlement are told in the aforementioned Landnámabók. There, one particular episode is mentioned in an aside that is hardly picked up in other historiography: Náttfari, a slave, together with a maid, leaves Garðar Svavarsson's party and stays near Húsavík when his master sails back south. Their settling place is assumed to be on the small bay of **Náttfaravík**, on the banks of the wide Skjálfandi Bay opposite Húsavík. This would make an escaped slave and a maid the first (permanent) settlers in Iceland.

An ice cold winter

The short visits of Naddoður and Garðar were soon followed by an attempt at settlement. **Flóki Vilgerðarson** started from the Norwegian Rogaland in the direction of Iceland. Preparing for a permanent settlement, he landed in the west of the island, on the northern shore of the Breiðafjörður. Neglecting to think about winter rations for the cattle with which he was travelling, Flóki promptly lost them all in the following winter. In the spring, he sailed back to his home country, but not without first giving the island a name: Iceland. After Thule, Snæland and Garðarshólmur, this fourth name proved to be the one that stuck.

Fight over a woman

The forbidding name didn't deter people: in 874 – as described in the Landnámabók – two Norwegians left their country to set about the final and permanent settlement of Iceland. **Ingólfur Arnarson and Leifur Hróðmarsson**, who grew up as brothers, fled: they killed someone in an argument over a woman, and both were threatened with the blood feud of the victim's family. Ingólfur, initially living in the south of Iceland on a spot that today bears his name, **Ingólfshöfði**, later moved to a bay where there is smoke – Reykjavík. According to tradition, on arrival Ingólfur threw two carved tree trunks into the sea off Iceland and had them searched for after landing. In the **Bay of Smoke** where they were washed ashore, he then established his new home.

Leifur settled just below the Mýrdalsjökull at a place that today is called Hjörleifshöfð. However, he was not allowed to enjoy his new home, as the slaves that he brought over from the west beat him to death. Subsequently they fled on to the islands lying within sight of the coast, giving them their name: islands of the men from the west – **Vestmannaeyar**. They, however, did not live to a ripe old age either, as Ingólfur took bloody revenge for his foster brother.

Leifur and the men from the west

Ingólfur was followed by a stream of people wanting to make a new life for themselves in Iceland. In roughly half a century, around 400 immigrant leaders arrived with their retinue. How many people came ashore in total can only be estimated; it is probably between 20,000 and 30,000, but a figure of 70,000 has been put forward too. »Ísland byggðist fyrst ýr Norvege á dogum Harallz ens hárfraga, Hálfdanar sonar ens svarta ...« (Iceland was first settled from Norway, during the time of Harald Finehair, son of Halfdan the Black ...), states the beginning of **Ari Þorgilsson's Íslendingabók**. The proven fact that many settlers came from the Norwegian possessions in Britain and Ireland does not invalidate Ari's statement; for him and his time, this was Norway. Genetic research confirms the Celtic influence: about every tenth Icelander of the founding generation is from the British Isles.

Iceland – a country of immigrants

ONE OF THE WORLD'S OLDEST PARLIAMENTS

around 930	End of the conquest of Iceland. The first Alþing convenes.
982	Erik the Red discovers Greenland.
around 1000	Christianization. Leifur, son of Erik, discovers America.

In 930, Iceland's colonization was practically complete and the available lands distributed. The first political structures emerged, initially at local level with the **Goðorðs** – domains of influence controlled by chieftains, or Goðar. The Goðar came from the ranks of rich landowners that ran a temple on their estates for the people of their region. In addition to looking after the temples, they were soon invested with secular powers, even the administration of justice. To support them, from around 900, regional **Þing assemblies** were established; these however were so autonomous that the law was interpreted differently in different parts of the country.

Emerging political structures

Alþing in Þingvellir

In order to achieve a uniform regulation of society, the first national Alþing convened in 930. Three years previously, a group of nationally-minded Goðar had sent a legally trained man, **Úlfljótur**, to Norway to put together a body of laws. After his return, he reports his version of new Icelandic law orally at the Alþing. In so doing, Úlfljótur founded a tradition that was to endure until the written codification of law in the early 12th century: the elected legislative speaker reported the entire law orally at the annual assembly of the Alþing. This gave him a prominent position, as he could even – as long as there is no dissent – change the law by presenting laws in a different way or omitting them. A meeting place was chosen in the southwest of the country, east of Reykjavík: **Þingvellir, the field of the þing**.

No executive powers

Governing the issues of the largest state in the region with relative sovereignty, the Alþing of the Icelanders was the most important þing in the North Atlantic area. Although its assembly had legal and judicial powers, the first Icelandic Free State forgoes an executive arm. Its citizens could gain legal titles, and the enforcement of law was a private issue, including the **carrying out of death sentences**.

Oligarchy rather than democracy

The parliament of today's Iceland is still called Alþing and sees itself in direct lineage to the assembly of the first Free State, and as such as the oldest existent national parliament in the world. However, the early Alþing represented an oligarchy, led by three to four dozen **Goðar**, whose followers were free men. In Iceland at that time, most people are either unfree, female or both, and hence not represented in the Alþing.

Voyage »from outside«

For those who did have the right to make decisions there, the early Alþing was a symbol of their freedom from the Norwegian king, although contact with Norway is maintained; travelling back to the old country was a part of life. The language documents this: in Old Icelandic, a ship sailing from Norway to Iceland is said to be sailing »út« – out – and in the other direction »útan« – from outside. For the sons of important Icelandic families, it was part of their career to have served at the king's court in Norway.

Harald Finehair's son Håkon founded an elite brigade, where many young Icelanders served, pledging allegiance to the king. Despite all this, for half a century the Icelanders were able to withstand Norway's attempts to influence the decisions of the Alþing. King **Olav I Tryggvesson** changed this and had all Icelanders who happened to be in Norway at the time arrested and baptised by force. He held four sons of important families as hostages to force the Alþing to accept the blessings of Christianity in Iceland too. This came to pass in AD 1000.

Soon after the beginning of Christianization around 1000, the church gained influence without becoming overpowering. Bishoprics were established in Skálholt and Hólar. For a while, the old and new religions existed side by side, sometimes even within one family. The most famous case is told in the saga of Erik the Red, who lead the European **settlement of Greenland**. Whilst Erik worshipped the old gods, his wife Þjodhlið embraces Christianity, to the extent that a small church was established in the grounds of their Brattahlíð estate in southwest Greenland, the first in the New World.

Duality of faith

Erik was one of the most colourful figures of the young country of Iceland. Early on he was forced to leave Norway together with his father Þorvaldur, settling in the Dalir district in West Iceland. There too, further crimes made him an **outlaw** – in order to survive, he had to leave the country. At the time, there were stories doing the rounds that there was more land a bit further west. Erik discovered it in 982, and called it Grønland, Greenland – for good publicity – when he turned up again in Iceland three years later. »Because he thinks people are more likely to want to move there if the country has a nice name«, said Ari Þorgilsson and other saga authors, revealing Erik's true intentions. His strategy bore fruit however: in 986, a band of some 500 people followed Erik to the »New World«. Only 300 arrived

Iceland as starting point to the New World

Made it! Leif Eriksson and his men land in America

though, as eleven of the 25 ships didn't make it. Outlawed in Iceland, Erik became the esteemed leader of the small colony. His son Leifur, born in the Dalir district of Iceland, ensured that his and his father's names become immortal: **Leifur Eiríksson** was credited with discovering America around the year 1000. For a long time only attested by quotes from various sagas, since the 1960s there has been archaeological confirmation of this through finds in L'Anse aux Meadows in Newfoundland. A pronounced worsening of climatic conditions – examinations of Greenland's inland ice suggest an extended cold spell between 1390 and 1550 – broke Iceland's connections to the west around 1400, consigning them to historical oblivion.

THE END OF THE FREE STATE

1262	Iceland is subjected to the Norwegian crown.
from 1302	Economic decline
1380	Iceland falls into Danish hands.
16th century	The Reformation leads to bloody conflicts.
1800	The Alþing is dissolved

From arbiter to ruler From the end of the settlement of the island into the new millennium, Iceland experienced years of peace and prosperity. Then, the Icelanders sealed their own fate, as disputes began between the powers that be. The Norwegian kings, initially welcomed as arbiters, later meddled without being asked for their advice. From 1152 onwards, on ecclesiastical issues Iceland was subject to the archbishopric of Nidaros, today's Trondheim. In 1238, for the first time, Norwegians occupied both Icelandic episcopal seats. In 1241, **Snorri Sturluson** – as writer and historian an indisputable authority, but as a power politician from one of Iceland's leading dynasties rather mediocre – fell victim to intrigue. In 1258, the Norwegian **King Håkon IV Håkonsson** managed to place a loyal administrator in Iceland – who received the title Duke of Iceland – and four years later, the work was done: the Icelanders pledged allegiance to the Norwegian king at the Alþing, with the duke becoming vice king. The Free State thus destroyed, Norway's power in the North Atlantic was at a peak, especially as the previous year the small colony of Greenland had already submitted itself to the Norwegian crown.

Economic decline The new rule only brought the Icelanders peace and prosperity for a short time. After a few years the economic upturn was finished. Trade became dependent on foreign ships, the **former Vikings** having neglected their own seafaring. Foreign ships only came if they thought they could make enough profit. From 1302 onwards, the Norwegian king restricted trade with Iceland to Norwegians only, later only to

merchants from Bergen. The latter mercilessly abused their monopoly, giving the Icelanders low prices for their goods and low-quality
goods for their money.

It is a woman who in 1376 shuffled the cards afresh in the north: Margaret, daughter of the late Danish king, and wife of the Norwegian
king Håkon VI, ensured that in the **elective kingdom of Denmark**
her six-year old son was chosen, as Oluf III Håkonsson, to be her father's successor. When Margaret's husband died in 1380, little Oluf
automatically became, as Olav IV Håkonsson, king in the unelected
kingdom of Norway and thereby ruler of the territories in the North
Atlantic. The death of the young king at 17 brought Margaret the formal regency which she had already been exerting in practice. The
centre of the Nordic Empire, which also included Sweden as part of
the Kalmar Union (1397 – 1448), rapidly shifted to Denmark.

> Iceland falls into Danish hands

As the Reformation spread north in the 16th century, Denmark officially became Lutheran in 1536, following a bloody civil war, and
began imposing Lutheranism on its outlying possessions. Meanwhile,
in Iceland, the two Catholic bishops used Denmark's internal problems to grab secular power. Violent clashes ensued, with loss of life
on both sides. In 1541 the **bishopric of Skálholt** in the south was
reformed by force, while in Hólar, in northern Iceland, the popular
Jón Arason was the last bishop in the whole of northern Europe to
remain faithful to Rome. Making the mistake of his life, he used force
to usurp the episcopal throne after the death of his Lutheran rival in
Skálholt, and reintroduced Catholicism. Soon afterwards he was
overpowered and beheaded, together with two of his sons.

> The Reforma- tion lets heads roll

As Denmark gained substantial influence on the island with this
bloody deed, Jón Arason was subsequently turned into a martyr for
Icelandic freedom; his death was avenged with the murder of many
Danes, while Arason's followers carried his mortal remains to Hólar.

> Martyr for freedom

The Danes soon took trade completely into their own hands and
eventually proclaimed the Northern Atlantic to be their state territory. In 1602, the Icelanders were even banned under threat of pun-
ishment from trading with third parties. The population was entirely
dependent on the mercy of the monopolists appointed by the king.
However, they were anything but merciful and the Icelanders went
through hard times. At this stage, **Árni Magnússon**, having come to
an arrangement with the Danes, safeguarded most manuscripts, en-
suring that the Icelandic literature of the Middle Ages survived. He
did not have much time, as the increasingly impoverished population
used the skins that the manuscripts were written on for all sorts of
things, and no longer just for reading. The manuscripts found their

> Hard times

way to Copenhagen, where some of them fell victim to fires in the city.

Natural disasters   In Iceland even nature now seemed to turn against the island's inhabitants. Diseases, some affecting animals and some humans, famines, harsh winters and constant volcanic activity regularly claimed victims. The **peak of the natural disasters** was reached with the eruption of the Laki fissure in southern Iceland in 1783/4. This caused the Eldhraun, »fire lava«, at 560 square kilometres/216 square miles the world's largest contiguous lava surface in historical times. On top of that, toxic gases entered the atmosphere. Witnesses described sulphuric clouds spreading over all of Iceland, known as the Móðuhar-

ðindi, or »Mist Hardships«. 9,000 people died as a result of the eruption, while nearly all the livestock perished. 910 years after the settlement, colonial civil servants in Copenhagen planned the evacuation of Iceland to give the survivors a new home on the heather moors of Jutland. Many did not have to be resettled as, following the catastrophe, the island had fewer inhabitants than at any point since its settlement. In the end, the survivors were

Hardly any country on earth suffers as many natural disasters as Iceland

left where they were and the cheaper option was selected: in 1786, the Danes eased the trade monopoly. Slowly life returned to the country – economically at least. Politically, the following years remained gloomy. **Dependency on the central government in Copenhagen** increased. In 1798 the nearly irrelevant Alþing met for the last time before being formally dissolved in 1800.

THE PATH TO INDEPENDENCE

1814	The Danish-Norwegian dual monarchy is dissolved.
1845	The Alþing convenes again.
1918	Iceland becomes an »autonomous« kingdom.
1944	Independence of Iceland; proclamation of the Republic
1986	Gorbachev and Reagan meet in Reykjavik.
2003/2006	Iceland takes up whaling again.
2012	After rigorous austerity measures Iceland's economy gradually begins to stabilize.

After the Napoleonic Wars, which raged in Europe, the Danish-Nor-
wegian dual monarchy was dissolved by the victorious powers –
Denmark fought on the side of France – at the end of the war in 1814.
Norway came under Swedish influence, then became independent.
But its old colonies – Greenland, Iceland and the Faroe Islands – remained with Denmark. In the meantime, the early 19th-century nationalist movements extend to the far north. Gathering in Copenhagen, Icelandic students and intellectuals were supported by liberal
Danes, united in their efforts for the preservation of Icelandic culture
and language, which was being supplanted by Danish. Soon they
turned political however, demanding the reinstatement of the Alþing
and gaining followers in Iceland. The young **Jón Sigurðsson**
(1811 – 1879), brought up as a pastor's son on a remote fjord in
northwestern Iceland, eventually became their leader. Unlike the ro-
mantics of the early movement, who aimed to revive the historical
Free State with a parliamentary assembly in Þingvellir, he was a political realist, envisaging a modern Iceland. He established this in
1845 when the Alþing convened as a modern **parliament in Reykjavík**, initially only in an advisory capacity. In 1874, a constitution-
al reform invested the Alþing with legislative powers, while the Danish king remained head of state. The latter appointed a governor who
reported to an Iceland ministry in Copenhagen. In the eyes of the
Icelanders this of course was only half the prize. In 1904, they were
given more with the dissolution of the Iceland ministry. In Reykjavík,
new political machinery took shape, reporting to the Alþing. From
1915, Iceland has flown its own flag and in 1918 a treaty of union
made the country an autonomous kingdom – in personal union with
Denmark.

In April 1940, the German Wehrmacht entered Denmark and Norway. British troops moved in to occupy formally neutral Iceland and
pre-empt a putative occupation by Germany, which in previous
years had shown a marked interest in the strategically positioned island. While protesting, Iceland's government still called on the population to stay calm and asked them to treat the British as guests. For
the Icelanders this was easy: the soldiers brought money into the
country and provided employment, overcoming the last consequences of the economic recession of the 1930s. In 1941, in order to ease
the pressure on Great Britain, the Americans took on the role of oc-
cupying force protecting the island, this time with the approval of the
Alþing who had demanded – and obtained – a declaration confirm-
ing the sovereignty of Iceland and promising a pull-out of the troops
as soon as the war ended. The Americans brought in even more
money, more jobs, new engineering techniques and much technical
know-how. The country enjoyed a real boom and made a rapid leap
forward in terms of development. Economically, the Icelanders also

did well, especially as they got to supply Great Britain with fish. The country itself was spared acts of war, but not its merchant fleet, so that in proportion to its population Iceland suffered a **high death toll** in the war.

Proclamation of the Republic

In 1943, the **Act of Union**, signed 25 years previously between Denmark and Iceland, expired. The Icelanders did not extend it but dissolved it unilaterally. Whilst technically within their rights to do so, many Danes today still question whether under the circumstances it was morally justified as well. On 17th June 1944, the 133rd birthday of the hero of Icelandic freedom, Jón Sigurðsson, the Republic is proclaimed at historic Þingvellir. 682 years after Håkon IV Håkonsson took power, the Icelanders regained their freedom.

NATO base at Keflavík

Apart from a short break between 1947 and 1951, American soldiers remained stationed in the country. From 1951, they began to expand Keflavík to a large **NATO base** and, backed by a defence agreement, were responsible for Iceland's national defence. Iceland joined NATO in 1949, but without possessing an army of its own. The country's contribution consists exclusively of its strategic position.

Extreme political unrest

For a long time, the arguments over the **pros and cons of the American presence in the country and the Keflavík base** dominated the political discourse in post-war Iceland, leading to the worst political riots the country has ever seen in front of the Alþing in Reykjavík during the vote on joining NATO. At a later stage, left-leaning government coalitions twice tried to cancel the contracts with the U.S. Americans and persuade them to leave the country. In 1956, the Alþing actually voted accordingly. However, Warsaw Pact troops then invaded Hungary and the Icelanders did not follow up on this resolution. With the end of the Cold War in 1989/90, the presence of the Americans became less of an issue, and finally they closed the Keflavik base in 2006.

Reykjavík at the centre of world politics

Internationally, Iceland made few political headlines, apart from an event of global significance in 1986, when the two most powerful men in the world, **Ronald Reagan and Mikhail Gorbachev**, met for the first time – on neutral soil in Reykjavík. This was the beginning of a political development that was to change the world forever (see above). Five years later, as one of the consequences of these geopolitical changes, Iceland was briefly thrust into the limelight again: the country was one of the first to give the Baltic states diplomatic recognition, prompting Russia to recall its ambassador from Reykjavík.

Crisis years

In fall of 2008 Iceland faced the **worst political and economic crisis since its independence**. Because of the dubious financial dealings of Icelandic banks the island republic was drawn into the maelstrom of the global financial and economic crisis; the country was virtually bankrupt and could only be stabilized with international financial support. From October 2008 the general public staged strong protests against the liberal-conservative government and the banks. In spring 2009 the government stepped down. Early parliamentary elections in April 2009 led to a change of power. The new head of government was **Jóhanna Sigurðardóttir**, who led a coalition of social democratic and left-green parties, supported a quick EU membership for Iceland. In the following years the Icelanders had to endure painful austerity measures, for private households and the government were under enormous financial pressure. But with the usual Icelandic calm the little island state survived the financial crisis better than many other countries. In 2011 already the OECD stated that Iceland's management of the crisis was exemplary and it predicted economic growth for the next year. Since then Iceland has good chances to be admitted into the EU, which many Icelanders view sceptically however. The main point of contention is the EU's demand that Iceland ban **whaling** (▶p. 22, 180/181). In December 2011 the accession negotiations were opened. In 2011 moreover, 25 Icelanders who were elected by the people drew up a draft for a new constitution – completely with-out any input by politicians. The group meetings are open to the public and all Icelanders can join in the conversation via Facebook.

Since 2011 the signs of economic success have become visible, especially in tourism, which for the first time in 2013 became the most important generator of revenue for the island, ahead of fishing and the fishing industry, and export of aluminium.

Signs of improvement

Parliamentary elections in April 2013 led to surprising results for an outsider: the conservatives, who were blamed for the financial and economic disaster of 2008, gained control of the state of Iceland again as part of a coalition government with the liberal party.

Arts and Culture

Iceland's Cultural Heritage

When did the Icelandic sagas emerge? What exactly is skaldic poetry? Who wrote the first Icelandic novel? Which motifs are favoured by the painter Jóhannes Kjarval? What stood in the way of the development of sculpture in Iceland? All will be revealed on the following pages.

Iceland's early cultural tradition was influenced by Scandinavia, and Norway in particular. Early on, conscious engagement with language and literature had an important role to play and was valued by large parts of the population. It should come as no surprise then that literature going back to the Middle Ages became an essential part of the country's cultural heritage. One prerequisite for this was the **introduction of the Latin written language**, which entered the country together with Christianity. Living for centuries without political freedom and in abject poverty, the Icelanders, also hampered by their geographical isolation, were not in a position to participate in the new trends of European arts and culture until late, if at all. Instead they immersed themselves in the medieval manuscripts. These only started to be systematically collected from the 17th century, with Árni Magnússon (1663 to 1730), the first Icelandic university professor in Copenhagen, playing an important role. On his travels through Iceland he collected **old manuscripts** and had them brought to Copenhagen. There they remained until 1971; only then did the Danish give the remaining manuscripts – a large part had perished in the flames of the 1728 Copenhagen fire – back to the Icelanders. For Iceland this was a historic event, marking the definitive regaining of their cultural sovereignty.

Norwegian influences

FROM THE SAGAS TO LAXNESS

Icelandic sagas belong to the outstanding works of world literature. Written between the 12th and 14th centuries, these works count among the most diverse medieval manuscripts in Europe – and all originating from a poor, remote island in the North Atlantic. It is assumed that the sagas were initially transmitted orally and only later written down. To this day it is not clear who wrote them; one of the reasons that attribution is difficult is that the originals no longer exist. Sagas are a combination of fiction and historiography

Icelandic world literature

Many people say that the glass façade of the new concert hall in the port of Reykjavík remind them of fish scales

? *Cultural sign posts*

The first Icelandic sagas were created between the 12th and 14th centuries; the first Icelandic novel was published in 1850. In the first half of the 19th century Jónsson and Sveinsson became the country's most important sculptors. 1950 is the year in which Guðjón Samúelsson, Iceland's most important architect, died. In 1955 Halldór Laxness was the first Icelander to receive the Nobel Prize for literature.

and bear witness to the high artistic ability of their authors. Copies, as well as embellished and reworked versions, have been preserved since the 13th century. The kings' sagas describe ruling Nordic dynasties going back to the 9th century. The most important amongst these is the **Heimskringla by Snorri Sturluson**, which, for the first time, tells history chronologically. The Icelanders' sagas were written down around the middle of the 13th century, i.e. not until 200 to 400 years after the events they describe. Considered the masterpiece of this classic period of Old Icelandic prose, the **Njáls saga** deals with more or less all human and societal conflicts. The Sturlunga saga is a literary reworking of the end of the Icelandic Free State in all its details and cruelties. As the Icelandic language has hardly changed since the Middle Ages, the sagas are still understood today and many Icelanders are familiar at least with the content of the most important works.

Edda/ Skaldic poetry

Early Icelandic literature also encompasses the Edda songs and skaldic poetry. Skaldic poetry came to Iceland from Norway and Scotland, while the older Edda songs deal with the fates of the Scandinavian and Germanic gods. The Younger (or Snorra) Edda gives insights into **Old Germanic mythology**. Written by Snorri Sturluson (1179 – 1241), it is at the same time a primer for the complex skaldic poetry. This form of poetry got its name from the skalds, courtly poets who praised their patrons' deeds to the skies, usually with musical accompaniment. After Iceland lost its independence, its literature entered a period of crisis when, apart from ecclesiastical writings, hardly any prose literature appeared up to the early 19th century.

Towards modernity

The modern era begins with the publication of the first Icelandic novel in 1850: *Boy and Girl* by **Jón Thoroddsen**. A love story, the book is at the same time a realistic depiction of rural Icelandic life at the time. All in all, the 19th century was the time of **national romantic** literature, describing the traditional ways of life in Iceland. One of the most famous exponents of this movement is **Gunnar Gunnarsson** (1889 – 1975), whose most successful novel, *Guest the One-Eyed*, appeared in three parts and tells a rural family saga. Gunnarsson wrote much of his extensive work in Danish, which gave him a certain recognition outside Iceland too. With the awarding of the Nobel

Prize to **Halldór Laxness** (▶Famous People, p. 55) in 1955, Icelandic literature finally regained international recognition. The fact that today some modern Icelandic authors are read abroad can probably be credited to him, although the towering figure of Halldór Laxness may have made it more difficult for young authors to make their mark at home.

It's said that every tenth Icelander writes a book at some point in his life. And when Icelanders are not writing then they're buying and reading books – an average of four a year per capita. Among the contemporary authors who have a following in English-speaking countries are, **Arnaldur Indriðason** (*1961), who created an Icelandic Wallander with the melancholy detective Erlendur from Reykjavík. Twelve of the fourteen novels have been translated into English. One of the most important authors of Icelandic contemporary literature is **Einar Kárason** (*1955). While several of his works have been translated into English he is best known for »Devil's Island«. **Steinunn Sigurðardóttir** (*1950) is currently one of the most translated Icelandic authors.

PAINTING AND SCULPTURE

Only in the 19th century did the Icelanders engage in painting more intensively. In 1863 **Sigurður Guðmundsson** (1833 – 1874) founded the National Museum of Iceland, and in 1900, Þorarinn Þorláksson was the first Icelandic painter to have a solo exhibition of his landscape paintings. Modern Icelandic painting begins with **Ásgrímur Jónsson** (1876 – 1958), with his landscapes, portraits and still lifes characterized by wonderfully atmospheric light. Another master of capturing the seascapes and fishermen bathed in the northern light was **Jóhannes Kjarval** (1885 – 1972). Many of the best works by one of the best-known Icelandic artists are exhibited in the municipal Kjarvalsstaðir Gallery in Reykjavík (▶p. 246), which was named after him.

For centuries, sculpture was very much a marginal art form in Iceland. Among the reasons were the lack of wood and the difficulties in working the predominantly volcanic rock. The medieval **church door of Valðjófsstaður** in East Iceland, dating back to the 13th century and adorned with plant and dragon decorations, is one of the few remaining wood carvings from the Middle Ages. During the Reformation, many Catholic relics were destroyed or moved to Denmark. Only a few wooden sculptures, as well as chests and cabinets with pretty tendril patterns, have been preserved from the time after the Reformation.

A scarcity of wood

Einar Jónsson and Ásmundur Sveinsson

The fame of Einar Jónsson (1874 – 1954) rests on his sculptures, heavily influenced by Nordic, Greek and Asian mythology. Visitors can't miss his works in the centre of Reykjavík, representing Iceland's first settler Ingólfur Arnarson, and Jón Sigurðsson, the fighter for national independence. Further works by Jónsson may be seen in a **museum in Reykjavík** that he designed himself. Born in West Iceland, the most famous sculptor is Ásmundur Sveinsson (1893 – 1982), who created his works – some on a monumental scale – following motifs taken from the Edda. Like a lot of Icelandic artists, Sveinsson also spent many years abroad, studying in Paris and Stockholm, among other places.

ARCHITECTURE: NO PALACES OR CASTLES BUT PEAT HOUSES

Plain, simple, functional

The magnificent churches, palaces and castles that can be found in their hundreds elsewhere in Europe were never built in Iceland, due to the lack of a rich upper class that could have financed this type of construction. Thus, all buildings were unadorned, simple and utilitarian. The oldest buildings still standing are two small churches in the south of Iceland dating from the 17th century. For a long time, the buildings most associated with Iceland were **peat houses with grass sod roofs** and characteristic front gables. Small and offering little living comfort, they were at least well insulated against the winter cold by their walls, several metres thick. Today, some of these houses stand in open-air museums. Jules Verne, whose famous novel *Journey to the Centre of the Earth* begins on Iceland, more exactly on Snæfellsnes Peninsula, wrote: »The Icelandic huts are made of earth and turf, and the walls slope inward; they rather resemble roofs placed on the ground. But then these roofs are meadows of comparative fertility. Thanks to the internal heat, the grass grows on them to some degree of perfection. It is carefully mown during the hay season; if it were not, the horses would come to pasture on these green abodes.« The first stone house was built in 1755 near the capital and today belongs to the National Museum. Wood and other construction materials have always been scarce in Iceland and had mostly to be imported, significantly raising building costs. This is why, to save money, in the early 20th century many houses were clad with corrugated iron when they needed to be protected from the elements. A good number of these houses characterize the urban image of Reykjavík. Together with the stone houses that were built later and the glass and concrete buildings, the capital does not exactly present a homogenous and architecturally successful cityscape. However, the brightly-painted houses do make it more attractive.

The outdoor museum Laufás on the eastern shores of the Eyjafjörður shows good examples for peat houses

A significant influence on Reykjavík's modern architecture was **Guðjón Samúelsson** (1887 – 1950), the architect who designed **Hallgrim's church**, the **National Theatre**, the **University**, the **Catholic church** and the **Hotel Borg**. Icelandic artist Olafur Eliasson has designed a spectacular façade for the **new concert hall** in the port of Reykjavik, which was designed by the Danish architect Henning Larsen.

Guðjón Samúelsson, Olafur Eliasson

JÓN ARASON (1484 – 1550)

Beheaded, together with two of his sons, at Skálholt in southern Iceland in 1550, during the course of the Reformation, the last Catholic
bishop of Iceland owes his reputation as martyr and freedom-loving
nationalist to his **resistance against Danish rule**. As bishop of
Hólar, the northern of the two Icelandic sees, Jón Arason held extensive estates. Therefore his fight for the pope and Catholicism wasn't
entirely altruistic, as not only goods, fiefdoms and tithes, but also
natural land rights such as fishing and hunting, as well as the gathering and use of driftwood, were claimed by the Reformation and sec-
ularisation or passed down to the Danish crown and its centralized
administration. In early 2003, the start of the Íslendingabók Internet
genealogy programme by Kári Stefánsson of the Íslensk erfðagrein-
ing genetic research company yielded interesting new information on
Jón Arason: the majority of Icelanders can trace their ancestry back
to the bishop, born in 1484. As fertile as he was belligerent – Rome
was far away and Iceland had its own laws – the Catholic dignitary
had numerous children both with his wife and several concubines.

Bishop and
»father« of
the
Icelanders

BJÖRK (BORN 1965)

No other person from the island in the North Atlantic is currently the
object of so much international media attention as musician and
singer Björk. At the tender age of eleven, Björk Guðmundsdóttir
launched her first record, landing a hit straight away. Still only 13, she
formed her first band, »Exodus«, with girlfriends, followed by Jam
80, Tappi Tikarrass and the nationally successful band KUKL, before
starting to gain recognition outside Iceland too, with the legendary
»Sugarcubes« (1986 – 1992). The precocious maverick child star has
developed into an independent composer, singer and pop artist.
Never in thrall to mainstream musical tastes, Björk joined forces with
a jazz trio in 1990 to release the album *Gling-Gló* in Iceland, a collection of songs in traditional interpretation – a long-running best-
seller in the island's record shops and a coveted Icelandic souvenir for
her fans all over the world. Leaving the Sugarcubes launched Björk's
rise to global stardom. The albums she since released as a solo artist
have met with much acclaim; her last, *Biophilia*, in 2011, was no exception. What is more, her songs have been released in countless re-
mixes, with Björk herself in most cases collaborating on the new versions. Time and again, Björk has also contributed songs and sound
tracks to films, amongst them *Tank Girl*, *The Young Americans*, *Mission: Impossible* and *Being John Malkovich*. In 1999/2000, she even

Musician,
singer, total
work of art

Björk Guðmundsdóttir is Iceland's best known singer

dabbled in acting under Denmark's eccentric star director **Lars von Trier**: in the film musical *Dancer in the Dark*, Björk plays the central character Selma, an immigrant in the US who is nearly blind through a hereditary illness. In her desperation to spare her child the same fate, she makes the ultimate sacrifice. Whilst the tabloid press relished the escalating arguments between the difficult director and the no less difficult pop star – Björk declaring she would never act again as she simply could not stand it – she was awarded Best Actress at Cannes 2000. Of course, Björk also composed the music for »Dancer in the Dark« and interpreted all the songs herself; in 2000 the title song *I've Seen It All* was nominated for an Oscar as Best Original Song. In 2010 Björk, together with the Italian film music veteran composer Ennio Morricone, received the Polar Music Prize. The prize was handed over by the king of Sweden in person. Married to the US-American artist and former football star Matt Barney, Björk Guðmundsdóttir has two children and divides her time between New York, London and Iceland.

LEIFUR ERIKSSON (c970 – c1020)

Discoverer of America

Leifur Eriksson, also called »Leif the Lucky«, must have come from a particularly feisty Viking family. Not only did his grandfather have to leave Norway and to go into exile in Iceland because of a murder, his father, Erik the Red, was also banished in 982, subsequently making tracks for Greenland with his son Leifur. Erik returned after three years to look for colonists that would accompany him to Greenland, eventually setting sail with 25 ships. Around the year 1000, Leifur Eriksson himself set sail in the direction of Greenland, but, after losing his way a few times, eventually landed, in all likelihood, near Boston – which meant that he **discovered America before Columbus** by a long way. After his return, the Vikings launched further voyages to America and most probably also founded some settlements there.

VIGDÍS FINNBOGADÓTTIR (BORN 1930)

Former President of Iceland

Born in Reykjavík, Vigdís Finnbogaðóttir finished high school in 1949 and went on to study in Grenoble and at the Sorbonne in Paris, at Uppsala in Sweden, and at the University of Iceland. At the presidential elections in 1980, Vigdís Finnbogaðóttir achieved victory over three male candidates by a slim majority. Her electorate was mainly to be found in the left-leaning sections of society and not least among women. Later on, she became a **president popular with all political camps**. As the world's first female head of state elected by

Extremely popular in all political camps until today: Vigdís Finnbogaðóttir

the people, Vigdís Finnbogaðóttir held office for four legislative periods, renouncing a new candidature after 16 years. During her presidency, Vigdís Finnbogaðóttir was a tireless ambassador abroad for Icelandic culture – the visual arts and contemporary literature in particular – and worked hard for women's equality.

HALLDÓR LAXNESS (1902 – 1998)

Over the course of a long writer's life, Halldór Kiljan Laxness authored 62 works – novels, drama, essays and short stories. What is more, he wrote countless newspaper articles to give his point of view on virtually any issue. For this small country he was not just the only Nobel Laureate but also the towering father figure of modern Icelandic literature, his extensive work shaping the 20th century. Born **Halldór Gudjónsson** in Reykjavík, he lived from the age of five on the Laxness farm near Mosfellsbær, later taking on this name. Never finishing high school, he started travelling, restlessly crossing the whole of Europe and also spending some time in America. In 1923 he fathered a daughter, converted from the Lutheran to the Catholic faith and took on the name of Saint Kilian. The novel *The Great Weaver from Kashmir* is a literary testimony to this period in his life. A long stay in the US turned Laxness into a staunch **follower of communism**, though he turned away from it again in the mid-1950s. The essay collection »The Book of the People« dates from this time. In the 1930s, Laxness wrote three epic novels that count among the most important books in Icelandic literature: using the fates of a girl living in a fishing community (*Salka Valka*), a farmer (*Paradise Reclaimed*) and a poet (*World Light*), he describes the problems and changes in Icelandic society. In the 1940s he wrote the novel *Iceland's Bell*, set in

Man of letters and Nobel Laureate

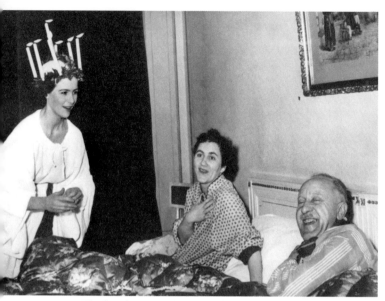

The day after: Lucia, the queen of lights, greets the freshly named Nobel Prize laureate

the 17th century, a time when Iceland was living in poverty and dependence on Denmark. In 1948, the novel *The Atom Station* was published, dealing with a controversial issue of its time: the agreement with the US that turned Iceland into a military base for the Americans. In 1955 Laxness was awarded the Nobel Prize for Literature. His grave is in the cemetery next to the church of Mosfell.

JÓN SIGURÐSSON (1811 – 1879)

Pioneer of Icelandic independence

No other Icelandic personality has been as continuously revered in Iceland as Jón Sigurðsson, pioneer of the country's independence. Born the son of a pastor in Hrafnseyri in the western fjords, Sigurðsson's role in securing the freedom of the country has made him an iconic personality and unassailable in every way. In 1833, he moved to Copenhagen to **study history and linguistics**. The revolutionary and democratic trends of Europe and America reached the Icelandic intellectuals living in Copenhagen, giving rise to Ny félagsrit (New Society Journal), an annual periodical published for the first time in 1841, edited by Jón Sigurðsson and appearing until 1871. Only in 1845 did Jón Sigurðsson return to Iceland, to take part in the resurrected Alþing as the elected representative of the Westfjords. Jón Sigurðsson was elected to be president of the parliament ten times, more often than any other parliamentarian in Iceland. His vehement commitment to independence for Iceland, and his indignant **We all protest**, which he flung in the face of the Danish monarchy, made him a cult figure. From 1852 onwards, Jón Sigurðsson led the Icelandic fight for freedom, again from Denmark. In countless letters, articles and contributions to almanacs he fired up his fellow countrymen in faraway Iceland. »The awakening of Denmark will make our position worse if we don't awaken too,« he warned his country-people. Thus, it was under his leadership that in 1855 the Danish trade monopoly over Iceland that had lasted for a good 250 years was ended. The constitution decreed by Denmark in 1874 for Iceland provided for a parliamentary monarchy under the Danish crown, leaving the country enough independence for Jón Sigurðsson to be able to call it »steps we can stand on«. Before reaching definitive independence in 1944, the country was to take quite a few more steps, but not Jón Sigurðsson, who died in Copenhagen as a result of an earlier bout of syphilis. The 17th of June, Jón Sigurðsson's birthday, is now Iceland's National Day, a major public holiday.

ÁSMUNDUR SVEINSSON (1893 – 1982)

Influenced by cubism, and later on by expressionism, the sculptor   Sculptor
Ásmundur Sveinsson spent his youth on the Kolsstaðir farm in the Dalasýsla district in the northwest of Iceland. Moving to Reykjavík in 1915 he began to work as a wood carver. Four years later, Ásmundur left Iceland to study at the State Academy in Stockholm. After finishing his studies in Paris and exhibiting several works at the Paris spring exhibition of 1929, he returned to Iceland. His interest in modern technology gave rise to metal works entitled *Electricity, Space Dragon, Flying Future* or *Yearning for Space*. In 1968, American astronauts, having trained in the lava deserts of Iceland and about to commence their journey to the moon, visited the visionary sculptor. Faithful to the school of thought that sees sculpture as part of the urban landscape, Ásmundur Sveinsson created large-scale sculptures that can be found at many places in Reykjavík, for instance The Water Carrier at the Meteorological Institute and Mother Earth in Sigtún, in eastern Reykjavík, home to Ásmundarsafn, the Ásmundur Sveinsson Museum, the artist's last residence and studio.

ENJOY ICELAND

Which Icelandic specialities should you by all means try?
Where can you celebrate with Icelanders? What are the best
shopping addresses? What accommodations are available on
this fascinating island?

Accommodation

Flexibility Beats All

»Þetta reddast« – it'll all work out somehow, is the motto of the Icelanders. For anyone who lives in a land where a volcanic eruption or an earthquake can change everything within a day, flexibility is a vital characteristic. »It'll all work out somehow« – this should also be the motto of anyone looking for accommodations in Iceland….

The **number of overnight guests** on the rough island in the north has **more than doubled** in the past ten years. Beds are scarce in many regions during the short summer months. Things don't always work out as planned when making reservations and the accommodations don't always live up to expectation. But never mind. It'll all work out somehow. At least those who have brought a sleeping bag along will always find a place to sleep. But anyone who wants to sleep in a tent had better have a warm sleeping bag. Temperatures at night can go below freezing in Iceland even during high summer. The **Icelandic hiking club Ferðafélag** keeps 38 huts in areas with attractive landscape in the Highlands and in southern Iceland. Anyone who wants to unroll his sleeping bag here should have booked at least a month in advance to be on the safe side. Many **guest houses, farms, youth hostels** with dormitories also have inexpensive sleeping bag quarters. Even some hotels allow you to use your own sleeping bag instead of their bedsheets and sometimes save up to 50 % of the price.

Sleeping bag quarters

There are 36 youth hostels **(farfuglaheimilin)** around the island, where guests of all ages are welcome. No two hostels are alike; in one you might stay in a former farmhouse while in another in a modern building. All of them have **family rooms** and **self-catering kitchens**.

Youth hostels etc.

One of the best hotels in Iceland is Hotel Buðir on Snæfellsnes Peninsula

Prices start at 3000 ISK per person and night in a multi-bed room. **Gistiheimili**, that is private guest houses, offer various levels of comfort and often a family atmosphere. Anyone who wants to be completely on his own could rent a typically Scandinavian **holiday cottage**.

Hotels   Hotel chains with huge concrete tourist hotels and standard service do not exist on Iceland. The Icelandic airline Icelandair has a network of hotels all over the island, which is divided into two segments: **Edda Hotels** are boarding school dormitories that are used as hotels during the summer school holidays. The rooms are furnished more functionally and the price at 20000 ISK for a double room with bathroom is quite reasonable by Icelandic standards. The nine **Icelandair Hotels** are more upmarket, and a comfortable room costs between

At Lake Jökulsárlón, the glacial lake on the southern

22,000 and 30,000 ISK and up to 40,000 ISK for the luxury version. Eight independent hotels got together to form **Fosshótels**; very differently furnished houses with prices starting at 30,000 ISK for a double room in the summer. The chain **Kea Hotels** has five hotels ranging from two to four stars. In past years a few **top class hotels** managed to get established in Iceland. The list »Áning«, a current overview of all accommodations in Iceland, can be downloaded at **www.heimur.is**.

But two things need to be remembered especially during the summer months: take along an **eye mask for sleeping** because of the light nights. And: always **book ahead** of time! It could happen otherwise that you won't find a place to stay.

Book early!

edge of Vatnajökull, Iceland seems like a fairy land

Holiday on the Farm

Many of the books by the Icelandic Nobel laureate Halldór Laxness are about the hopeless battle of the farmers against cold, forces of nature, poverty and hunger. Even today, almost 100 years later, Icelandic farmers still have to work hard. But new technology has changed their working day fundamentally and many have discovered a second source of income: tourism.

Around the year 1900 almost 80% of the Icelanders lived in rural areas. Today it is only 8.5%, and these live and work very differently from their forefathers. While sheep used to be the main source of income for farmers, beef and pork have been added, as well as horse breeding and gardening. The ground is still barren, the summers short and the winters long. But in times of hot running water, hot houses, central heating, four-wheel drive and modern methods of communication life on the remote farms has lost much of its hardness. What remains is the **solitude, life with nature,** the **wideness of the landscape** and the **work with animals**. These are values that many modern city people long for. No wonder that »farm holidays« in Iceland are booming. Anyone who rents a room on an Icelandic farm can **get away from his own everyday life** and get to know this land and its people in a special way.

Paradise is so Close

For breakfast the milk might well have come from the cows grazing outside of the window. Then visit the newborn lambs, calves or foals, book a jeep tour or go horseback riding. The evening dinner is served family-style followed by a bath in the hot spring. This sounds like paradise – and it is. The association **Icelandic Farm Holidays** has joined 160 farmers together to offer guests a total of 4,100 beds in sleeping bag quarters, country hotels, guest houses, farms or holiday cottages on the whole island. It also arranges holiday activities like riding, fishing, hunting or golf. On many farms contact with the family is included, English works well almost everywhere.

Four Categories

Most farms have guest houses with all the amenities. In so-called **country hotels** an en suite bath is a matter of course, **holiday cottages** also have a self-catering kitchen. All accommodations are divided into four categories, from simple to comfortable. Prices for a double room on a farm, however, are not necessarily cheaper than a hotel room in the city.

For Every Taste

A wonderful country hotel, which can be booked via the home page of Farmholidays, is for example **Hotel Anna** in Moldnúpur at Eyjafjöll. Sheep, horses, dogs and cats remind you that you are in the country. In the seven rooms, all en suite and lovingly furnished with antiques, you're more likely to feel

This local museum in Olavsvik on Snæfellsnes Peninsula gives a good impression of the good old days

like you've gone back in time.

Horses and ecology – these two subjects are the focal point on **Eldhestar Farm** Vellir near Reykjavík. More than ten years ago a comfortable eco-hotel was opened right next to the farm – the first in Iceland, which was awarded the **Nordic ecology seal**, the **swan**. The farm also offers log cabins with sleeping bag accommodations for up to 20 guests. Horse fans can take part in riding treks for one or more days, while others can go hiking, fishing or play golf.

On **Vogafjos farm** at Lake Mývatn you can help with the farm chores, like milking the cows; on **Hólmur** **farm** in Mýrum in the south-west of the island there is a petting zoo with Icelandic farm animals; at **Neðra-Vatnshorn farm** in northern Iceland you can experience the lambing in May and help gather the sheep and horses in the fall. Incidentally, the owner is from Germany; anglers are in the right place on **Hlíð farm** at the Walfjord in the east.

FURTHER INFORMATION, BOOKING ONLINE
Icelandic Farm Holidays
Sidumuli 2, Reykjavík
Tel. 5 70 27 00
www.farmholidays.is

The most important addresses

CAMP GROUNDS
Visit Iceland
Borgartún 35, Reykjavík
Tel. 5 11 40 00
www.visiticeland.com

HUTS
Ferðafélag Íslands
(Icelandic hiking club)
Mörkin 6, Reykjavík
Tel. 5 68 25 33, www.fi.is

YOUTH HOSTELS
Hostelling International Iceland
Borgartún 6
Reykjavík
Tel. 5 75 6700

HOTEL CHAINS
Hótel Edda
Hlíðarfotur, Reykjavík
Tel. 4 44 40 00
www.hoteledda.is

Fosshotel Iceland
Sigtun 38, Reykjavík
Tel. 5 6240 00
www.fosshotel.is

Icelandair Hotels
Nautholsvegur 52
Reykjavík, Tel. 4 44 40 00
www.icelandairhotels.com

IKEA Hotels
Hafnarstraeti 87–89, Akureyri
Tel. 4 60 20 50, www.keahotel.is

Recommended hotels

PRICE CATEGORIES
for a double room
££££ over 35,000 ISK
£££ up to 35,000 ISK
££ up to 25,000 ISK
£ up to 15,000 ISK

LUXURY
Hotel Glymur *Insider Tip*
££££
Hvalfjörður, Akranes
Tel. 4303100
www.hotelglymur.is
Located around 30km/24mi north-east of Akranes, the Glymur is one of the most beautiful hotels on Iceland. It lies in a remote, wildly romantic setting on the Walfjord. The 22 rooms each have a bathroom and living area in the lower floor and the beds are on an inner balcony. The two suites each have a terrace and sound system as well. All of the rooms are individually furnished with Italian furniture and works of art. There are also six luxury cottages for self-caterers, all of which have an outdoor whirlpool.

TIMELESS CLASSICS
Hotel Borg ££££
Posthusstræti 11
Reykjavík
Tel. 5511440, www.hotelborg.is
Centrally located, Hotel Borg attarcts with its timeless elegance. It is the most historic hotel in the city – during a renovation a few years ago it lost some of its Art déco charm but definitely gained in elegance and comfort.

UNUSUAL
Hotel Phoenix £££ Insider Tip
Laugavegur 140
Reykjavík
Tel. 5 11 50 02
www.phoenix.is
The somewhat different hotel in Reykjavík: a charming little bed & breakfast with nine lovingly furnished rooms, ideal for a romantic weekend for two. The unusual mix of antiques and kitsch gives every room its own character; the breakfast is excellent, and the owners have many tips on special places to visit in Reykjavík. Not that cheap, but unique!

COSY-COMFORTABLE
Kex Hostel £££/££££
Skúlagata 28
Reykjavík
Tel. 5 61 60 60
www.kexhostel.is
This hostel used to be a factory – where the finest biscuits were produced and today it is a comfortable meeting place for the young and the still young. The appealing mixture of factory and student flats is definitely a hit – in the summer reservations are definitely a must.

LUXURY & NATURE
Hótel Búðir £££/££££
Snæfellsnes, Tel. 4 35 67 00
www.hotelbudir.is
Located east of Arnarstapi this hotel stands out not only for its variety of luxurious extras and – thanks to its solitary location – ecological far-sightedness, but also for the breath-takingly beautiful view of the sea and the mountains. It also has a successful mixture of old and new in the comfortably furnished rooms as well as cooking that celebrates the best food.

PURE NATURE
Youth hostel
Fljótsdalur A
Fljótshlíð
861 Hvolsvöllur
Tel. 4 87 84 98 / 4 87 84 97
www.hostel.is
This youth hostel is located between the glaciers Eyjafjallajökull and Mýrdalsjökull in a rustic old peat house. If you're looking for comfort, this is the wrong place: the 15 beds are in three large bedrooms – the shower is in the garden! But the house and the landscape are unique and in the evening you can page through the many books and periodicals on Iceland that are collected here. Open mid March until early November.

Camp ground Skaftafell A
Skaftafell National Park, Visitor Centre, Tel. 4 70 83 00,
May – Sept.
www.vatnajokulsthjodgardur.is
The camp ground is often very busy – no wonder as the location is ideal for visits to the national park – to see the glacial lagoon Jökulsárlón for instance.

Children in Iceland

Holiday Fun for the Whole Family

Vikings, volcanos, bubbling mud pots, whales, seals, Icelandic horses – for children Iceland is a gigantic adventure playground and so an ideal country fro taking holidays. The only condition: this adventure playground is really big, so be prepared for long drives.

Ever since the most recent financial and economic crisis Iceland is no longer one of the richest countries in Europe, but it is still one of the countries with the **most children**. With an average of 2.2 children per woman the island nation can keep its population stable through its fertility rate alone (U.K. 1.9 children per woman). Families with three, four or more children are not uncommon. An important reason for this is that the conditions for parents and children are ideal here.

Optimal conditions

According to a report by the organisation »Save the Children« Iceland is one of the three most mother-friendly countries worldwide. Along with the good medical care and educational opportunities the good **family policies** of the government brought about this rating. Icelandic parents are entitled to a total of nine months off per child, three of them specifically for the mother, three of them for the father, and the rest can be divided up as the parents wish. During this time the parents get 80 percent of their income. If the father does not take his share of the time it is forfeited. In Iceland employers have to take into account that the men as well as the women will take time off when a child is born, so the opportunities and the risks are accordingly divided up between them.

Mother-friendly nation

All of this leads to a relaxed and completely natural attitude towards children. There are rarely special offers for kids but they are welcome everywhere and everyone is open for their questions and needs.

Relaxed attitude

Up to the age of four, children are admitted at no charge almost everywhere and most of the attractions for adults are also exciting for children. Farms make for wonderful holiday accommodations for children. Anyone who prepares for long drives and bears in mind that in Iceland not all cliffs, rivers or promontories can be fenced off will find a child's holiday paradise here.

Free almost everywhere up to 4 years old

Vikings everywhere: father and son at the culture night in Reykjavik on the Austurvöllur, one of the most popular places in the city centre

Tips for Kids

Volcano Show

Red Rock Cinema
Hellusund 6 A
101 Reykjavík
Tel. 8 45 95 48
Fiery volcanos: Whenever a volcano erupted in the past decades the nature cinematographer Villi Knudsen was there and filmed it. His Volcano Show can be seen in Reykjavík in the Red Rock Cinema.

Volcano Tours Insider Tip

Vikurbraut 2, Grindavík
Tel. 426 88 22
www.volcanotours.is
around 35,000 ISK per person
By Jeep into the region of the **Eyjafjallajökull** – tours like these can be booked with Volcano Tours. In eight hours you cross 30 rivers, see waterfalls, lava fields, and explore breath-taking gorges. For anyone travelling on their own in Þórsmörk, the visitor's centre on the **Þorvaldseyri** farm at the foot of Eyjafjallajökull is recommended. It has information on the volcanic eruption of 2010 (www.icelanderupts.is).

Wild Vikings

www.fjorukrain.is, www.leif.is
An almost authentic Viking ship, a replica of the »Íslendingur«, can be seen in the **Vikingaheimar Museum** in Reykjanes.

Eating and living like a Viking: **Iceland's only Viking hotel** is in **Hafnarfjörður**, about a 30 minute drive from Keflavík Airport. The rooms are furnished with tree-trunk-like furniture and Viking accessories. But the restaurant which serves Viking food is expensive!

About 150km/90mi north of Reykjavík there is the **open-air museum Eiríksstaðir**. The seafarer and chief Eric the Red is supposed to have lived in a house like this replica of a Viking long-house. His son Leif Eriksson was born here too; the first European to set foot on the North American continent.

Horse dreams Insider Tip

Renate Hannemann and
Arnar Jónsson
Herríðarhóli, Hella
Tel. 487 5252
www.herridarholl.is, www.holar.is
The stable **Herríðarhóli** has great conditions for small equestrians. The owner's wife is German, her two daughters who love riding.

An exhibit in the former **stables of Hólar** sheds light on the historical significance of the Icelandic farmer's most important helper, the Icelandic horse.

Ghosts, witches and magical creatures

www.Reykjavík871.is
Reykjavík 871 is an exciting museum in the nation's capital city. A multimedia exhibit in a replica of the city's oldest house has previous residents appear as ghosts carrying out their usual everyday activities.
In the museum **Icelandic Wonders** in **Stokkseyri** floating elves, sleeping trolls and flickering

Children too kann explore Iceland on horseback

northern lights can be seen. There is also a ghost museum in the same building.

The **witch museum** in **Hólmavík** is only for older children and adults and not for the faint of heart. The history of 17th century Icelandic witch hunts is told; another subject is magic rituals.

Food and Drink

Enjoy your Meal!

Horror stories about Icelandic cooking are making the rounds, but don't let them stop you. In fact Icelanders love to eat well – especially lamb and fish dishes have an incomparable aroma on this northern island.

»**Takk fyrir matinn**« – »Thank you for the meal« – is what is said to the hosts in Iceland after a meal. This custom comes from times when food was scarce on this barren island, and all of the Icelandic dishes that are described with shudders in newspaper articles and online come from this time: spoiled shark meat, black pudding tortes, whole sheep heads that stare at you with glassy eyes from the plate and of course the notorious sheep's testicles.

An old custom

Many of the domestic animals that Vikings brought along in their boats more than 1,000 years ago could not cope with the rough island climate. There was no local game, fruit, vegetables or grain, so Icelanders had to make do until into the 20th century with **berries, herbs, mushrooms, mutton** and **horse meat** as well as **seabirds** and **fish**. When a sheep was slaughtered all of the parts that were somehow edible had to be used, including the head. Food had to be preserved for the winter by means of drying or smoking, with salt or sour. But these dishes are only served now in Iceland in connection with commemoration of old traditions, like during the winter festival **Þorrablót**, or when something unusual is to be offered to tourists. But the often mentioned »fermented shark« is a myth: Icelanders do not bury sharks and dig them up months later to eat them. When you order **hákarl**, you will get a foul-smelling dish that was made by pressing and drying the meat of grey sharks. Since cartilaginous fish have urea, the meat ferments and develops its characteristic smell of ammonia.

Traditional food

Today Icelandic menus also include fruit, vegetables, and exotic fruits – geothermally heated hot houses make it possible. **International cooking trends** have also taken root, especially Italian and Asian cooking. Fast food is available everywhere, even in the back of beyond, and Icelanders especially like **pylsur**, that is hot dogs. Most of the time they are ordered »**eina með öllu**« – one with everything that the stand has to offer: ketchup, mustard, mayonnaise or roasted onions, sometimes also fresh vegetables.

Today

Blue hour with blue cocktails in the Blue Lagoon near Grindavik on the Reykjanes Peninsula

Vegetables preferred? A new generation of Icelandic chefs is specialising more and more in **reinterpretations of typically Icelandic dishes**. Lamb, fish and lobster continue to be the focus, flavoured with Icelandic herbs, berries, lichens and algae. Reindeer specialities also play an important role as they were brought to Iceland in the 18th century. Wild birds like puffins, razor bills and guillemots are also tasty. **Vegetarians** need not fear that they won't get enough to eat. In Reykjavík there are excellent restaurants for lovers of meatless cooking while in smaller towns there are always pasta dishes and salads. **Vegans** might have more of a problem and might have to become self-caterers in the rural areas.

Saving cash Because of the **high price** of eating out in Icelandic restaurants it's wise to keep closer tabs on expenses: an Icelandic menu including drinks can cost the equivalent of up to £55 per person. This amount can be reduced by skipping the alcoholic drinks and going out to eat at noon. Icelanders eat their main meal in the evening, so many restaurants offer **affordable menus at noon** especially for tourists. Since **tipping is not customary** in Iceland this money can be saved too. The important thing is to say thank you for the meal afterwards with the words »Takk fyrir matinn.«

Unusual and practical: the Laundromat Café in the old city of Reykjavík combines an Art deco café with a laundromat

Recommended Restaurants

Anyone travelling to Iceland these days can look forward real culinary pleasures. The capital city Reykjavík has meanwhile become an insiders' tip among gourmets.

PRICE CATEGORIES
for a main dish without drinks
££££ from 4500 ISK
£££ up to 4500 ISK
££ up to 3000 ISK
£ up to 2000 ISK

Baejarins Beztu Pylsur £
Tryggvagata 10, **Insider Tip**
Reykjavík,
www.bbp.is
Reykjavíks legendary hot dog stand is easily recognizable at midday by the long lines at the counter. Even former US President Bill Clinton and James Hetfield, singer with the band »Metallica«, have already been to this probably world's best sausage stand (▶ p. 231).

Gullfoss Kaffi ££/£££
Gullfoss, 801 Selfoss
Tel. 486 65 00, www.gullfoss.is
An excellent kjötsúpa is served here!

Gamli Bærinn ££/£££
660 Mývatn,
Tel. 464 4170
Informal, somewhat nostalgic pub opposite Hotel Reynihlíð (▶ p. 204).

Klausturkaffi ££/£££
Skriðuklaustur, Tel. 471 29 92
www.skriduklaustur.is
The monastery café is known for a varied lunch and cake buffet as

! *Black, sweet death* **Insider Tip**

MARCO ⊕ POLO TIP

When there was too much to eat it can be washed down with one or more glasses of brennivín from the label **Svarti Dauði** (Black Death). This is an aquavit made from potatoes with a malty caraway flavour and slightly sweet aftertaste. Brennivín has an alcohol content of about 40 percent. It's better to leave the car parked after trying it!

well as the excellent clam soup that is served here (▶ p. 155).

Einar Ben £££/££££
Veltusundi 1, Reykjavík
Tel. 511 50 90
One of the best addresses in town: The restaurant is located in one of the oldest trading houses in Reykjavík and still emanates some of the nostalgic charm of the 19th century. Typical Icelandic dishes are served here – fish, seabirds, game, lamb (▶ p. 235).

Dill Restaurant £££/££££
Sturlugata 5, Reykjavík
Tel. 552 15 22
www.dillrestaurant.is
The Norse house near the university was built by the Finnish star architect Alvar Aalto. The Icelandic star chef Gunnar Karl Gislason, one of the pioneers of New Nordic Cuisine does the cooking here (▶ p. 235).

Lækjarbrekka £££/££££

Bankastræti 2
Reykjavík
Tel. 551 44 30
www.laekjarbrekka.is
Old wooden house in the city
centre with cozy furnishings and
excellent cooking (▶ p. 235).

Hotel Hólt £££/££££

Bergstaðastræti 37,
Reykjavík
Tel. 552 57 00, www.holt.is
Not very attractive on the outside,
but the inner value is all the greater: first class cooking and a wine
cellar with 4000 varieties
(▶ p. 236).

Hotel Búðir £££/££££

Snæfellsnes, Tel. 435 67 00
www.hotelbudir.is
The finest cooking is celebrated in
this hotel, which was reconstructed after a fire (▶ p. 268).

Humarhöfnin £££/££££ Insider Tip

Hafnarbraut 4, Hornafirði
Tel. 478 12 00, http://humar
hofnin.is/
Lobster soup, lobster pizza, lobster baguette and grilled lobster
are served here. Watch the boats
from which the lobsters are
bought arriving and leaving
through the windows. The lamb,
duck and fish are also regional
products (▶ p. 178).

**Plain on the outside, really cosy on the inside is the top restaurant
Lækjarbrekka in Reykjavík's Bankastræti 2**

The Island of the Lambs

Icelandic sheep are different from other sheep. They are the direct descendants of Viking sheep and they are kept today just like their ancestors were kept more than 1,000 years ago. This can't necessarily be seen – but it can be tasted!

In Iceland there are almost twice as many sheep as people. In the summer around one million members of the species Ovis orientalis graze on the meadows and pastures. The Icelandic **wild sheep** is a member of the Nordic short-tailed sheep family that was once spread out from Greenland and Iceland through Great Britain and Scandinavia all the way to the Ural Mountains. Most of these old species of sheep have been replaced in the meantime by more modern species that yield more meat. But in Iceland the **Vikings' sheep** have been allowed to multiply for around 1200 years almost without any cross-breeding.

Species-appropriate and Organic

In June shortly after lambing the mother sheep and their offspring are driven into the mountains, where they can graze and look for their own food all summer without supervision. The lambs know no barns, get no industrial feed, no antibiotics and no growth hormones. Their life consists of fresh air, fragrant herbs, clear mountain water, playing with their own kind and the dangers that sheep face in the wilderness in all kinds of weather. During the **Réttir**, the sheep drive in September, the farmers ride on Icelandic horses into the mountains and drive the sheep back into the valley, where they are sorted in pens according to their markings and returned to the owners. Most of the lambs are then slaughtered and land as delicacies on plates or in deep freezers. Their meat does not taste like our usual lamb's meat, but rather it is spicier, like game.

The Best Lamb

In Reykjavík's gourmet restaurants lamb can be enjoyed in all its varieties. The best addresses include **Restaurant Dill** in the Nordic House (▶p. 75), which was built by the Finnish star architect Alvar Aalto. The menu varies with the seasons. Filet of highland lamb is served here in the summer, for example, on a bed of spinach with sorrel sauce.

Lamb is also an important subject in **Lækjarbrekka** (▶p. 76) in Bankastræti. Here the meat is marinated with blueberries as an appetizer or served as a main dish in fine thyme sauce. In the Gallery Restaurant of **Hotel Hólt** (▶p. 76) lamb is spiced with caraway and served with stuffed fennel. Outside of the capital, the **Hotel Búðir** (▶p. 76) on Snæfellsnes Peninsula serves a small, but very fine selection of lamb dishes.

Typical Dishes

Other countries, other customs: the taste of the Icelandic speciality
hákarl reminds German star cook Vincent Klink of »overly ripe cheese,
like Romadur in its final stages with a shot of horse urine«. But this did
not stop him from making a culinary voyage of discovery: »Isn't cooking
and eating together the best way to get to know people?« Just so. Try it
here…

Farm owner Hildibrandur Bjarnason on the shark farm Bjarnarhöfn with a
piece of grey shark, which is served – fermented – as »hákarl«

Skyr, a low calorie mixture of yoghurt and quark with a thousand-
year tradition, is typically Icelandic.
In supermarkets skyr is generally
available in two varieties: »hraert«,
that is stirred, and »óhraert«, not
stirred. The latter has to be diluted
with milk or cream. Skyr is ideally
eaten with fresh fruits, preferably
blueberries, as a tasty dessert or at
breakfast.

Súrmjólk, a thick sour milk, is always on every Icelandic breakfast
table. Traditionally it is sprinkled
with brown sugar.

Everywhere on Iceland's coasts
wooden scaffolding can be seen
with fish dangling in the wind. After the fish is dried, it is rolled,
stripped and sold as **harðfiskur**. Its
smell takes getting used to, but

the taste is comparatively mild. Icelanders spread butter on harðfiskur before eating it.

Hangikjöt is less controversial than harðfiskur: it is strongly smoked, salted lamb that might remind you of gammon steak. Birch wood or dried sheep dung is used to make the smoke. Icelanders eat their »hung meat« in thin slices on bread or on holidays with a white sauce, peas and sweetened mashed potatoes or glazed potatoes.

Kjötsúpa, a lamb stew, is a kind of Icelandic national food that simmers in many cafés, snack bars and even petrol stations in a large pot on the cooker. Every cook and every homemaker has a unique recipe, but the main ingredients lamb, potatoes, turnips and cabbage are always included.

Every Icelandic child knows how to make **Lummur**, small thick pancakes, since it is part of the curriculum in the fourth school year. The ingredients are wheat flour, oats, baking powder, salt, sugar and lemon rind. Mix everything in a bowl, make a depression in the centre, into which milk, súrmjólk, oil and an egg are added. Mix

these in well in circular movements from the centre. Then bake them in a hot griddle. On the first side bake them for two minutes, then on the other side only briefly. Lummur taste best hot with butter, cinnamon and sugar.

Rúgbrauð is a somewhat sticky black rye bread reminiscent of pumpernickel. It is not baked but either dried for 24 hours at 100°C/212°F or steamed over hot springs (seytt rúgbrauð). It tastes sweet, but it is nevertheless served with salted butter and savoury sliced meats. It is also served with soups. Very nourishing and ideal for backpackers!

Celebrating and Feasting

Even if Icelanders sometimes act Nordic cool, they love to celebrate and do it often. There are many occasions. Some of them go back to pre-Christian times, others have religious origins, while others again are based on historic dates. Food, drink and laughter are always involved, often also music, singing or dancing. Traditional festivals are usually celebrated in the family or with friends, but colourful street festivals are also popular.

The Icelandic year begins already with a festival: Christmas time ends on January 6 with fireworks and bonfires. Twelve days later the old Icelandic month of **Þorri**, when Icelanders celebrate **Þorrablót**, a revived traditional sacrificial feast. People gather in families or with friends to eat traditional Icelandic »delicacies« like sheep's testicles, Hákarl (fermented shark) and Svið (seared mutton head). Anyone visiting a restaurant in Iceland between January 18 and February 26 should study the menu more carefully than usual. Food also plays an important role in the **Icelandic carnival**. On Shrove Monday children hit their parents with colourfully decorated sticks so that they will give the children »**bollur**«, a kind of cream cake. **Shrove Tuesday** is called »**Sprengidagur**« (burst day), and this name says it: everyone eats pea soup with salted lamb to the bursting point. Only on **Ash Wednesday** do the children wear costumes and go singing from house to house to collect sweets.

Specialties to feast on

> **!** *Food & Fun* **Insider Tip**
>
> MARCO POLO TIP
>
> In Iceland celebrating well often also means eating well. During the annual **Food & Fun Festival** in February gourmets get what they want, too, as international and local chefs present their creations in many restaurants. At Easter there are not only large praline eggs on the breakfast table – traditional **roast lamb** is also served to celebrate the day. In the many street festivals during the year love (for the festival) also goes through the stomach: there's always enough to eat.

In the past Iceland only had two seasons, **summer** and **winter**. For this reason for Icelanders summer traditionally begins on the third Thursday in April, even if there is still snow and ice on the ground outside. People exchange summer gifts on the »first day of summer« and wish each other a happy summer. The start of the long, light days is also a welcome occasion for street festivals and parades with brass bands. On the first Sunday in June ships gather in all of the harbours and Icelanders remember all drowned seamen on Seaman's Day.

Two seasons

Sun in (Culture) Night takes place every year in August in Reykjavík

Most important holiday

The most important Icelandic holiday is **Independence Day** on June 17. On this day Icelanders commemorate June 17, 1944, the birthday of the freedom fighter Jón Sigurdsson, on which the Republic of Iceland was founded. There are speeches, colourful parades, music and dancing. A few days later the **summer solstice** takes place. The longest day of the year, June 21, is not as important in Iceland as it is in Scandinavia however. But it is still a chance to celebrate, mostly with dancing events in rural areas. **»Bank holiday«** is celebrated on the Monday after the first weekend in August. All Icelanders have the day off and on the long weekend they flock to holiday cottages, campgrounds or one of the many festivals that take place everywhere.

Sheep drive

In September the Icelandic highland farmers drive their sheep and horses together, which spent the summer on the free range. They are driven together into the valleys and sorted into paddocks. This stock drive, **Réttir**, marks the end of summer, which for Icelanders is a welcome occasion to hold merry festivals. The third Sunday in October is traditionally the »first day of winter«. This is not a day for lively

Live music in Reykjavík

celebrations, but rather to gather together as a family and get a little melancholy. Christmas in Iceland is also celebrated with a tree and presents, and New Year's Eve is celebrated everywhere with fireworks.

The **Christmas season** lasts **26 days** in Iceland however. The reason is that Iceland does not have one but **13 Santa Clauses**. These are the sons of the **troll woman Gryla**. Starting on December 12 one of these odd fellows visits the families at home, where he stays for 14 days, brings gifts, but also makes mischief. There is, for example, the »door slammer«, the »pot scraper«, the »sausage pincher«, the »window starer« or the »door gap sniffler«. Starting on December 25, one of the sons of Gryla disappears every day until all are finally gone on January 6, so that the Icelanders can begin the new year with a merry feast again.

Thirteen Santa Clauses

Calendar of events

PUBLIC HOLIDAYS
January 1 (New Year), Maundy Thursday, Good Friday, Easter Sunday, Easter Monday, 3rd Thurs in April (beginning of summer), May 1 (Labour Day), Ascension Day, Whit Sunday and Monday, June 17 (National Day), 1st Monday in August (Commerce Day), December 24 – 26 (Christmas), December 31 (New Year's Eve (from midday))

FESTIVALS AND EVENTS
Critics claim: Whenever Icelanders get even a little bored they go to a festival or organize one themselves. Indeed life on Iceland is pleasantly marked by the many large and small events on almost every weekend of the year. The most important festivals are held in Reykjavík, but not only there. Here is a small selection.

JANUARY/FEBRUARY
Þorrablót
A mid-winter festival without a fixed date, it is usually celebrated between January 18 and February 16 and it goes back to Viking times. It is a welcome chance to drive away the winter blues. Traditionally Icelanders eat food on this date that for non-Icelanders takes some getting used to, like Hákarl and Sviö, fermented shark meat and seared sheep's head.

FEBRUARY
Winter light festival
In mid or late February the end of the cold time of year is celebrated in Reykjavík with atmospheric illumination of buildings, fireworks and a torch procession (www.vetrarhatid.is).

MARCH
Beer Day
For 75 years the consumption of beer was not allowed in Iceland, only on March 1, 1989 was the ban lifted. On this day Icelanders celebrate Bjórdagurinn (Beer Day) in pubs and restaurants, most often with a Rúntur: am old-fashioned pub crawl in a group,

where you stop and drink one beer per pub.

APRIL
Sumardagurinn Fyrsti
On the third Thursday of this month Icelanders celebrate the beginning of summer, especially in Reykjavík, with colourful festivities and parades.

Aldrei fór ég suður
»I never went south« (»Aldrei fór ég suður«) is the name of a legendary music festival in Ísafjörður, which transforms the town in the Westfjords into »Rock City« every year – a counter-programme to the cultural programme in the capital city in the south. The festival (www.aldrei.is) generally takes place after the ski week (www.skidavikan.is) held every year at Easter; it is held in the harbour warehouse. Improvisation means everything here. There is no set programme, no fee and no admission charge: Feel free!

MAY
Sumardagurinn Fyrsti
But then everyone goes south, where the **beginning of summer** is celebrated with a cultural festival in Reykjavík (www.listahatid.is), for example. For more then two weeks the capital becomes the showplace of national as well as international film shows and theatre performances, concerts and art exhibits.

JUNE
Seaman's Day
In the fishing villages Seaman's Day, Sjómannadagurinn, is the largest festival of the year.

At Gay Pride Festival in Reykjavík

Viking Festival
Hafnarfjörður

Every year in mid June around 200 »Vikings« lay siege to the city of Hafnarfjörður. The Viking festival has Norse-style markets, music on ancient instruments, dancing and Viking food (www.hafnarfjordur. is).

JULY/AUGUST
Music festivals

High summer is high season for festivals like Culture Night in Reykjavík. Jazz is played in Egilsstaðir, classical music in the south-west, rock in Borgarfjörður Eystri, country music in Skagaströnd, folk music in Siglufjörður.

Other festivals

An alternative to hearing music in high summer is eating – in Höfn, for example, there is a **lobster festival** and in Dalvík Fish Day is celebrated. Horse lovers meet at the Icelandic horse spectacle **Landsmót**, and anyone who likes things colourful and extravagant enjoys **Gay Pride** in Reykjavík. The most important summer festival of Iceland is held on the Westman Islands: During Þjóðhátíð Heimaey Island turns into one big party for three days on the first weekend in August (www.dalurinn.is).

SEPTEMBER
Night of Lights

During the **Night of Lights** in Reykjanesbær fireworks flow down the cliffs into the harbour like lava.

Réttir

The **sheep drive** and the return of the horses from the highlands in September mark the end of summer.

October

The music festival **Iceland Airwaves** in the capital city Reykjavík is the venue for five days for new bands from all over the world.

Individual and Creative

The French word »flâner« (stroll) only has French roots at first glance. In fact the French verb »flâner« goes back to Old Icelandic »flana«, which means as much as »strolling around without a destination«. And really, you make the best finds in Icelandic shopping areas when you do just that: stroll around without a destination.

People don't go to Iceland to hunt for bargains. Everyday necessities are much too expensive there for that. But many of the things that make life nice and colourful should be bought here, simply because they are only available here and nowhere else in the world.

Good and expensive

Take **fashion**, for example: Icelandic women are known for their unique, extravagant style. Creativity is important here, and a new generation of young designers places value in original ideas. In and around Reykjavík not only the large shopping centres Kringlan and Smáralind (Kópavogur) attract. Almost every Icelandic fashion label has a boutique in the capital city. One of these belongs to **Sara María Eyþórsdóttir**. In 2005 she opened the shop »Naked Ape« and collected fans all over the world with her creations. »Naked Ape« has been closed since 2011 and the designer has started a new label called Forynja. Everything from fashion to bedsheets to furnishings is available here, shrill, colourful and unique (Laugavegur 12, www.forynja.is).

What elves wear today

»I have two hands, a brain, many ideas and a very good sense of humour«, says the Icelandic designer **GAGA Skorrdal** about herself. In her shop in Reykjavík she sells dresses, hats, caps and pullovers unlike any others in the world (Vesturgata 4, www.gaga.is).

The two designers **Bjork** and **Vala** deliberately sell their wares in Iceland. For their label **Spaksmannsspajrir** they design »clothing for wise girls«, inspired by Iceland's landscape and history, a mix of Gothic style and folklore in high quality materials combined with handwoven fabric. This is what elves would wear today (Bankastraeti 11, www.spaksmannsspjarir.com)!

Flowing fabrics and elegance in layers are what mark the Icelandic label **ELM**, which also has its own shop in Reykjavík. The UK is ELM's largest foreign market (Laugavegur 1, www.elm.is).

Jewellery that fits Iceland's natural landscape is made from lava stone by the goldsmith **Dýrfinna Torfadóttir**. Her studio is in Akranes

Unique & chic = unique Chic

(Stillholt 16–18, www. diditorfa.com), but pieces from her collection can also be bought in Reykjavík (in shops including the Airport Shop Keflavík and in the souvenir shop in Hotel Saga). Another good address for jewelry and design is **Kirsuberjatréð** (Vesturgata 4, www.kirs.is). Ten designers got together here. They sell bags made of fish skin, colourful fashion jewellery, extravagant lamps, ceramics and glass, fashion and accessories. The cult flea market **Kolaportið** in the former coal store near the harbour (Geirsgata) is a real treasure trove, as is **Kraum Gallery** in the oldest house in Reykjavík, which sells exquisite furniture, jewellery, clothing and accessories by Icelandic designers (Aðalstræti 10, www.kraum.is).

Music shops in Reykjavík are also worth visiting. Take lots of time for **Smekkleysa** (»bad taste«, Laugavegur 28, www.smekkleysa.is) and for **12 Tónar** (Skolavorðustígur 15, www.12tonar.is). Here you can not only browse through the great variety from the Icelandic music scene, but also enjoy coffee and newspapers during the day and live music in the evening, and with lots of luck you might even meet Björk, if she happens to be in Iceland, or one of the members of the band Sigur Rós.

> **!**   *Tax free!!*   Insider Tip
>
> MARCO ⊕ POLO TIP
>
> Watch for the »**tax-free shopping**« sign in windows to save money: When your purchase is worth more than 4000 Icelandic Kroner (at the airport: 5000 Kroner) ask for the tax-free form when you pay. If you stay no longer than three months the **value-added tax**, which can be up to 15% of the purchase price, will be **refunded**. It is important to remember the following two points: Apart from woollen products everything has to be in the **original packaging** and presented to customs before checking in. The **refund coupon** can be cashed in directly at the Landsbanki Íslands (bank teller window) in the departure hall.

Even smaller villages nearly always have a grocery store or supermarket; larger petrol stations also often sell groceries. The choice of fruit and veg is significantly smaller and more expensive than in other countries, with almost everything **imported or grown under glass**.

Opening times
: Shops are usually open Mon – Fri 9am – 6pm, Sat 9am – 2pm or 6pm. Large supermarkets often stay open until 11pm, in Reykjavík even round the clock. Icelandic banks are open Mon to Fri from 9.15am until 4pm.

Get Your Knitting on: More than a Souvenir

No Icelandic closet is without a hand-knit Iceland pullover. The woolly wonders protect against the cold, wind and rain, are lighter than down jackets, more breathable than microfibres and relatively easy to care for. The versatility of the typical Icelandic knitted pullovers comes from a few Icelandic specialities in the production.

A real Iceland wool pullover can be recognized at first sight: the wide **decorative band** around the chest is its trademark. The rest is solid coloured, apart from decorative bands at the bottom edge and sleeve ends. Another important detail sets it apart from Norwegian pullovers with their T-pattern: it is made on circular knitting needles in one piece. First the body and the sleeves are made. Then the stitches are all taken up onto the needle and **knit together** from that point on. This leads to the Icelandic wool pullover's first unique characteristic: it has no irritating seams.

The Lopapeysa

Icelandic traditions mostly have roots that go back to Viking times. Iceland wool sweaters are different. Even though these warm, thick pullovers that are called »lo-

Typical of Iceland wool sweaters are the broad, patterned chest band

papeysa« can be found in every closet in Iceland they are no more than a few decades old. For centuries knitwear in Iceland had been made of firmly spun wool yarn and the clothing was rough and heavy. But in the 1920s Icelandic needlework magazines for the first time presented pullovers made of loosely turned lopi wool yarn and loosely knit in the characteristic pattern. These seaters were light and yet **warm**.

Natural Product

But the Icelandic sheep, from whose wool the sweaters are made, do have roots that go back to the Vikings. As already mentioned they are descendants of Nordic short-tailed sheep that came to Iceland with the Vikings around 1200 years ago. Thanks to the island's location they have been able to preserve their special character until today. This applies to their wool as well: the wool of the Icelandic wild sheep consists of long, water resistant outer hair and short, soft inner hair with excellent **insulating properties**. Both types of hair are mixed and loosely turned to produce lopi, traditional knitting yarn. This produces the mohair-like quality of the yarn. Even when this yarn is knitted in loose stitches the sweaters are still **wind-proof** and **water resistant**. The natural lopi wool has a natural antibacterial function. Odours can be removed by airing it and many spots can be brushed out. **Alafoss lopi** is what the thick yarn is called in Iceland, which is usually used for outdoor Iceland pullovers. Thinner pullovers are made from lett lopi

and these can be worn under a jacket. These kinds of yarn are produced in Iceland's only spinning mill, named **Istex**. Factory sales in Mosfellsbær, 17km/10mi north of Reykjavík, is especially interesting for knitters who need material for their own creations.

Shopping Tips

A lopapeysa can be bought in every souvenir shop. Sweaters are also produced and sold on many farms, like the horse farm **Hrafnkelsstaðir** near Borgarnes (www.reiten-in-island.de), or **Eiríks-staðir**, about 80km/50mi northeast of the town Egilsstaðir (www.eiriksstadir.com). Depending on size, style and design prices start at GBP80 (€100), sometimes much more. But this is not much in view of their versatility and long life span when cared for properly.

Incidentally: anyone who does not want to give himself away as a tourist in Iceland never wears his lopapeysa at temperatures above 10°C/50°F. That's when t-shirt weather starts in Iceland!

Alafoss Factory Outlet Insider Tip
Alafossvegi 23, Mon – Fri 9am to 6pm, Sat 9am – 4pm
www.alafoss.is
With some luck you can find a bargain here and the selection of yarn types and colours is big. Knitwear is also sold but at similar prices to the rest of Iceland.

Þingborg Wool Center Insider Tip
On the Ring Road, 8km/5mi east of Selfoss, Tue – Fri 1pm – 4.30pm
www.thingborg.net

The sweaters sold here are made from hand-spun wool from house-own sheep. The sweaters are considered to be especially soft.

Farmers & Friends
Hólmaslóð 2, 101 Reykjavík, Mon to Fri 10am – 6pm, Sat 11am – 4pm; www.farmersmarket.is
Many boutiques carry items from the local label »Farmers Market«, which specialices in traditional Icelandic zig-zag patterns from the 1950s. The small family-owned business even has a flagship store in Reykjavík.

Islandic Hand-knitting League
Skólavörðustígur 19, 101 Reykjavík

Mon – Fri 9am – 6pm, Sat 10am until 4pm, www.handknit.is
Wide selection, competent sales staff, cheaper than souvenir shops.

Market and bazaar in Reykjavík
Fleamarket Kolaportið in the former coal store at the harbour, Sat/Sun 10am – 5pm; Thorvaldsen's Bazaar, Austurstraeti 4, Mon – Fri 9am – 6pm, Sat/Sun 10am – 2pm
Affordable prices can be found in the capital in Kolaportið flea market or in Thorvaldsen's Bazaar, one of the oldest shops in the city. The sweaters here are all handmade, the staff volunteers and the profit is given to charity.

Well-prepared for wind and cold weather with these sweaters

Sport and Outdoors

Fit by Nature

Waterfalls surrounded by wisps of fog, grass-covered turf ho-
zuses nestled against green hills, lava deserts, coastal cliffs,
glacial lakes. No matter where you are in Iceland nature is
overwhelming and ubiquitous. And wherever you want to be
active during your holidays you always travel closely with nature – or battling against it …

It might sound odd at first, but it's true: the only holiday-makers on
Iceland who do not depend on the weather are the ones who go
swimming. When you're relaxing in hot water, the snow and ice at the
edge of the pool are far from your mind. And rain and fog don't
bother you when you're wet already. Everywhere in Iceland a **heated
pool, hot spring, hot pot, water park** or even a **heated beach**
with year-round swimming pleasure is not far away. Anyone looking
for peace for body and soul, impressive surroundings to relax in will
find them here.

Swimming paradise Iceland

Reykjavík was even named »**Spa City**« by the European Spas Association. Here you will find heated outdoor pools, mineral pools and
wellness spas for every taste. The »**Blue Lagoon**«, about 25 minutes
from the capital, is legendary; there you can splash in warm salt water
between lava fields and snow-capped peaks while lifeguards on the
edge of the pool wear rain jackets. In **Laugardalur**, the valley of hot
springs, a large spa facility has been built. According to the newspaper »Guardian« the **most beautiful exotic spa** in Europe is located
in Reykjavík: at the golden beach of **Nauthólsvík** geothermally heated water is fed into a small bay, and the water temperature in the
summer is between 15 and 19°C (59 and 66°F). There is no lack of
opportunities outside of Reykjavík either, like the **lagoon** at Lake
Mývatn.

Wellness spas for every taste

WATER SPORTS

No one thinks of scuba diving in Iceland. But they ought to since Iceland has become an insider's tip for divers. In **Þingvellir National
Park** divers have the unique opportunity to dive between two continents. In the **Silfra rift** the continental plates of America and Asia
drift apart, and the glacial melt water is so clear that there is visibility

Insider's tip for divers

A trip to the Krafla region (here with Leirhnjúkur rift and lava fields) is
spectacular, but it can also be dangerous.

Diving in Þingvellir National Park: the ice cold glacial water is so clear that visibility is over 100m/330ft

up to 100m/330ft in the underwater lava fields and the many branches of the underwater cave system. **Akureyri** offers another diving adventure that is unique: just under the water's surface in the Eyjafjord lies »Strýtan«, a more than 50m/165ft-high underwater chimney that spews hot water. These hydrothermal springs, which are called »white smokers«, usually only exist in the ocean. Despite the **extreme environmental conditions** that prevail in the hot water, bacteria, worms, clams and starfish live in the chimney. Scientists consider them to be **models of how life developed** on earth.

Rafting

Rafting is a water sport that can be carried out in many of the rivers in Iceland. **Hvítá** and **Jökulsá** Rivers are especially popular.

Angling

For those who prefer to sit next to the water and fish rather than moving around in or on it, Iceland has one-of-a-kind fishing in crystal clear rivers whose courses are not disturbed by power plants. **Angling for salmon** has its price, though. On some rivers a day of fishing costs 600 to 800 British pounds (800 to 1000 euros). A licence for trout fishing is cheaper. The Icelandic fishing card, **Veiðikortið**, allows fishing to one's heart's content in 35 lakes for around GBP 30 (€40). Disinfect your fishing gear before bringing it along. Further information: www.mast.is

ON THE TRAIL

Hardly anywhere is the expression »sudden temperature change« as fitting as it is here: In Iceland the weather can change dramatically and quickly – even in the summer situations come up that usually occur in other seasons in the more moderate zones, with downpours, storms, frost and even snow. Paths can turn into mud and rivers swell to twice their normal size. Anyone trekking by bike or on foot should get accurate and reliable information beforehand and not save on his equipment. For people not bothered by the weather hiking or mountain biking can be an unforgettable adventure, the likes of which cannot be experienced elsewhere.

On foot and on a bike

Iceland's most famous hiking route is the **Laugavegur** from Landmannalaugar to Þorsmörk. For 54km/32mi that can easily be covered in four days hikers pass through all the kinds of landscape that Iceland is known for. These include lava fields, mountains, mossy meadows, volcano peaks, bubbling mud pots and hot springs. In the summer months things can get quite »busy« for Iceland – by all means reserve sleeping places in the huts in good time beforehand.

Iceland's best-known hiking trail

On many other routes in Iceland it can happen that no other people are seen for days. The Icelandic hiking and mountain biking clubs will help organize tours (addresses ▶ p. 102).

Pleasure alone

WATCHING WILDLIFE

Anyone who wants to observe wildlife in Iceland need not worry about predators or snakes. Unlike other Nordic countries there are no bears, wolves, lynxes or adders. The only form of life interested in human blood is the mosquito, which becomes a plague in only a few areas on the island. Arctic terns and sea gulls can get very unpleasant when they are defending their nests however.

Harbour seals and other seals live everywhere along the coasts of Iceland, as they love the salmon-rich river mouths, mud flats or sunny beaches. One of the country's largest

seal colonies lives in Hindsík Bay on Vatsnes Peninsula. The animals have been protected here for decades and are very friendly, which makes them easy to photograph. Near Ósar there is a stone wall to hide behind and to be able to watch the seals. With some luck **Arctic ringed seals** can also be seen. These shy individuals can be recognized by the light rings around dark spots on their grey fur. On the coast near Akureyri **hooded seals** with the typical bladder between forehead and nose can be seen sometimes. **Grey seals** can easily be spotted in northern Iceland. They can be distinguished from harbour seals by their more pointed heads. Harbour seal colonies also live in the mud flats of Héraðssandur in northeastern Iceland and on the southern coast.

Whales and dolphins
(▶MARCO POLO Insight p.180)

Anyone who wants to help save the whales and dolphins should book a **whale safari** in Iceland as the booming whale tourism is the main reason for many Icelanders to stop hunting them. Despite international protests and even though there is hardly any demand in the market for whale meat Iceland refuses to comply with international bans on whale hunting. This means that every year numerous fin and minke whales are slaughtered in Icelandic waters. This, of course, cannot be done in front of tourists, so the organizers of whale watching tours are actually a lobby in favour of the gentle ocean giants. But booking a whale tour by boat is not just a political statement, it is also an unforgettable experience. Minke whales and hump-backed whales are the most common whales around Iceland. But fin whales, orcas and porpoises as well as dolphins also show up. And with lots of luck an extremely rare blue whale might surface. In Reykjavík several tour organizers leave from the old harbour. Elding, for example, offers four to six whale tours per day during the summer months, the price is around 8000 ISK per person. From the harbour in Keflavík the M.S. Moby Dick starts every day during the summer around 9am for a three-hour tour for around 4000 ISK. On the Westman Islands Vikingtours offers trips for which the time is set according to the time and number of participants. Here mainly orcas and dolphins can be seen. In the north, in Húsavík, the success rate is especially high, at 98%. Gentle Giants and North Sailing offer whale safaris several times a day (addresses ▶ p. 103).

Birds

In Iceland there are around 300 kinds of birds – and that is not many considering that the classification »bird« contains more than 10,000 species, which makes it the largest class of land animals. But in Iceland the density and composition or the bird population make them unique.

The rarest and most protected bird in Iceland is the **gyrfalcon**. Its popularity as a hunting falcon and global warming have lead to this, the world's largest species of falcon, being in danger of extermination.

In Iceland approaching the nests without special permission is not allowed. Icelandic gyrfalcons grow to be around 50cm/20in tall and are usually dark grey. Among the rare birds on Iceland is also the **sea eagle**, with about 30 pairs living on Snæfellsnes Peninsula and around the Breiðafjörður.

Lake Mývatn (fly lake) is an area especially suited for birds; 16 different kinds of ducks alone brood there, including **harlequin ducks** and the **Barrow's goldeneye**, both of which are rare in Europe. The bird cliffs in Iceland's coastal cliffs are also meccas for bird lovers. **Puffins, northern fulmars, guillemots, razorbills, kittiwakes** and **cormorants** brood here. **Northern gannets** can also be seen. The best known bird cliffs at the Látrabjerg coastal cliffs in the Westfjorden, at Hafnaberg on Reykjanes Peninsula and on the islands Lundey, Eldey and Heimaey. Bird cliffs should be visited from mid May to July, as many of the birds are out at sea when they are not brooding.

MARCO POLO INSIGHT

?

Protection in the wrong territory

In areas with large numbers of birds it can happen that you accidentally enter the territory of **Arctic terns** or **skuas**. While they are brooding these birds attack all enemies that get close to their nests. While terns usually only warn by flying at the enemy, the buzzard-sized skuas actually attack; but they rarely cause serious injuries. Since the birds always aim for the enemy's highest point they can be diverted from your own head by holding up a stick or umbrella.

The most important addresses

SWIMMING/WELLNESS SPAS

Laugar Spa
Sundlaugarvegur 30 a
Reykjavík
Tel. 5 53 00 00
www.laugar.com

Blue Lagoon
Grindavík
Tel. 4 20 88 00
www.bluelagoon.com

Geothermal beach
Ylströnd
Nauthólsvík
Tel. 5 1166 30
www.nautholsvík.is

Jarðböðin
Jarðbaðshólar
Mývatn
Tel. 4 64 44 11
www.jardbodin.is

DIVING

Strýtan Divecenter
Huldugil 25
Akureyri
Tel. 862 2949
www.strýtan.is

DIVE.IS
Hólmaslóð 2
Reykjavík
Tel. 6 6328 58
https://www.dive.is

Across Lava and Ice on Viking Horses

When the Vikings loaded their dragon boats in the 9th century in order to settle on Iceland, they took their toughest horses along. In the isolation of island life a very special race of horses developed here in the course of centuries, the robust, intelligent and willful Icelandic horse.

»Gæðingur«, dream horse, is what Icelandic riders call their best mounts. But any layperson who watches a herd of Icelandic horses at pasture cannot understand this enthusiasm. All you see is some shaggy, elemental ponies grazing lethargically. Only when they are saddled is the energy in their lively eyes to be seen, their zeal and quick mind. Only when riding them through the wilderness are their surefootedness, their soft gaits and their strong nerves evident.

Horse or Pony?

By modern definition the Icelandic horse's around 140cm/56in height actually makes it a pony. But Icelandic horse lovers all over the world do not like to hear this as these horses are the descendants of medieval horses and back then the horses simply were no bigger than this. In the fans' ears »pony« sounds too much like a petting animal for children, and that's not what Icelandic horses are. While these horses are good mounts for small and large children but thanks to their sturdy bones they can easily carry adults, too, and their very special style of gait makes them tireless sports partners in tournaments.

At the Right Gait

Nowadays horses »only« know three gaits: **walk, trot** and **gallop**.

But this was not so during the Middle Ages. At that time so-called **palfreys** were popular – light horses that could amble, which is the gait that is now called »tölt«. Unlike the trot or the gallop there is **no springing phase**. With each step of the horse at least one of the horse's feet is touching the ground, so the rider does not feel any jolting. Women used to prefer such palfreys as they could hardly stay in a ladies' saddle when the horse was trotting. But travellers also preferred tölting horses over long distances. When better roads were built on the European mainland in the course of centuries, large draughting horses were needed instead of light, comfortable ones to pull coaches. So in the course of time horses were bred away from the tölt. But there were no paved roads on Iceland for a long time and the genetic disposition to tölt remained. Many Icelandic horses are even capable of a fifth gait, the flying pace.

On a Horse

This kind of riding represents the oldest form of cooperation between humans and horses. Being released from civilization, the close contact with the rider, the slow travelling speed and **experiencing** one's own boundaries **intensively** leads to **experiences of nature** that

Seeing Iceland on a horse: riding tour near Hafnarfjörður

are rarely to be had in the 21st century. By the way, exploring Iceland's nature on the back of a horse is a means of transportation that is both ecologically friendly and typical of Iceland.

Íshestar and **Eldhestar** are the two big riding centres on Iceland, which have been offering day rides and adventure tours for tourists for some decades. Both have their own horses at their home bases near Reykjavík and leave from there on tours of the area. They also work together with farmers all over Iceland and can thus offer tours in other parts of the country. There are also many smaller farms and horse breeding stables on Iceland that emphasize personal service and individual tours, from rides for beginners to more strenuous rides for experienced riders ("addresses p. 99). Popular tours for experienced riders run straight across Iceland via the ancient highland routes Kjölur and Sprengisandur with their fascinating contrasting landscapes. With daily stages up to ten hours riders and horses are both »put through their paces«, overnight stays are often in Lappland-style tents or mountain huts. But there is also the easy way: on many farms riders can tölt through beach or lava landscapes during the day and relax in the hot pot in the evening.

Horseback Riding on the Edge of the Arctic

When the Vikings came to Iceland in the 9th century they brought along their toughest horses. On the chilly island the weather-proof and sure-footed horses were the only help in covering long distances. In this way a very special breed of horses developed in the course of time: the robust, intelligent but also wilful Icelandic horse.

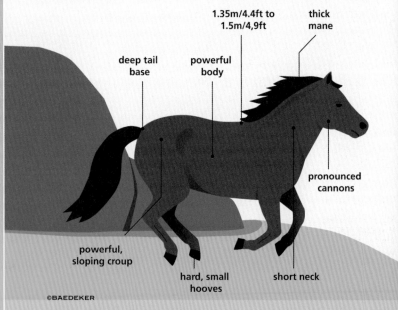

1.35m/4.4ft to 1.5m/4,9ft

thick mane

deep tail base

powerful body

pronounced cannons

powerful, sloping croup

hard, small hooves

short neck

©BAEDEKER

▶ **Gaits of Icelandic horses**
Unlike most horses Icelandic horses use two additional gaits, the tölt and the »flying pace«. For centuries these horses were the only means of transport on the island. As parts of Iceland are still not accessible by road horses are still a common alternative.

Walk
The walk is a four-beat gait. Feet move in the order back left, front left, back right, front right, and the horse moves forward slowly.

Trot
The trot is a two-beat gait. Diagonal pairs of legs move forward together.

▶ **Trekking on horseback**
There are many organizers of horse treks on Iceland. The distances vary from day rides to treks taking several days. Riders should be experienced and in good physical condition.

Some Trails on www.ishestar.is

Horse drive

Ride on the Wild Side

Odyssey of the north

Mountain and beach ride

REYKJAVIK

Power of creation

Other organisers
www.eldhestar.is
www.egilsstadir1.com
www.abbi-island.is
www.lysuholl.is

www.strandir.is
www.polarhestar.is
www.lythorse.com
www.husey.de

▶ **The Landsmot**
In 1950 Icelandic horse fans met for the first time in the Landsmot. There were horse races, horse judging and presentation of tournament horses. Meanwhile more than 1,000 horses can be admired during Iceland's largest tournament; it takes place every two years at different locations.

The Gæðingakeppni
The most common form of competition involving horses is in harmony with old traditions. Attractiveness, temperament, power and gaits are the decisive competitive criteria.

Event sites on www.landsmot.is

Gallopp
The gallop is a three-beat gait. Feet move in the order one back leg, one back and one front leg together, one front leg followed by a suspension phase.

Tölt
The horse runs quickly and upright, with the feet moving in the same order as with the walking gait. One foot is always on the ground. Jolt-free riding.

Flying pace
Icelandic horses are also capable of this extremely strenuous pace in which the pairs of legs on the same side move forward together.

! *Rules for riders* **Insider Tip**

Since many contagious animal diseases are not endemic to Iceland there are special rules for **bringing along your own riding clothes:** Used clothing must be washed, dry cleaned or disinfected. Consult your veterinarian for more details on disinfection. The cleaning or disinfection should be carried out **at least five days** before contact with Icelandic horses. Saddles, bridles and similar accessories made completely of leather may not be brought into Iceland under any circumstances, according to the Icelandic veterinary office. More information with the Icelandic veterinary office at **www.mast.is**

ANGLING
National Angling Association
Baendahollinni, Hagatorgi
Reykjavík
Tel. 5 53 15 10
www.angling.is

Lax-A Angelclub
Akurhvarf 16, Kópavogur
Tel. 5 31 61 00
www.lax-a.is

RAFTING
Arctic Rafting
Laugavegur 11, Reykjavík
Tel. 5 71 22 00
Brekkugata 5, Akureyri
Tel. 4 61 18 41
www.nonnitravel.is

HIKING
Ferðafélag Íslands
(Icelandic hiking club)

Mörkin 6, Reykjavík
Tel. 5 68 25 33
www.fi.is

Útivist
Laugavegur 178
Reykjavík
Tel. 5 62 10 00
www.utivist.is

MOUNTAIN BIKING
Icelandic mountain bike club
Brekkustíg 2
Reykjavík
Tel. 5 62 00 99
www.fjallahjolaklubburinn.is

Hike and Bike
Múlavegur 1
Mývatn
Tel. 8 99 48 45
www.hikeandbike.is

BIRDWATCHING
Ferry Herjólfur to Heimaey
Básaskersbryggja
Vestmannaeyjar
Tel. 4 81 28 00
https://de-de.facebook.com/gavia.travel

Gavia Travel
Álfaheiði 44, Kópavogur
Tel. 5 11 39 39
www.gaviatravel.com

WHALE WATCHING
Elding Whale Watching
Ægisgarður 7
Reykjavík
Tel. 5 55 35 65
www.elding.is

Viking Tours
Suðurgerði 4
Vestmannaeyjar

Tel. 4 88 48 84
www.vikingtours.is

Gentle Giants
Harbour Húsavík
Tel. 4 6415 00
www.gentlegiants.is

North Sailing
Hafnarstett 11, Husavik
Tel. 4 64 7272
www.whalewatchinghusavik.is

RIDING
Lýtingsstaðir
Varmahlið
Tel. 4 53 80 64
www.lythorse.com

Lýsuhóll
Snæfellsbær
Tel. 4 35 67 16
www.lysuholl.is

Íshestar
Sörlaskeið 26
Hafnarfjörður
Tel. 5 55-70 00
www.ishestar.is

Eldhestar
Völlum
Hveragerði
Tel. 4 8048 00
www.eldhestar.is

Pólar Hestar
Grytubakki II
Akureyri
Tel. 4 63 31 79
www.polarhestar.is

Húsey
Hróarstunga
Egilsstaðir
Tel. 4 71 30 10
www.husey.de

TOURS

A whole circuit of Iceland – or just sticking to the southwest?
Looking for solitude in the northeast or plunging into the
nightlife of Reykjavík? We take you on tours showing all the
different aspects of Iceland.

Tours Through Iceland

Thundering waterfalls and geysers, black lava deserts and ice blue glacier lakes, snow-capped peaks and green valleys, add a few sheep and horses, lots of solitude in nature and colourful encounters with people in picture book towns: our suggested tours will show you the most beautiful sides – and places – on the island.

Tour 1   A good all-rounder

Doing a circuit around Iceland on the almost fully-tarmacked Ring Road is the easiest way to explore many of the island's sights. Visitors with a bit more time on their hands can add little side trips to the highlands or into the Western fjords.

►page 110

Tour 2   Into the wild west

On the Snæfellsnes Peninsula and the extremely sparsely populated Western fjords, an abundance of natural spectacles await the visitor. Snæfellsjökull, mighty fjords and magnificent sandy beaches never fail to work their magic.

►page 113

Tour 3   Glaciers and geysers

This tour leads to some of the most famous highlights in Iceland and, even outside the main tourist season, can easily be combined with a short but interesting visit to Reykjavík.

►page 116

Tour 4   Iceland for specialists

Starting at Seyðisfjördur ferry harbour, this round trip leads to the extreme north, where Arctic foxes outnumber people. Taking in Húsavík, Goðafoss, Akureyri, Mývatn, Ásbrygi and Dettifoss, this tour encompasses some of Iceland's greatest sights.

►page 120

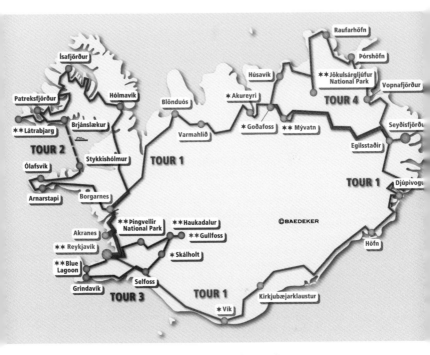

Out and About in Iceland

Iceland is a destination for individualists. The most important factors in planning the trip are time, budget and the choice of means of transportation. Everything else more or less happens on its own.

Personalized travel

Anyone who wants to travel in high summer and plans his trip late will soon discover that most of the accommodations are full. Whoever wants to travel by bus will need less money but more time on the ring route; it might be better to do just part of the tour instead of all of it. The tours described in this chapter thus can only offer a rough guide to individual planning. But they do give an impression of what you can experience in the different regions and how much time you'll need.

For the past few years insiders have been raving about **Reykjavík's pub scene**, and rightly so – prepare to be amazed at what goes on at summer weekends in the city! It seems like rivers of beer – and not just beer – flow through Reykjavík, and the whole city seems to be

City tour to Iceland?

out and about, as if the light-filled summer nights have to make up for the long dark winter. Gastronomically, Reykjavík also has plenty to offer: visitors undeterred by the high prices have the choice between a surprising number of first-class restaurants. However, few visitors just come for a **city break to Iceland** – most are attracted by the fascinating nature of the Atlantic Ocean island.

Sublime scenery and few people

It is the combination of fire and ice – the intensity of which no other country in Europe can match – that is the biggest draw of a holiday to Iceland. Where else to find such a **sparsely populated country** that offers such extreme landscapes? Only the coast is settled to any degree; often many kilometres lie between the farmsteads, and even settlements that on the map seem to promise a modicum of urban flair turn out to be villages with no more than 100 or 200 inhabitants. Visitors leaving the narrow, often green, coastal strip and driving into the **highlands**, find themselves after only a few kilometres in a landscape devoid of people, desert-like in places and only negotiable during a few months in summer by all-terrain vehicles with a high clearance. But even those keeping »only« to the Ring Road will not tire of the landscape, large swathes of which are pretty extreme. A drive through Iceland presents all conceivable **forms of volcanic activity**, as if the country were an open textbook. There are lava fields, sometimes black and hostile, sometimes covered by thick green cushions of moss, plus steaming fields of solfataras, that with their rich colours and inhospitable terrain could serve as **film sets for science fiction movies**. Contrasting beautifully with this are the largest glaciers in Europe, with countless jagged breaks and tongues; even lagoons can be found here, with dozens of icebergs swimming in them. Few countries can offer this kind of variety.

Hot spots and fjords

Visitors looking for extreme volcanic landscapes will find what they are looking for along a line between the Reykjanes peninsula and the Mývatn, as this is the location of the **island's hot spots** – most of the geothermally active areas. Life is quieter if no less spectacular in the Western fjords and on the fjord coast of east Iceland. Here, the **mighty fjords** dominate the landscape, carved by the glaciers of the last Ice Age. Surprisingly, many of these bays consist of sandy beaches stretching for miles, some of which do merit the sobriquet »dream beach«. No matter where travels might lead, don't forget to pack hiking boots and swimming togs. Even visitors to Iceland who are no great fans of extensive **trekking tours** have countless opportunities for shorter and simpler walks, often leading to the most beautiful waterfalls, gorges and areas of geothermal activity. The endless empty beaches are also ideal hiking territory. To make up for the somewhat chilly sea, which even the hardy Icelanders never set foot in, nearly every town has a public swimming pool. As there is little shortage of hot water, the pools are nearly always cosily warm, and the hot tubs that form part of every public pool have at least bath-tub temperature. An ideal place, where even the legendary Icelandic low pressure area cannot drag you down.

Choosing the Right Transport

The most comfortable way to travel in Iceland is of course by car. Visitors can either bring their own car – which means arriving in the east of the island, at the Seyðisfjörður ferry terminal – or, for shorter stays, consider the time-saving option of **arriving by plane** in Reykjavík and hiring a car. All routes described below may be negotiated without problems in a regular saloon car, while bearing in mind that longer sections off the Ring Road have not been tarmacked yet. It has to be said that the Icelanders are investing a lot of money in road improvements, so that every year many kilometres of gravel road are covered with asphalt. It is also possible to take the Ring Road around Iceland by bus, although travellers will need to factor in more time. A visit to the **Þingvellir National Park** and the **Geysir and Gullfoss** is no problem without a car, as they can nearly always be reached as day trips from Reykjavík. In principle, a trip into the **Western fjords** and around the Melrakkaslétta peninsula is also doable by public transport, if somewhat cumbersome. Here, a hire car opens up a lot more options for detours to more far-flung sights.

Most comfortable by car

Touring Iceland's highlands

Tour 1 A Good All-Rounder

Length of tour: 1,375km/854 miles
Duration: min 14 days

Full of variety, at some points running right next to the sea, at others heading inland for a stretch, the Ring Road leads through towns and past lakes, volcanoes, glaciers, meanders through lonely plateaus and steaming solfatara fields. The Ring Road runs once around the island and leaves travellers lots of opportunities to design their own tour.

The (side) trip is the reward

This tour can be completed in ten days by car, but then you will miss many worthwhile side trips, which actually give the tours its charm. To do justice to the tour you will need two, more likely three weeks. That way you can stop for a day's hiking or absorb some local culture. A four-wheel drive vehicle is necessary for trips away from the main road.

Off we go!

For anyone who arrives by airplane the tour begins in Keflavík. Staying at least one night in ❶****Reykjavík** is recommended in order to get used to the climate and locality, after that leave the capital city heading north. In Kópavagur in Smáralind shopping centre you can even shop on Sundays for everything you need on supplies and provisions. If you're in a hurry cross the fjord Hvalfjörður through the tunnel Hvalfjarðargöng (tolls are charged). But driving around the fjord leads through much more charming landscape. The detour of about 60km/36mi leads though a romantically wild, hardly settled region. Near Saurbær is the stylish Hotel Glymur in a remote location but still one of the best hotels in the country.

❷**Akranes** is worth a stop for its extensive local museum and to climb the mountain of Akrafjall, which gives great views of the Walfjord. ❸**Borgarnes** is modern and offers the chance to go shopping again before turning off onto the Ring Road into the interior of the

Highlights of Tour 1

▶ **Reykjavík**
Good museums, top-class pub scene, excellent restaurants

▶ **Reykholt**
In the footsteps of Snorri Sturluson

▶ **Glaumbær**
The outdoor museum gives interesting impressions of life in past times.

▶ **Mývatn**
Vulcanism in all variations, and: paradise for ornithologists

▶ **Vatnajökull/Skaftafell**
Sheer endless ice and nature pur

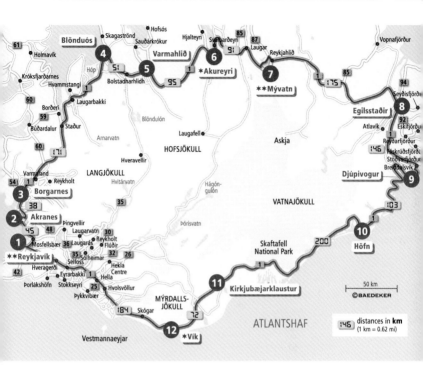

country. Anyone interested in Egil's Saga should visit the Land-námssetrið (Settlement Centre) near the bridge to Brákey Island for detailed information.

A larger but truly worthwhile side trip on the following part of the tour is the drive to Reykholt. The important Icelandic poet and historian Snorri Sturluson once lived in this historically rich village – a museum and several buildings are reminders of the influential **Goðorðs** in the Middle Ages. Follow the side road eastwards and soon the lava stream Hallmundarhraun and the Hraunfossar will appear, the most beautiful waterfalls in Iceland, which bubble out of black lava in hundreds of small streams.

Iceland's most beautiful waterfalls

Back on the Ring Road, the drive soon passes the imposing lava field of Grábrókarhraun, a bizarrely cleft moonscape, and shortly after Staður on the Hrútafjord returns to the coast. The northern part of the Ring Road, which you have now reached, offers lots of opportunities to see animals, but some side trips are necessary for this. If your time doesn't allow a seal tour on Vatsnes Peninsula, at least leave the

Bizarre moonscapes

Sidetrip to Húsavík to watch whales

Ring Road to go to Hóp Lagoon, where seals and sea birds live. The little stone church of Þingeyrar can also be visited here; it has a valuable medieval altar.

Iceland's oldest hotel

Shortly after ❹**Blönduós** the Ring Road leaves the coast once again and turns towards the interior. The next side trip is a must: ❺**Varmahlíð** on the [75] towards Sauðárkrókur. First visit the wonderful little peat church Víðimýri. And do not miss out on one of the best preserved peat farmyards on Iceland, the museum farm Glaumbær. In Sauðárkrókur then the subject is horses. Almost every farm in the area raises Icelandic horses and in Hólar you can not only study horses but also visit a horse museum. For riders there are also many opportunities here for unforgettable rides. You can stay in Hotel Tindastóll, Iceland's oldest hotel, in rooms with old-fashioned nostalgic charm. A boat trip to the bird island Drangey is also an experience.

Colourful cultural scene

The next stop is ❻***Akureyri**, the undisputed capital of northern Iceland, which boasts numerous museums and an interesting cultural scene, alongside some historic buildings. Plan in some time for the next stops.

On the way to the bird paradise **⓻** ∗∗ **Mývatn** and its touristic centre   Relax in the
Reykjahlíð, consider taking a look at the **Goðafoss** – the »waterfall   »new« blue
of the gods«. The detour to **Húsavik** is longer but it's worth it. Here   lagoon
you can go on a whale-watching tour with an astonishing success rate
of 98%. Try to schedule in a few days for the Mývatn as well, as nowhere else presents so many different forms of volcanic activity.
Mighty lava flows, pseudo craters, solfatara fields and the Krafla volcano turn the area into a fairy-tale landscape. To relax sink into the
milky blue waters of the »new blue lagoon« Jarðböðin and enjoy the
spectacular view of the sea.

From the Mývatn, the Ring Road leads through the country's inte-   Stocking up
rior to **❽ Egilsstaðir**, which lies on the elongated **Lagarfljót** lake,
where you can stock up on supplies again. There's not much to see
here but the lively town is a great starting point for side trips to the
east coast, which is characterized by deep fjords that stretch to the
south of **❾ Djúpivogur**. Anyone looking for solitude, horseback riding and watching seals and birds can spend a few days on **Húsey**.

Shortly after Egilsstaðir the road reaches the coast again and follows   Sublime
it. Natural spectacles take up more and more of the panorama here.   nature
The coastal town of **❿ Höfn** is already influenced by the huge **Vatnajökull**, its glacier tongues and outwash (broad plains of glacial out
wash) offering a breath-taking natural spectacle. The highlights of the
drive along the southern coast are the glacier lagoon of **Jökulsarlón**
with its icebergs, and **Skaftafell National Park**. When the weather
is good make sure to hike to **Svartifoss**, the black waterfall. The small
town of **⓫ Kirkjubæjarklaustur** is the best base for a trip to the Laki
fissure. The landscape around the Grassodenhof Núpsstaður nearby
is among Iceland's prettiest. Other highlights on the route are the
black beach at **⓬ ∗Vík í Mýrdal** and the waterfall **Skógafoss**. If you
have any time left go to **Heimaey**, in the Vestmannaeyar, from
Landeyjahöfn and explore the beautiful island before returning via
Hveragerði to **Reykjavík**.

Into the Wild West   **Tour 2**

Length of tour: 1,185km/736 miles
Duration: min 10 days

Tiny colourful villages against a backdrop of deeply-cut fjords,
mighty mountains and gorgeous sandy beaches to enchant
any nature lover. Here, climate and landscape are even harsher
than elsewhere in Iceland, and the solitude boundless.

Highlights of Tour 2

▶ **Snæfellsjökull**
Picture book glacier on the western
end of Snæfellsnes Peninsula

▶ **Látrabjarg**
Millions of sea birds brood on a cliff
up to 440m/1450ft high. A special
experience of natural.

This circular tour also takes the capital of ❶**Reykjavík** as its starting point. Leaving Reykjavík in a northerly direction follow the Ring Road to the town of ❷**Borgarnes**, which is closely linked to the Egillssaga. Immediately after Borgarnes, the [54] road branches off from the Ring Road and, just before turning west towards the Snæfellsnes Peninsula, leads through the lava field of **Eldborgarhraun**, from which the red »fire castle« (Eldborg) rises up. From here the road runs along the sparsely populated southern coast of the Snæfellsnes Peninsula to ❸**Arnarstapi**. This small village is one of the best bases from which to explore the glaciated volcanic cone of **Snæfellsjökull**, credited by some with magical powers. Due to its beautiful location on the steep coastal cliffs fringed by bird rocks, Arnarstapi itself is well worth a visit.

Rounding the tip of the peninsula provides many opportunities for both short and longer walks, before the old trading centre of ❹**Ólafsvík** is reached. Driving along the northern coast brings visitors to the fishing town of ❺**Stykkishólmur**. From here, a ferry crosses the Breiðafjörður to ❻**Brjánslækur**, significantly shortening the drive to the Western fjords. After this, heading west from Brjánslækur, serpentine roads wind past lonely, sandy beaches against the backdrop of mighty fjords, leading to Iceland's most impressive bird cliff, the ❼**Látrabjarg**, which shelters millions of breeding sea birds in the summer.

Sorcery and
magic From here, continue along partially-gravelled roads snaking their way through a grandiose, extremely sparsely populated landscape of

fjords to ❽**Patreksfjörður**, which was already a trading post at the time of the Hanseatic League (an alliance that monopolized trade along the coast of Northern Europe from the 13th to 17th centuries; it took control of trade with Iceland in the 16th century). On the way to ❾**Ísafjörður**, the largest town in the Western fjords, visitors really should make a stop at the Dynjandi waterfall. Ísafjörður, worth seeing for its blend of historic and modern houses, presents a near-urban bustle. The maritime museum reminds visitors of the hard life of fishermen. The reward for a lengthy drive along many deeply-carved, lonely fjords is ❿**Hólmavík**, with its biggest attraction, the

In summer the glacier cap of Snæfellsjökull melts
almost completely

unusual Icelandic Museum of Sorcery and Witchcraft. Having taken in part of the western bank of the **Húnaflói** (bay) and the **Hrútafjörður**, the tour eventually rejoins the Ring Road and heads back to its starting point of Reykjavík.

Tour 3 Glaciers and Geysers

Length of tour: 350km/217 miles
Duration: min 3 days

This tour is well suited for a short trip to Iceland – and not only in the summer high season, as the sights along the route are accessible in winter too. In fact, when covered in snow and ice the Gullfoss is at least as spectacular as in the summer.

A magical place

Starting in ❶ ✶✶**Reykjavík**, take the [36] via Mosfellsbær to the Þingvallavatn and the national park of ❷ ✶✶**Þingvellir**. For Icelanders Þingvellir is a magical place inextricably linked with their history, as it was here that over 1,000 years ago already, around 930, the first »assembly of free men of Iceland« was held. Out in the open innovations and changes that affected the whole nation were discussed – like in 1000 when they decided to accept Christianity voluntarily.

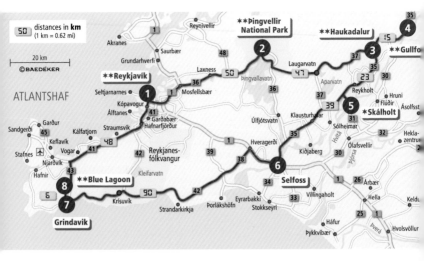

In the **Almannagjá Gorge**, running through the landscape like a gaping wound, visitors can experience up close the fact that Iceland lies right on the more than 20,000 kilometre-long Mid-Atlantic Ridge. The North American and the Eurasian Plates drift apart along this plate boundary at an average speed of two centimetres per year. This gap in the ocean floor makes it possible for magma to reach the surface regularly, which in turn closes the gap again. Plate tectonics is nowhere as visible as it is on this border between America and Europe. The 60km/37-mile drive around the Þingvallavatn on the winding, hilly road is very rewarding for the pretty views it repeatedly offers of the lake and the surrounding mountains.

Life at the edge (of the plate)

Highlights of Tour 3

▶ **Þingvellir**
The historical assembly site of the oldest parliament in the world is part of the UNESCO World Heritage.

From the Þingvallavatn, the road leads to the small village of Laugarvatn, with its natural saunas and hot tubs, and on to the geothermal area of ❸**Haukadalur** and then to the ❹**Gullfoss**. Virtually every tour bus stops for the most famous Icelandic geothermal field. Steam and hissing sounds emerge from various fissures, but the still, blue pools of hot water are remarkable too. The biggest attraction here though is the **Strokkur**, a fountain geyser which erupts several times an hour, sending a mighty column of water skywards. The large **Geysir** nearby, which incidentally gave its name to all erupting springs, was completely inactive for a long time; however, since an earthquake in 2000 the "father of all geysers" does surprise visitors with occasional eruptions.

▶ **Haukadalur**
Don't miss Strokkur Geyser.

▶ **Gullfoss**
The »Golden Falls« – beautiful and mighty!

▶ **Blue Lagoon**
a warm bath is always welcome!

On the way back, consider taking a detour along the Hvítá river to the former bishopric of ❺*Skálholt, which for centuries was an important centre of power. Road [35] eventually leads to ❻**Selfoss** and the Ring Road. Drivers with time to spare before their return to Reykjavik can make a detour on the Ring Road to **Vík** (135km/84 miles), worth seeing for its impressive plunging coastline, a beach which has been described as one of the most beautiful on earth, and its proximity to the Mýrdalsjökull. It might also be worth considering a short stop en route at the **Skógafoss** or a detour to the **Þórsmörk Valley**, particularly popular with hikers. Drivers heading directly for ❼**Grindavík** and on to Reykjavík from Selfoss should not miss taking a dip in the ❽**Blue Lagoon** – the most pleasant part of this tour and a fitting close.

Aurora Borealis

Aurora borealis or northern lights in the colours white, yellow, green are not uncommon on Iceland. These illuminated paintings in the sky always appear when there is increased solar activity – most recently in spring 2012.

▶ **Where do the northern lights come from?**
Polar lights appear at both of the earth's magnetic poles at the same time. On clear nights the conditions for watching polar lights in Iceland are ideal in the months September, October and March.

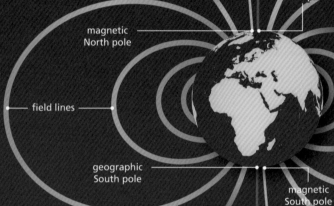

Dipolar axis

Earth's axis

geographic North pole

magnetic North pole

field lines

geographic South pole

magnetic South pole

▶ **How are polar lights formed?**

©BAEDEKER

1 After strong eruptions on the sun electrically charged particles flow as solar wind towards Earth.

Solar wind

Sun

Polar light in Iceland (film)

A phenomenon at great heights

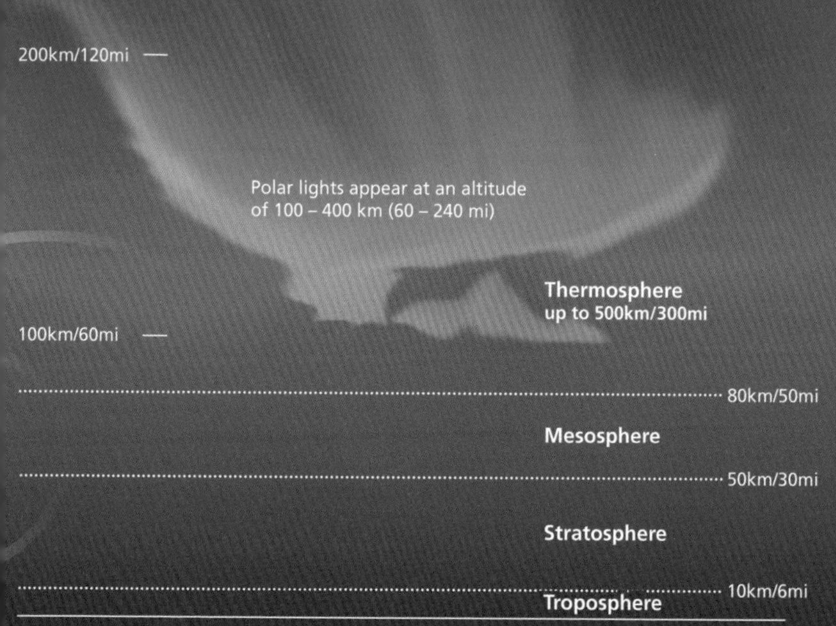

200km/120mi —

Polar lights appear at an altitude
of 100 – 400 km (60 – 240 mi)

Thermosphere
up to 500km/300mi

100km/60mi —

··· 80km/50mi

Mesosphere

··· 50km/30mi

Stratosphere

··· 10km/6mi

Troposphere

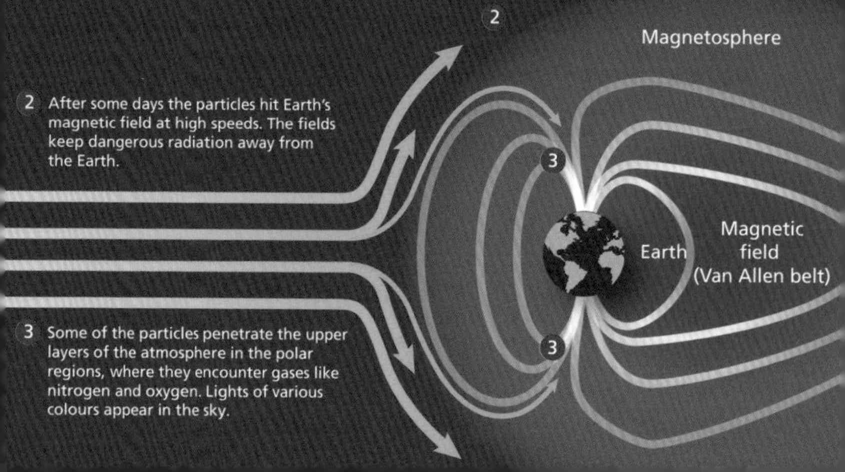

2

Magnetosphere

2 After some days the particles hit Earth's
   magnetic field at high speeds. The fields
   keep dangerous radiation away from
   the Earth.

3

3

Magnetic
field
(Van Allen belt)

Earth

3 Some of the particles penetrate the upper
   layers of the atmosphere in the polar
   regions, where they encounter gases like
   nitrogen and oxygen. Lights of various
   colours appear in the sky.

Tour 4 Iceland for Specialists

Length of tour: 705km/438 miles
Duration: min 10 days

On this tour, lonely hikes on the Langanes Peninsula and a drive around the practically uninhabited Melrakkaslétta Peninsula contrast with the popular tourist attractions of Húsavík, Goðafoss and Mývatn.

For those taking the ferry and their own car to Iceland, ❶ **Seyðisfjörður** on the east coast is the first point of contact with the island. They could not wish for a more beautiful introduction, as the town with its colourful houses and the fjord with its green mountain slopes and peaks flecked with snow even in summer, together form a magnificent backdrop. From the ferry harbour, the road leads over a pass to ❷**Egilsstaðir**, the busy hub of the region with its extensive East Iceland Heritage Museum. Before heading north, consider a drive around the **Lagarfljót** lake, with a walk in Iceland's largest forest and a hike up to the **Hengifoss** waterfall.

A drive north via ❸**Vopnafjörður** leads to ❹**Þórshöfn**, an ideal starting point for hikes on the abandoned **Langanes Peninsula**, one of the loneliest corners of Iceland. Afterwards, the [85] road leads around the **Melrakkaslétta Peninsula**, hugging the coast practically all the way. The extreme north of Iceland is sparsely populated and

Highlights of Tour 4

▸ **Langanes**
A hike on this deserted peninsula is balm for the soul.

▸ **Jökulsárgljúfur-National Park**
Unique canyon landscape with Ásbyrgi canyon as the highlight.

▸ **Mývatn**
Craters, solfatara fields and our feathered friends await visitors.

Insider Tip

No hour of life is wasted …

… that is spent on the back of a horse, according to Churchill. For that reason we are recommending a **tour on horseback**. Where the peninsulas Snæfellsnes and Westfjorde meet lies the **region of Dalir**, translated »valleys«. These are off the tourist routes and there are hardly any roads here – ideal conditions for a tour on sure-footed, tölt-paced Icelandic horses. **Information** is available from organizer Arinbjörn Jóhannsson, Brekkulækur, Hvammstangi, Tel. 4 51 29 38, **www.abbi-island.is**

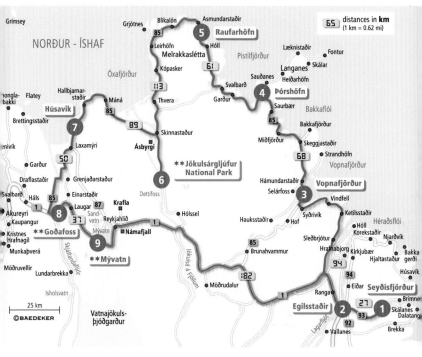

the coastline, littered with driftwood, has a rugged, austere beauty. Visitors looking for solitude but not wanting to forgo all comforts, should put up in the hotel of ❺**Raufarhöfn**. After a drive around the peninsula, ❻**** Jökulsárgljúfur National Park** offers good hiking options; don't under any circumstances miss the enormous, horseshoe shaped canyon of **Ásbyrgi** or one of the largest waterfalls in Europe (in terms of volume of water), the **Dettifoss**.

From the national park, return to the coast and drive to ❼**Húsavik**, to take part in a **whale-watching safari**. A good stopping-off point on the way to the Mývatn is at the ❽***Goðafoss**. A drive around the ❾****Mývatn** really requires at least two days, in order to explore the solfatara field at the Námafjall, the geothermal area shaped by the numerous eruptions of the Krafla volcano, the black lava towers of Dimmuborgir and of course the lake with its rich birdlife. A good base for exploring is the small town of **Reykjahlíd**. The Ring Road eventually leads back to Egilsstaðir, and after another 21km/13 miles to the tour's departure point at Seyðisfjörður.

SIGHTS FROM A TO Z

Iceland is what a land must look like just after creation: volcanoes, glaciers, waterfalls, erupting geysers, whales surfacing off the coast. Civilisation can be found in tiny villages and in Reykjavík, the island's captal.

Akranes

✶ C 6

Region: West Iceland
Population: 6500

Ever since the Hvalfjarðargöng Tunnel was built the small harbour town Akranes is only a 45-minute drive away from Reykjavík. While the towers of the cement factory, which can be seen for miles, are not very attractive at first sight the town at the foot of Mount Akrafjall has a beautiful beach, an interesting local museum, a romantic lighthouse and a small but fine shopping street.

WHAT TO SEE IN AKRANES

City stroll
Wandering around town, the two **lighthouses** on the tip of the promontory catch the eye, while the old harbour quarter is also worth a detour. The long sandy beach also has its charms, with only the nearby factory spoiling the view somewhat.

The **church of Akranes** dates back to the year 1896. Inside, look out for the golden baptismal font, the altar piece by Sigurður Guðmundsson, and the painted ceiling and walls executed in 1966 by Greta and Jón Björnsson.

*Akranes museum complex
East of the town centre lies one of the largest regional museums in Iceland, with four sections. Opened in 1959 and housed in the former Garðar farmstead, the **Folk Museum** forms the oldest part of the museum complex. On display is an extensive collection of items connected to the history of Akranes, including a rowing boat dating back to 1874, various model ships, a fully equipped blacksmith's workshop, the town's oldest wooden house (1875) and its first concrete house, the small school building from the early 20th century, as well as the restored Sigurfari coastal sailing boat.

Insider Tip
The rock and minerals collection is the most extensive in Iceland, with thousands of items. Next to it is an exhibition telling the story of the Hvalfjörður Tunnel, which, since its construction in 1998, has considerably shortened the road link with Reykjavík.

The **Sports Museum** looks at the history of Icelandic sport, showing photographs, sporting equipment and trophies. In addition, since 2003, the National Land Survey of Iceland has been presenting the history of cartography and the latest land survey techniques.

❶ June – Aug. daily 10am – 5pm, otherwise daily 1pm – 6pm, admission 800 ISK, www.museum.is

Akranes

INFORMATION
In the Garðar Museum
Tel. 431 55 66
www.akranes.is

WHERE TO EAT
Restaurant in Hotel Glymur **££££**
Hvalfjörður, tel. 430 31 00
The hotel is well known for its excellent
cuisine, with the extensive Italian buffet
a speciality. More affordable is the
superb buffet lunch (non-residents need
to book ahead).

Garðarkaffi **£**
Garðar, tel. 431 55 66
A good spot for a cup of coffee and a
slice of freshly baked cake. The shell and
sand compositions under the glass panes
covering the tables are also worth a look.

WHERE TO STAY
Hotel Glymur **££££**
Hvalfjörður, Akranes
Tel. 430 31 00
www.hotelglymur.is
Hotel Glymur, located around

30km/18mi north-east of Akranes, is
one of the most beautiful hotels in all of
Iceland. The hotel is in an isolated loac-
tion in wildly romantic landscape on the
Walfjord. The rooms on two stories are
individually furnished with Italian furniture and artworks. From the hot pot
there is a fabulous view of the fjord.

Litla gistihúsið við sjóinn –
The little guesthouse on the sea **£**
Bakkatun 20, Akranes
Tel. 6 95 62 55
https://is-is.facebook.com/media/set/?set
=a.10150089194783928.287173.1557
28753927&type=3
Three lovingly furnished private rooms
in the ground floor of this pretty fisherman's house near the old city centre.
The host Johanna Leopoldsdottir also
serves breakfast when desired.

Gistihúsið Móar **£**
Tel. 431 13 89
Situated 7km/4.3 miles east of Akranes
on the [51], with five imaginatively
designed doubles in a cosy guesthouse.

Behind the town, the prominent basalt mountain of Akrafjall is di-   Akrafjall
vided in two by the Berjadalur. The southern peak, **Háihnjúkur**
(555m/1,821ft), can easily be reached in an hour from the parking
area at the foot of the mountain near the geothermal power plant.
Climbing the western peak of **Geirmundartindur** (643m/2,110ft)
does not take much longer. Both peaks offer views of Faxaflói Bay and
the mountain ranges on the Reykjanes peninsula.

Penetrating inland for some 30km/18.5 miles, the Hvalfjörður,   Hvalfjörður
4–5km/2.5–3 miles wide, is the longest fjord on the southwestern
coast. It also counts amongst the most beautiful fjords in the country,
due to its steep rock walls and the high massifs on its banks. In the
Second World War, both the British and the Americans maintained
naval bases here, of which some traces can still be seen. After the war,

the fjord became well known for its large shoals of herring and its **whaling station**. Since the opening of the tunnel (toll charged), the interior of the fjord has been fairly quiet. In **Saurbær** the small church is worth seeing, built in honour of Hallgrímur Pétursson (1614 – 1674), who was pastor here while working on his Passion Hymns. At the end of the fjord, a gravel track leads into the **Botnsdalur**, with its impressive birch forest. From the car park, a not completely undangerous path (slippery tree trunk as bridge over stream, loose rope as railing) takes about two hours to lead to the **highest waterfall in Iceland**, the **Glymur**, some 200m/655ft in height. Options for longer walks are the Herringfishers Trail (Síldarmannagötur), which also begins at the end of the fjord.

✴ Akureyri

⊹ G 3

Region: North Iceland
Population: 17,500

Whilst the capital of the North lies nearly within the Arctic Circle, it has an exceptionally mild climate with little rain, and surprises with vegetation that by Icelandic standards is positively lush. Some good museums, a long Summer Art Festival, fine old wooden houses, and good shopping options are combining to steadily increase the number of visitors.

Iceland's second largest settlement At the end of the Eyjafjörður, which reaches far inland, and at the beginning of the green valley of the same name, this is Iceland's largest urban area outside the capital. Probably the first settler was **Helgi the Lean**, who settled around 10km/6.2 miles south of today's town in the 9th century, calling his farmstead Kristnes. He is commemorated by a statue north of the centre at the end of the Brekkugata, from where visitors have a good view of the town. Even at the time, the favourable climatic conditions and the relatively fertile soils allowed for productive agriculture. The first document mentioning Akureyri – today a university town but then only a village – dates back to 1562.

WHAT TO SEE IN AKUREYRI

Akureyrarkirkja Perched on a hill in the centre of town, the cathedral, with its tall towers, is the symbol of Akureyri. From the outside, the visual impact of the concrete edifice – designed by Icelandic architect **Guðjón Samúélsson** and consecrated in 1940 – is not exactly delicate, and the interior, too, is kept very simple. Similarly to Hallgrim's Church in Reykjavík, the towers are reminiscent of basalt pillars. The stained-glass windows here are remarkable: the one in the chancel is 400 years old and was brought here from Coventry Cathedral, which was subsequently destroyed in the Second World War. The windows in the nave show events from the life of Christ and Icelandic ecclesiastical history.

❶ June – Aug daily 10am – noon and 2 – 4pm

Akureyri may be the second-largest city in Iceland, but it can easily be explored on foot. A good starting point for a stroll is the **Aðalstræti** at the southern end of the city, which forms the original core of Akureyri. Heading further north on this road leads to the heritage museum, the Nonnahús and several lovingly kept, old wooden houses. The southern part of the next street, **Hafnarstræti**, is also characterized by traditional wooden houses, which are around 100 years old. The conspicuous light-blue building at no. 3 Hafnarstræti used to be the city's phone exchange. A little bit further north lies the inconspicuous **Laxdalshús** of 1795, which is considered to be the oldest house in Akureyri. At the beginning of the 20th century, Hafnarstræti merited its name, as the houses were still by the water; however, subsequent earth deposits have meant that the shoreline has moved a fair distance away from the harbour road.

*Historic centre

The northern parts of Hafnarstræti, Rádhustorg and Brekkugata, are mainly pedestrianized, forming the **town's commercial centre**, with numerous shopping opportunities, restaurants and pubs. From an architectural point of view, this part is less interesting, as the few old houses are virtually crushed by the surrounding modern concrete architecture.

Town commercial centre

Lying high above the town and the fjord, the Botanical Gardens (Lystigarður Akureyrar), or »Pleasure Garden«, are also a public park. Locals like to use this **tranquil green oasis** for a short stroll or a picnic. 4,000 foreign and 400 indigenous types of plant thrive in the park. On a warm sunny day, the colourful flower beds in bloom and the trees offering shade suggest much warmer climes, belying the city's proximity to the Arctic Circle. The park was originally laid out in 1911 by women who wanted to beautify Akureyri; in 1957 the Botanical Gardens were integrated into the park.

Botanical Gardens

❶ June– Oct weekdays 8am – 10pm, Sat/Sun 9am – 10pm

The town and its surroundings offer many hiking opportunities, like the **Glerárdalur** valley and on the **Vaðlaheiði** plateau. The forest Kjarnaskogur is also a popular destination for hikers. One popular and well-marked route leads up to the local mountain, **Súlur**, whose pyr-

Walks in and around Akureyri

Akureyri

INFORMATION
Menningarhús Farm
Strandgata 12, Tel. 4 50 10 50
www.nordurland.is

TRIPS
The Ferðafélag Akureyrar hiking club (www.ffa.is) offers day trips and longer trekking tours. There are also scheduled flights to various destinations with Air Iceland (www.airiceland.is). Ferry to Hrísey from Árskógsströnd (8 x daily). The ferry to Grímsey (Mon, Wed, Fri) departs from Dalvík at 9am, with a crossing time of 3.5hrs, plus a 3-hr stay.

EVENTS
At the end of July, the officially northernmost 18-hole golf course in the world hosts the international Arctic Open tournament in the light of the midnight sun.

WHERE TO EAT
❶ *Rosagarðurinn* **£££**
89 Hafnarstræti, tel. 460 20 00
The Rosagarðurinn on the ground floor of the KEA hotel is a top restaurant in the best hotel in town. The wine list is impressive too. The dining room is relatively large if not particularly cosy.

❷ *Strikið* **£££**
Skipagata 14, tel. 462 71 00
First-class restaurant in the town centre. The view from the dining room over the city and across the fjord is outstanding.

❸ *La Vita è Bella* **££**
Hafnarstræti 92, tel. 461 58 58
Italian restaurant with tasty pizza and pasta dishes. Good wine list and fresh home-made bread.

❹ *Bautinn* **£**
Hafnarstræti 92, Tel. 4 62 18 18
In one of the oldest and most beautiful houses in Akureyri. On cold days the veranda with a view is the best choice.

❺ *Bláa Kannan* **£**
Hafnarstræti 96, tel. 461 46 00
A wonderfully cosy interior, with lots of wood, and a terrace on the main shopping street. Serving tasty (cream) cakes, rather pricey coffee, fresh bread in the mornings, a nicely-priced soup of the day and daily specials.

WHERE TO STAY
❶ *Hótel Kea* **£££**
Hafnarstræti 87–89
Tel. 460 20 00, www.hotelkea.is
This four-star hotel in the centre is considered the best establishments in town.

❷ *Gistiheimili Akureyrar* **££** Insider Tip
Hafnarstræti 104
Tel. 462 56 00, www.nett.is/guest
19 rooms, furnished in a light and modern style, plus a fantastic buffet breakfast every morning on the top floor, giving a splendid view over the town!

❸ *Hótel Edda* **££**
Hrafnagilstræti, tel. 444 49 00
www.hoteledda.is
Summer hotel in a high school, rooms with or without bathroom, serving a hearty buffet and à la carte meals in the evening.

❹ *Farfuglaheimili Akureyri* **£**
Stórholt 1, tel. 462 36 57
storholt@simnet.is
Cosy youth hostel with modern furnishings just north of the town centre.

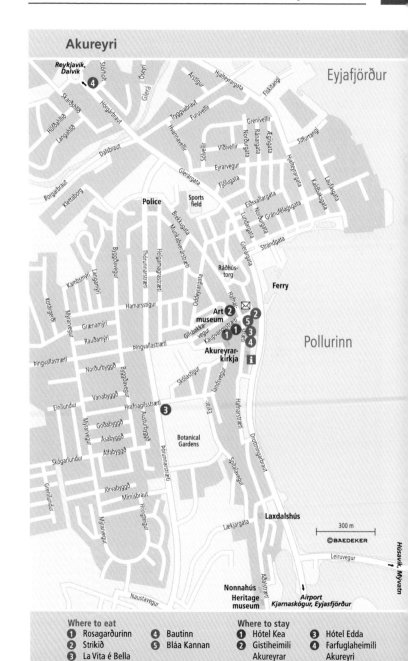

Akureyri

Reykjavik, Dalvik

Eyjafjörður

Pollurinn

Police

Sports field

Art museum

Ferry

Akureyrar-kirkja

Ráðhús-torg

Botanical Gardens

Laxdalshús

300 m

©BAEDEKER

Nonnahús Heritage museum

Airport Kjarnaskógur, Eyjasfjörður

Húsavik, Mývatn

Where to eat
1 Rosagarðurinn
2 Strikið
3 La Vita é Bella
4 Bautinn
5 Bláa Kannan

Where to stay
1 Hótel Kea
2 Gistiheimili Akureyrar
3 Hótel Edda
4 Farfuglaheimili Akureyri

amidical summit area often has pockets of snow even in summer. Beginning at the parking area of the municipal waste disposal site, the path to the summit ascends around 900m/2950ft, becoming rockier and steeper along the way. Allow at least five hours for the return trip. In good weather, hikers can see as far as Grímsey Island from the summit.

Winter sports in Akureyri The Eyjafjörður region counts among the best skiing areas in Iceland, both for cross-country and alpine skiing. The ski centre, with its four lifts, is situated at the **Hlíðarfjall** mountain, only 7km/4.3 miles west of the city, and lies at an altitude of 500 – 1,000m/1,640 – 3,280ft.

MUSEUMS AND EXHIBITIONS

Nonnahús A life-size statue of the writer and Jesuit priest **Jón Sveinsson** (Jon Svensson), better known as Nonni (1857 – 1944), stands directly on the road in front of the red house belonging to the Zonta Club. Visitors have to pass this house however to see the small, black-tarred Nonnahús (Aðalstræti 54), where he lived. Inaugurated in 1957 to honour the centenary of Nonni's birth, the museum shows the constricted conditions of Jón Sveinsson's childhood. The interior is fitted out with 19th-century furniture and presents Nonni's books in many different languages (including Chinese and Esperanto!), as well as photos and memorabilia. Today, the memory of Nonni books such as At Skipalón, An *Icelandic Boy's Adventures* in the mid-19th century or *Nonni's Voyage Around the World* is somewhat faded; fifty years ago however, they were bestsellers.

● June – Aug daily 10am – 5pm, otherwise by appointment, tel. 462-35 55, www.nonni.is

> **! MARCO ⊕ POLO TIP**
>
> **Insider Tip**
>
> *A long summer of the arts*
>
> »Listagil«, the »art canyon« in Kaupvangsstræti is the city's artistic and cultural centre. The former factories now house the art museum, the school of art, galleries and studios. From the middle of June to late August the heart of the »**Listasumar**«, the summer of art, beats here with performances and exhibitions by local and foreign artists. The highlight of the summer of art is the **Akureyravaka** festival in August, which combines art and entertainment (www.listagil.is, only in Icelandic).

Heritage museum Akureyri's heritage museum (Minjasafnið á Akureyri) is housed in the **Villa Kirkjuhvoll** (Aðalstræti 58), built in 1934, and shows two worthwhile permanent exhibitions on the history of the city and the Eyjafjörður area from the first settlement to the present day. Some 100 years ago, the first tree nursery in Iceland was established here, on the site of today's museum garden. The small wooden church was erected in 1846 at Svalbarð, on the fjord's eastern banks, and has been

The children's book author Jón Sveinsson lived here as a little boy

standing in the **museum gardens** since 1970. Every Friday during the summer, the church is the starting point for a historic city walk (tickets from Aktravel, Rádhústorg 3, tel. 460 06 00).

Minjasafnið á Akureyri: June – mid-Sept daily 10am – 5pm, otherwise Sun 2 – 4pm, admission free, www.akmus.is

City walk: tickets at Aktravel, Rádhústorg 3, Tel. 4 60 06 00

Since the nomination of Hannes Sigurdsson a few years ago as director of the art museum (Listasafnið á Akureyri), the dynamic Icelander's exhibits have put the efforts of big cities in the shade. For instance, in 2002 he brought a major exhibition of Dutch masters including 30 Rembrandts to Akureyri, while the presentation of 80 Goya drawings was a minor sensation. It remains to be seen which works by Icelandic and foreign artists he will in future choose for the display space of the former dairy (Kaupvangsstræti 24).

Akureyri Art Museum

➊ daily except Mon noon – 5pm, free admission.

Safnasafnið Since 2001, the white house on the eastern banks of the Eyjafjörður (Svalbarðsströnd), with a view of Akureyri, has been home to a lovingly put together selection of modern Icelandic folk art. On display are drawings, sculptures, dolls, toys and much more. The imaginative figures outside the entrance alone merit a closer look.

❶ Mid-May – early September daily 10am – 6pm

AROUND AKUREYRI

Vaglaskógur In the fertile valley of **Fnjóskadalur**, branching off the Ring Road some 30km/18.5 miles east of Akureyri, spreads Vaglaskógur, one of the most beautiful birch forests in Iceland.

*Laufás As far back as pre-Christian times there was a settlement at Laufás on the eastern banks of the Eyjafjörður. With Christianization, the place became a parish with a rectory, while today's church dates from 1865. The oldest parts of the neighbouring farmstead, which was inhabited up to 1936, are thought to date back to the 16th and 17th centuries. This typical Icelandic **grass sod farm** is much larger than most farms worked at the time and occupies a beautiful position between fjord and fell. The frontage, clad with white clapboard and built sometime in the late 19th century, seems to suggest that Laufás at that time was a rich estate. Not only was the rectory surrounded by fertile soil, fishing and the sale of eiderdown brought in additional money. The eider duck on the roof of the storehouse is a reminder of this sideline. On average, there were 20 to 30 people living on the farmstead, as the large estate required a lot of labour. Today, Laufás is run as a regional museum, with the interiors reflecting the time around 1900.

❶ **Laufás farm:** Mid-May – mid-Sept. daily 10am – 6pm, otherwise by appointment: tel. 463 31 96, admission 700 ISK

Grímsey Its position directly on the Arctic Circle lends the island of Grímsey – 5.3sq km/2 sq miles in area and 41km/25 miles off Iceland – a certain cachet. The barely 100 inhabitants of this northernmost settlement in Iceland share the verdant island with a large number of seabirds, for whom the rocks of the eastern coast (up to 105m/344ft high) make ideal nesting conditions. The islanders live first and foremost by fishing and fish processing, but since the island has had an airport and regular ferry connections, many tourists join them, drawn here by the »real« **midnight sun**.

*Goðafoss Some 50km/31 miles east of Akureyri, the Skjálfandafljót river forms the Goðafoss waterfall, which might boast only a modest height of 10m/33ft, but the way the water gushes over a lip 30m/98ft wide into the gorge below is highly photogenic. As the **»Fall of the Gods«** occupies a logistically strategic position on the Ring Road, it counts among the most popular sights in Iceland. The fall got its name from the Goði Þorgeir, who converted to Christianity at Þingvellir in the year 1000, whereupon he threw his statues of pagan gods into the waterfall.

The **extensive peninsula** between Eyjafjörður and Skjálfandi used to be densely populated, but nowadays is completely abandoned. Hardly in use now, the paths provide a good option for longer walks. One pretty stretch leads from Grenivík and hugs the coast all the way to Gjögurtá at the furthest tip of the peninsula.

Látraströnd

The farmstead of Möðruvellir, situated 1km/0.6 miles north of Akureyri in the Hörgárdalur valley, is one of the most historic places in northern Iceland. From 1296 up to the Reformation there was an **Augustinian monastery** here; afterwards it served as the seat of the provincial governor. Today, Möðruvellir houses an agricultural research institute and a handsome church dating from the year 1865. It is also the birthplace of the writer Jón Sveinsson (»Nonni«).

Möðruvellir

Goðafoss: exalted, like the gods made it

Is Herðubreið the seat of the gods?

Dalvík   Dalvík on the western banks of the Eyjafjörður was almost completely destroyed by a major earthquake in 1934 and rebuilt in a modern
style. The **heritage museum** shows a pretty decent natural history
collection. The museum also honours the memory of Jóhann Pétursson, who was born in 1913 in Dalvík and at 2.34m/7.6ft remains, to
this day, the tallest man Iceland has ever known. Dalvík is also the
point of departure for **whale-watching tours** and trips to the island
of Hrísey.

Heritage museum: June – Aug daily 11am – 6pm, admission 500 ISK
Whale-watching tours: tel. 7 71 76 00,

** Askja · Kverkfjöll
—————————————————————— ✦ J 4/5
Region: Highlands north of the Vatnajökull

**Icelandic highlands at their best! The area north of the Vatna-
jökull with the prominent table mountain of Herðubreið, the
crater cauldron of Askja, the volcanic crater of Víti – which
invites travellers to take a bath in its milky-white water – and
the geothermal area at the Kverkfjöll, is among the most interesting regions of Iceland, and will stay in the memory of
any visitor.**

[F 88] and   Not all paths lead to the caldera of Askja, but many do. Most drivers
[F 910]   choose the **Öskjuleið** [F 88], which turns south off the Ring Road

30km/18.5 miles east of Reykjahlíð am ►Mývatn. Running parallel to the raging glacier river **Jökulsá á Fjöllum**, the [F 88] is – along with all other access roads to the Askja – only passable by jeep. Visitors travelling west on the Ring Road from ►Egilsstaðir are best served by the [923], turning off 34km/21 miles past Egilsstaðir. This access road first leads through the **Jökuldalur to Brú**, where it joins the [F 910], which can be followed briefly north, then westwards to the Askja. Sandy passages and a few easy fords have to be negotiated on the [F 910], while the raging **Kreppa** is bridged. The scenic beauty on both sides of the [F 910] is unforgettable: an area characterized by pumice deserts, basalt formations and dark expanses covered in volcanic ash, where sea lyme grass and sea starwort, oyster plant and sea campion maintain tender islands of vegetation. The **US astronauts Aldrin and Armstrong** trained here in 1968 for their moon landing a year later. Alternatives to the [923] as access road to the [F 910] are the [901] and [F 905], or indeed the [901] and [907]. A general recommendation is to get to experience both the [F 88] and the [F 910], one of them on the way there, the other on the way back.

✶ HERÐUBREIÐ – THE »BROAD-SHOULDERED«

This mountain dominates the scenery of an entire region, being ever-present on the horizon here: the Herðubreið, or »broad-shouldered«, table mountain displays its distinctive outline in the east of the lava desert **Ódáðahraun**. Whether approaching the Askja area from the north on the [F 88] or from the east on the [F 910], the Herðubreið is a constant presence and point of reference on the way to the highlands north of the Vatnajökull. Standing at 1,682m/5,518ft tall, the mountain towers above the high plateau at its base by some 1,000m/3,280ft, making it an unmissable landmark which is often shrouded in cloud. With its abundant vegetation, the oasis of **Herðubreiðarlindir** makes a pleasant contrast to the barren countryside east of the Herðubreið: a speck of land blessed with a wealth of plant life amidst an expanse of desert landscape. **Herðubreiðarlindir** lies right on the [F 88], 60 km/37 miles south of the turning off the Ring Road, and is the starting point for hikes and tours at the foot of the »Queen of Mountains« – another name for the Herðubreið. Accommodation is provided by a lodge with campsite run by the Akureyri hiking club. Way-marked trails lead through the sur-

? MARCO POLO INSIGHT *Did you know...?*

... that in Norse mythology the Herðubreið – under the name of **Asgard** – is the seat of the divine dynasty of the æsir (Norse gods)? However, the first people to reach the sacred summit area were the German Hans Reck and the Icelander Sigurður Sumarliðason in 1908.

Askja · Kverkfjöll

INFORMATION
►Egilsstaðir
►Mývatn, Reykjahlið

EXCURSIONS Insider Tip
In high season (25 June – 31 Aug), Mývatn Tours offer excursions to the Askja daily. Duration: approx. 12 hours. Departure in Reykjahlið at Mývatn. www.myvatntours.is

WHERE TO STAY
Herðubreiðarlindir: Þorsteinskáli lodge/campsite £
Tel. 462 27 20 (book ahead for lodge!) Lodge (floor mattresses, cooking facilities) and campsite in a green oasis on the [F 88] dirt road near the Herðubreið.

Askja/Dyngjufjöll: Dreki lodge/campsite £
Tel. 462 27 20 (book ahead for lodge!) Small lodge in an impressive location at the entrance to the Dragon Gorge; campsite somewhat exposed to the wind and on stony ground, but offering good sanitary facilities, partly adapted to special needs.

Kverkfjöll: Sigurðarskáli lodge/campsite £
Tel. 853 62 36 (book ahead for the lodge at the Ferðafélag Ísland Icelandic hiking club: tel. 853 62 36, www.fi.is) Lodge at the northern edge of the Vatnajökull. Grass areas set up for tents.

rounding countryside, including one to a lava cave where the legendary outcast **Fjalla Eyvindur** is said to have spent the harsh winter of 1774/1775. Herðubreið may also be climbed from Herðubreiðarlindir, but the route is considered very difficult. Even those with alpine hillwalking experience and the right equipment should check the conditions on the mountain with the staff at the lodge before setting out.

** A BATH IN THE VOLCANO: ASKJA

Dragon Gorge
Our next stop is anything but a green oasis such as the one at the Herðubreið. In harsh surroundings at the foot of the Dyngjufjöll massif, 30km/18.5 miles southwest of Herðubreiðarlindir, there is just a mountain hut and campsite. The Dreki lodge lies at the entrance to the **Drekagil**, the **Dragon Gorge**, which ends with a waterfall plunging down a rock face. A trail leads through the entire gorge. The Dreki lodge is the start of the [F 894], a dead-end road leading through a lava field which only appeared in 1961 – this is a volcanic area that remains active to this day! – to a parking area at the northeastern edge of the Askja caldera. The Askja's **crater cauldron** (caldera) was formed just under 5,000 years ago by the emptying of a magma chamber and the subsequent subsidence of the ground.

From the car park a footpath offers a 20-minute stroll to the interior of the caldera, and on to the Víti crater and the Öskjuvatn. Both are much younger than the Askja caldera: following a major eruption in 1875, the southeastern part of the Askja subsided further and gradually filled with water – giving birth to the Öskjuvatn. At the same time, further eruptions formed the Víti crater. A bath in its milky-white, lukewarm water is a very special experience. A monument at the crater's edge honours the memory of the geologist **Walther von Knebel** and the painter **Max Rudloff**, who in 1907 as part of a research trip set out to the Askja area, and despite advance warning put out on the Öskjuvatn in a small boat. Neither of them was ever heard from again.

**Víti crater, Öskjuvatn

** KVERKFJÖLL: HOT SPRINGS IN THE ETERNAL ICE

The Kverkjökull glacier with the up to 1936m/6388ft Kverkfjöll mountains is a textbook example of the combination of volcanic activity and glacial phenomena, of fire and ice. Whilst volcanic activity below Iceland's glaciers is not unique by any means and other geothermal extrusions from the perpetual ice do exist elsewhere, it is only at the Kverkfjöll that they are accessible with relatively little effort. Two tracks lead to the Kverkfjöll, so that one can be used for access and the other as the return road. Starting from the Askja, drive east, and later southeast, on the [F 910], until reaching the [F 902] (Kverkfjallaleið). Three kilometres/1.8 miles further on, the [F 903] (Hvannalindavegur) turn off south, leading through the **Hvannalindir**, an oasis of green vegetation. Some 25km/15.5 miles further south the two tracks join again. The last 17km/10.5 miles to the lodge and campsite at the Kverkfjöll are shown as [F 902].

Fire and ice

Öskjuvatn with the Víti crater in the foreground

At the small harbour of Bakkagerði

First impressions — Visitors arriving at the **Sigurðarskáli** lodge at the Kverkfjöll usually start by checking the facilities or setting up their tents on one of the grassy spots. The surroundings are so impressive that it is tempting to gain a first impression straight away. So why not don the hiking boots and follow the path leading to the mountain at the back of the campsite? From up here, there are splendid views of the nearby glaciers, of a world shaped by ice.

Ice cave — From the lodge it is not far, on a bumpy track and crossing a ford, to the car park right next to the Kverkjökull. From here, visitors can reach the largest ice cave in Iceland on foot. For many years, the cave could be entered, but **volcanic activity and glacier movements** have caused parts of it to collapse. Heavy blocks of ice work themselves loose at regular intervals to smash into pieces on the ground. Entering the cave is extremely dangerous, and visitors should keep clear even of the entrance area.

*Hveradalur — The parking area is also the starting point for glacier tours to the bubbling mud pots, fumaroles and solfataras of Hveradalur, the **»Valley of Hot Springs«**. One route leads to Hveradalur via the Kverkjökull, while another, easier one, goes west around the glacier tongue. None of the tours are entirely risk-free however: quickly changing weather and fog make orientation difficult, not to mention the dangers of the glacier itself. Any tour should be discussed in advance with the staff at the Sigurðurskáli lodge. Visitors with no experience of glaciers can join an organized **glacier hike**. For more information, contact the staff at the lodge.

Bakkagerði · Borgarfjörður

 ✳ M 3/4

Region: East Iceland, Eastern Fjords
Population: 150

The inhabitants of Bakkagerði village have to exercise caution, as at the Borgarfjörður elves and trolls live everywhere, and indeed Álfaborg is where the queen of all Icelandic elves resides. But visitors should not let this stop them, as the wild mountain countryside and the coasts around here are among the best trekking areas in Iceland.

The easternmost of the eastern fjords, the Borgarfjörður, is short and wide and fairly unspectacular. The inland mountains by contrast are very impressive. In geological terms, this is the border between the dark **basalt mountains** in the west and, in the east, the **liparite mountains**, resplendent in their strong colours. The only settlement of note in this otherwise virtually deserted swathe of countryside is Bakkagerði, which on some maps appears as Borgarfjörður eystri. Until 1950, Bakkagerði did not even have a road link, and today it is still situated at the end of a cul-de-sac. However, it's worth a visit for

Bakkagerði

INFORMATION
At Álfasteinn
Tel. 472 99 77
www.borgarfjordureystri.is

WHERE TO EAT
Fjarðarborg £
Tel. 472 99 20
This restaurant serves mainly simple but delicious dishes.

WHERE TO STAY
Gistiheimilið Borg £
Tel. 472 99 62, gisting-borg@visir.is
Simple, excellent-value hostel right in the centre of town

Ásbyrgí Farfuglaheimili £
Tel. 472 99 62
Small and fairly cosy youth hostel in Bakkagerði with 17 beds

the excellent birdwatching on offer. The best spot is Hafnarhólm, where a hill provides a good vantage point for watching gulls, eider ducks and puffins.

❶ Hafnarhólm, closed in May for the protection of breeding birds, in June and July accessible between 11am – 7pm, www.puffin.is

WHAT TO SEE IN BAKKAGERÐI

Álfaborg
At the edge of town, the protected Álfaborg (»Elf Hill«) rock formation, around 30m/18.5ft high, is a prominent landmark. It is closely associated with elves, as Álfaborg is said to be the home of the Icelandic **elf queen**. However, elves being what they are, so far no one has really seen her. Which is why it is assumed that she has no problem with visitors climbing to the summit of the hill to enjoy the view. The Álfaborg however is only one of the many places associated with the »huldufólk« (hidden people) – elves, invisibles and trolls – and so the locals tell many **stories of strange encounters and events**.

Bakkagerðiskirkja
Whilst not that interesting from an architectural point of view, the church of Bakkagerði, dating from 1901, draws many visitors for its altarpiece, created by **Jóhannes Sveinsson Kjarval** (1885 – 1972). One of Kjarval's most famous works, it shows Jesus' Sermon on the Mount being held at the elves' castle.

Alfasteinn
This is where minerals from the Börgarfjörður area are made into souvenirs such as stone trolls. The **rocks and minerals exhibition** is also worth seeing. In the Alfacafé everything is made of stone: tables, plates, accessories.

❶ Mon – Fri 10am – 6pm, Sat, Sun 1 – 6pm

One of the best hiking regions in Iceland
Over the past 12 years, the local tourist association has waymarked a network of hiking trails of some 140km/87 miles, allowing tours all the way to ►Seyðisfjörður and turning Borgarfjörður into one of the best walking areas in Iceland. On the way to **Seyðisfjörður** to the south, walkers can avail themselves of simple mountain huts in Breiðavík and Húsavík (reservations required, tel. 471 20 00). The Á Víknaslóðum (1:75 000) hiking map is helpful for longer expeditions, offering information on the most important routes. One popular and fairly simple tour leads to the mighty boulders at **Stórurð** – the result of a landslide on the western flank of the Dyrfjöll. Marked trails begin at the [94] road near Skeggjaklettur and near Vatnsskarð, with the routes taking approx. 5 hours there and back. With a height of some 600m/1,970ft, the **Staðarfjall** gives a nice mountain viewpoint. Best climbed from the northeast, its summit offers superb panoramic views across the fjord.

Blönduós

E 3

Region: Northwest Iceland
Population: 900

Húnaflói, the largest bay in the north of Iceland, separates the western fjords from the rest of the island. Lying on the eastern banks of the bay, the modern and fairly sober Blönduós provides the commercial and service hub of the region. A few kilometres south of town, Húnaflói Bay joins the fertile valley of Vatnsdalur, reaching inland for 25km/15.5 miles.

The town stretches along both sides of the mouth of the **Blanda** glacier river, which has its source at the Hofsjökull glacier and, with a length of 125km/78 miles, counts among the longer rivers in the country. The Blanda has long been famous as one of the best salmon rivers in Iceland, frequently yielding over two thousand salmon per summer. Right in the middle of town, the river forms **Hrútey Island**, which is protected because of its bird population but may still be explored on several shorter hiking trails.

WHAT TO SEE IN BLÖNDUÓS

The Textile Museum has moved into a new home, an architecturally interesting house on the riverbank (Árbraut 29). It shows a collection of handmade rope and textile goods, besides various costumes and changing exhibitions featuring well-known textile artists. Part of the

Textile Museum

Blönduós

INFORMATION
Brautarhvammi
Tel. 452 45 20
www.northwest.is

WHERE TO EAT
Við Árbakkann £
Húnabraut 2
Tel. 452 46 78
Conspicuous blue house with terrace in the centre of town, serving snacks such as sandwiches and pancakes.

WHERE TO STAY
Hótel Blönduós ££
Aðalgata 6, tel. 557 61 00
www.hotelblonduos.is
Small hotel in the historic centre of Blönduós right on the Ring Road

Glaðheimar ££
Melabraut 21, Tel. 8 20 13 00
www.gladheimar.is
Seven well-appointed holiday cottages sleeping 3 to 8

museum, the Halldórustofa, is dedicated to **Halldóra Bjarnadóttir** (1873 – 1981), the oldest Icelandic woman on record.

❶ June – Aug daily 10am – 5pm

Blönduóss-kirkja
Consecrated in 1993, the **parish church of Blönduós** was designed by Maggi Jónsson. Taken to symbolize the surrounding nature, the conspicuous concrete building has excellent acoustics and is often used for concerts. The altarpiece is the work of Jóhannes Kjarval.

AROUND BLÖNDUÓS

Þingeyrar
It was in 1133 that in Þingeyrar, 25km/15.5 miles southwest of Blönduós, the first **Benedictine monastery** in Iceland was founded. Remaining active for some 400 years up to the Reformation, the monastery held a lot of land in the surrounding countryside. It was also an important cultural centre where many historic books were written. Thus, the abbot **Arngrímur Brandsson** wrote down the history of Bishop Guðmundur the Good, containing the oldest known description of Iceland. Various sagas of the Húnavatn region, such as the Heiðarvíga Saga, were also recorded in this monastery. Today, the stone church built between 1864 and 1877 in the Neo-Romanesque style is the only reminder of this once important religious site. Inside, look out for the **alabaster altarpiece**, probably dating back to the 13th century, the pulpit (1696) and the silver baptismal font.

Vatnsdalur
Situated between the Víðidalsfjall (993m/3,258ft) and the Vatnsdalsfjall (1,018m/3,340ft), the green valley of Vatnsdalur, 25km/15.5miles long, has a lot of good pasture and is traversed by the Vatnsdalsá river. Rich in salmon and with its source in the highlands, this river forms a deep gorge and numerous waterfalls on its way to the sea. At the exit of the valley, near the Ring Road, lie a bizarre group of hills (Vatnsdalshólar), formed by a massive avalanche from the **Vatnsdalsfjall** long before the settlement of the country. The hills have different colours and shapes, some quite conspicuous. North of the Ring Road, three striking hills (Þrístapar) lie close together. This is where, on 12 January 1830, the last execution in Iceland took place. Waymarked hiking trails lead through the Vatnsdalshólar.

> ! MARCO ⊕ POLO TIP
>
> *King of Country* **Insider Tip**
>
> The **Kántrýbær** country music restaurant in Skagaströnd is unique in all of Iceland. Owner Hallbjörn Hjartarson calls himself the only cowboy in Iceland, running his own radio station (FM 96.7 and 100.7) and often organising live performances in his rustic venue. Hólanesvegur, tel. 452 29 50.

Near the harbour of Borgarnes the artist Bjarni Þór created this sculpture, which is dedicated to the mythic figure Thorgerdur Brak

From Blönduós, consider a drive around the sparsely populated Skagi Peninsula, on the [74], [744] and [745] (length of drive around 140km/87 miles). On the coast at **Skagaströnd** near **Spákonufellshöfði** some fine basalt pillars can be found. One of the most striking mountains in the area is the Spákonufell (646m/2,119ft), which got its name (»Mountain of the Seeress«) from the clairvoyant Þórdís who in the 10th century lived on the farm of the same name at the foot of the mountain.

From the **Brandaskarð** farm, a hiking trail leads to the summit, with good views in all directions. Also north of Skagaströnd, between Króksbjarg and Kálfshamarsvík, there are cliffs of up to 50 metres/165ft in height, featuring basalt pillars that are worth seeing. In the north of the peninsula, at **Selavíkurtangi**, seals can often be spotted on the rocks from the shore.

Skagi Peninsula

Basalt pillars and seals

Borgarnes

 D 5

Region: West Iceland
Population: 2000

Borgarnes appears as far back as the Egil saga under the name Digranes, which is why all the roads here are named after personalities from this saga. With the construction of the bridge over the Borgarfjörður in 1980, the town became a transit hub between Reykjavík and the North.

WHAT TO SEE IN AND AROUND BORGARNES

Skallagríms-garður In the small Skallagrímsgarður park in the town centre a burial mound shelters the remains of Egil's father, **Skallgrímur Kveldúlfsson**, who was buried, Viking-style, with his horse and weapons. A relief by the Danish artist Anna Marie Brodersen shows Egil with his dead son Böðvar, who is also said to have been buried here.

Safnahús The Safnahús museum complex (Bjarnarbraut 4–6) houses the **Art Museum**, showing works by Icelandic artists, the **Natural History Museum** with an extensive collection of stuffed birds, as well as the **Heritage Museum**, showing historical dress and tools of daily life from the region.
  🕐 Mon – Fri 1 – 6pm, Tue til 8pm

On the settlement history The **Settlement Museum** attractively shows the history of the Settlement of Iceland. The exhibit on the ground floor shows how the »Norsemen« left their erstwhile home Norway and discovered Iceland. The Egil exhibit in the basement shows the most important and most adventurous chapters from the life of Egil Skalla-Grimsson, one of the most unusual personalities from the time of the Settlement.
  ℹ June – Sept. daily 10am – 9pm

Borg à Mýrum The Borg à Mýrum farm at the end of Borgarvogur Bay, west of Borgarnes, is the birthplace of the famous skald (poet) **Egil Skallgrímsson** (900 – 983). In front of the small wooden church (1885) stands the Sonatorrek (Lament for the Sons) sculpture by **Ásmundur Sveinsson**, representing the loss of Egill's two sons Gunnar and Böðvar. The great poet **Snorri Sturluson** (1178 – 1241) also lived for a while in Borg before moving to Reykholt.

Deildartunguhver Some 20km/12 miles north of Borgarnes, the [50] branches off the Ring Road, leading through a wide, green agricultural valley, surrounded by gently rising hills. Shortly after the **Hvitá** river crossing, the Deildartunguhver thermal spring, with a length of several hundred metres, produces around 11,000 litres/2,905 gallons of near-boiling water per minute. This makes it the most productive hot water spring in Iceland, but not the only one, as these gently steaming springs – tamed these days – can be seen everywhere, providing the farmers with cheap energy.

Viðgelmir lava cave After this detour, head back across the Hvitá and follow the [523] leading along the northern banks of the river. There, the **Fljótstunga farmstead** is the starting point for a visit to the Viðgelmir lava cave, one of the largest lava caves in the world. As a protected site, the cave may only be visited as part of a guided tour. At the **Kalmanstunga**

Borgarnes

INFORMATION
Hyrnutorg
Tel. 437 22 14
www.vesturland.is, www.west.is

EVENTS
The Reykholt Festival in July sees classical music performed on historic soil.
www.reykholt.is

WHERE TO EAT
Restaurant in the Borgarnes Hótel £££
Egilsgata 14-16, tel. 4 37 11 19
www.hotelborgarnes.is
Good Icelandic cuisine

Hredavatnsskali Restaurant & Café £
Norðurárdal 311, Borgarnes
Tel. 4 35 00 11, www.hredavatnsskali.is
This Restaurant is located in Bifröst, below the Grábrók Crater and the volcano Baula; it serves inexpensive soups, snacks, salads, fish and meat dishes

WHERE TO STAY
Icelandair Hotel Hamar £££
By the golf course, Borgarnes
Tel. 4 33 66 00
www.hotelhamar.is
Golfhotel with a view of a spectacular mountain panorama. While the Hamar looks like a motel on the outside, rooms and service are quite personal.

Hótel Reykholt ££
Tel. 4 35 12 60, www.fosshotel.is
Modern hotel near the museum, also offering spaces for sleeping bags. Open all year round.

Guesthouse Bjarg £
Tel. 437 19 25, Fax 437 19 75
bjarg@simnet.is
Old farmstead a little outside Borgarnes, with a total of 14 beds, amongst them a studio apartment.

Ferðaþjónustan Húsafelli £
Tel. 435 15 50
www.husafell.is
Cabins with spaces for sleeping bags, and a pretty campsite in the birch forest of Húsafell, open all year round. With swimming pool, horse riding, hiking and golf.

Fljótstunga £   Insider Tip
Tel. 4 35 11 98
www.fljotstunga.is
Farm on Road [518], north of Húsafell, camping huts with kitchens, 3 double rooms. Tour of the lava cave Viðgelmir from here.

farm, a track branches off to two other caves, **Surtshellir and Stefánshellir**, which may be explored independently.

Shortly before reaching Húsafell, the [F 550] highland road (▶Kaldidalur) leads to ▶Þingvellir; in good weather, it is passable with a regular saloon car. Húsafell makes a good base for walks in the surrounding area. Past Húsafell, the [518] follows the southern banks of the river until, a few kilometres later, a parking area announces the Hraunfossar waterfalls. Under the **Hallmundarhraun** lava flow, which

Húsafell, Hraunfossar

formed around 800BC and is mentioned in the saga of Grettir the Strong, countless waterfalls gush forth along a stretch of around one kilometre/0.6 miles, to flow into the Hvitá. A little further upriver lies the **Barnafoss** waterfall, named »The Children's Waterfall« in memory of two children who drowned here.

*Reykholt   The [518] eventually leads to the parish of Reykholt, which also has a school, in the **Reykholtsdalur** valley, one of the most important historic places in Iceland. This is where the most famous Icelandic poet and historian, **Snorri Sturluson** (around 1178 – 1241) lived and worked. With the Heimskringla, Sturluson composed a detailed historical analysis of his time. Even more important however is his skaldic manual, detailing the rules of the poetic art of the time and many Norse myths. Snorri Sturluson was not merely a poet and historian however, he also ranked among the most influential men of his time. He ruled over two goðorð, sat in the Alþing and was twice appointed law speaker, at the time the highest office in the state. A power politician, Sturluson had good connections to the Norwegian royal dy-

Hraunfossar: uncounted waterfalls feed the Hvitá

nasty and was probably involved in several intrigues, leading to his murder in Reykholt in 1241. Today, he is remembered with a statue in front of the school by Gustav Vigeland, a present from the Norwegian royal family. Behind the building lies the small round **Snorralaug** swimming pool, which dates back to the time of Snorri Sturluson and is fed by a hot spring. From there, a partially preserved underground passage leads to the dwelling. Snorri was probably buried in the cemetery next to the small wooden church, but the exact spot is not known. For the past few years, extensive archeological digs have been attempting to shed more light on medieval Reykholt. The **Snorrastofa cultural centre**, housed in the basement of the modern church, documents the life of Snorri Sturluson.

❶ **Snorrastofa:** May – Aug. daily 10am – 6pm, www.snorrastofa.is, admission 1200 ISK

Djúpivogur

⚹ L 5

Region: East Iceland
Population: 450

The merchants of the Hanseatic League were among the first to trade here, taking advantage of the good natural harbour. Following on from them, the Danes came and made Djúpivogur one of the most important fishing ports in the eastern fjords. Today Djúpivogur is a charming fishing village with colourful houses and a small yacht harbour.

Djúpivogur lies on the relatively flat promontory of Búlandsnes, pushing out far to sea between the fjords of Hamarsfjörður and Berufjörður and petering out in numerous rocky islands. Inland, the regular, pyramid-shaped outline of the **Búlandstindur** (1,068m/ 3,504ft) draws the eye. The mountain is supposed to possess strong magical powers. Legend has it that after Iceland's conversion to Christianity, the old pagan statues and idols were cast into the depths from a rocky ledge on the eastern side at an altitude of 700m/2,300ft, called Goðaborg.

WHAT TO SEE IN AND AROUND DJÚPIVOGUR

The long red house above the harbour is said to be one of the oldest   Langabúð
trading houses in Iceland; with parts of it dating back to the year 1790, it served as the economic centre of Djúpivogur until the 1950s. Around the year 1850, another timber-framed house was erected,

Djúpivogur

INFORMATION
Langabúð
Tel. 478 82 20

TRIPS TO PAPEY ISLAND
daily 1pm, duration approx. 4hrs.
Tel. 478 81 19

WHERE TO EAT
Restaurant in Framtíð Hotel **£££**
Tel. 478 88 87
Lovely little restaurant in the old part of the house serving excellent Icelandic

food with gourmet aspirations, a good wine list and cellar bar.

Langabúð **££**
Tel. 478 82 20
The museum café serves coffee and cakes in a snug setting.

WHERE TO STAY
Hótel Framtíð **£/££**
Vogalandi 4
Tel. 478 88 87
www.hotelframtid.com
The hotel, named »Future«, was built in 1905 right on the harbour. A modern annexe does detract from the charm of the old house. Comfortable rooms in the new building, as well as rooms without a bathroom and sleeping-bag accommodation.

Farfuglaheimili Berunes **£**
Tel. 478 89 88, www.simnet.is/berunes
Simple and very cosy accommodation in a former farmhouse on the northern side of the Berufjörður, with views across the fjord. Also campsite and holiday cottages.

which stands in front of the Langabúð to this day. Today, the Langabúð's interior houses two collections: the works of the sculptor **Ríkarður Jónsson** (1888 – 1972), who was born in Djúpivogur, and memorabilia of the minister **Eysteinn Jónsson** among other Icelandic politicians. The attic is given over to an informative museum of regional history.

❶ **Museum:** Mid May – mid Sept daily 10am – 6pm

Papey   Lying off the promontory of Búlandsnes alongside numerous other islands and skerries, Papey – measuring some two sq km/three quarters of a sq mile – was in all likelihood inhabited by Irish monks before the arrival of the Vikings. The name of the island could be a pointer, as the **Vikings** called the Irish monks »Papar«. The monks were followed on the island by farmers supplementing their income by collecting eggs and the down from eider ducks. Today the island is uninhabited and given over completely to the shrieking seabirds. In the water and on low rocks seals enjoy life. The house of the last island dweller, plus one of the smallest wooden churches in Iceland, dating from 1807, serve as reminders of the times when the island was still inhabited.

Teigarhorn

The coast at the Teigarhorn farm, 3km/1.8 miles north of Djúpivogur, has been known for 300 years as a great site for attractive minerals and crystals; in particular, it is world-famous for its zeolite deposits. Today, the entire area is in private hands and its natural beauty **protected**. A collection of minerals for sale is on display at the farm, comprising finds exclusively from the area, mainly zeolites. Opening times: daily 9am – 9pm. Behind the building housing the mineral collection stands the old Teigarhorn dwelling, which was imported in 1880 by Niels Weyvadt, the head of the Ørum & Wulff trading company, as an assembly kit from Norway. His daughter Níkolína (1848 – 1921) learned to be a photographer in Copenhagen and studied mineralogy. Taking over the farmstead after the death of her father, she had a photographic studio built next to it where she worked successfully for many years. **Nicoline Weyvadt** is considered the first female photographer in Iceland; her work is held by the National Museum which also, in 1992, took over her residence in Teigarhorn, planning to extend it into a photography museum. Some reproductions of Nicoline's photographs can be seen in the Framtið Hotel in Djúpivogur.

❶ **Mineral collection:** daily 9am – 9pm

Foggy scene near Djúpivogur

Eyjólfsstaðir About 20km/12.5 miles northwest of Djúpivogur, a cul-de-sac branches off and leads for some 2km/1.25 miles to the Eyjólfsstaðir farmstead in the Fossárdalur. The **Fossá valley**, making its way to the fjord over numerous basalt steps and waterfalls, is framed by mighty, terraced, predominantly green mountain slopes. The Ring Road or the farm can both serve as starting points for a hike, either along the river or, more easily, on the jeep track leading uphill through the valley.

Eastern Fjords

 L/M 3-6

Region: East Iceland

Around a dozen fjords are arranged along the coast of East Iceland, with the largest of them, the Reyðarfjörður, penetrating for some 30km/18.5 miles inland. The eastern fjords are similar to those in the west, just that everything here is on a slightly smaller scale. The eastern fjords are also relatively old geologically and far removed from the volcanically active zones of the island. Which is why the typical rock here is the dark, often multilayered basalt wrought by the Ice Age glaciers.

Past times The chain of fjords starts in the north with the relatively small Borgarfjörður and continues south to the Álftafjörður. On the good natural harbours along the coast a relative proliferation of settlements have sprung up over time, the largest being **Neskaupstaður** and **Eskifjörður**. Until around 1900 they were all able to live comfortably off herring fishing. Today, fishing and fish processing still form the area's economic basis, but the golden times of the herring boom are long over.

A stranded fishing boat at an eastern fjord

Up to now, tourism has not taken on the role that was hoped for, which is why local people are trying to increase the choice of activities for visitors. A start was made with a few new cafés, giving a bit of life to the very quiet villages. Waymarked trails and a generally improved infrastructure are in place to lure more hikers into the region, who will find ideal conditions for short routes, but also for longer expeditions through a spectacular landscape. There is now also a map showing all the waymarked trails.

Eastern Fjords

INFORMATION

Eskifjörður
Verkstæði Kötu, Strandgötu 29
Tel. 8 94 93 06

Neskaupstaður
Café Nesbær, Egilsbraut 5,
Tel. 4 77 11 15

WHERE TO EAT

Neskaupstaður: Restaurant in Hótel Capitano ££
Hafnarbraut 50, tel. 4 77 18 00
Blues corrugated metal house from 890 by the water. The furnishings are not very imaginative, but the food is good.

Reyðarfjörður: Tærgesen £/££
Buðargata 4, Tel. 4 70 55 55
The artist's café in an old house on the harbour serves pizza and hamburgers. Very relaxed. Lots of pictures on the wall, which are all for sale.

Neskaupstaður: Egilsbúð £
Egilsbraut 1, Tel. 4 77 13 21
Inexpensive pizza followed by draught beer and billiards in the pub. Youth meeting place on weekends.

Fáskrúðsfjörður: Fransmenn á Íslandi £
Búðavegi 8/Chemin de Budir 8
Tel. 8 64 27 28
Small, cosy museum café with French atmosphere.

Fáskrúðsfjörður: Café Sumarlína £
Búðavegur 59, Tel. 4 75 15 75
Relaxed café, which also serves light meals like fish soup. Furnished with love, View of the harbour.

WHERE TO STAY

Neskaupstaður:
Hótel Edda ££/£££
Tel. 4 44 48 60, www.hoteledda.is
Summer hotel right by the water in wonderful location, 29 comfortable double rooms

Reyðarfjörður: Fjarda hótel
Reyðarfjörður ££ /£££
Tel. 4 74 16 00
20 double rooms with bath, telephone and TV, open all year. Excellent restaurant, open for non-residents too. Affordable daily special in the evening, but also lamb and fish à la carte.

Breiðdalvik: Café Margret £/££
Tel. 4 75 66 25
Beautiful isolated location north of the town. New log cabin with terrace and fjord view. Horst and Margret offer 4 comfortable double rooms and a varied menu.

Reyðarfjörður £
Tel. 8 95 16 39
Three small new huts for two people with simple furnishings. Near the campground.

Stöðvarfjörður: Kirkjubær £
Fjardarbraut 37a, Tel. 8 92 33 19
The church was converted into a sleeping bag accommodation for ten people. Comfortable furnishings, kitchen and bathroom. Moderately priced. The interior can still be clearly recognized as a church, altar and pulpit are still there, the choir loft is the sleeping area. Elevated location with view of fjord.

NESKAUPSTAÐUR

The largest town in East Iceland has held town status since 1929 and does have a certain urban flair – at least compared to the other settlements along the fjord coast. The main road, running close to the water, has not only the obligatory petrol station and supermarket but also a selection of other shops, down to a small furniture store. Neskaupstaður also boasts a hotel, a restaurant and a fairly cosy café. The town lies on the northern banks of the small **Norðfjörður** – with a view of the uninhabited **Barðsnes peninsula** – and directly below steep mountainsides, which avalanches often thunder down in winter. The last major disaster hit Neskaupstaður in December 1974, when twelve villagers were killed by an avalanche.

Náttúrugripasafnið
The natural history museum shows, over two floors, a collection of Icelandic minerals as well as a number of stuffed animals. The **birchwood chess figures** were made by Sófus Sveinsson and were even displayed at the 1939 World Exhibition in New York.
❶ Miðstræti 1, daily 1–5pm

Neskaupstaður Nature Reserve
The local hiking club has by now marked many trails around Neskaupstaður and published a walking map covering the area between Seyðisfjörður and Reyðarfjörður. At the exit to the town the campsite marks the beginning of the nature reserve, which in 1972 was the first to be established in Iceland. Here is the starting point of a one-hour hike through blossoming wetland meadows along the coast to Hundsvik. At **Páskahellir** the trail passes a cave carved out by the swell. The interesting thing about it is the small holes inside, which stem from trees that some 12 million years ago were covered by lava.

ESKIFJÖRÐUR

Colourful houses
Eskifjörður, situated on the small, eponymous branch of the **Reyðarfjörður**, on the road to Reyðarfjörður, makes for a pretty sight. The colourful houses strung out along the town appear tiny in front of the impressive mountain backdrop. The town is somewhat hemmed in by the steep mountainside which in the winter often causes avalanche danger alerts. At a height of 985m/3,232ft, the **Holmatindur** is one of the most impressive mountains in the area, dividing the two fjords of Eskifjörður and Reyðarfjörður. Taking a stroll through Eskifjörður, some old houses still catch the eye between the new buildings. A monument by Ragnar Kjartansson on the main road honours the memory of the drowned mariners from Eskifjörður.

The East Iceland Maritime Museum is housed in the **Gamla Búð**, Eskidfjörður's old trading house dating back to 1816. In front of the museum visitors will find some old tools, an around 200-year-old anchor from a sailing ship, cast-iron pots which would have been used for boiling cod-liver oil, and even a steamship propeller. On the ground floor, a faithfully reconstructed old grocery store may be viewed, as well as collections on whaling, shark hunting, and herring fishing. On the upper floor, the **heritage museum** shows a model of Eskifjörður town from the 1920s, all kinds of traditional working tools and equipment for the production of sweets. All in all, the museum gives a vivid idea of what life was like in the town during the time of the herring fisheries. Fittingly enough, the aroma wafting over from the fish-processing plant also provides a connection between the past and the present. Another part of the museum is a herring-processing plant from 1890, which can be visited in the eastern part of the town.

Maritime Museum

Gamla Búð

❶ **Sjóminjasafn Austurlands:** Strandgata 39 b, June – Aug. daily. 1pm – 5pm

FURTHER SETTLEMENTS

During the first half of the 20th century, Reyðarfjörður was the main trading centre for the farmers of the Fljótsdalshérað area, and during the Second World War, there was an **Allied base** here with over 3,000 soldiers. Today, Reyðarfjörður appears fairly sleepy. A war museum was established in 1995, to mark the 50th anniversary of the war ending. Without aspiring to provide an in-depth historical analysis of WWII, it shows how the soldiers lived here and how the population of Reyðarfjörður adapted to their presence.

Reyðarfjörður

❶ **War museum:** June – Aug daily 10am – 5pm

At the entrance to the town of Fáskrúðsfjörður, the French flag can be seen flying, and all street names are in both Icelandic and French. This is in memory of the up to 5,000 French fishermen who from the mid-19th century came here every year to fish. At the time, Fáskrúðsfjörður was the most important settlement of French fishermen in the eastern fjords; they even kept up a consulate and built a church and hospital. There is a small cemetery on the edge of town, where 49

Fáskrúðsfjörður

French and Belgian mariners lie buried. The exhibition **»Fransmenn á Íslandi«** has put together all kinds of memorabilia from this era, and with the help of the map available at the museum, visitors may explore Fáskrúðsfjör- ður in the footsteps of the French.

❶ **Museum**: Buðavegi/Chemin de Budir 8, Juni – Aug daily 10am – 5pm

Stöðvar-fjörður

For some time now, **rock collector Petra Sveinsdóttir** has ensured that every year 20,000 visitors stop in the small town of Stöðvar-fjörður, which they would otherwise most probably bypass. As long as the old lady is not out indulging her collector's zeal, she is happy to show visitors her house and garden. Here are rocks, and nothing but rocks, not collected from a scientific perspective, but a purely aesthetic one. The passionate collector is naturally unable to pass up some other choice items such as bleached skull bones or an old hob. These are used for **arrangements in the front garden**. Also worth a visit is the **Snærós Gallery** near the church, where Austrian artist Richard exhibits and sells his work and that of his wife Sólrun.

❶ **House of rock collector Petra Sveinsdóttir**: Fjarðarbraut 21, daily 9am – 7pm

Egilsstaðir

 L 3

Region: East Iceland
Population: 2300

Visitors expecting sites of architectural interest in Egilsstaðir will be disappointed, as the town only developed some 60 years ago from a large farmstead. Its rise to become the transit and service hub of East Iceland finally started properly with the construction of the bridge over the Lagarfljót.

By Icelandic standards, there is an unusual bustle to Egilsstaðir. Icelanders come from all over the surrounding area to shop here, and many tourists also use the place as a stopping-off point, in particular between the arrival and departure of the weekly ferry from Seyðisfjörður to the Färöe Islands.

WHAT TO SEE IN AND AROUND EGILSSTAÐIR

Heritage museum

The East Iceland heritage museum (Minjasafn Austurlands; Laufskógar 1) displays finds from a **Viking tomb** discovered in 1995, which counts among the most important archaeological excavations in Iceland. The museum also exhibits period furniture, ecclesiastical items,

Egilsstaðir

INFORMATION

East Iceland Regional Information Centre, Miðvangi 1–3 Egilsstaðir, Tel. 4 71 23 20
www.east.is

EXCURSIONS

Trips on the Lagarfljót on the Lagarfljót-sormurinn pleasure boat. Daily 9pm departures from Atlavík; on-board restaurant with music.

WHERE TO EAT

Klausturkaffi ££/£££

Skriðuklaustur, tel. 471 29 92
www.skriduklaustur.is
The monastery café is known for its varied lunch and cake buffets, as well as the excellent clam soup served here.

Café Nielsen ££

Tel. 471 26 26
Old wooden house hiding behind tall trees. Quiet, sunny terrace, tasty cream cakes and traditional Icelandic dishes such as fish soup.

WHERE TO STAY

Hótel Hallormsstaður ££

Tel. 471 24 00
www.hotel701.is

Summer hotel with 35 comfortable double rooms, some of which have a lake view, in the middle of the forest with a swimming pool right next to it. Good restaurant, with value-for-money dish of the day in the evening.

Gistihusið Egilsstöðum £££

Tel. 471 11 14
egilsstadir@isholf.is
Wonderfully quiet and idyllic location on the lake, despite being only a few hundred metres from the main road. Carefully restored, comfortable farmhouse built in 1903 with plenty of atmosphere and a good restaurant. Open all year round.

Húsey: Tungnahreppur £/££

Tel. 471 30 10
www.husey.is
Small youth hostel with 16 beds. Ideal for holidays on horseback, as each guest gets his own horse.

Fellabær: Skipalækur í Fellum £/££

Tel. 471 13 24
En suite room in the farmhouse, campsite and five cabins which are basic, but right on the lake.

---

clothing and tools from the area. Information on transport links in East Iceland round off this successful heritage museum.

❶ Laufskógar 1, in summer Tue – Sun 11am – 5pm, otherwise 1pm – 4pm

Fed by the Vatnajökull, the Lagarfljót river forms a lake, some 25km/15.5 miles long and at its widest 2.5km/1.5 miles wide, south of Egilsstaðir, known as **Lögurinn**. At a depth of 112m/367ft and with a sediment layer up to 100m/328ft thick the bottom of the lake is the deepest point in Iceland. A muddy-grey colour due to the glacier water, the lake is the **Loch Ness of Iceland**, as its freezing waters are said

Lagarfljót

Hengifoss plunges about 118m/389ft into the deep

to shelter the lake monster Lagarfljót worm, also called **Laggi**, which guards a hoard og gold. But the monster should be a ripe old age indeed, as he was already sighted in the 13th century. Incidentally, Laggi is just as camera-shy as its relative in Loch Ness, which is why there is now a prize for the first photo of the monster. Some 11km/7 miles south of Egilsstaðir, the [931] turns off to lead around the lake (approx. 90 km/56 miles).

Old birches   Iceland's most extensive forest area on the eastern bank of the Lagarfljót at Hallormsstaður with its up to 160-year-old birches has been looked after and nurtured since 1899. As far back as 1903 the first trials began with the **planting of foreign trees**; since then 90 types of tree have been tested for their suitability to Icelandic life, of which only ten made the grade. The Atlavík campsite lies in the middle of the forest on the banks of the lake.

Hengifoss   Shortly after crossing the bridge in the north of the Fljótsdalur, the waters of the Hengifoss plunge down 118m/387ft, which gives it the distinction of being the third-highest waterfall in Iceland. Below the Hengifoss, the **Litlanesfoss**, 30m/98ft high, features an unusually beautiful basin lined with basalt columns. From the car park at the western riverbank, a path leads uphill for roughly 2.5km/1.5 miles to the Hengifoss. Two kilometres/1.2 miles south of the waterfall, the [F 910] jeep track branches off to the 1,863m/6,112-ft **Snæfell** at the foot of the Vatnajökull (57km/35 miles).

Kárahnjúkar power station   The road [F 910] turns off before Skriðuklaustur to the new dam of the Kárahnjúkar power station. There are beautiful views of the glacier on the way. There is a visitor centre in the valley after Skriðuklaustur and it informs on the significance of the power station.

Originally, the farmstead in the Fljótsdalur was simply called Skriða (landslide), but following the foundation of an Augustinian monastery in the late 14th century, Klaustur (monastery) was added to the name of the place. It was the only monastery in East Iceland and also the last to be founded in Catholic times. In 1938, the poet **Gunnar Gunnarsson** (1889 – 1975) bought Skriðuklaustur and had a German architect design a stately home in the Bohemian style. Due to financial and health-related problems, Gunnarsson and his wife had moved to Reykjavík by 1948, where he lived until his death. He bequeathed Skriðuklaustur to the state, stipulating its use for cultural purposes. Today, his wish has been granted, and every year the Gunnar Gunnarsson Institute organizes several exhibitions in the prestigious house, beautifully located on the hillside.

Skriðu-
klaustur

❶ daily. 12pm – 5pm

** Golden Circle

— ✳ D/E 6

Region: Southwest Iceland

Cultural and historic sites with breathtaking nature: the Golden Circle route takes in the region's touristic highlights east of Reykjavík, including Þingvellir, Geysir, Gullfoss and Skálholt.

The starting point for the Golden Circle route is usually ▶Reykjavík. Taking the Ring Road from the Icelandic capital via Hveragerði soon leads to Selfoss. Here the circuit turns off northwards to the [35], leading past the Kerið explosion crater, stopping at the church of **Skálholt** – in medieval times the spiritual centre of the country – and eventually reaching the geysers in the **Haukadalur** and, a few kilometres away, the **Gullfoss**, the »Golden Waterfall«. The return to Reykjavík passes the hotel village of Laugarvatn, where visitors can find accommodation, and through ▶Þingvellir National Park. Sightseeing coaches need about eight hours to complete the 250km/155-mile round trip. Visitors with their own car can build in additional side trips – for instance to the town of Selfoss or into the ▶Þjórsárdalur – and detours such as returning to Reykjavík along the Þingvallavatn lake via Nesjavellir.

TO SOUTHERN ICELAND VIA THE RING ROAD

At the start of the Golden Circle, driving southeast from Reykjavík, the landscape seems to become more primal, raw and inhospitable by the minute. The dominant feature is black lava with minimal veg-

Hellisheiði

etation. Soon after the [39] turns off towards the Þorlákshöfn ferry harbour, the [1] Ring Road leads uphill to the Hellisheiði. On the western edge of this high plateau the Ring Road cuts through the very lava flow which in the year 1000 gushed out of an eruption fissure at the nearby **Hengill** massif when not 30km/18.5 miles north of here, in Þingvellir, the medieval parliament resolved to introduce Christianity, which resulted in the lava flow being dubbed **Kristnitökuhraun**, »Christianization lava«. To the east, the Hellisheiði ends abruptly and winds steeply downhill. An attraction on the Hellisheiði is **geothermal power station Hellisheiðarvirkjun** (214 MW), which is located 18km/11mi north-west of Hveragerði and which started operating in 2008; it has a very worthwhile ***Mexhibit on geothermics**.

❶ daily. 9am – 5pm, admission 800 ISK, www.orkusyn.is

Hveragerði Situated right below the slope, Hveragerði is a spa and greenhouse town with some 2,000 inhabitants. There is no better place to witness the know-how of the Icelanders in outsmarting the vagaries of the Northern Atlantic climate using geothermal energy: local hot springs are used to heat innumerable **hothouses**, with even tropical fruit ripening under their glass roofs. Flower and vegetable cultivation are of more economic relevance. Iceland's hothouse gardeners – with their state-run horticultural college in Hveragerði – largely satisfy the country's demand for cucumbers, peppers and tomatoes. After an earthquake in 2008 a **new high temperature area** developed east of town at the foot of the Reykjafjall. North and north-west of Hveragerði lies the Hengill Thermal Area, where outdoor enthusiasts like to hike and swim in the well-tempered natural thermal pool

Insider Tip

Selfoss Selfoss lies off the Golden Circle route, which turns off to the north before reaching the entrance to the town. With its nearly 6500 inhabitants Selfoss is Iceland's largest inland town, despite having merged with the coastal villages of Eyrarbakki and Stokkseyri to form the municipality of **Árborg** during a local government reorganization in the late 1990s. The town's history begins in the late 19th century, with the construction of the first suspension bridge over the Ölfusá river. Selfoss owes another growth spurt to the founding of an agricultural cooperative in the 1930s, from which originated one of the biggest dairies in Northern Europe.

Þorlákshöfn, Eyrarbakki and Stokkseyri These three towns on the southern coast, with fewer than 2,500 inhabitants between them, live mainly by fishing. The biggest employer however is the Litla Hraun Icelandic state prison at the eastern edge of Eyrarbakki. Of the three towns Þorlákshöfn has the best harbour; at least once a day the car ferry from the Westman Islands docks here. Since the building of the bridge spanning the mouth of the Ölfusá, many fishermen from Eyrarbakki and Stokkseyri also land their catch here, saving themselves having to enter the small harbours of their towns, the stronger swell making them a trickier proposition. More information on the fishing business in the region can be found in Eyrarbakki's **maritime collection**. Eyrarbakki might seem insignificant today, but the place can look back on a proud past as a commercial port for the southern coast of Iceland during colonial times. Built in 1756, the trading house of the Danish monopoly trader in the Eyrargata, called **Husið** for short, is now used as a heritage museum, showing the culture and history of the region. In Stokkseyri the museum **Icelandic Wonders** knows all about elves, trolls, ghosts and Christmas elves.

Maritime Collection: Túngata 59, Eyrarbakki, mid May–mid Sept 11am–6pm
Husið: Eyrarbakki, mid May–mid Sept 11am–6pm, www.husid.com
Icelandic Wonders: Hafnargata 9, Stokkseyri, June–Aug 10am–8pm, admission 1000 ISK

Golden Circle

INFORMATION
Hveragerði tourist office
Breiðamörk 2, Tel. 483 46 01
https://www.south.is/en/

In the Geysir Center
Tel. 480 68 00, www.geysircenter.is

WHERE TO EAT
►Reykjavík, ►Þingvellir

WHERE TO STAY

Guesthouse Frost and Fire **££/£££**
Hverhamar, Hveragerði, Tel. 4 83 49 59
www.frostandfire.is
14 elegant doubles with a wonderful view of the Varma River.
The room walls are decorated with works by 20th century Icelandic artists. The hotel has hot pots on the riverbank; there is also a 12m/40ft-long heated pool and a sauna.

Geysir Center **£/£££**
Tel. 480 68 00, www.geysircenter.is
With hotel, restaurant, pool, multimedia

show, horses for hire and campsite, the Geysir Center offers tourists everything they need. There is also space for sleeping bags.

Hveragerði: Hótel Eldhestar **£££**
Völlum Hveragerði, tel. 480 48 00
www.eldhestar.is
Small hotel with ten comfortable double rooms furnished in a rustic style. With all the riding excursions on offer, horse lovers will be particularly happy here.

Skálholt: Skálholtsskóli **££/£££**
Tel. 486 88 70, fax 486 89 90
www.skalholt.is
The modern school building of Skálholt offers 18 comfortable double rooms, with another 35 beds in a neighbouring building.

Selfoss: Gesthus **£**
Engjavegur 56, Selfoss
Tel. 482 35 85, www.gesthus.is
Eleven bungalows with kitchen, bathroom and TV, campsite.

Kerið – crater at the roadside
A few kilometres north of Selfoss, the Golden Circle route crosses the Sog river on the [35]. Soon after, lying on the eastern side of the road, the Kerið explosion crater is a textbook maar (a broad volcanic crater). With a depth of 55m/180ft and a very regular shape, almost like an amphitheatre, it counts among the most beautiful of its kind in the country and has even been used as a **concert arena**. For that occasion, a pontoon was lowered into the crater lake to serve as a stage, and the acoustics proved to be excellent.

* SKÁLHOLT: IN THE LAND OF THE BISHOPS

Stronghold of faith
The bridge at the Brúará river marks the transition to the region of **Biskupstungur**, the »Bishop's Tongue«, an area stretching like a tongue between the Brúará and Hvítá rivers and reaching inland to the highlands. The religious reference is due to the ancient episcopal see of Skálholt, whose large church stands isolated, towering above the surroundings and visible from afar. From 1056 until the Reformation reached southern Iceland in 1541, Skálholt was the spiritual – and eventually also the secular – centre of Iceland. For centuries, the associated elite school was the only one in the country that offered higher education. When, in 1106, a second bishop's seat was established at Hólar in northern Iceland, Skálholt remained the country's leading episcopal office.

> ! **MARCO POLO TIP**
>
> *Anthroposophic, ecological* **Insider Tip**
>
> By turning off at Borg, the [354] allows a 10km/6-mile detour via Sólheimar. This eco-village with 100 inhabitants and a dedicated special needs project has been run since the 1930s along the principles of anthroposophy (an educational, therapeutic and creative system established by Rudolf Steiner). Workshops sell crafts, candles and organic vegetables grown in their own hothouses. Guests also have access to the Grænakannan (Green Can) café and the Brekkukot guesthouse. (Tel. 480 44 00; www.solheimar.is)

Significant events
Many significant events in Icelandic history and culture are closely linked with Skálholt. Thus, it was at its monastic school that the secret translation of the Bible was made; when printed at the end of the 1530s, this became the first book in the Icelandic language. And it was here that a good decade later the last Catholic bishop of Northern Europe lost his head: **Jón Arason**, who was actually bishop of Hólar, anticipated that the new faith would strengthen the influence of the Danish crown in Iceland and thus wanted to change the course of history with a counter reformation. In 1549, he subdued – more by the power of the sword than the Bible – the episcopacy of southern Iceland, which had been Protestant for some years. This proved a step too far: Lutherans faithful to the

king arrested him, and in 1550 he was decapitated near the church of Skálholt together with two of his sons. The place where the bloody deed happened is today marked by a memorial stone. In 1785, an earthquake damaged the old cathedral and the school to such an extent that the bishop and his retinue moved to Reykjavík, where soon a unified diocese for the whole country was established. For a century, Skálholt was reduced to a simple parish church, although now it is once again the official seat of a suffragan bishop.

The first stone for today's church was laid in 1956 for the 900th anniversary of the foundation of the Skálholt diocese; it was finally completed in 1963. Excavations suggest that the church is probably the eleventh on this site. Although little is left from the old days, one gem was discovered when a crypt was excavated during the construction of the last church: a stone coffin dating back to the early 13th century containing the remains of the well-known saga personality, bishop **Páll Jónsson**, in full array. The sarcophagus is shown as part of a small exhibition. Otherwise, well-known 20th-century artists have contributed a lot to the style of the modern church. **Nína Tryggvadóttir** (1913 – 1968) created the dominating mosaic on the back chancel wall as an oversized altarpiece, while **Gerður Helgadóttir** designed the colourful stained-glass windows. In front of the church, two stone tablets by the sculptor **Páll Guðmundsson** show two famous men of the church, Gissur the White, who had the first church in Skálholt built, and Ísleifur Gissurarson, the first Icelandic bishop (1056).

Modern style dominates

MARCO POLO TIP

! **Whitewater rafting**   *Insider Tip*

It is obvious from the white spray of the Hvítá that its water is not in the business of flowing gently by, as one set of rapids follows another. Thus, the »White River« is also popular with rafters. An extensive programme of lessons and tours is offered by Arctic Rafting, Laugavegur 11, 101 Reykjavík, tel. 562 70 00, www.arcticrafting.com

** GULLFOSS, THE GOLDEN FALLS

To head in the direction of Gullfoss and Geysir, either go back to the [35] or take the [30] east of the mighty Hvítá, which is crossed at Laugarás. Thanks to hot springs, this village also has a flourishing business in **horticulture under glass**. Travellers with children should pay a visit to the small pet zoo at the Slakki farm. From the [30], another possible detour runs to the ▶Þjórsárdalur, the valley of the Þjórsá; otherwise, after only a few kilometres, the road reaches Fluðir. From here, the Gullfoss is some 30km/18.5 miles away.

Laugarás

Natural wonders
With a double-cascade flowing across two tiers, at right angles to each other, the mass of water from the river Hvítá plunges down 70m/230ft into the ravine of **Gullfossgljúfur**. In an average summer, 130 cubic metres/over 34,300 US gal of water thunder down the fall per second, while record quantities of 2,000 cubic metres/over 528,300 US gal have been recorded. The streams of visitors are led to a car park above the gorge where a **mini exhibition in the Sigrídarstofa visitor centre** has information on the waterfall and the surrounding landscape. Passing the parking area, the [35] carries on as the so-called ►Kjölur Route through the highlands to northern Iceland.

** HAUKADALUR – »VALLEY OF THE SURGING WATERS«

The Big Geyser
Gullfoss marks the turning point of the Golden Circle route. Just under 10km/6.2 miles back west on the [35], Haukadalur represents **Iceland's most famous geothermal active area**, usually only referenced by the name of its most famous spring, **Geysir** (► MARCO POLO Insight p. 162/163). This proper name, derived from the Old West Norse word for »gush«, has become the generic term for gushing springs all around the world, whereas in Iceland they are called »goshver«; only the one in Haukadalur is actually called »Geysir«, or to be exact, **Stórigeysir** – the Big Geyser. Reports on the time of the settlements don't mention it, even though **Ári Þorgilsson**, the most important chronicler of that era, lived for many years on the Haukadalur farm right next to it. Analysing sinter deposits around the vent, geologists estimate Geysir's age to be at least 10,000 years. It is probable that the Stórigeysir, when the first settlers arrived, was experiencing an extended period of calm, until woken by one of those earthquakes that frequently rocked southern Iceland at the end of the 13th century, and which repeatedly continued to influence it later on.

Woken from a deep sleep
In its heyday the Big Geyser sent its column of water up to 60m/195ft high, accompanied by ghostly rumblings in the ground. As far as reliable descriptions are available, the intervals between the eruptions varied over the years between 30 minutes and several weeks. In the 19th century, an earthquake stoked the Stórigeysir to a phase with very violent eruptions, only to calm down and go to sleep entirely between 1916 and 1932. There have always been attempts to artificially stimulate the natural spectacle: for a short time, lowering the water level or adding large quantities of soft soap stimulated some activity – a trick used for tired geysers worldwide. The soap changes the water's surface tension, thus encouraging eruptions. However, the Icelandic Nature Conservation Council banned this »aphrodisiac« and

On the Golden Circle: between Þingvellir and Laugarvatn

any other aids in the Haukadalur in 1992. What humankind could not achieve was successfully brought about by an earthquake in June 2000: the Stórigeysir woke up again and has been active since, if only with small eruptions that remain far behind its major displays of the past.

**Strokkur

There is no need to worry though – every visitor to Haukadalur will see the column of water from a geyser shooting towards the sky, courtesy of Strokkur. The »butter tub« might only achieve heights of between 10 and 20m/33 and 65ft, but does so reliably every few minutes. What is fascinating about Strokkur's eruptions is the **water bell** which starts off every eruption, and from which the jet of water and steam shoots skyward. There are numerous other springs in the thermal field of the Haukadalur, of which some bubble away quietly, while others are just luke-warm puddles of water. Care should be taken anywhere though, as all the springs at Haukadalur have become more active – and, more importantly, hotter – since the last earthquake and many are visibly boiling. Warning signs are there for a reason, and putting a foot wrong can lead to seriously burnt toes.

Geysir Center

As Geysir and Strokkur count amongst the most visited sights in Iceland, it's no surprise to find an extensive service infrastructure in place: a hotel with cabins by the river, plus four luxury rooms, a campsite and a restaurant for hungry geyser spotters, as well as a large cafeteria and souvenir shop at the petrol station. Next to this, the multimedia Geysir Center serves up a popular scientific presentation of **Iceland's geological phenomena**. Here visitors can even have themselves rattled by an earthquake.

❶ **Geysir Center:** summer daily 10am – 5pm, otherwise 12pm – 4pm, admission 1000 ISK, www.geysircenter.is
Geysir Thermal Area: daily 10am – 5pm, admission 600 ISK

MARCO ⊕ POLO INSIGHT

Gushing Springs

Hot springs that are fed by underground water are called geysers. From time to time they eject a column of water explosively. How does a geyser like this work?

❶ Water column

In 1880 the chemist Robert Wilhelm Bunsen from Göttigen, Germany developed a theory on the functioning of geysers; its basics are still considered to be valid today. Geysers are part of the underground water system, which runs to great depths. There is a deep shaft under the surface opening which contains a column of water that is heated by the earth's warmth. Because of the pressure of the water column the boiling point is much higher than 100°C (212°F). The decisive factor in the creation of a geyser is that the water is heated up to much more than 100°C (212°F), but it cannot boil because of the great pressure deep in the earth.

❷ Vaporisation

When the pressure become too great, steam rises abruptly to the surface, expands more and more, carries the water above it along, and causes an explosive vaporisation, which is the driving force behind the fromation of the rising water column.

❸ Funnel

The water access channel expands to a funnel at the surface.

❹ Water access channel

After the eruption water flowing back into the ground together with underground water refill the shaft in a few minutes.

Strokkur in Haukadalur: effects and lifespan of a geyser depend on the amount of water that flows into it from the surface and underground

Hafnarfjörður

INFORMATION
Strandgata 6
Tel. 585 55 55
www.hafnarfjordur.is

WHERE TO EAT
❶ Fjörugarðurinn £££/££££
Strandgata 55
Tel. 565 12 13
www.fjorukrain.is
In the town where the Vikings are the centre of all the attention, naturally visitors also partake of their food like them – in the Fjörugarðurinn. The food on offer ranges from hearty and rustic to quality traditional fare, and is of course washed down with at least one »Black Death«. Booking in advance is recommended, as the Fjörugarðurinn is popular with tour groups.

❷ A. Hansen ££
Vesturgata 4
Tel. 565 11 30
Located in one of the oldest houses in town, the restaurant does offer excellent Icelandic fish and lamb dishes, but the house speciality is the elf menu. Visitors who have always been curious to know what elves like to eat have come to the right place – and will be surprised by the good taste of the invisibles.

WHERE TO STAY
❶ Hótel Viking ££
Strandgata 55
Tel. 565 12 13
www.fjorukrain.is
Sleep like the old Vikings, in rooms named after ancient gods or chiefs. In the former smithy the comfort of guests is ensured by rooms with bathroom and TV, plus of course the hot pots.

❷ Helguhús £
Lækjarkinn 8
Tel. 555 28 42
helguhus@helguhus.is
A ten-minute walk from the town centre, this guesthouse offers bright rooms under the roof and two more in the lower floor. Breakfast and friendly atmosphere come at no extra charge.

centre, which presents, under the name of Hafnarborg, works from their own collection as well as various changing exhibitions – it is well worth having a look at the programme or paying a visit to the museum café. **Insider Tip**

❶ Strandgata 34, daily except Tues 12 – 5pm, www.hafnarborg.is

More modern art can be seen in the Víðistaðatún sculpture park north of the town centre, where the campsite is. Most of the sculptures were made as part of an arts festival in 1991. **Sculpture park**

The town is still active in promoting the arts, for instance by **providing artists' studios** on the Straumur farm, just west of the Straumsvík aluminium factory, instantly recognizable by its numerous gables. **Promoting art**

** Hekla

 F 6/7

Region: Highlands north of Mýrdalsjökull

Numerous legends surround one of the most famous volcanoes on earth; it has even been said to be the mouth of hell, the dwelling-place of lost souls. One thing is certain however: the currently 1491m/4920ft-high Hekla is very active, and always »fired up«.

Always ready for an eruption (▶MARCO POLO Insight p.172)

Its foundations were laid under the glaciers of the last Ice Age – approx. 20,000 years ago. Over the course of the following millennia, a volcanic fissure some 5km/3.1 miles in length has expanded to form an impressive **central volcano**, a ridge stretching from southwest to northeast with a current summit height of 1,491m/4,892ft at the Toppgígur crater. This is not guaranteed to remain the same however, as during one eruption in 1947 the mountain grew by nearly 40m/131ft, and the Hekla is always ready for a new eruption. Typical for the Hekla are fissure eruptions stretching along different sections of its ridge, like the one which occurred in 2000, at nearly 7km/4.3 miles in length. In spring of 2104 the magma chamber was full again.

February 2000: Volcano Hekla spewing fire

Hekla

INFORMATION
Hvolsvöllur
Hildavegur 16, tel. 4 87 80 43
www.hvolsvollur.is

Hella
Suðurlandsvegi 1
Tel. 487 51 65, tourinfo@rang.is

WHERE TO EAT/ WHERE TO STAY
Hella: Hekluhestar £
Austvadsholt, Tel. 487 65 98
hekluhestar@islandia.is
Guesthouse with 18 beds (plus sleeping bag accommodation) in a house built in 1990 in the traditional Icelandic style. Varied activities on offer include riding tours and trips to the Hekla. Open all year round.

Hvolsvöllur: Hótel Hvolsvöllur ££
Hliðarvegur 7, tel. 487 80 50
www.hotelhvolsvollur.is
Small hotel with 28 rooms, some en suite. Pleasant breakfast room in the conservatory. Sauna, jacuzzi, bar and restaurant inside the main house. Various trips may be organized from here.

Leirubakki £/£££   *Insider Tip*
Tel. 487 65 91
www.leirubakki.is
Equine holiday farm on the [26], with comfortably equipped cabins, plus sleeping bag accommodation for up to 50 people. Also a good restaurant, hot pots, sauna and Viking bath, covered riding arena, horses for hire and various organized trips.

»FIRE MOUNTAIN« AND »HELL'S MOUTH«

Turning off the Ring Road 7km/4.3 miles northwest of Hella on the [26] and heading north, visitors will notice that the further inland they penetrate, the more strongly the scenery is dominated by the Hekla. From the south, it is the »Fire Mountain«'s narrow front end that first becomes visible, but to see the Hekla's true dimensions revealed, visitors need to view its flanks. Whilst the mountain is often likened to a boat floating bottom up, it has more similarities to the spine of a huge reptile, a dragon maybe, as it is not reluctant to spew fire.

Dragon's back

Using **tephrochronology**, (Greek téphra: ashes) dating layers of volcanic ash, proved that the Hekla has erupted over 100 times now, in five major cycles. In between there have been breaks lasting centuries, but always ending in a particularly violent eruption. Thus, the biggest volcanic eruption that Iceland experienced after the last Ice Age, in the 10th century BC, is likely to have marked the beginning of one of Hekla's eruptive periods. The ash from that eruption – scientists have projected its volume to be 9 billion cubic metres/nearly 2.4 trillion US gal – can be detected in the soil of some 80 % of the surface of Iceland, all the way from the western fjords to the extreme east of the country.

9 bil. cubic meters of ash

Fire versus Ice

Ever since the settlement of Iceland 1,100 years ago a volcano has erupted on the average of once every five years. First material collects in a magma chamber, then the pressure rises and finally it is released in an eruption. The massive ice shields that cover many of Iceland's volcanoes may be able to delay the eruption, but they cannot prevent the masses of volcanic ash from being thrown more than 20km/12mi into the atmosphere during the explosive eruptions

▶ **Iceland's three most active volcanoes**
eruptions since 1500

HEKLA	KATLA	GRÍMSVÖTN
2000		
1991		
1980	KATLA	
1970	1860	GRÍMSVÖTN
1947	1823	2004
1845	1755	1998
1766	1721	1902
1693	1660	1873
1636	1625	1598
1597	1612	1783
1510	1580	1598

Reykjavík

▶ **Profile Eyjafjalla – Katla**

Eyjafjalla, Fimmvörduha ls and Katla are mostly covered by glaciers. Eyjafjalla last erupted in spring of 2010. The ashes that were thrown up to 13km/8mi high caused massive delays in air traffic in may parts of Europe.

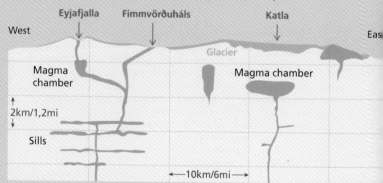

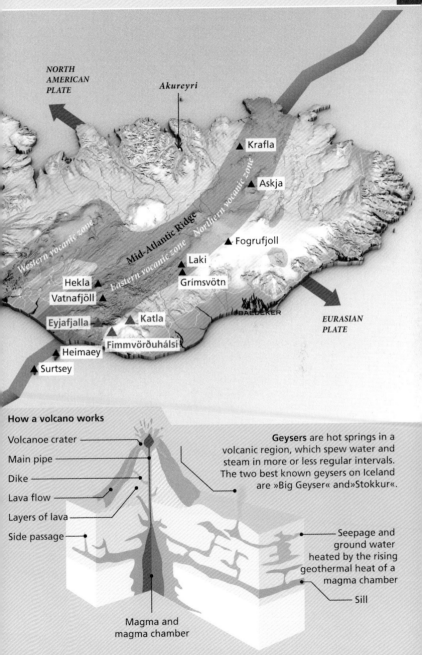

NORTH
AMERICAN
PLATE

Akureyri

▲ Krafla

▲ Askja

Western volcanic zone

Mid-Atlantic Ridge

Eastern volcanic zone

Northern volcanic zone

▲ Fogrufjoll

Laki
▲
Grímsvötn

Hekla ▲
Vatnafjöll ▲

Eyjafjalla ▲ Katla
△
Fimmvörðuhálsi

▲ Heimaey

Surtsey

BAEDEKER

EURASIAN
PLATE

How a volcano works

Volcanoe crater

Main pipe

Dike

Lava flow

Layers of lava

Side passage

Geysers are hot springs in a volcanic region, which spew water and steam in more or less regular intervals. The two best known geysers on Iceland are »Big Geyser« and »Stokkur«.

Seepage and ground water heated by the rising geothermal heat of a magma chamber

Sill

Magma and magma chamber

Active cycle The last eruption cycle, continuing to this day, was triggered in 1104 by the eruption that extinguished nearly all life in the ►Þjórsárdalur under a thick layer of pumice ash. All in all, since 1104 the Hekla has blown around 7 billion cubic metres/nearly 1.9 trillion US gal of ash into the skies – enough to fill some 115 million ship containers – and spewn around 8 billion cubic metres/over 2 trillion US gal of lava from its craters and fissures. Shorter active phases within the large cycles also usually begin with an explosive **initial eruption**, followed by prolonged lava flows. The eruption in late March 1947 is classified by scientists as such. Without warning the mountain blew an ash cloud into the atmosphere that took less than half an hour to reach a height of some 30,000m/nearly 100,000ft, and over the following days rained down over Scandinavia all the way to Finland. In 1970, the ash from a smaller eruption proved fatal to thousands of sheep in northern Iceland, as it deposited toxic compounds onto their pastures. The eruptions of 1980/1981, 1991, and the most recent on 27 February 2000, brought almost solely lava to the surface, which spread itself over uninhabited areas of the mountain.

Gateway to hell? Early European travellers often described the Hekla as the gateway to hell, from whence the cries of the lost souls could be heard. Old Icelandic literature however does not mention Hekla as a gateway to hell – this is the fruit of the imaginations of early, religiously-motivated visitors to Iceland. Legends and scientific facts on the Hekla are presented by the volcanological edutainment centre at Leirubakki farm. The centre uses a multimedia concept. The architecturally extravagant building consists of walls made from lava blocks and shows the subject of the exhibition, reflected in large windows, at different times of the day and year. The exhibition is part of the Leirubakki tourist centre on the [26].
❶ daily 10am – 10pm

Climbing the Hekla Visitors can get closest to the Hekla on the Landmannaleið track [F 225] running north of the volcano. Two turnings lead off from the [F 225] to the foot of the volcano, from where the Hekla can be climbed on a waymarked route. All this effort is rewarded by a fantastic view of the **volcanic landscape** spreading out below. It should be kept in mind however that the wind on the Hekla sometimes reaches gale force and mist severely reduces visibility on the lava fields.

HELLA AND HVOLSVÖLLUR

Alongside the tourist hub of Leirubakki (see above), other starting points for exploring the Hekla region are the villages of Hella and

Hvolsvöllur. Counting some 600 inhabitants, the village of Hella only started developing from the 1920s onwards around the bridge that had been built at this site over the **Ytri Rangá**. The accommodation and restaurants on offer here only tempt the odd tour group to schedule a short stop in Hella.

Marginally bigger, Hvolsvöllur suffers a similar fate, hard though it tries to interest tourists with a saga centre. The exhibition, with many text-heavy panels and displays but few exhibits, is only really worth visiting in bad weather. More fun are the trips organized by the saga centre to the sites of the famous **Njáll's Saga**, which can be identified everywhere around Hvolsvöllur.

Hvolsvöllur Saga Centre

❶ Jun – Aug daily 9am – 6pm, Sat/Sun only from 10pm.

The historic settlement of Keldur near Hvolsvöllur is well worth a look around. One of the houses belonging to the farmstead, the 12th-century **Keldnaskálinn**, is considered the oldest surviving building in Iceland. Another was built around a spring, hence the name Keldur – spring. More recent excavations uncovered an **escape tunnel** dating back to the 12th century, which led from the farmstead to the river. This tunnel is mentioned in the Njál's Saga. Keldur can be found near the western approach to the Fjallabaksleið Syðri [F 210] dirt road, accessible via the [264], which turns off inland 5km/just over 3 miles west of Hvolsvöllur and leads to the Ragnávellir valley.

*Keldur historic farmstead

❶ June – Sept. daily 10am – 15pm, other times on appointment, tel. 487 84 52, admission 500 ISK

At the Keldur farmstead, the **Fjallabaksleið Syðri** [F 210] turns off in an easterly direction. The road winds its way through spectacular mountain scenery, offering superb visibility, past three glaciers, the large **Mýrdalsjökull** and its smaller neighbours **Torfajökull** and **Tindfjallajökull**. With suitable vehicles, this can be used as a route through southern Iceland as an alternative to the [1] Ring Road. The road does actually have this function in official emergency plans in case the Katla volcano below the Mýrdalsjökull should erupt and flood the foreland, including the Ring Road, all the way to the coast with one of its feared glacier runs. The [F 210] does require the crossing of several watercourses and fields of quicksand and should only be attempted with well-equipped jeeps, preferably in convoy.

GOING EAST ON THE RING ROAD

Driving further east along the coast from Hvolsvöllur, the Eyjafjöll massif, formed from volcanic rock and some 1,666 m/5,465ft high, marks the end of the more densely populated southwest of Iceland.

Eyjafjöll

The summit region is topped by a mighty icecap covering some 100 sq km/39 sq miles, the Eyjafjallajökull, and hides below it a massive volcanic crater that was last active in March/April 2010, with gigantic clouds of ashes that hindered international air traffic and created news headlines all over the world.

Seljalands-foss and Gljúfurárfoss

At the southwestern corner of the Eyjafjöll, at the spot where the access road to ▶Þórsmörk turns off the Ring Road, two **unusual waterfalls**, each very different from the other, mark the transition from the mountains down into the flat foreland. The Seljalandsfoss is visible from afar, and at night even illuminated, and it is possible to »go behind its back« – with whoever you like – while a few hundred metres further north at the edge of the Hamragarðar campsite the Gljúfurárfoss furtively slips into a moss-covered crack in the rock and cannot be reached without getting one's feet wet.

Seljavallalaug

One valley, the Seljavellir, pushes particularly far into the southern flank of the Eyjafjöll. This is a worthwhile detour, as amid the wonderful mountain panorama a quaint little swimming pool, the Seljavallalaug, looks rather inviting. This water used in this pool (currently closed) stems from a warm spring further up in the mountains, where there was a geothermic pool as early as the 1920s. Where the Ring Road goes around the Eyjafjöll in the south, back in the mists of

Nature as drama at Seljalandsfoss

time the sea broke against the steep cliff, clearly discernible in many places, and gouged some caves into the rock. These were used as shelters in the early days of the settlement, and to this day serve as stables or sheds. Good examples such as the **Rútshellir** and the stable caves of **Drangshlíð** can be seen on the southern slopes of the Drangshlídarfjall, a small mountain spur situated shortly before Skógar.

The regional museum of Skógar counts among the most interesting in Iceland and is the life work of one man: **Þórður Tómasson** not only brought – and furnished – old turf houses, a school and a church to Skógar, he also left the museum countless items of daily life. Next to the museum, the nearby **Skógafoss** waterfall is the town's biggest attraction. The deluge of water plunges down 60m/over 195ft across a width of 25m/82ft. According to legend the settler Þrasi hid a box full of gold in a cave behind the waterfall, which today has protected status. The Skógá river, with its source at the Fimmvörðuháls highland pass, forms a lot more waterfalls further upriver, some of them fairly big.

*Skógar

Höfn

 K 6

Region: East Iceland
Population: 1,700

Höfn means harbour in English and this gave the town its significance for a long time. Today the convenient location is what brings tourists to the town. Along with the harbour the nearby Ring Road and the airport make the town the starting point for many tours of south-eats Iceland.

WHAT TO SEE IN HÖFN

Höfn í Hornafirði, to give the town its full name, is not exactly a highlight on the tourist circuit. It's mainly the proximity to the Vatnajökull which (temporarily) attracts travellers, who tend to overnight here – and then move on. Nevertheless, Höfn does play host to three cultural institutions that are worth seeing. Upon entering the town, to the left Höfn's oldest building catches the eye. A merchant called **Ottó Tulinius** had it erected in 1864 as Gamlabúð trading house – not here however, but in a place called Papós on the banks of neighbouring Skarðsfjörður. Papós only existed briefly however; by 1897 there was only one merchant living there – the aforementioned Ottó Tulinius. Tulinius moved it to the harbour of Höfn at the **Hornafjörður**. In 1978, the house once again found itself on the wrong

Gamlabúð heritage museum

Höfn

INFORMATION
Hafnarbraut 25
Tel. 478 26 65, www.east.is

WHERE TO EAT   Insider Tip
Humarhöfnin £££/££££
Hafnarbraut 4, Hornafirði
Tel. 4 78 12 00
https://humarhofnin.is
The »lobster harbour« is known for its good lobster dishes. Lobster soup, lobster pizza, lobster baguettes and grilled lobster are served. Through the window watch the boats that bring in the lobster arrive and depart. The lamb, duck and fish that are also served all come from the region and all dishes are flavoured with Icelandic herbs.

WHERE TO STAY
Arnanes £££
Nesjum 6km/3.7 miles west of Höfn
Tel. 478 15 50
Fax 478 18 19
www.arnanes.is
Guesthouse near the Ring Road, with 16 rooms in five small cottages, some en suite. There is also a restaurant and art gallery.

Nýibær Farfuglaheimili £
Hafnarbraut 8
Tel. 478 17 36
Youth hostel with friendly service in the town, 33 beds in 2 to 6-bed rooms. A lot of wood in the rooms makes for a cosy atmosphere.

spot. Having been dismantled and put up again at its current location in Hafnarbraut, filled with period furniture and objects from the region, it is now open to visitors as a museum of local history.
❶ **Gamlabúð:** mid May – mid Sept 1pm – 6pm, July/Aug 9am – 6pm

Glacier show   In the town centre (Hafnarbraut 30), words and images, films and slides, paintings and other artworks, plus historical and contemporary tools and material on glacier research, give visitors an attractive insight into the **icy world of the Vatnajökull.**
❶ Jun – Aug 10am – 6pm

Pakkhúsið   In the basement of the Pakkhúsið (Krosseyjarvegur, right on the harbour), the heritage museum shows its maritime collection: boats and exhibits from the field of shipping. More interesting is the **Hanraðin Hafnarfirði** shop on the top floor, offering crafts, Icelandic jumpers and jewellery.

Stokksnes   6 km (3.5 mi) east of Höfn, at the entrance to the tunnel through the Vestrahorn, a 7km/4mi.long side road branches off to Stokksnes, the stormy south-easternmost point of Iceland in front of an imposing mountain backdrop. There is a lighthouse here as well as the highly modern antenna and telecommunication facility of the NATO listening post Stokksnes.

Húsavík

H 2

Region: Northeast Iceland
Population: 2,400

There are probably few better places to spot small and large whales than Húsavík. Which is why the small town proudly wears the self-proclaimed title of »whale watching capital of Europe«.

Húsavík lies in a gently curved bay with a beach of dark sand, part of the larger Skjálfandi Bay. Every year the small town attracts 80,000 visitors, a third of whom come in order to take part in a **whale-watching safari**. Just approaching the town reveals a strong smell of fish in the air, an unmistakable sign that this place too cannot live purely from tourism and still has to partially rely on fishing and fish processing.

WHAT TO SEE IN HÚSAVÍK

The biggest attraction in Húsavík is the whale watching safaris that in the summer run several times a day. **North Sailing**, founded in 1995 by a local family, was the first Icelandic company to offer whale watching tours. Two years later, the Whale Centre was opened, presenting sound scientific research on whales in an accessible way. Since the tours began the probability of spotting whales has stood at 99 % – a rate that is achieved nowhere else in Europe.
In the summer, whales and dolphins find ideal conditions in Skjálfandi Bay, thanks to, among other things, the depth of water on the western side, the rivers flowing into the bay, its sheltered location protected by high mountains and the minor tidal variations. So far, **twelve different kinds of whale** have been spotted, amongst them humpbacks, with their impressive size, sperm whales and fin whales. Very rarely blue whales can also be seen.

**Whale watching (▶MARCO POLO Insight p. 180/181)

Housed in a former abattoir, the museum (Hvalamiðstöðin, Hafnarstétt) gives extensive information on the giant sea dwellers. Much space is given over to presenting the various species of whales as well as their development. There is also information on whaling, beached whales and whale watching. Nine whale skeletons form a »whale walk«.
❶ June – Aug 9am – 7pm, May and Sept 10am – 4pm, www.whalemuseum.is

Whale museum

Camera Instead of Harpoon

Whaling has not been economically viable for some time, but still almost two thirds of the Icelanders are in favour of it. They often use their long tradition as an argument – but in the old sagas whales are neither caught nor eaten.

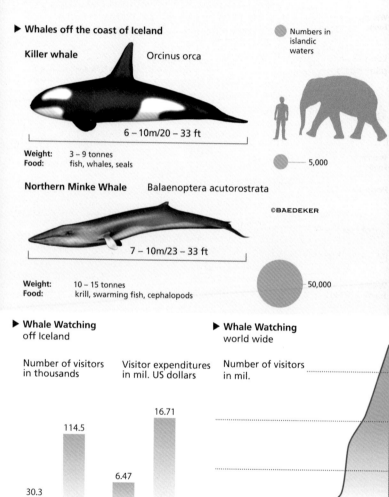

▶ **Whales off the coast of Iceland**

Killer whale Orcinus orca

Numbers in islandic waters

6 – 10m/20 – 33 ft

Weight:	3 – 9 tonnes
Food:	fish, whales, seals

5,000

Northern Minke Whale Balaenoptera acutorostrata

©BAEDEKER

7 – 10m/23 – 33 ft

Weight:	10 – 15 tonnes
Food:	krill, swarming fish, cephalopods

50,000

▶ **Whale Watching**
off Iceland

Number of visitors in thousands

Visitor expenditures in mil. US dollars

▶ **Whale Watching**
world wide

Number of visitors in mil.

114.5
30.3
1998   2008

16.71
6.47
1998   2008

1960   1970   1980   1990   2000

Northern bottlenose whale   Hyperoodon ampullatus

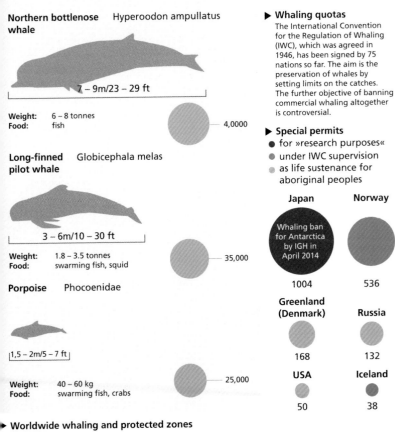

7 – 9m/23 – 29 ft

Weight: 6 – 8 tonnes
Food: fish

4,0000

Long-finned pilot whale   Globicephala melas

3 – 6m/10 – 30 ft

Weight: 1.8 – 3.5 tonnes
Food: swarming fish, squid

35,000

Porpoise   Phocoenidae

1,5 – 2m/5 – 7 ft

Weight: 40 – 60 kg
Food: swarming fish, crabs

25,000

▶ **Whaling quotas**
The International Convention for the Regulation of Whaling (IWC), which was agreed in 1946, has been signed by 75 nations so far. The aim is the preservation of whales by setting limits on the catches. The further objective of banning commercial whaling altogether is controversial.

▶ **Special permits**
● for »research purposes«
● under IWC supervision
● as life sustenance for aboriginal peoples

Japan
Whaling ban for Antarctica by IGH in April 2014
1004

Norway
536

Greenland (Denmark)
168

Russia
132

USA
50

Iceland
38

▶ **Worldwide whaling and protected zones**

■ Whaling zone   ■ Protected zone

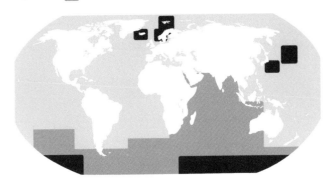

Safnahúsið The regional museum (Stóragarði 17) houses several sections and collections, such as the interesting **regional folk museum**, the **maritime museum**, the **art museum**, which shows mainly works by local artists, and a natural history collection. Opening times: in the summer daily 10am – 6pm.

i Stóragarði 17, summer daily 10am – 6pm, admission 500 ISK

Harbour promenade Erected between 1997 and 1999 from driftwood, the buildings on the **harbour promenade**, amongst them the »Gamli Baukur« fish restaurant glow in the sunlight in wonderfully warm hues. The terrace with a view of the harbour is the ideal spot for an afternoon coffee. The substantial lunchtime sea food buffet offered by **»Gamli Baukur«** is worth trying. Visitors looking to indulge in some nostalgia will very much enjoy the ship lanterns, compasses and steering wheels of the nautical collection.

Husavík

INFORMATION
Húsavíkurstofa
Garðarsbraut 7
640 Húsavík
Tel. 464 43 00
www.visitnorthiceland.is

WHALE WATCHING EXCURSIONS
North Sailing
Tel. 4 64 72 72
www.northsailing.is
Departures 10am, 1.30pm, 5pm, 8.15pm, on demand also at 9am, 12.30pm
North Sailing offer whale watching and other boat trips in restored oak boats and an Icelandic coastal sailboat

Gentle Giants
Tel. 4 64 15 00
www.gentlegiants.is
daily 9.45am, 1.15pm, 4.45pm, 8.15pm
Sail out in small boats where in the summer up to two dozen different kinds of whales can be watched.

WHERE TO EAT
Salka ££
Garðarsbraut 6
Tel. 464 25 51
Cosily furnished wooden house from the late 19th century, serving mainly fish dishes.

WHERE TO STAY
Fosshótel Húsavík £££
Ketilsbraut 22
Tel. 464 12 20
www.fosshotel.is
Mid-range hotel right in the centre of town, all rooms en suite and TV, some with views across the bay. Good hotel restaurant with fair prices.

Kaldbakskot, Kaldbakur ££
Tel. 464 15 04
www.cottages.is
A dozen camping huts of varying sizes south of Húsavík. Comfortably furnished, with kitchen and terrace. Superb location with sea views and a short stroll to the water's edge.

Hvammstangi

 E 4

Region: Northwest Iceland
Population: 600

This quiet village off the Ring Road has a nice mountain view-point, a gallery with high-quality crafts and a large selection of woollen goods. A drive around the Vatsnes peninsula offers many opportunities to spot seals.

WHAT TO SEE IN HVAMMSTANGI

Iceland's biggest **woollen-ware factory** is located in Hvammstangi; its outlet, »Ísprjón« (Höfðabraut 34), not only offers a large selection of Icelandic jumpers, but also many other woollen goods for sale. Strolling through the village, the **goldsmiths' workshop** of Einar H. Esrason (Eyrarland 1) is also worth a visit. The »Gallerí Bardúsa« (Brekkugata) has **crafts** of a high quality for sale, with part of the building additionally serving as a museum consisting mainly of an old grocery shop. Above Hvammstangi, the bizarre rock formation of **Káraborg** (476m/1,562ft) offers a good view over the village and surrounding mountains. The track up to the summit starts in Helguhvammur; on foot the climb takes about 2 hours.

High-quality souvenirs

 Insider Tip

Hvammstangi

INFORMATION
www.northwest.is

WHERE TO EAT
Café Sírop £
Norðurbraut 1
Tel. 451 27 17
Good value, varying dish of the day, soups, sandwiches and cakes. Also internet access, guesthouse and shop.

WHERE TO STAY
Hótel Edda Laugarbakki ££
Ketilsbraut 22
Tel. 444 49 20

www.hoteledda.is
Summer hotel with 28 furnished rooms and 30 spaces for sleeping bags.

Gistiheimili Hönnu Siggu ££
Garðarvegur 26
Tel. 451 24 07
gistihs@simnet.is
Four doubles, where guests feel part of the family in the house of Jóhanna Sveinsdóttir and Ólafur Guðmundsson. Breakfast with freshly baked bread, a large living room with TV, use of the garden, and views across the fjord.

*Selasetur A special attraction is the **Icelandic seal centre**, which opened in 2005, which explains everything there is to know about these North Atlantic mammals.

● June – Aug 9am – 4pm, Sept & 15th – 31st May 10am – 3pm
11.000 ISK, tel. 4 51 23 45, www.selasetur.is

WHAT TO SEE AROUND HVAMMSTANGI

Reykir The regional museum, some 22km/14 miles south of Hvammstangi, mainly documents the shark-fishing carried out in Húnaflói Bay in the 19th and up to the 20th century. The most important exhibit is the open **Ófeigur shark-fishing boat**, built entirely from driftwood and rowed by eight to ten men. Also on view is a »Baðstofa«, the communal living and sleeping room of a traditional Icelandic farm.

● **Regional museum:** June – Aug daily 10am – 6pm

Bjarg Still cultivated today, the Bjarg farm in Miðfjörður, south of Hvammstangi on the [704], is the birthplace of **Grettir the Strong**, who entered Iceland's history books as the country's most famous outlaw. Probably born around the year 1000, he spent his childhood on the farm, but even when he was an outlaw, he kept returning to his mother Ásdís. Grettir was eventually beaten to death on Drangey, an island in the Skagafjörður. His murderers brought Ásdís his head, which she in all probability buried on the farm. On the way to the farm stands a monument with reliefs by **Halldór Pétursson**, showing scenes from the Grettir saga.

Lighthouse on Vatsnes peininsula

The roughly 80km/50-mile trip around the **Vatsnes Peninsula** takes the [711] along the predominantly flat coast. In many places, such as in the bay of Hindisvík on the northern tip, or at Ósar,, lazy seals lie in the sun. At **Ósar**, in the east of the peninsula, rubble has been piled up to form a wall, which allows visitors to get a closer view of them. As the seals have enjoyed protected status for decades, they don't really let any curious visitors get in the way of a lazy life.

Vatsnes Peninsula

Hvítserkur (»White Shirt«) is a 15m/49ft-high rock bathed by the swell on the eastern side of Vatsnes at Húnafjörður. The rock takes its name from the colour of the excrement of the main birds breeding here, the cormorants and kittiwakes. Of course, the Hvítserkur is also at the centre of a story involving trolls. This time one of them is supposed to have thrown stones at the monastery of Þingeyri, only to have been surprised, as is wont to happen, by the sun, and since then has had to stand here petrified and suffer the screeches of the breeding birds. Just before the Ring Road, consider a detour via the [717] to **Borgarviki**, where basalt columns up to 15m/49ft high, arranged in a circle, are reminiscent of a castle.

Cormorants and kittiwakes

** Jökulsárgljúfur National Park

✳ J 2/3

Region: Northeast Iceland

Over the course of the millennia, the grey floodwaters of the Jökulsá in the Jökulsárgljúfur National Park have dug into the basalt, creating a deep canyon, which, with the Dettifoss plunging into it, receives the waterfall with the highest volume of water in Europe. The Grand Canyon and the Niagara Falls might be much larger, but the Icelandic version of those natural wonders is hardly less impressive. Another scenic highlight of the national park is the horseshoe-shaped Ásbyrgi Gorge.

In 1973, the gorges of the Jökulsá á Fjöllum river and the Ásbyrgi Gorge were protected by the establishment of the Jökulsárgljúfur National Park, covering 120 sq km/46 sq miles. To the east, the borders of the national park follow the course of the river from the Dettifoss to the [85], while the western border runs in a relatively straight line from the Eilífur in the south to the [85] in the north. At 25km/15.5 miles in length, 500m/1,640ft wide and with a depth of up to 120m/nearly 400ft, the Jökulsárgljúfur (the gorge of the Jökulsá) is the

Iceland's most massive erosion gorge

Jökulsárgljúfur

INFORMATION
At the campsite in Ásbyrgi
Tel. 465 21 95
www.ust.is
National park administration:
Tel. 465 23 59

WHERE TO EAT
Skúlagarður £
Kelduhverfi
Tel. 465 22 80
Guðrún Helga Sigurðardóttir and Andrés Júlíus Ólafsson create a homely atmosphere in this guesthouse and restaurant 12km/7.5 miles west of the national park.

WHERE TO STAY
Campsite Ásbyrgi £
Tel. 465 23 91
Pretty area at the entrance to the gorge, with good sanitary facilities.

Campsite Vesturdalur/ Hljóðaklettar £
Basic facilities in a very scenic location.

Grímstunga i Fjallahreppi £
Tel. 464 42 94
Small house in a quiet location, shortly after the [864] turns off the [1], 27km/17 miles south of the Dettifoss.

mightiest **erosion gorge** in Iceland. Its river is one of the longest in the country at a length of 206km/128 miles, and also carries one of the highest volumes of water. With its two-pronged source at the Vatnajökull glacier, the Jökulsá becomes a single river south of Herðubreiðarlindir. With little gradient initially, at the edge of the highlands the current becomes stronger, and near the Dettifoss the waters, by now dark-grey through the sediment they carry, plunge into the depths via several waterfalls. The rock walls shelter a thriving and – by Icelandic standards – **lush vegetation**, and in places the trees reach considerable heights. The largest forest areas, consisting of birches, willows and rowan trees, lie near Ásbyrgi, otherwise shrub forest and heather dominate the scenery.

WHAT TO SEE IN THE NATIONAL PARK

Ásbyrgi The Ásbyrgi Gorge is approx. 3.5km/just over 2 miles long, one kilometre/0.6 miles wide and 100m/328ft deep. The »Eyjan« wedge protruding into the gorge from the north lends it the shape of a horseshoe. It comes as no surprise then that according to legend it was created by a **hoofprint of Odin's eight-legged steed Sleipnir. Scientists also spent a long time wondering how this imposing rock formation with its vertical walls might have come into being. The solution to the mystery could lie in two waterfalls that once sat very close to each other but were eventually joined through erosion of the crest

Hiking trails lead to the three waterfalls (here: at the Dettifoss) in the national parks

lines, leaving only the wedge in the middle of the gorge. The course of the riverbed also later changed, as today it flows some 3km/1.9 miles further east. From the campsite, a hiking trail leads onto the island in the gorge and then on to its southern end. It is only from up here that the horseshoe shape of the Ásbyrgi Gorge becomes clear. The rock projection also allows a good view of the sandy flats stretching north all the way to the sea (trail length 5km/3.1 miles, approx. 1.5hrs). Several other hiking trails start from the parking area inside the gorge; one simple walk leads to the Botnstjörn lake and then on to a viewpoint. Somewhat more challenging is the trail from the campsite through the **Tófugjá Gorge**, as the only way up to the plateau from the valley floor is by means of a rope. Afterwards the trail continues east to the Jökulsá Gorge and around the wooded Áshöfði back to the starting point (approx. 2hrs).

Roughly in the middle of the national park lies Hljóðaklettar. The starting point for the following walks are the parking area or the campsite, both easily reached on a track. The circular hike to the »Echo Rocks« (Hljóðaklettar) takes about an hour, leading through an imposing volcanic landscape with bizarrely eroded remains of volcanoes, strange basalt formations, »petrified trolls« and a large cave. Another short walk leads from the parking area to »Karl og Karling« (Man and Wife), supposedly two petrified trolls standing on a gravel bank by the Jökulsá river.

Hljóðaklettar

Dettifoss The Dettifoss might only measure 45m/148ft in height, but as the vast quantities of grey water plunge over the edge, some 100m/328ft wide, into the depths below in a foam of spray, it is one of the most impressive waterfalls in the northern hemisphere. Above the Dettifoss lies the **Selfoss, with a height of 10m/33ft, and below the **Hafragilsfoss**, at 27m/88ft; all three waterfalls are connected by a hiking trail. In this area, the Jökulsá river has eaten particularly deeply into the dark basalt, forming a spectacular gorge. From the Dettifoss waterfall a way-marked trail leads along the western side of the gorge, time and again offering spectacular views to the campsite at Ásbyrgi. The complete hike takes two days and is relatively simple apart from the narrow Hafragil canyon and the Tófugjá Gorge at Ásbyrgi. Access to the Dettifoss from both north and south is via the [864], which has recently been paved. The [862], on the western side of the gorge, is also fine from the north to the Dettifoss, but after that point it turns into a track only suitable for off-road vehicles.

Kaldidalur

✳ E 5/6

Region: West Iceland

At just 40km/25 miles, the Kaldidalur [F 550] is the shortest road traversing the highlands. As there are no deep rivers to cross and in good weather the track can be negotiated with a regular saloon car, it is also called »highlands for beginners«.

Through the wild Kaldidalur The Kaldidalur route is the shortest link between ▶Þingvellir and the north and west of Iceland – which is why it has been used since the time of the settlements to ride to the Alþing. Drivers coming from the south follow the [52], the **Uxahryggjavegur**, from Þingvellir for 23km/14 miles north to Brunnar, where the [F 550] track turns off. East of the road the striking 1,060m/3,477-ft **Skjaldbreiður** shield volcano catches the eye. Onwards through the Kaldidalur, the cold valley lying between the glaciers of **Ok and Þórisjökull** does indeed do merit its name. After that the road goes uphill, leading eventually to the head of the pass, Langihryggur (727m/2,385ft). A little to the north lies Skúlaskeið, of which the saga reports that it was here the lawbreaker

Skúli, condemned to die at the Alþing, escaped his pursuers after fleeing Þingvellir. He owed his life to his fast horse Sörli, which at the end of the flight in Húsafell collapsed and died from exhaustion. Grímur Thomsen tells the story of this flight in his poem Skúlaskeið. From the top of the pass the road eventually leads down into the **valley of the Hvitá**, and the barren highlands, devoid of vegetation, change into the small birch forests at Húsafell.

Kirkjubæjarklaustur

G 7

Region: South Iceland
Population: 150

Nuns still play an important role here, although there have not been any resident in Kirkjubæjarklaustur for a long time. An odd monument in the middle of the village, rocks and lakes – which are said to guard strange secrets – and even the only restaurant here, act as reminders of the nuns of old.

Whilst Kirkjubæjarklaustur might only count 150 inhabitants, it is the largest settlement for miles around. Formerly called just Kirkjubær, for a long time it was a rich farm. This formed the core of today's village, which locals simply call »Klaustur« (convent). Klaustur can look back on a long history, as according to the **Book of Settlement** there were Irish hermits living here before the Norse Vikings arrived. It is said that when the hermits left, they cast a spell on the place to fall on any heathens there. After the Irish, **Ketill the Foolish** settled in Kirkjubær, owing his nickname to the fact that he had turned his back on the Norse gods to become a Christian. According to one legend, the unbaptized Hildir Eysteinsson is said to have tried later to settle in Kirkjubær; however, when he reached the edge of the village, he dropped down dead. The next important event was the founding of a convent by the Benedictine order which remained active up to the Reformation. That convent is also at the centre of several legends. Thus, the graves of two nuns **burned at the stake** are supposed to be at Systrastapi, a rock formation west of Klaustur. One is said to have pledged her soul to Satan and shared her bed with men, the other to have blasphemed against the pope. Incidentally, the reputation of the latter was rehabilitated following the Reformation, as the flowers on her grave were in bloom, whilst the grave of the promiscuous nun stayed barren. As there was a monastery fairly nearby at Þykkvibær at the time, with mutual visits probably a daily occurrence, these stories may well contain a kernel of truth.

Myths and legends

WHAT TO SEE IN KIRKJUBÆJARKLAUSTUR

Kirkjugólf Just outside the village, on the [203], the so-called »church floor« can be found: a few square metres of perfectly paved ground right in the middle of a meadow. These are the ends of basalt columns, polished smooth by water and ice.

Walk to the Systrafoss and Systravatn This hike starts at the campsite and leads on the main road through the village, past the odd **monument of the two nuns** carrying a huge stone on their heads. At the end of the village lies the Systrafoss, the »Waterfall of the Nuns«. A short steep path leads to the edge of the high plateau, with a good view of Klaustur and the green pseudo crater south of the Ring Road at Landbrot. The path then carries on along the edge past Systravatn, the **»Nuns' Bathing Lake«**, and into the valley to the »church floor«. From here it is not far to another waterfall, the Stjórnarfoss.

AROUND KIRKJUBÆJARKLAUSTUR

Dverghamrar The odd formation of the Dverghamrar, some 12km/7.5 miles east of Klaustur, consists of several basalt columns and was probably created around the end of the last Ice Age, when the tide was still nibbling away at the coast. Since time immemorial the superstition has persisted that this is the place where supernatural beings come out into the light of day. Not far away from here, and visible from the Ring Road, is a pretty waterfall, the **Foss á Síðu**. A little bit further on in

Kirkjubæjarklaustur

INFORMATION
Kirkjuhvoll
Tel. 487 46 20, www.klaustur.is

WHERE TO EAT
Systrakaffi ££
Klausturvegur 12, tel. 487 48 48
This restaurant right in the village centre is always busy. Homely atmosphere and good food, for instance the fish soup.

WHERE TO STAY
Hörgsland á Síðu ££
Tel./fax 487 66 55, www.horgsland.is

13 new, very well equipped holiday cottages sleeping 6 people each. 5km/just over 3 miles east of Klaustur in an attractive location on a green hillside.

Farfuglaheimili Hvoll £
Tel. 487 47 85,
Youth hostel 24km/15 miles east of Kirkjubæjarklaustur, 2km/1.2 miles off the Ring Road towards the coast. Large former farmhouse with 70 beds, mainly in doubles and three-bed rooms, with daily tours to Núpsstaðarskógur.

the direction of Núpsstaður, the road crosses the **Brunahraun** lava flow.

The farm of **Núpsstaður** was made famous by the post rider Hannes Jónsson (1880 – 1968), who for over 50 years led travellers safely through the dangerous labyrinth of rivers of the Skeidarársandur. His grave is located behind the small 17th-century church which was completely refurbished in 1972. This is the smallest **grass sod church** in Iceland, only fitting 30 visitors who can hardly stand up straight inside. At a height of 767m/2,516ft, the striking **Lómagnúpur** mountain has one of the highest steep-faced walls in Iceland. All in all, the landscape around Núpsstaður counts amongst the **most beautiful and most extreme** that Iceland has to offer: bizarre lava mountains, sometimes dark and hostile, in other places covered by a thick green carpet, huge congealed lava flows, dozens of glacier tongues flowing down to the valley from the Vatnajökull, and desert-like outwash plains crossed by countless rivers, all creating a grandiose and dramatic scenario.

MARCO ● POLO TIP

Lakagígar craters Insider Tip

Even visitors travelling without an off-road vehicle can easily reach the most important destinations in the highlands via high-clearance buses. Between June and August daily tours leave Skaftafell (departure 8am) and Klaustur (departure 9am) to Lakagígar, leaving 3.5hrs for exploring (Austurleið, tel. 545 17 17).

TO THE LAKAGÍGAR CRATER ROW

Five kilometres/just over three miles south of Klaustur, the [F 206] turns off the Ring Road to lead more than 42km/26 miles north to the Lakagígar crater row. After about 3km/1.8 miles a track branches off, leading after one more kilometre/just over half a mile to a parking area at the entrance to the Fjaðrárgljúfur Gorge. Up to this point the road is still passable by regular saloon car, whilst the stretch to Lakagígar is a mere **off-road track** requiring vehicles with a high clearance. Some 2km/1.25 miles long and 100m/330ft deep, the Fjaðrárgljúfur gorge consists of tuff stone, lava and igneous rock intrusions. This deeply-carved gorge was formed by the river and processes of erosion over the course of two million years. A path leading uphill

Fjaðrárgljúfur

from the car park on the eastern edge of the gorge gives many good views of the river as it snakes its way down below.

*Lakagígar   From Fjaðrárgljúfur, the track to Lakagígar leads steadily uphill, through a landscape which is initially green but becomes ever more barren and inhospitable. Along the way lies the Fagrifoss, the pretty waterfall where the **Geirlandsá** river plunges into the depths. In 1783, the Lakagígar crater row on the high plateau of Síðumannaafréttur became the **scene of the biggest volcanic eruption in recorded history**. On 8 June, in the so-called fissure land between Mýrdalsjökull and Vatnajökull a 25km/15-mile chasm of fire opened up. With more than 100 craters it produced an overall mass of 14 billion cubic metres/3,700 billion US gal of lava. At the time, the jets of lava, several hundred metres high, could be seen for miles around and a huge gas and ash cloud hung over the area. The lava flow poured in two streams onto the plain, where it widened and carried on flowing in the beds of the Skaftá and Hverfisfljót rivers. When the lava finally stopped eight months later, the biggest lava flow since time immemorial had buried over 300 sq km/115 sq miles of countryside. However, the biggest catastrophe only happened after the end of the actual eruptions, as the ash and sulphur clouds covered large parts of Iceland with highly toxic dust. As a consequence, nearly all the horses and sheep died, and harvests fell dramatically. In the following years, around a quarter of the population fell victim to the biggest **famine** that Iceland has ever seen. Today, large parts of the impressive crater landscape of Lakagígar are covered in moss. The best view of the crater row can be had from the summit of the 818m/2,684-ft Laki mountain.

* Kjölur · Kjalvegur

✳ F 5

Region: Western highlands

The Kjölur Route [35] – also called Kjalvegur – is considered to be one of the easier ways to cross the highlands: by Icelandic standards the track is in good shape and all fords are bridged, so that the Kjölur is manageable with a regular saloon car. At the same time, the track's washboard character can make the drive in a saloon car a tortuous experience. A jeep, whilst not essential, makes the drive a lot more comfortable.

Kjalvegur   The Kjalvegur [35] starts in the south at the Gullfoss. The last opportunity to fill up with petrol is at the geothermal area of Haukardalur. Visitors coming from the north should fill up in Varmhalíð or Blön-

Kjölur

BUS CONNECTIONS
Daily from Reykjavík via the Kjölur to Akureyri and back, with stops in Hvítárnes and Hveravellir. Bus companies: SBA-Norðurleið (tel. 550 07 70, www.sba.is) and BSÍ (tel. 591 10 20, www.bsi.is).

WHERE TO STAY/ WHERE TO EAT
Áfangafell £
Cottage at the Blöndulón reservoir
Tel. 854 54 12
Sleeping-bag accommodation in shared rooms, hot showers.

Hveravellir £
Two lodges/campsite
Tel. 854 11 93, 452 46 85

www.hveravellir.is
One of the two lodges is reserved for groups, the other has a large dormitory. Coffees and the occasional hot snack can be had in the main lodge. The campsite is stony and the sanitary facilities scant, but the hot pot makes up for this.

Kerlingarfjöll £
Managed cottages
Tel. 852 42 23
www.kerlingafjoll.is
Sleeping-bag accommodation in the large dormitory as well as smaller cottages sleeping up to twelve. Hot pot and camping. Dinners need to be booked in advance, otherwise snacks only.

A sidetrip leads from the Kjölur to the geothermal area Kerlgarfjöll

MARCO ● POLO TIP

! *Only half* Insider Tip

Travellers crossing the highlands but also wanting to go around Iceland on the Ring Road are presented with a problem: it is difficult to go around something that one is traversing at the same time! The drive from the Gullfoss on the [35] to Hveravellir and – ideally after one or two overnight stays locally – back on the same road, has the advantage of offering an experience of the highlands without having to forgo the classic circumnavigation of Iceland in full. Turning back in Hveravellir is made easier by the fact that the Kjölur Route north of the geothermal area has little to offer.

duós, although there is the possibility of an **emergency tankful at Hveravellir** in the middle of the highlands. The total length of the stretch from the Gullfoss to the Ring Road in the north is about 180km/110 miles. Back in the time of the settlements, the north-south link between the Langjökull and Hofsjökull glaciers was of major importance. It was only after the **death of the Reynistaðir brothers** (1780), two farmers who were trying to cross the highlands on the Kjölur, that the passage was consigned to oblivion. A curse that, according to local folklore, was visited upon the farmers brought a quiet life to the Kjalvegur. Today, this stretch is again much frequented, by highlands standards, and the curse nearly forgotten. However, when gale force winds make breathing difficult, swirling dust restricts visibility, and an icy cold penetrates the limbs, visitors will get an idea of the kind of curse that afflicted the two brothers.

FROM THE GULLFOSS TO HVERAVELLIR

Detour to the Hagavatn

Let's start this trip with a detour only suitable for off-road vehicles: 10km/6 miles north of the Gullfoss, the [335] turns off west, and after 15km/9 miles of typically desolate Icelandic highlands, brings drivers to the small Hagafell refuge at the foot of the **Jarlhettur mountain range**. Beyond a ford that is not without its challenges, the track leads steeply uphill to the glacier lake of Hagavatn. It is better to leave the car at the refuge and attempt the climb beyond the ford on foot.

Bláfell, Hvítárvatn

Back on the [35] main route, after a few kilometres the track leads uphill to the **Bláfellsháls**, the high pass west of the Bláfell mountain, situated at an altitude of around 700m/2,300ft. Below the pass, the view opens up of the lowlands lying far below, dominated by the glaciers of Langjökull in the west and Hofsjökull in the east. Two kilometres/1.2 miles beyond the bridge over the Hvítá, a track (jeeps only!) branches off to the left, leading along the Hvítárvatn lake to the oldest lodge of the Ferðafélag Ísland Touring Association in an area called **Hvítárnes**. After 12km/7.5 miles, the track rejoins the [35].

At kilometre mark 62 (counting from Gullfoss), the [F 347] turns off **Kerlingarfjöll** east towards the summer ski and geothermal area of Kerlingarfjöll. Striking rhyolite mountains and several steam springs in the **Hveradalur**, the »Valley of the Hot Springs«, make the 16km/10-mile drive (only possible by jeep) worthwhile.

Back on the [35], the Kjalvegur runs along a lava field by the name of **Kjalhraun** Kjalhraun, which was created after the glaciers of the last Ice Age receded. A cul-de-sac leads some 7km/4.3 miles into this wasteland to the **Beinahóll**. It was here, on »Bone Hill«, that the mortal remains were found of those sheep and horses that in 1780 had been herded through the Kjalhraun by the two farmers. Where exactly the two men died is not known. After this tragedy, the Kjölur route was shunned for a long time, and later its course moved further east. A **memorial stone** on the Beinahóll commemorates the brothers' fate.

At the northern edge of the Kjalhraun the sound of bubbling and ***Hveravellir** hissing, the unmistakable smell of sulphur, and the retreating clouds of steam vapour announce the geothermal area of Hveravellir. Getting closer to the **»Plain of the Hot Springs«**, the first impression is rather sobering: not only is the environment barren and desolate, but the two huts of Hveravellir with a couple of parked cars outside, a »campsite« on rocky ground and probably also a strong wind – its strength meticulously recorded by the nearby weather station – don't exactly seem inviting. However, a **stroll through the geothermal field** with its bubbling springs and hissing miniature volcanoes, as well as a fantastic hot pot that is hard to leave once in, make Hveravellir appear in a different light.

Bubbling ground in Hveravellir, the »plains of the hot springs«

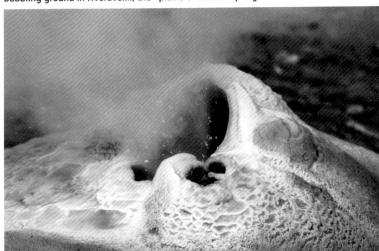

! Caves, craters and outlaws _Insider Tip_

Past the lava cave (Eyvindarhe-llir) of Fjalla Eyvindur, a legend-ary 18th-century outlaw who spent years in isolation here with his wife Halla, past a lava fissure, a natural pen in which Eyvindur Jónsson, to give him his full name, kept sheep, a **hiking trail leads from Hveravellir** into the Kjalhraun **to the crater of the Strýtur shield volcano** (duration one way: approx. 2hrs). This is a hike through a lava desert with highly interesting vegetation. The return is either done on the same trail or via the Þjófadalir lodge to the west. For more information and maps, contact the lodge staff in Hveravellir (tel. 452 42 00) or visit the following website: www.hveravellir.is.

Auðkúlur-heiði, Blöndulón — Going north on the Kjölur from Hveravellir, beyond the bridge over the Seyðisá, the desert-like conditions gradually give way to a tundra landscape called Auðkúlurheiði. Parts of the Auðkúlurheiði have been flooded by the dammed lake of **Blöndulón**, which feeds the Blönduvirkjun hydroelectric plant. The highland crossing ends with the drive down into the valley of the Blanda, which welcomes visitors after 180km/110 miles of desert and scree with occasional lush greenery. After this the [35] turns into the [732], which in turn leads to the Ring Road.

** Landmannalaugar
✳ F/G 6/7

Region: Highlands north of Mýrdalsjökull

Famous for its rhyolite mountains and hot springs, Landmannalaugar lies at the centre of a unique hiking area and is the start and finish point of one of the most popular trekking tours in Iceland, the Laugarvegur.

Landmannalaugar, including its surroundings, enjoys special protec- **Getting there**
tion as Fjallabak Nature Reserve. The drive to Landmannalaugar is
either done via the **Fjallabaksleið Nyrðri** track [F 208], just under
90km/55 miles long, or via the **Landmannaleið** [F 225]. From the
[26], past the Sigölduvirkjun hydroelectric plant, the [F 208] is also
passable by off-road vehicles right up to the Landmannalaugar campsite, with only the last ford through the Námskvísl being occasionally very difficult. That ford can however be rounded on foot, as there
is space to leave the car. From the south, the stretch to a ford just
under an hour's walk from the Eldgjá can be done with an off-road
vehicle. Both sections are however **dirt roads**. The Landmannaleið
[F 225], the southern shortcut of the [26] to Landmannalaugar, still
has some fords and is not suitable for regular cars. Visitors who do
not want to subject their car to the drive to Landmannalaugar can
leave it at various points along the Ring Road and make a day trip
there by bus. On the Landmannalaugar – Skaftafell – Reykjavík run,
there is a daily bus in June, July and August, with pick-up points in
Selfoss, Hella and Kirkjubæjarklaustur amongst others. The buses
make stops for sightseeing in the Eldgjá and in Landmannalaugar,
leaving enough time there for a dip and a short stroll (www.aus-
turleid.is or www.bsi.is).

WHAT TO SEE EN ROUTE

The interesting and varied Landmannaleið [F 225] leads first through   ***Land-**
the **Svölvahraun** lava plain. No other track gets visitors as close to the   **mannaleið**
▶Hekla and her younger lava fields. Two turnings lead to the foot of
the volcano, from where the Hekla can be climbed. But back to the
Landmannaleið: scenic highlight of this old access road to Landmannalaugar are the picturesque, sheltered – and therefore relatively
green – valleys south of the **Löðmundur**, over 1,100m/3,600ft and
extremely steep. Amid this landscape, a campsite and a mountain hut
can be found at the **Landmannahellir** caves. The way there runs parallel to the [F 225], which branches off in the middle of a ford: drivers
wishing to take the direct way to Landmannalaugar should keep
right, while drivers wishing to go via Landmannahellir, keep left.

Coming from the north, the Fjallabaksleið Nyrðri [F 208] reaches the   **Fjallabaksleið**
Fjallabak nature reserve at the spot where drivers come closest to   **Nyrðri**
the Tungnaá. River and track run at the same level, and in this dread
landscape the grey of the water seems like camouflage. Afterwards
the [F 208] crosses an imposing, barren wasteland of black ash. To the
east, accessible by short detours, keep an eye out for two deep crater
lakes with steep ash walls, the **Hnausapollur** and the much larger **Ljó-
tipollur**.

Landmannalaugar

INFORMATION
Available from the lodge keepers.

WHERE TO EAT
Fresh fish and some staple food items are sold in the green bus at the campsite in Landmannalaugar (June/July – Aug).

WHERE TO STAY
Hiking lodge £
Tel. 8 60 33 35, geöffnet Juli – Sept
The basic lodge run by the Iceland Touring Association has space for about 100 guests. (Make sure to book in advance.) Guests can use a self-catering kitchen. A (stony) campsite is situated near the refuge; further campsites can be found in Landmannahellir and Hrafntinnusker.

Lodges in the area: £
Landmannahellir, (tel. 853 84 07, 893 84 07)
Hrauneyar (tel. 487 77 82)
Áfangagil (tel. 854 95 00)
Hólaskjól (tel. 854 99 77, 894 99 77)
Hólaskógur (tel. 820 87 84).

THE »HOT SPRINGS OF THE MEN OF LAND«

In all the colours of the rainbow

Landmannalaugar's popularity is understandable, with its brook being heated by hot springs, allowing visitors to lie in it for hours and look up into the sky, by day or night. Back in the times of the sagas, the men from the region who herded cattle called the area northwest of Hella »Land«. Therefore, Landmannalaugar translates as »the Baths of the Men of Land«. The banks of the warm brook are lined with green marshland. On one side, a black wall of glass-like obsidian lava pushes up, as high as a house – the **Laugahraun**. On the other, the vista opens up across the wide bed of the **Jökulgilskvísl**, all in light shades of yellow and ochre. Further on, the eye sweeps across a bleak but fascinating mountain landscape in all the colours of the rainbow – rhyolite, an acidic, extrusive rock, is famous for its colours and nowhere else in Iceland does it cover such a large area.

Climbing Bláhnúkur

Climbing Bláhnúkur is best attempted when the skies are clear. The route begins only a few metres past the campsite, and involves a climb of 350m/1,150ft. At the summit, a panoramic dial helps visitors get their bearings, all the way to the Vatnajökull. The way down – passing the hot vapour springs of the **Brennisteinsalda** and cutting across the Laugahraun back to the campsite – can be done in four to five hours, but leaves impressions that will last a lifetime. When the mountains are hidden by clouds, the hike into the gorge **Grænagil**, which divides the foot of the blue-green Bláhnúkur from the jet-black Laugahraun, might not be quite the real thing, but at least gives a good idea. Hikers can pick up a walking map of the area around Landmannalaugar FÍ hut.

View from Bláhnúkur onto Landmannalauguar

** LAUGAVEGUR – THE FOUR-DAY-TREK

Iceland's most famous long-distance hiking trail covers just under **Ascent** 50km/31 miles from Landmannalaugar to ▶Þórsmörk. It is usually walked from north to south with three overnight stops. En route there are only smaller brooks to ford, as all larger ones are spanned by pedestrian bridges. The four to six-hour stages are prescribed by the **Fí mountain huts**, as staying overnight is only possible in these or – for hikers who have brought their own tent – at dedicated camping areas nearby; wild camping along the way is not allowed. Spaces in the huts have to be booked in advance; for summer dates this is best done in the spring (tel. 568 25 33, www.fi.is). In season, there is always somebody looking after the lodges, but there is no food provision, so hikers need to bring their own supplies.

A potpourri of colours It is on the first day that the track is most demanding, with the ascent of the Landmannalaugar – a good 600m/1,970ft – to the mountain hut, which lies at an altitude of nearly 1,100m/3,610ft at the **Hrafntin-nusker**. But there is plenty of variety too, such as the Laugahraun with its obsidian lava, the sulphur springs of Brennisteinsalda, colourful rhyolite mountains and the Stórihver hot spring. On the second day, the route leads mainly downhill, although there are sections which can have snow even in the peak of summer. At the end of the second day, there is a choice between two huts: one at the **Álftavatn** – the »Swan Lake« – and, a good hour further on, at the **Hvannagíl**. On the third day, the track leads through more flat terrain, a few kilometres of which run parallel to the Fjallabaksleið Syðri [F 210] highland track. From the stage destination, the Botnar hut in Emstrur, take a stroll to the largest river of the region, the Markarfljót. Here its grey waters, which come from Torfajökull and Mýrdalsjökull amongst others, squeeze through the narrow canyon of **Markarfljótsgljúfur**. On the last day of the hike the landscape becomes progressively greener as the route nears the end point of Þórsmörk with its national forest. There are several lodges and campsites available here, as well as a bus service back to civilization.

* ELDGJÁ – THE FIRE FISSURE

Going south from Landmannalaugar on the Fjallabaksleið Nyrðri [F 208], some 30km/18.5 miles southeast of Landmannalaugar the track crosses the Eldgjá »fire fissure«. Nearly 40km/25 miles long, up to 600m/1,970ft wide and in parts 200m/650ft deep, this is currently the **largest eruption fissure on earth** and a textbook example of the fissure volcanism of the region. At least one eruption is known for certain to have happened after the settlement of the country. A cul-de-sac running 2km/1.2 miles leads from the F 208 to the fire fissure. Shortly before a parking area at the end of the road, the »unconquerable« **Ófæra** has to be forded. From the car park, it takes about 30 minutes by footpath to the Ófærufoss.

Ófærufoss Up to 1993, the multi-tiered Ófærufoss waterfall was one of the country's most-photographed sites and would appear in every one of the older coffee table books on Iceland. The lower fall was spanned by a natural **basalt bridge** which visitors could even walk on. However, as the first tourists arrived in the spring of 1994, after a harsh winter, it had disappeared! It is not known whether the iconic landmark was blown up by frost or blocks of ice plunging down the fall with the first meltwater had taken the bridge with them. The destruction of the bridge meant the waterfall lost its special charm – it is still pretty, but no longer exceptional.

* Melrakkaslétta

J/K 1/2

Region: Northeast Iceland

Only a few tourists make the detour to the far north of Iceland. Visitors who can take the loneliness of a primal landscape will be enthralled by the deserted beaches covered in driftwood and the company of the screeching seabirds.

The circumnavigation of the Melrakkaslétta peninsula, the Plain of the Arctic Foxes, is done on the [85] or the [867]. The route, some 110km/68 miles long, leads mainly along the coast through an extremely sparsely populated, ancient landscape, to the northernmost point of Iceland. The west of the peninsula is dry, and the sparse greenery is often broken by dust and scree. Sprinkled with small lakes and moors, the east appears a little more welcoming.

Plain of Polar Foxes

WHAT TO SEE IN THE MELRAKKASLÉTTA

Shortly before the road hits the Öxarfjörður, Núpur offers a pretty view of the wide Jökulsá delta. Carry on along the coast to reach Kópasker, which despite only having 130 or so inhabitants, is actually one of the larger settlements in the Melrakkasléttat, owing its survival to shrimp fishing. A fairly imposing church, a field with many creative scarecrows and a small **heritage museum** provide variation. The pride and joy of the museum is the **book collection**, donated by a book lover who bound and gilded them all by hand.

Kópasker

At the northwestern corner of the peninsula, a dead end leads to the Rauðinúpur bird cliffs. The last section in front of the parking area at the farm is the terrain of the Arctic terns, who in early July feed their young right next to the road and welcome anybody who so much as dares to stick their head out of the car window with mock attacks, often only missing by inches. With a height of 73m/239ft, the Rauðinúpur rocks break off vertically to the sea and serve as a breeding ground for numerous sea birds, of which the **puffins**, as always,

Rauðinúpur

Melrakkaslétta

INFORMATION
Raufarhöfn
In the Norðurljós Hotel, Aðalbraut 2
Tel. 465 12 33 www.raufarhofn.is

WHERE TO EAT
Raufarhöfn: restaurant in the Norðurljós Hotel £££
Aðalbraut 2
Tel. 465 12 33, www.raufarhofn.is
When the sun is shining, a coffee on the terrace, with a view across the port and the lighthouse, is a must. In stormy weather, the views from inside are not far behind.

WHERE TO STAY
Raufarhöfn: Hotel Norðurljós £££
Aðalbraut 2
Tel. 465 12 33, fax 465 13 83
ebt@vortex.is www.nat.is
16 modern and functionally furnished guestrooms at the end of the world are a pleasant surprise.

Kópasker: Farguglaheimili Kópasker £
Akurgerði 7, Tel. 465 23 14
The fact that there are only four rooms is made up for by the friendly, personal atmosphere.

occupy the uppermost echelons. Note the red colour of the rock, owing to layers of volcanic slag; it looks particularly beautiful in the evening light. Just off the coast stand two columns of rock, Karlinn and Sölfavöf; until 1962 the latter was connected with Rauðinúpur by a rock bridge.

Hraunhafnartangi A fairly inhospitable place, Hraunhafnartangi was long held to be the northernmost point of Iceland. New measurements however have come to the conclusion that the rocks at Rifstangi a little further west stick out northwards that bit more. From here it is only 2km/1.2 miles to the – imaginary – line of the Arctic Circle. In Hraunhafnartangi, a jeep track leads to the beach and on to the **lighthouse**, which for once is not painted bright orange, but stands as a simple, white concrete building on the headland.

> **! MARCO POLO TIP**
>
> *Kajaking ...* **Insider Tip**
>
> ... into the midnight sun. The owner of the Norðurljós Hotel in Raufarhöfn is an enthusiastic kayaker and also rents out some of his boats in the shed. On one of his tours along the coast he once discovered the mighty skull bone of a blue whale, which now has pride of place outside the house.

Life in the »capital« of the Melrakkaslétta, in **Raufarhöfn**, proceeds as serenely as if there were hardly anybody living here. The times when Raufarhöfn was significant for herring and as a port of export seem to have been irretrievably consigned to history. Today, the factories are quietly rusting away and no one seems to have come up with any ideas to improve the situation.

★★ Mývatn

──────────── ✦ H/J 3

Region: Northeast Iceland

The Mývatn offers a landscape as varied as they come, primarily consisting of volcanism in all its forms, colours and smells. There are bubbling mud pots, glowing sulphur fields, hissing solfataras, mighty petrified lava flows, perfectly circular wall craters, mysterious pseudo craters and dark lava castles. In the middle of it all lies a lake with islands and bays, partially framed by lovely green meadows and populated by thousands of birds.

The Mývatn, with its many little islands and bays, was created during two volcanic eruption phases 3,700 and 2,300 years ago, when a lava field blocked a river in the Laxárdalur. Today, at 37 sq km/14.2 sq miles, it is the **fourth-largest inland lake in Iceland** and despite its size no more than 4.5m/15ft deep, and on average only 2.5m/8ft. The Mývatn has few surface inlets, but many springs on the bottom of the lake. The only larger outflow, the Laxá, is a good salmon river, while the lake itself is known for its trout stocks. In the summer, the lake fully merits its nickname of »**Midge Lake**«, as huge swarms of the pests are out and about. A closer look reveals non-biting midges and blackfly. As they don't sting, the midges are relatively harmless unless they stray into the eyes, ears or mouth, and of the blackflies, it is only the females that are out for blood. And another bit of good news: the two midge generations hatch in June and August each year, so that there are significantly fewer of them about in July. One thing to bear in mind is that without these swarms of midges the Mývatn would not have such a rich bird life, and the trout too enjoy the insects.

Islands and bays

The Mývatn lake and the Laxá river have enjoyed protected status since 1974, which means wild camping and putting up for the night just anywhere, off-road driving, boat traffic, and entering the breeding grounds on the northwestern banks from mid-May to mid-July are all prohibited. Despite this, the Mývatn area still suffers from a number of environmental problems, mainly through erosion and the extraction of kieselguhr. Erosion is particularly problematic on the eastern side of the lake, threatening to silt up the **Dimmuborgir** a few years ago. The extraction of kieselguhr, a siliceous material used as a filter aid, requires mud to be sucked from the bottom of the lake, increasing the water's depth and thereby changing the fauna on the bottom of the lake, which in turn affects birdlife.

Conservation and protection of the natural environment

Mývatn

INFORMATION
In Reykjahlið supermarket

WHERE TO EAT
Reykjahlíð: Gamli Bærinn ££
Tel. 464 41 70
Cosy pub with a nostalgic touch opposite the Reynihlíð Hotel. A good-value choice is fish soup or fish and chips. Guests are also allowed to play the piano!

Skútustaðir: Restaurant in Gígur Hotel £££
Tel. 464 44 55
For trout with a lake view, look no further than the Gígur Hotel in Skútustaðir. The view from the restaurant sweeps across the lake and the pseudo craters. Visitors in the mood for a gourmet experience should splash out on the three-course meal.

WHERE TO STAY
Reykjahlíð: Hótel Reykjahlíð £££
Tel. 464 41 42
www.reykjahlid.is
Small hotel right on the lake, with some rooms and the breakfast room offering good views.

Reykjahlíð: Fossótel Laugar £££
Tel. 464 63 00
www.fosshotel.is
Summer hotel in a quiet location, an ideal base for day trips to Húsavik, Mývatn, Goðafoss and Akureyri.

Reykjahlíð: Hlíð £
Tel. 464 41 03
A little outside Reykjahlíð, and enjoying a sea view due to its elevated location. Some 50 good-value sleeping-bag accommodation places in a large house, plus cabins of varying sizes and a campsite.

SPORT
Mývatn Marathon
Information, Sel Hotel Mývatn
Tel. 464 41 64
www.myvatn.is
Every year the Mývatn Marathon takes place around the lake in late June.

Flora and fauna
The flat, heavily indented banks of the Mývatn with their rich nutritional value offer ideal conditions for **many birds** to breed. The ducks are particularly famous with bird-lovers, as of the 15 different species of duck to be found in Iceland, all except the eider duck breed around the lake. Apart from the seabirds, nearly the entire range of Icelandic species is present on the Mývatn. One speciality is the **Barrow's Goldeneye**, an immigrant from America that breeds nowhere else in Europe. Bird stocks have consistently declined over the past decades however; among the suspected reasons are increasing traffic and tourism, minks that have become feral, and disturbances caused by the kieselguhr extraction.

Geology and volcanism
The Mývatn area lies exactly on the border of the Eurasian and American tectonic plates, which are drifting apart. The resulting gap is

continually filled up by rising lava, so the landscape is shaped by various kinds of volcanic activity, with, at its centre, the **Leirhnjúkur**. A hundred thousand years ago, the mountain was still a volcanic cone producing large quantities of lava and ash; at some stage however, it gently collapsed, giving it the rather flat appearance it has today. There is however, at a depth of some 3km/1.8 miles, still an **active magma chamber** which is liable to expand and break open. This lessens the pressure in the chamber, resulting in the earth's surface sinking again. This change can repeat every few months over many years. Over the past centuries there have been two major eruptions in the Mývatn area. The so-called **Fire of Mývatn** started in 1724 with a massive eruption, resulting in the creation of the **Víti crater**, and continued with earthquakes and eruption on the **Krafla**. In 1729, lava flowed all the way to the Mývatn, destroying parts of Reykjahlíð. The lava flow, with hardly any vegetation on it even today, is still clearly visible. During the **Krafla fires** in 1975, the volcano of the same name came to life, causing numerous eruptions up to 1985. The effects of this active phase may still be seen in Leirhnjúkur today.

> **MARCO POLO TIP**
>
> **Insider Tip**
> *Total relaxation …*
>
> … and a real alternative to the Blue Lagoon are the new **Mývatn Nature Baths** between Reykjahlíð and Námaskarð. The water in the generously-sized open-air pool is milky-blue and blissfully warm, with a superb view over the lake for good measure. Whether in the light of the midnight sun or the pale glow of the northern lights, a dip in the new Blue Lagoon is always a treat. (June – Aug daily 9am – midnight, Sept – May daily noon – 10pm, tel. 464 44 11, www.jardbodin.is

WHAT TO SEE AROUND THE MÝVATN

Visitors coming in from the west on the Ring Road soon reach Skútustaðir, after Reykjahlíð the biggest tourist centre at the Mývatn. In spite of this, Skútustaðir has kept its character of a tiny, sleepy settlement of old. Worth seeing here are the **pseudo craters**, which can only be found in Iceland and show up particularly well at Skútustaðir. They were formed by rivers of lava flowing across wet ground such as flat lakes or fenland. Heat made the water below the lava evaporate in an explosion-like way, sometimes blasting craters of up to 300m/985ft in diameter into the landscape. This explains why pseudo craters, as opposed to »real« volcanoes, have no chimney. The campsite at Skútustaðir is the starting point for a short walking trail through the **crater landscape**, largely covered by grass.

*Skútustaðir

The best view of this landscape is to be had from Hverfjall, an ash cone with a tuff stone crater and a ring wall that rises up 170m/560ft

*Hverfjall

and is visible from far off; it is possible to walk around the crater on the wall. The ascents as well as the path around the top have steel cables as railings.

*Dimmu-
borgir

At Geiteyjarströnd, roughly in the middle of the eastern banks, a cul-de-sac branches off towards Dimmuborgir. This area might only measure approximately one square kilometre/a third of a square mile, but it is full of the most bizarre **lava formations**. The »dark castles« consist of towers, bridges, caves and overhangs, some of which look like petrified trolls. Not much imagination is required to read all kinds of stone figures into the jagged rock. A little over 2,000 years ago there was a dammed lava lake at this place. When the water below the lava evaporated and the steam made its way up to the surface, the lava solidified into a bizarre **variety of shapes**. At some point the dam broke and the still liquid lava ran down to the Mývatn, leaving the already solidified towers behind.

In the Krafla power station geothermal energy is produced

This village on the northeastern banks of the lake is the tourist hub of the Mývatn area, with hotels, guesthouses and campsites. During the **Mývatn fire in 1729** the inhabitants of Reykjahlið narrowly escaped diaster, as the lava flow destroyed their homes, but spared the church on the hill where they had taken refuge. Today, the lava flow can still be made out clearly near the village.

Reykjahlið

Once the Ring Road leaves the Mývatn to go east, after a few kilometres it reaches the head of the pass at **Námaskarð**, and shortly after, at the foot of the Námafjall mountain, unfolds the most impressive solfatara field in Iceland: Hverarönd. This natural spectacle's assault on the senses starts at the parking area at Hverir. The barren plain and the mountainside glow in strong shades of yellow, orange and brown, a vista reminiscent of photos from Mars. Everywhere white plumes of steam escape from cracks, some of which force their way onto the surface with a loud hissing and spitting. Hot **mud pots** bubble and boil away, with a pervasive smell of rotten eggs.

*Námafjall

From the parking area, a steep path leads onto the 485m/1,591-ft Námafjall, offering a panoramic tour through this unreal landscape. The path leads part of the way along the ridge, and eventually ends on the top of the pass at the Ring Road.

Panorama tour

Shortly after passing Námafjall, the [863] track branches off from the Ring Road and leads to the **Krafla power station**, the Viti crater and the Leirhnjúkur lava field. Travellers interested in taking a look inside the plant should head for the **Visitor Centre**, which offers a lot of information on the construction of this facility and how it is run.

With its diameter of 300m/984ft, the Viti crater was created during a mighty explosion at the beginning of the Mývatn fire in 1724. Over 100 years after this eruption, a mud pot bubbled in the crater, where today there is a green lake at its bottom. From the car park a path leads to the crater's edge and then runs along the ridge. After the creation of the Viti crater the **Leirhnjúkur fissure** opened up further west, producing large quantities of magma. The parking area is the starting point for a walk of approximately an hour across the gloomy, steaming lava field.

Viti crater, Leirhnjúkur

Promised Land of Renewable Energy

Iceland, the volcanic island in the North Atlantic, is the »promised land« of renewable energy. Residents of Reykjavik, like four fifths of the whole country, get their hot water out of the ground: from a cheap, safe and especially an environmentally friendly source.

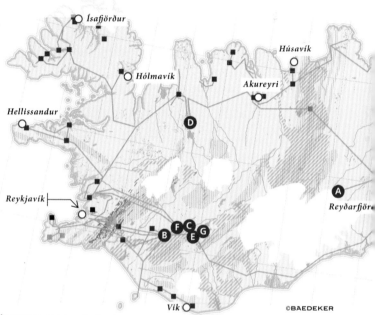

Ísafjörður
Húsavík
Hólmavík
Akureyri
Hellissandur
D
Reykjavík
A
Reyðarfjör...
B F C G
E
Vik

©BAEDEKER

▶ **Waterpower on Iceland**
The second most important source of energy on Iceland is hydropower. The many rivers that run from the large glaciers into the sea are an inexhaustible reservoir of energy.

▶ **Distribution of use of electricity** in %

74	Aluminium industry
6	Public energy supply
5	Ferrosilicon industry
5	Private households
4	Other businesses
4	Other industries
1	Agriculture, gardening

▶ **Waterpower and industry** Ⓐ
In the Alcoa plant, which opened in Reyðarfjörður in eastern Iceland, up to 346,000 tonnes of aluminium are produced every year – using a large amount of energy. Aluminium production uses up to 5,000 GWh of electricity every year. A large part of the necessary energy is supplied by the nearby power plant Kárahnjúkar, one of the largest hydroelectric plants in Europe.

(A) Kárahnjúkar (690 MW)

(B) Búrfellsstöð (270 MW)

(C) Hrauneyjafosstöð (210 MW)

(D) Blöndustöð (150 MW)

(E) Sigöldustöð (150 MW)

(F) Sultartangastöð (120 MW)

(G) Vatnsfellsstöð (90 MW)

■	Hydroelectric power station
▨	Geothermal power station
■	Petroleum power station
▨	Geothermal fields
▨	Plate tectonics
—	Power grid

▶ **Energy from under ground**
Geothermal energy is used on Iceland in two ways:
geothermal plants supply warm water for heating,
while geothermal power stations produce electricity.

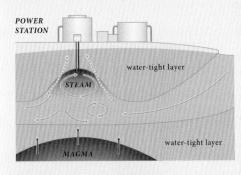

▶ **Use of geothermal energy on Iceland**
in %

Room heating 45

Melting snow 4

Aquaculture, fish processing 4

Greenhouses 2

4 Swimming pools

39 Producing electricity

2 Other industries

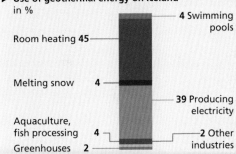

690 MW
Output

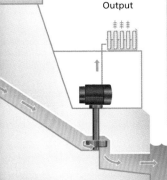

▶ **Use of energy**
Development from 1940 to 2010

Jahr
40 50 60 70 80 90 00 10

150 PJ

100

50

GEOTHERMAL

COAL   PETROLEUM   WATER POWER

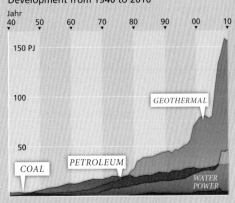

Gren-
jaðarstaður
folk museum

On the way from the Mývatn to Húsavik, consider a short detour off the [87] to the **Grenjaðarstaður** folk museum in the Aðaldalur, presenting a large grass sod farm with a collection of historical exhibits. The farmstead dates from the 19th century and was inhabited into the middle of the last century.

❶ Grenjaðarstaður: June – Aug daily 10am – 6pm

＊ **Reykjanes Peninsula**

✦ C/D 6/7 ●

Region: Southwest Iceland

Reykjanes Peninsula is an Iceland in miniature, with just the glaciers missing. Signs of volcanism – lava areas, old craters, geothermic fields – are everywhere. The porous lava soil is hardly able to hold the copious rainfall, and most water quickly seeps away into the depths. There are no rivers worth mentioning, only a peculiar lake, Kleifarvatn, with no major inlets or runoffs.

The horn to
the north

The proper name for the Reykjanes peninsula – pushing far out into the North Atlantic in the southwest of Iceland, its shape resembling a rhino – is really **Suðurnes**. However, it is more commonly named after the furthest point – Reykjanes. The rhino's horn pointing north with Iceland's international airport Keflavík has its own (if seldom used) name: **Miðnes**.

Paradise for
bird-lovers

The peninsula is fringed by steep cliffs, smooth, black sandy beaches and ecologically valuable rocky mud flats. These coasts are inhabited by countless seabirds, including all kinds of guillemots, razorbills and fulmars as well as gulls. Of the two largest bird cliffs, the one at **Hafnaberg** south of Hafnir is easier to get to and offers better views than the larger **Krysuvíkurberg** on the southern coast. At a height of 77m/252ft, and situated some 14km/just under 9 miles off the southwesterly point of the peninsula, Eldey rock island, the dormant remains of a volcano, is home to one of the largest gannet colonies in the northern hemisphere. Until the last of its kind was shot in 1844 on Eldey, great auks were living there too. Eldey is now a conservation area and not freely accessible to the public. However, the gannets also show up on the southwestern point of Reykjanes on the Valahnúkur.

Insider Tip

Whale
watching

The waters around Reykjanes are a favourite haunt of dolphins and whales, which with a little luck may even be spotted from the banks. For a better chance of seeing them, consider a whale watching tour. Between April and mid September, the **Moby Dick** sets sail at least

Reykjanes

INFORMATION
Keflavík Tourist Information Center
Leifur Eiríksson Airport
Tel. 425 03 30
www.reykjanes.is

WHERE TO EAT
Grindavík:
Blue Lagoon Restaurant £££
Svartsengi
Tel. 420 88 00
The views through the large glass-panelled frontage onto the steaming Blue Lagoon, and the clear lines of the Scandinavian-designed furniture frame this exceptional and highly-praised restaurant. Here too, fresh fish dishes form the basis of the cuisine; for instance, there is an excellent Mediterranean bouillabaisse or salmon in lemon sauce at very fair prices.

WHERE TO STAY
Kevlavík: Hótel Kevlavík £££
Vatnsvegur 12
Tel. 420 70 00
www.kef.is
Luxury four-star hotel near the airport, ideal for a comfortable first or last night in Iceland. The hotel restaurant, which also serves breakfast, is among the best in the country.

Grindavík:
Northern Light Inn £££
Blue Lagoon Road
Tel. 426 86 50
www.nli.is
Not far from the airport and the Blue Lagoon, this small hotel with 21 rooms offers comfortable and quiet accommodation in the middle of a barren volcanic landscape. The substantial breakfast buffet and dinner in Kristjana's Kitchen do not disappoint either.

Keflavík:
B&B Guesthouse £
Hringbraut 92
Tel. 421 89 89
Fax 867 44 34
Fairly good-value guesthouse with seven double rooms in the centre of Keflavík, only five minutes from the airport.

Njarðvík:
Farfuglaheimili Njarðvík £
Fit Hostel
Fitjabraut 6A/6B
Tel. 421 88 89
www.hostel.is
Recently expanded and modernized youth hostel near the airport.

once a day from Keflavík or, in suitable weather, from Sandgerði or Grindavík.
Dolphin & Whalespotting, tel. 421 77 77 or toll-free 800 87 77; transfer service from Reykjavík with the option to take a dip in the Blue Lagoon

The name Reykjanes, »**Smoke Peninsula**«, leads visitors to suspect the existence of geothermal springs. Indeed, steam emerges from the ground in a lot of places, sometimes more or less naturally as in the

Intersection of the continental plates

solfatara field of Krysuvík, sometimes from boreholes as at the Svartsengi power plant, with its »effluents«, cooled down to swimming temperature, filling the Blue Lagoon, Iceland's most famous thermal spa. Geologically, Reykjanes is considered the surface continuation of the Mid-Atlantic Ridge, the restless boundary between the continental plates of America and Eurasia. In principle, in the southeast of the peninsula visitors stand on European soil, and in the northwest on American. South of Hafnir, the **»Bridge between the Continents«** spans a crack in a lava field – a clever idea to visualize the continental drift.

KEFLAVÍK AND NJARÐVÍK – THE TWIN TOWNS

Varied tour   Starting from Reykjavík, the Reykjanes peninsula can be explored in a varied round trip. Follow the [41] road west from Reykjavík, to arrive after a good 40km/25 miles at the town of **Keflavík**. Practically now one entity, seamlessly grown together, the towns of Keflavík and Njarðvík – the latter consisting of larger Ytri Njarðvík, dominated by the harbour, and the smaller, more rural Innri Njarðvík – enjoy a protected position on **Stakksfjörður**, a side bay of the large Faxaflói. Along with Hafnir, the twin towns form the greater community of **Reykjanesbær**, boasting not one but three important ports, namely those in the two parts of Njarðvík town, plus the port of Helguvík (north of Keflavík).

Duushús   A reminder of a long maritime tradition are the buildings of a former trading base, the Duushús, above Keflavík's old port of Grófin (Duusgata). There, the regional museum **Byggðasafn Suðurnesja** shows a collection of nearly 60 models of Icelandic ships, assembled by a true seadog, skipper Grímur Karlsson. Opening times: May – Sept. daily 11am – 6pm. Next door, in good weather, the outside terrace of the Kaffi Duus with its views over the harbour makes a good stopping-off point.
   ❶ **Byggðasafn Suðurnesja:** daily 11am – 5pm

Fisherman's   Between the old part of Keflavík around the Duushús and the new
Memorial   town centre next to the Hafnargata, right on the seafront a monumental sculpture catches the eye. The Fisherman's Memorial by Ásmundur Sveinsson commemorates the fishermen drowned at sea.

Vikinga-   From Road [41] from Keflavík to Reykjavík a futuristic glass struc-
heimar/   ture can be seen, which has housed the Vikingaheimar museum since
Íslendingur   2009. The museum is located right on Faxaflóibucht and displays parts of the millennium exhibit of the Smithsonian Institute in Washington on the Vikings and sea travel. The museum also holds the

Íslendingur, a faithful reproduction of a Viking ship, which covered some 4,400 nautical miles across old routes from Iceland via Greenland all the way to New York in 2000, to celebrate the thousandth anniversary of the discovery of America by Leifur Eiríksson.

❶ May – Oct daily 11am – 6pm, otherwise 12pm – 5pm, admission 1000 ISK

That Reykjanes historically had more than just this maritime side is shown by the **agricultural section of the Byggðasafn Suðurnesja**, with a typical farmhouse from the 19th century: Stekkjarkot, its walls made from lava stones and grass sods, lies between the two parts of Njarðvík, at the end of the bay of the same name.

Stekkjarkot

THE NORTHWEST OF REYKJANES

At the entrance to Sandgerði town, the modern, heavily symbolic sculpture **Álög by Steinunn Þórarinnsdóttir** welcomes visitors: a man made from rusting iron stands in front of three large waves made from stainless steel – a transient Human in front of the Eternal Sea. The people of Sandgerði understand this sculpture only too well; their chief workplace for generations has been out there on the Atlantic. In Sandgerði, which has had the right to call itself a town since 1990, the fishing industry is the main employer, using the good harbour on the western coast. The landmark of the town is an extremely unusual **lighthouse**; showing the way to the harbour, it sticks out of the roof ridge of a warehouse. The **Sandgerði Nature Center Fræðasetrið** (Garðvegur 1) works in close conjunction with the maritime reseach institute under the same roof. Sea, coast and bird life are presented with high educational standards. Opening times: Mon – Fri 9am – 5pm, Sat/Sun 1 – 5pm.

Sandgerði

Sandgerði Naturcenter Fræðasetrið: Garðvegur 1, June – Aug. daily 9am – 5pm, otherwise Mon – Fri 9am – 5pm, Sat/Sun 1pm – 5pm, admission 300 ISK

The mudflats and the beach off the northeastern point of Garðskagi are ideal spots to watch Icelandic birds as well as migrants, and sometimes seals can be seen basking in the sun. But even without birds, the views on clear, light summer nights are incredible, most of all when the **outline of the Snæfellsjökull** – rising up a good 100km/62 miles away on the other side of the Faxaflói – becomes visible on the horizon. Two lighthouses mark out Garðskagi: the older one, decommissioned long ago, was built in 1897 and is today accessible as an observation tower, while its younger colleague, a good bit taller, was put into service in 1944. In an annex to the new lighthouse, the **Byggðasafnið á Garðskaga heritage museum** shows mainly tools and motors from fishing and seafaring, amongst them one of the open

Garðskagi

boats that used to be rowed for fishing. Opening times: in summer daily 1 – 5pm.

● Byggðasafnið á Garðskaga: im Sommer daily 1pm – 5pm

ON THE [425] INTO THE SOUTH OF REYKJANES

Hafnir With its 120 inhabitants, Hafnir is the small adjunct of the larger Reykjanesbær municipality, situated at a distance of 10km/6.2 miles from the two other »districts«, Keflavik and Njarðvík, in a lonely location on the western coast. Before motorized fishing cutters and trawlers, Ósar Bay, north of Hafnir, was an important base for the fishing industry and a busy stretch of coast. Even the Hanseatic League had a representation for a while on the northern banks of the bay. The downward spiral was triggered by a storm flood destroying the Danish trading post of Básendar in January 1799.

> **?** MARCO POLO INSIGHT
>
> *No sign of life*
>
> In 1870 the schooner Jamestown beached in Ósar Bay north of Hafnir with neither man nor mouse aboard. The **ghost ship**'s wooden cargo was more than welcome in treeless Iceland – today, many houses still feature beams and planks from this mysterious shipwreck. The anchor of the Jamestown is rusting away in front of the tool shed of the local coastguard.

South of Hafnir, soon after the fish farm of Kalmannstjörn, the coast pushes up the bird cliffs of **Hafnaberg** like a protective shield against the waves of the Atlantic. Whilst these cliffs might not be as high and spectacular as the ones at Krysuvíkurberg on the southern coast, the birds are easier to watch here. In this section, the [425] runs a bit further inland, so visitors should schedule in an hour for a walk along the waymarked trails from the parking area to the cliffs. South of the cliffs, at the **Stóra Sandvík** – »Great Sandy Bay« in English – the coast becomes flat and sandy again. In good weather, the locals practise proper beach life, except it is nearly always too cold for swimming. The flat beach lakes in the dunes are good spots for bird watching.

Bridge between the Continents Level with the Stóra Sandvík, east of the [425], an 18m/59-ft long steel-and-wood bridge spans the **Alfagjá**, the continental gorge, described by local tourism managers as »one of the major wonders of the world«. While this is a bit of an exaggeration, the cut, a good 6m/20ft deep, is undoubtedly worth seeing, particularly as it is embedded in a **dramatic lava landscape**. The gorge was formed, as were others in the surrounding area, as a consequence of continental drift. Here, the continental plates of Eurasia and North America drift apart by up to 2cm/0.7 inches per year, according to geologists' measurements. The bridge is named after the first European who stepped onto American soil in the 11th century: Leifur heppni, Leif the Lucky, better known as **Leifur Eiríksson**. What many a tourist might at first glance consider a folly with no discernible function, holds such significance for Icelanders that its inauguration on 3 July 2002 was attended by the head of the government no less, alongside the foreign and transport ministers who made their way from Reykjavík to step onto the bridge.

While the [425] turns off east, a cul-de-sac leads to the most southwesterly point of Reykjanes. The last kilometres should be driven carefully, without leaving the car, as the road crosses a colony of belligerent Arctic terns (once you reach the coast there is no need to fear their attacks). At the end of the track, rising above the banks, the Valahnúkur is clearly recognizable as **part of a volcano crater**. Towards the sea it shows vertical cliffs, towards land a steep but eminently climbable slope. A lighthouse used to warn seafarers from its peak, but in 1887 an earthquake destroyed the tower. Its successor has been pointing skywards from Bæjarfell hill just inland since 1908. The rugged coast gives excellent views on to the sea, and from here it is easy to observe the seabirds, usually gannets, nesting in their thousands on the off-shore rock island of Eldey.

Valahnúkur

Valahnúkur lighthouse

Looking back inland, columns of steam reveal the existence of a high-temperature area. Part of the latent energy is harnessed to boil seawater for the extraction of salt. The factory lies near the main road, while a cross link to the road leading west passes a relatively unspoilt field of hot springs surrounding the legendary Gunnuhver, **Gudrun geyser**. This is supposedly the place to which the spirit of an argumentative woman was banished.

A warm bath in the Blue Lagoon ...

Grindavík Towards Grindavík, the road crosses some more inhospitable lava fields, eventually reaching the green outskirts of the port town, and as so often happens in Iceland, as soon as there is a blade of grass, a golf course appears! Grindavík is an important base for the fishing industry, with large processing facilities. The great fishing and fish-processing tradition in Grindavík is documented in Magma – House of Culture and Natural Resources. The geology of the region, volcanism and its geothermic potential and uses are its other topics. Different techniques for geothermic drilling are also presented. Incidentally, driving through Grindavík gives food for thought: in the modern town centre alongside the church, supermarket and sports centre with swimming pool, seemingly historical walls catch the eye. The ostensibly ancient is in fact modern art: this sun temple was built between 1995 and 1997 by the esoterically inspired multimedia artist and »earth house architect« **Tryggvi Hansen** (born 1956).

Insider Tip

✱✱ BLUE LAGOON · SVARTSENGI POWER PLANT

Svartsengi About five kilometres north of Grindavík, visitors might think they've found themselves on a **science fiction film set**: shiny steel

… which lies between Keflavík and Grindavík

towers, modernist concrete architecture, hissing steam, and thick reddish-brown pipelines, the whole thing framed by black lava and whitish-blue expanses of water. The Svartsengi power plant is however very much of this world, even if its technology has a futuristic touch. It provides the entire west of Reykjanes with energy and heat, and while it's by no means inconspicuous, it is certainly environmentally friendly.

The technology: from boreholes nearly 2,000m/6,561ft deep, a mixture of water and steam, with a temperature of 242°C/467°F, shoots up. The fact that it is not just steam, as might be expected at this temperature, is due to the pressure down below, which significantly increases the water's boiling point. The **mix of water and steam** coming out of the ground is saline and full of minerals, as the porous lava soil allows salt water from the surrounding Atlantic to seep into the subsoil of Reykjanes. This makes the hot liquid unsuitable for electricity turbines and long distance heating pipes; it is however, by a process of heat exchange, heating clear spring water. Condensed and cooled to approx. 70°C/158°F, at the end of the process at least a million litres/nearly 265,000 US gal of perfectly clean »wastewater« per hour flows into the surrounding lava.

Until well into the 1980s hardly anybody took a second glance at the shimmering blue lake forming in the cooled-down lava. The lake

**Bláa Lónið – Blue Lagoon

owes its colour to a special mix of silicic acid, minerals and algae covering the jagged lava lake floor as a smooth, dense layer of sediments – as if it were lined with a synthetic material. It was young people who first discovered the lake for late-night parties and to splash around in. Workers from the nearby power plant would also sometimes use their breaks for a dip. When one of them noticed an improvement in the psoriasis that had been plaguing him for a long time, the situation promptly changed, and the »wild« swimming lake was turned into an orderly bathing establishment named **Bláa Lónið**, the Blue Lagoon, with a treatment section for psoriasis patients.

In 1999 the original lagoon had to make way for the expansion of the power plant. A little bit further west a new, rigorously planned spa complex was set up, with lava grottoes and islands, as well as small sections of beach, steam baths in a lava cave, a white-tiled luxury bath, various spa facilities, a service centre with changing rooms, souvenir shop and tourist information, catering, conference centre and Hotel Northern Light Inn (►Reykjanes, p.210). From this perspective a wastewater lake created by chance has become one of the most popular tourist attractions in Iceland. Whether under the summer sun or in a snowstorm, a soak in the Blue Lagoon is always an experience, and a very healthy and invigorating one at that: the **curative powers of the water** for psoriasis have by now been scientifically confirmed, and the mineral-rich mud has long been for sale in a broad range of skin care products under the »**Blue Lagoon**« label.

❶ **Bláa Lónið:** Jan – May & Sep – Dec daily 10m – 8pm, June & mid Aug – end Aug daily 9am – 9pm; July – mid-Aug daily 9am – 11pm; admission €48 – €89, tours daily 1pm & 3 pm, ticket €15, daily bus shuttle from Keflavík airport and Reykjavík; www.bluelagoon.com

VIA KRYSUVÍK BACK TO REYKJAVÍK

Krysuvík From Grindavík, the rough and not yet tarmacked [427] winds its way east along a wild coastline and through lonely lava fields. Way-marked trails lead into the surrounding mountains and to the coast where the cliffs of the **Krysuvíkurbjarg**, nearly 7km/4.3 miles long and up to 70m/230ft high, are a special attraction. Near the parking area, where the hiking trail to the cliffs starts, the road passes the small **Krysuvíkurkirkja**, the remains of an estate of some importance in the Middle Ages. Old documents show that there was a church here as early as 1100. The current one was built in 1857, but used as a residence for decades in between until it was reconsecrated in 1964. The name Krysuvík is also used for the geothermal steam, sulphur and mud springs around the area.

Also of volcanic origin is the Grænavatn, a turquoise crater lake, barely 1km/0.6 miles north of where the [427] joins the [42], which is in a significantly better state.
Seltún, the best-known geothermal field in Krysuvík, lies another 1.5km/0.9 miles further north and is easily accessible via paths and platforms.

Grænavatn

Krysuvík is an enclave of the town of ▶Hafnarfjörður, reached by taking the [42] leading north. The same road going east crosses a section of the coast which is deserted today, where only the **Strandakirkja**, or »good-luck church«, steeped in legends, is a reminder of happier times.

Strandakirkja

On the way north, the 10 sq km/3.8-sq mile Kleifarvatn mountain lake soon presents a real conundrum: the lake has hardly any inlets and no visible outlets, yet the water level rises and falls at regular intervals. After an **earthquake in 2000** it was even feared that somebody had pulled a plug deep down below, as the water level fell rapidly, only to stabilize again after a few months. The road running along the banks of the lonely lake is a scenic route.

Kleifarvatn

Level with the aluminium smelter of Straumsvík the [42] joins the main road connecting Reykjavík with Keflavík airport. The aluminium works represents Iceland's largest industrial firm, set up in the late 1960s. Since the end of 2000 the company has been part of the Canadian aluminium and packaging group Alcan. In Straumsvík about 500 people produce some 170,000 tons/187,400 short tons of aluminium per year for Alcan Iceland.
The electricity needed for the production is provided by the hydroelectric plants on the **Þjórsár** at such a good price that it is worth transporting the raw material, alumina, from the Alcan mines in northern Australia halfway around the globe to Iceland, and to subsequently ship the end products to the markets in North America and Europe. Visitors to the area can't miss the red and white striped silos, next to the long factory workshops, where the alumina is stored.

Straumsvík

** Reykjavík

⸺ ✦ D 6

Region: Southwest Iceland
Population: 120,000 (metropolitan area: 200,000)
Internet: www.Reykjavik.is

By international standards Reykjavík is at best a »small city«. But the world's northernmost capital has the diversity and creativity, the cultural range and the nightlife of a cosmopolitan city. But Reykjavík's charm is usually only seen when you look twice.

Reykjavík is the country's dominating city. Two thirds of all Icelanders live in the metropolitan area – and the number is growing. The most important cultural and educational facilities are at home here, the leading media, the largest banks and economic enterprises as well as the centres of political power: Reykjavík is the centre of a centralized government. Meanwhile the metropolitan area consists of not only one but seven independent communities. These are so intertwined that their borders within this conglomeration of settlements are hardly recognizable to outsiders. Moreover almost half of the residents of the city of Reykjavík itself live in suburbs like Árbær, Breiðholt, Hraunbær or Grafarvogur, which are even farther from the city centre than neighbouring towns like Kópavogur or Seltjarnarnes. While other regions of the country have to deal with declining populations due to migration the capital's metropolitan region is growing regularly. The population of Reykjavík only passed the 1000 mark in the 19th century and the 100,000 mark in the 1990s; about 120,000 people live in the city today.

Two thirds of all Icelanders live in the capital

While at first glance Reykjavík seems modern and – thanks to the multicoloured roofs – very colourful, it also has something quite American about it. This is the Reykjavík that shows itself mostly in the shopping malls such as **Kringlan**, the centre of the New City. Visitors looking for the true character of Iceland will be disappointed by these temples to consumerism, by the spreading concrete architecture and the broad main roads tailored to the needs of cars, and often don't spend enough time in the city to discover its charm. The Reykjavík that knows how to please shows its face in the **Old Town** and the **shopping streets of the city centre**, with small shops, trendy boutiques, cosy cafés and noisy pubs, in the traditional residential areas with their little houses clad in corrugated iron, or at the Tjörnin, the lake where some four dozen types of bird may be spotted.

Discovering the city's charm

Hallgrímskirkja and the roofs of Reykjavík

CITY HISTORY

A look back It would have been hard to predict from Reykjavík's history that it would achieve the importance it has today. The city can however look back on **Ingólfur Arnarson**, Iceland's first permanent settler, who settled in 874 at **»Smoky Bay«** – which is the English translation of the name »Reykjavík«. Two carved tree trunks that Arnarson had thrown into the sea just before he first landed on the coast of southern Iceland, were washed ashore here. For Ingólfur, this was a sign from the gods to take up residence at this place; today, the coat-of-arms of the city of Reykjavík shows the two trunks in the sea's waves. Archaeologists reckon that Ingólfur's farmstead used to stand round about where the Aðalstræti joins the Túngata, only a few metres from today's town hall and the parliament. However, the farm did not play an important role in the settlement phase and the period of the sagas, but rather always stood in the shadow of Bessastaðir on the Álftanes peninsula. More important in the end was Viðey Island, the site of an influential Augustinian monastery from the 13th century to the Reformation.

Years of A good two centuries after the monastery was razed by marauding change Danish troops, 18th-century Viðey moved back to the centre of Icelandic politics. This was where **Skúli Magnússon** (1711 – 1794) had his Viðeyarstofa residence built, today the oldest stone house in town. Change came with Skúli in 1749, the year that he was appointed governor, the highest administrative civil servant of the colony. Skúli was the first Icelander to hold this position and as such was able to stand up to the interests of the Danish monopoly traders for nearly one-and-a-half decades. During this time, he started the development of independent economic structures in the country, which was starving, exploited and completely dependent on its colonial masters. Inspired by the fresh wind of the Enlightenment, he established a company to invest in a programme of industry and infrastructure for Iceland. Where today the Aðalstræti runs through the Old Town, Skúli had apartments and companies for wool and fish processing as well as for shipbuilding – the roots of the metropolis.

Rise When the monopoly traders took over Skúli's life work in 1764 and disempowered him, the seeds of Reykjavík's rise were already planted, even if the big breakthrough had not yet come. When the Danish king officially founded the town of Reykjavík by royal decree in 1786, its inhabitants were counted and found to total 167.

Reykjavík
becomes the In 1784, the bishop of Iceland moved his seminary to Reykjavík from
centre of Skálholt, which had been largely destroyed by earthquakes. With the
power consecration of the cathedral in 1796, the town officially became the

»Sólfar« – »Sun Ship« – is what artist Jón Gunnar Árnason named his sculpture on the coast promenade

bishop's see for the island. In 1819, secular power joined the spiritual, as the governor turned the prison at the Lækjartorg, finished in 1771, into his personal and official residence. After 1874, as Iceland gained more of its own institutions and administrative tools with every step towards independence, these too established themselves in Reykjavík; for instance in 1885 the national bank was formed, and in 1911, the university founded, with the merger of several higher education colleges. The biggest push however came with the start of **self-governance of the country** in 1904. The city was by now growing quickly and continuously, the nearly 7,000 inhabitants (Greater Reykjavík some 9,500) representing 12 % of the entire Icelandic population. From 1909 onwards, water and gas provision was secured, and between 1913 and 1917 the port was built. In 1921, a power plant at the Elliðaár began feeding homes with electricity, and from 1928, geothermally heated water was put to use; by the end of the 1930s,

View from the steeple of the Hallgrimskirkja
over the old city of Reykjavík

the hot-water provision covered the entire country. No other town in Iceland benefited so much from the economic boom that the British and later the American troops brought to the country during the Second World War. From this, Reykjavík developed into the undisputed economic and administrative centre of Iceland, and the population figures, still rising today, attest to the continuing appeal of the metropolis.

The financial crisis and its consequences In the summer of 2007 economic life in the capital came to an abrupt end. The local banks, which had grown strongly from inscrutable dealings mainly in foreign currency, were drawn in 2008 into the whirlpool of the international financial crisis and were practically ruined. They could only be »saved« by being nationalized and left the general public with a massive mountain of debt. The Icelandic Kroner lost great value, which led to impoverishing of large parts of the city population. The consequences were weeks of protest by enraged citizens and early parliamentary elections. Free towels for all public pools, a polar bear area for the zoo and the promise not to keep any promises – this was the »campaign platform« of a fake political party in 2010 during the election campaign for mayor of Reykjavík. What nobody would have believed: this party actually got the majority of the votes. Since then the TV comedian and ex-punk rocker Jón Gnarr has been mayor of Reykjavík, and until now he has indeed not kept any of his promises. There are still no free towels at the swimming pools, and the undernourished polar bear that washed ashore in spring of 2011 was shot because after the financial crisis there was no money for a polar bear area in the zoo. But Jón Gnarr did achieve one thing: he brought a fresh breeze into the Reykjavík city administration and that was probably what the city residents wanted most in the election.

CULTURE IN REYKJAVÍK

Most visitors miss out on the variety of culture, which in Reykjavík is vastly superior to many European cities of a similar size, as during the main summer holiday season the performing arts largely take a break. The season of the major **theatres** and the **opera** – Reykjavík boasts ten stages at seven venues – as well as the Icelandic Symphony Orchestra, run from October to May. Some actors do use this free time to stage historical material from the times of the sagas, or scenes from folk culture in a tourist-friendly format. Light Nights is a well-established production of this kind in English, and another is staged in the Skemmtihus chamber theatre at the Laufásvegur; the Tourist Information knows the current programmes and performance times.

The summer lull

Highlights Reykjavík

▶ **Old Town**
A stroll through the streets and small lanes between the harbour and Tjörnin is a walk through the heart of Reykjavík.
▶page 230

▶ **Municipal Art Museum**
Museum spread over three sites. Icelandic art from Erró via Kjarval to Sveinsson.
▶page 237, 246, 250

▶ **National Art Gallery**
For those that want to see more (Icelandic) art. Landscape and nature paintings are well represented.
▶page 240

▶ **National Museum**
A journey through the history and culture of the country.
▶page 245

▶ **Árbæjarsafn open-air museum**
Historical buildings and demonstrations of traditional trades – an excellent and authentic museum.
▶page 247

▶ **Nightlife**
Reykjavík is famous for its bars, pubs and clubs. In Iceland's capital, night owls have come to the right place!
▶page 231, 234, 237

New Start at the Harbour

Reykjavík's new trademark is the concert hall Harpa, which is located right by the harbour. The building was designed in the shape of a harp by the renowned Copenhagen architectural office of Henning Larson. Most spectacular is the façade, which enfolds the angular building complex, by the Icelandic light artist Olafur Eliasson.

Arnarhóll Hill with the statue of Ingólfur Arnarson offers the best view of the city's latest attraction, the conference centre and concert hall Harpa. The asymmetrical Cubist building right on the sea is conspicuous not only for its enormous size but also for the glass façade with its honeycomb-like windows.

The construction of the new concert hall took an estimated 200 mil. euros

High-flying Plans

The building, which has room for 1800 visitors, was planned in economically strong times. Money did not appear to be an object when building began at the start of the new millennium. Reykjavík was booming and everyone believed in a golden future. But it was all ove practically overnight – financial crisis, banking crisis, government bankruptcy. Further high-flying plans like a new bank building, a luxury hotel and even a World Trade Center were quickly put to rest in the »boulevard of shattered dreams«, as the street that ran past the Harpa was called. But Icelanders did not want to have to look at the unfinished Harpa every day as the symbol of their bankruptcy, so the city and the national government decided to at least complete a more moderately priced version of the building. Visible from far off and a little lost on its own the Harpa is a reminder of the times when the small Iceland was still allowed to play along in the worldwide economic poker.

Symbolic Power

But construction after the economic collapse was difficult and controversial. But the name of the concert hall has symbolic power:

The Icelanders brought up a Viking-like resolve in order to complete their new showpiece on the harbour despite the financial crisis.

»Harpa« is not only the Icelandic word for harp but also the first month of spring in the Norse calender. The name also means new beginnings. In 2011 the building was completed and given the World Architecture Award. You can't help but agree when you stand in front of it and get the full impact of the façade. The glass blocks imitate the black basalt columns that are so common in Iceland's landscapes. There are exactly 956 glass blocks of which no two are supposed to be alike; for the varied reflective and light-breaking effects the artist did not rely on nature but on highly mathematical calculations. Or the building front might remind you of fish scales – in Iceland this is also not out of place and one that shows what a Ger-

man journalist nicely expressed, that Eliasson's façade adjusts to every interpretation – »the mirror surfaces show the viewer what he wants to see in them«.

Outside Posh, Inside: Too

But inside the concert hall, which is painted in dark lava red, shows that Iceland's new landmark has more to offer than a glittery exterior: The acoustics – which are not unimportant in a concert hall – are excellent.

More information: www.harpa.is or tel. 5 28 50 50. Both the bistro and the concert hall restaurant serve Nordic specialties. Tours are also possible in the summer months.

MARCO ◉ POLO TIP

> **!** *Top information!* **Insider Tip**
>
> Events information, entrance fees for museums and other attractions, as well as reviews of restaurants, pubs and nightlife can be found in the brochures **What's on in Reykjavík** and **Reykjavík this Month**. Published in a new edition every one or two months, they can be picked up free from the Tourist Information as well as from most accommodation places

Since 1970, in even-numbered years cultural life has stayed vibrant up to the beginning of the travel season, thanks to the »**Listahátíð í Reykjavík**« biannual arts festival with its broad-ranging programme of good national and international events (www.artfest.is). In early/mid-June however, this festival too nears its end. After the first weekend in August, with the following Monday a holiday which nearly all city-dwellers celebrate somewhere in the countryside, leaving Reykjavík quiet and sleepy like no other day, the city wakes up again. On the two subsequent weekends, the carnival atmosphere of the gay and lesbian procession **Gay Pride Reykjavík**, and the long, colourful Menningarnott culture night following the **Reykjavík Marathon**, set the pulse of the city racing again.

REYKJAVÍK – CITY OF THE MANY SPAS

Whiff of the exotic
Is there one thing that the visitor absolutely has to do in Reykjavík? While the museums are undoubtedly interesting and worth seeing, in global terms they are second rate. The position of the city, with a mountain panorama on one side and the sea on the other, is impressive but not unique. Some tourism PRs might characterize the nightlife as a global hot spot, but in reality it is probably rather the whiff of the exotic than a real comparison with Berlin, London or New York that makes it attractive. One thing however is truly unique: **Reykjavík's spa life**. Don't leave the city without visiting one of the many pools. Surveys of foreign visitors who enjoyed a bathing experience here show their attractiveness: 98 % would definitely go bathing again if they came back to Reykjavík.

Warm bath on the Arctic Circle
Elsewhere, any treasurer of a city with 100,000 inhabitants would need several relaxing baths a day if they had to finance the running of seven thermal spas all year round, only one of them with a roof. However, in Reykjavík this is no problem despite the proximity to the Arctic Circle. Heating costs are hardly worth mentioning, particularly when weighed against the nearly 2 million visitors per year – far more than the baths of a much bigger city might attract. And the seven spas in Reykjavík are complemented by another half a dozen in the suburbs. In terms of size and facilities most reach standards

only offered elsewhere by more expensive recreational baths; in Reykjavík, by contrast, a visit to the swimming pool is an **inexpensive pleasure** compared to other living costs. And as the open-air pools have fairly long opening hours even in winter, there is a good chance to take a bath after dark under the Northern Lights.

Alongside normal swimming pools with water temperatures rarely below 29 °C/84°F, most baths also have steam saunas, whirlpools, warm water pools and hot pots, or **heiti potturinn**. Stepping into these mini pools, with steam temperatures of 37 – 42 °C/98 – 107 °F, has a similarly relaxing effect to a sauna. Beginners should however be sure to start by testing the »coldest« of the pots, as for bodies not used to it, water temperatures over 40 °C/104°F can seem scaldingly hot. Also, don't spend any longer than 15 minutes in the hot pots, and

Hot pots

Starting point of the Reykjavík Marathon every year in August is Lake Tjörnin in the city

Women only!

Baðhúsið is a health spa for women only, which was opened in 1994 by Linda Pétursdóttir – a former Miss Iceland and Miss World – and offers massages, beauty treatments, jacuzzis and much more. Every day, some 1,000 women allow themselves to be pampered in these wonderfully relaxing surroundings (Reykjavík, Brautarholti 20, tel. 561 51 00, www.badhusid.is).

cool off afterwards in an outdoor or normal swimming pool. And lastly, don't schedule in too much for the evening – hot pots are tiring!

The population statistics show the results of the Icelandic passion for swimming: health experts are convinced that Icelanders' life expectancy, high by international comparison, is partly due to the country's spa culture. Thermal spas are credited with **curative powers** for degenerative diseases, such as arthritis, as well as for modern stress-related illnesses. However, the whirlpools and hot pots don't just promote health but also communication: the cosily warm pools are a meeting place for the people of the city to chat about daily life or politics, to gossip about neighbours or celebrities, and are also where it is easiest for visitors to get chatting to the locals or other guests. **Laugardalslaug**, the main swimming pool of the city next to the campsite in the Laugardalur (Sundlaugarvegur), offers an open-air competition pool with 50-meter lanes as well as six hot pots, plus a sauna and steam bath area. Close to the centre, in the west of the city, is Sundlaug Vesturbæjar (Hofsvallagata), while the baths of Kópavogur and Seltjarnarnes are also easily accessible.

❶ For further details of all the baths in terms of facilities, opening times and bus connections, check www.visitreykjavik.is for »Tours and activities« and click on »Health & Wellness«.

✳ THE OLD TOWN BETWEEN THE HARBOUR AND TJÖRNIN

Grjótaðorp The streets, lanes and squares in the centre between the harbour to the north and the Tjörnin lake on the southern side are the oldest part of Reykjavík. Visitors will notice this most clearly west of the Ingólfstorg in the so-called Grjótaðorp, a block of streets with small crooked lanes and houses from the early days of the town in the late 18th and early 19th centuries.

The building at **Aðalstræti 10** is considered the oldest house. It was built in 1752 for one of the small enterprises with which Skúli Magnússon stimulated Iceland's economy. Skúli, in this sense the real founder of the city of Reykjavík, stands as a monument at the corner of Aðalstræti and Kirkjustræti. Practically at his feet, extensive archaeological ground surveys were made during preparations for the construction of a new hotel, which revealed the foundations of the first buildings in Reykjavík.

The fact that in this quarter which lies so far west, the most important shopping street is called **Austurstræti**, i.e. East Street, is due to the historical development of the city: when the name was chosen in the mid-19th century, it was leading eastwards out of town! There is also a counterpart going in the other direction: leading west, the Vesturgata is a road lined with small shops selling arts and crafts.

Shopping street

The quarter between the harbour and Tjörnin stays extremely lively until late at night. Here, visitors will find several institutions of the café, pub and restaurant scene, such as Reykjavík's legendary hot dog stand Baejarins Beztu Pylsur (»best hot dogs in town«) an Tryggvagata 22, which can easily be recognized at lunch time by the long queues going to the counter. There's photographic evidence: even Bill Clinton was here already. The Guardian has even chosen this stand as the best one in Europe. A hot dog costs 280 ISK. With their outdoor tables on summer days, bistro cafés such as the **»Paris«** and the **»Thorvaldsen«** at the Austurvöllur, the Mexican bar **»Tabasco's«** at the Ingólfstorg or the **»Kaffi Reykjavík«** right around the corner from the Vesturgata, even manage to exude a near-Mediterranean vibe which clashes somewhat with the woollens shops at the Ingólfstorg or along the Hafnarstræti.

Best hot dogs in town

Insider Tip

One of the most conspicuous houses in the area, the Falcon House on the northern side of the Ingólfstorg, is shared by the Café Victor and one of these shops. Carved falcons on the roof crest are a reminder of its role in colonial times, when coveted gyrfalcons from the whole country were collected here before being shipped off as presents from the Danish kings to delight European aristocracy.

Falcon House

The cafés, along with several restaurants of the Old Town, change character in the evening and turn into bars. At least at weekends, nearly all offer **entertainment** as well, with either a DJ getting people moving on the dance floor or live musicians performing on a little stage somewhere. The largest of those where better-known names of the national music scene perform, belongs to the »Gaukur á Stöng« (www.gaukurinn.is). Visitors not wanting to spend their weekend evenings queuing outside trendy venues or paying inflated entry fees and alcohol prices, can choose open-air entertainment: bikers and young skaters meet at the **Ingólfstorg**, and in the streets cars cruise through the night in an endless convoy – the Icelanders' name for this activity is »rúnturinn« – with at the wheel a fair few Icelanders old enough to have a driving licence, but not to step inside a pub let alone drink alcohol.

Entertainment

Reykjavík

Hólmar

ÖRFIRSEY

0,25 mi
500 m
©BAEDEKER

Vikin
(Maritime
Museum)

Höfn

Grandabryggja

Eyjarslóð
Holmaslóð
Fiskislóð
Djúpsl.
Jarnbraut
Norðagarður
Grandagarður

Bátahöfn

Selgjarnaners

Ægisgarður
Faxagarður
Ingólfsgarður

Seljavegur
Ánanaust
Mörargata
Nýlendugata
Vesturgata
Bakst.
Bræðraborgarstígur
Öldu-
Rán.
Bárugata
Holtsgata
Brekust.
Drist
Mar.
Öldu-gata
Seljavegur
vegur
Vesturg.
Framnes-
Sólvallagata
Ásvallagata
Blómvallag.
Háhvallagata
Túngata
Nýja-vallag.
Grjótag.
Geirsgata
Mjóstr.
Aðalstr.
Grófin
Austurstr.
Tryggvagata
Hafnarstr.
Hverfisgata
Lindargata
Sölvhólsgata
Skúlagata
Sæbrú
Faxagata
Kalkofnsvegur

Eiðsgrandi
Lág v.
Grandavegur
Álagrandi
Hringbraut
Vestyg.
Reynim.
Mel.
Gren.
Mel.

Town Archive
Hafnarhús
Lækjartorg
Ísl. Óperan
Safnahúsið

Rékagr.
Boðagr.
Álagrandi
Bárugr.
Fjörugr.
Flyðugrandi
Mestaravellir
Frostaskjól
Frostaskjól
Kaplaskólsvegur
Granaskjól
Nesvegur
Sörlaskjól
Faxaskjól
Eiðismelur
Hagamelur
Furumelur
Hofsvallagata
Melhagi
Tómasarhagi
Ásvegi
Dunhagi
Fornhagi
Fálkagata
Grímsh.
Lynghagi
Starhagi

Landakotskirkja

Sundlaug

KAPLASKJÓL

Alþingishús
Town Hall Dóm-
Tjanar-
bær
kirkjan

National
Library

Tjörnin

National Gallery
of Iceland

Kirkjst.
Kirkjst.
Suðurgata
Skothúsvegur
Melatorg
Bjarkar-
gata
Skothúsvegur
Bjarnar-
gata
Sóleyjargata
Fríkirkjuvegur
Skálst.
Þingholtsstr.
Óðinsgata
Bergst.
Týsgata
Njálsg.
Grettisg.
Laugavegur
Hverfisgata
Skólavörðustígur
Bókhlöðust.
Klappastígur
Barónsstígur
Smiðjustígur
Snorra-stígur
Frakkastígur
Bragi
Nönnug.
Mímisv.
Baldursg.
Urðarst.
Mánag.
Mógilsá

Volcano
Show

Hallgrímskirkja

Einar
Jónssonar
Museum

Neskirkja

Guðbrandsg.
Birkimelur
Birkimelur
Aragata
Oddagata
Eggerts.
Fjölnisv.
Hljomskálinn

Ásgrimur
Jónsson Coll.

4

National
Museum

Hagatorg

Fjölnisvegur
Laufásvegur
Njarðargata
Njarðargata
Smáragata
Freyjugata
Bergstaðast.
Laufásvegur
Þórsgata
Hringbraut

University

Árni
Magnússon
Institute

Tele-
communications
Museum

Fjallhagi
Hjarðarhagi
Aragata
Suðurgata
Oddagata
Suðurgata
Njarðargata
Vatnsmýrarvegur

3

Norræna
Húsið

BSÍ
Coach Terminal

Skerjafjörður

VATNSMÝRI

Brú
Hólar
Hörpug.
Góug.
Þóragata
Skerplug.
Rvk.
Skerplug.
Fossag.
Þórsg.

National
airport
✈
Hotel Loftleiðir

Flugleiðir
Flugvallar-
vegur
Flugvallar-
vegur

Where to eat

① Perlan
② Einar Ben
③ Dill Restaurant
④ Humarhúsið
⑤ Þrír Frakkar
⑥ Lækjarbrekka
⑦ First Vegetarian
⑧ Mokka
⑨ Shalimar
⑩ Stofan Kaffihús

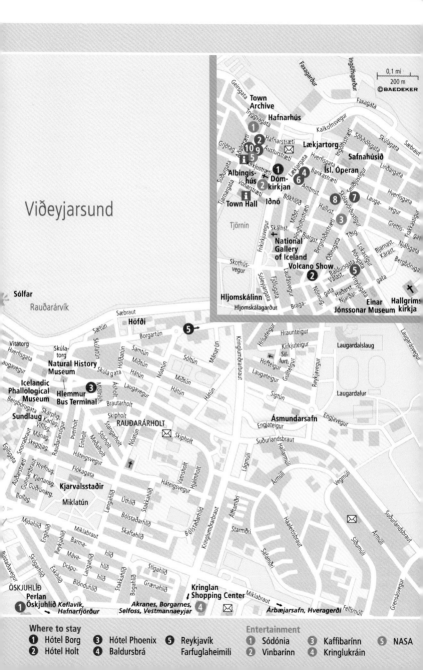

0,1 mi
200 m
©BAEDEKER

Faxagarður
Ingólfsgarður
Geldagata
Tryggvagata
Town Archive
Faxagata
Kalkofnsvegur
Sölvhólsgata
Skúlagata
Sæbraut
Hafnarhús
Hafnarstræti
Lækjartorg
Ingólfsstræti
Lindargata
Gröftag.
Austurstræti
Safnahúsið
Hverfisgata
Hverfisgata-vegur
Kirkjustræti
Lækjargata
Ísl. Óperan
Albingis-hús
Bankastræti
Lauga-vegur
Dóm-kirkjan
Amtmst.
Smiðjustígur
Grettis.
Vonarstræti
Bókhlöð.
Laugar-vegur
Town Hall
Iðnó
Hallvst.
Mjóst.
Tjörnin
Skálhst.
Þingholtsstræti
Hallvst.
Tóg.
Bjargst.
Grjótagata
Njálsgata
Bergþóru.
Friðrikjuvegur
National Gallery of Iceland
Óðinsgata
Lokastígur
Bjarnast.
Karast.
Bergþóru-gata
Skothús-vegur
Volcano Show
Baldursgata
Freyjugata
Sóleyjargata
Fjólugata
Nönug.
Valast.
Hljómskálinn
Laufásvegur
Braga-
Hafnarst.
Njarðar.
Einar Jónssonar Museum
Hallgríms kirkja
Hljómskálagarður

Viðeyjarsund

Sólfar
Rauðarárvík

Sæbraut
Höfði
Borgartún
Hrauneigur
Laugardalslaug
Laugarásvegur
Vitatorg
Skúla-torg
Sætún
Skúlatún
Höfðatún
Samtún
Sóltún
Mánatún
Kringlumýrarbraut
Hrísateigur
Kirkjuteigur
Síl-turt
Höfteigur
Hverfisgata
Laugavegur
Natural History Museum
Miðtún
Hátún
Miðtún
Hátún
Skúla gata
Ásholt
Laugavegur
Laugateigur
Gullteigur
Reykjavegur
Laugardalur
Engjavegur
Laugardalslaug
Icelandic Phallological Museum
Hlemmur Bus Terminal
Brautarholt
Skarphg.
Karlag.
Víffilsg.
Skeggjag.
Mánag.
Stangarholt
Skipholt
RAUÐARÁRHOLT
Skipholt
Ásmundarsafn
Engjavegur
Sundlaug
Snorrabraut
Rauðarárstígur
Einholt
Meðalholt
Stórholt
Nóatún
Suðurlandsbraut
Egilsgata
Auðarstræti
Guðmundarbraut
Hrefnug.
Kjartansg.
Guðrúnarg.
Bollag.
Háteigsvegur
Flókagata
Skipholt
Hjálmholt
Vatnsholt
Lágmúli
Ármúli
Vegmúli
Kjarvalsstaðir
Miklatún
Langahlíð
Stakkahlíð
Úthlíð
Háteigsvegur
Bólstaðarhlíð
Kringlumýrarbraut
Starmýri
Bólstaðarhlíð
Afðamýri
Háteigsvegur
Lágmúli
Suðurlandsbraut
Mjóahlíð
Engihlíð
Reykjahlíð
Barma-
hlíð
Máva-hlíð
Drápu-hlíð
Langahlíð
hlíð
Miklabraut
Skaftahlíð
Ármúli
Sólumúli
Bogahlíð
Stigahlíð
Safamýri
Háaleitisbraut
Grensásvegur
ÖSKJUHLÍÐ
Perlan
Öskjuhlíð
Keflavík, Hafnarfjörður
Akranes, Borgarnes, Selfoss, Vestmannaeyjar
Kringlan Shopping Center
Miklabraut
Árbæjarsafn, Hveragerði
Fellsmúli

Where to stay
1 Hótel Borg
2 Hótel Holt
3 Hótel Phoenix
4 Baldursbrá
5 Reykjavík Farfuglaheimili

Entertainment
1 Sódónia
2 Vinbarínn
3 Kaffibarínn
4 Kringlukráin
5 NASA

Reykjavík

INFORMATION
Adalstræti 2 tel. 519 15 50
www.visitreykjavik.is

TRANSPORT
The yellow city-centre buses run on 20
lines between 7am – midnight, in the
daytime every 20 minutes, in the evenings and at weekends every half hour.
The main interchange points are Lækjartorg in the historical centre, Hlemmur,
Grensás, Mjódd and Ártún. A town map
showing the bus routes can be picked
up from the tourist office. Single tickets
cost about 250 Icelandic króna, and
transfer tickets are called »skiptimiði«.
Two hours before every international departure, an airport bus leaves from Hotel
Loftleiðir for Keflavík airport. The overland buses run by the BSÍ company depart near the Hringbraut; tickets may be
bought between 7.30am and 10pm.

REYKJAVÍK WELCOME CARD
24 hrs 1900 ISK, 48 hrs 2400 ISK,
72 hrs 2900 ISK

The Welcome Card gives free entrance
to all thermal spas and nearly all museums and galleries, free internet access,
various shop and restaurant discounts
and unlimited travel on Reykjavík's buses. The card can be bought at the tourist
office, bus station, Hotel Loftleiðir and in
the youth hostel.

GOING OUT
Reykjavík has become a hot spot of
good cheer in the far north. On summer
weekends in particular, there are high
jinks into the small hours, lubricated by
rivers of alcohol. Which locality is the
»in« place can be judged from the
length of the queue at the door. Don't
be too disheartened however, as the
turnover is usually fairly high, with the
locals preferring to drift from pub to
pub. Don't expect much to be happen-
ing before midnight though; Icelanders
start the party at home, drinking one or
three beers before coming out – not
such a bad idea given the price of a beer
in the pubs.

❶ Sódóma
Tryggvagata 22
Tel. 8 60 22 16
From Wednesday until Saturday Icelandic bands play the best live music here; afterwards it becomes a disco

❷ Vinbaríinn
Kirkjutorg 4, Tel. 5 52 41 20
Relaxed bar with excellent wine list. A good place to wind down the evening.

❸ Kaffibarinn
Bergstaðastræti 1
Tel. 551 15 88
This is where the cult movie 101 Reykjavík was filmed, which might explain why it is always so full. Or it might be to do with the good music that the DJs put on at the weekends. In any case, the Kaffibarinn is a good place for Icelandic celebrities.

❹ Kringlukráin
Kringlan
Tel. 568 08 78
This is where theatre goers meet before and after performances for a snack or drink in a cosy pub atmosphere. Live music at the weekends.

❺ NASA
Austurvöllur 101   **Insider Tip**
Tel. 511 13 13
The largest club in Iceland, playing the hottest music – incredibly »in«.

WHERE TO EAT
❶ Perlan ££££
Öskjuhlíð, tel. 562 02 00
International gourmet cuisine in a spectacular setting. The view across the city changes constantly, as in one hour the revolving restaurant in the glass dome –

above the huge silver, gleaming hot water tanks – completes its turn. One floor below the restaurant, the café has a terrace with panoramic views.

❷ Einar Ben ££££
Veltusundi 1, Tel. 5 11 50 90
www.einarben.is
One of the best addresses in town: The restaurant is located in one of Reykjavík's oldest trading houses and has 19th century charm. The menu is Icelandic: fish, sea birds, game and lamb.

❸ Dill Restaurant ££££
Sturlugötu 5, Tel. 5 52 15 22
www.dillrestaurant.is
The Norse house near the university was built by Finnish star architect Alvar Aalto. Icelandic star chef Gunnar Karl Gíslason, one of the pioneers of »New Nordic Cuisine«, cooks here.

❹ Humarhúsið
Amtmannsstígur 1
Tel. 561 33 03
Lobster is the speciality in this stylishly furnished establishment – as a soup it is pretty good value even. Other fish specialities are served too however.

❺ Þrír Frakkar
Baldursgata 14
Tel. 552 39 39
Cosy restaurant in the Old Town specializing in fish. Highly praised chef Úlfar Eysteinsson likes to give traditional Icelandic recipes a contemporary makeover.

❻ Lækjarbrekka ££/£££
Bankastræti 2
Tel. 551 44 30
Old wooden house in the centre with extremely cosy, slightly old-fashioned

furnishings. Excellent cuisine, mainly lamb and fish dishes. Daily tourist menu and home-made cakes. Expensive gourmet menu in the evening.

❼ First Vegetarian £/££
Laugavegur 20b, tel. 552 84 10
Inexpensive, frequently changing, vegetarian meals, often with an Indian flavour. Good selection of cakes.

❽ Mokka £/££
Skólavördustígur 3a
Tel. 552 11 74
Reykjavík's oldest café, which has been looking after its regulars since 1958. Popular meeting place for artists and intellectuals.

❾ Shalimar £/££
Austurstræti 4, tel. 551 02 92
Good selection of Indian and Pakistani dishes, inexpensive lunch and dinner specials.

❿ Stofan Kaffihús ££ Insider Tip
Aðalstræti 7, Tel. 5 67 18 81
Not just good coffee, but also outstanding tortes, cakes and other fine pastry are available at this presently very popular coffee house.

ACCOMMODATION
❶ Hótel Borg ££££
Pósthússtræti 11
Tel. 551 14 40, www.hotelborg.is
Four-star hotel, built in 1930 in the Art Déco style and restored in 2007. Offering modern rooms, individually styled.

❷ Hótel Holt ££££
Bergstaðarstræti 37
Tel. 552 57 00, www.holt.is
In a quiet and central location, no great beauty from the outside. However, the interior more than compensates: the corridors, 30 rooms and 12 suites house the largest private art collection in Iceland of paintings and sculptures by Icelandic artists.

❸ Hotel Phoenix ££ £
Laugavegur 140, Tel. 5 11 50 02
www.phoenix.is
Charming little hotel with nine carefully furnished rooms, ideal for a romantic weekend for!

❹ Baldursbrá Guesthouse
Laufásvegur 41
Tel. 552 66 46, fax 562 66 47
This guesthouse offers an experience of pure cosiness. Eight large, welcoming rooms in a central location, with a hearty breakfast buffet. In the garden a hot pot awaits guests.

❺ Reykjavík Farfuglaheimili
Sundlaugavegur 34, tel. 553 81 10
Modern youth hostel near the public swimming pool.

Nostalgic charm in Hotel Borg

From Thursday to Sunday, there is more going on late at night on the streets of the Old Town – as well as at the Laugavegur – than during business hours. Visitors wanting to get the full experience need a lot of stamina though, as the evening seldom starts before 11pm. One famous **nightlife attraction** has now lost its shine however: as there has effectively been no enforced closing time since 2002, the **Lækjartorg** no longer suddenly fills with noisy revellers continuing the party, as it did when all establishments had to close on the stroke of three o'clock. Despite this, the square is still full of activity all night long, as it is here that people order the last hot dogs, pancakes or waffles from fast-food stalls, before catching a taxi or night bus home.

No closing hour

Until 1915, larger ships could only moor off Reykjavík; people and goods had to be brought ashore or landed by tender boats that anchored on the banks level with today's Hafnarstræti. The area lying in front of it today was only created by the expansion of the port between 1913 and 1917. Meanwhile, the modern container and freight port of **Sundahöfn** a few kilometres further east, has considerably reduced the role of the more central Reykjavíkurhöfn, which has however kept the fish trawlers and coastguard boats. A long quay right in front of the city centre on Geirsgata is reserved for small and mid-size cruisers, while the really big ones have to go into deeper Sundahöfn. The old steam engine standing on the quay is a favourite climbing frame for children. Having been used during the construction of the harbour for transporting material, to this day it has remained Iceland's only train.

City harbour

Right opposite the »Crusaders' Quay« at weekends the gate to the underground car park in the **Tollhusið** (Customs House) is opened for the Kolaportið weekly market and flea market, with its colourful mix of food and junk on display: cucumbers and peppers grown in private greenhouses, potatoes and home-baked pancakes from a farm in southern Iceland, dried or fresh fish from a fishing village on the Reykjanes Peninsula, as well as sweets and all kinds of bric-a-brac, antiques and second-hand goods, mobile phone accessories and neckties.

Kolaportið

A former fish factory in the northwest of the old harbour uses fishing to tell the story of Icelandic seafaring. The 1970s cod war also gets a mention.

*Víkin

❶ July – Sept daily 10am – 5pm, otherwise closed Mon; admission 1650 ISK; internet: www.sjominjasafn.is

The most recent and certainly the most attractive branch of the Municipal Art Museum (Listasafn Reykjavíkur), which shows its treasures at two more addresses in the city (Kjarvalsstaðir ▶p. 246 and

Hafnarhús

Ásmundarsafn ▶p. 250), fills the Hafnarhús at Tryggvagata 17. Modern architecture, inspired by Minimalism, has turned the office and warehouse of the harbour administration building from the 1930s into a **temple of the arts**. Steel and concrete are the dominant materials, and six exhibitions rooms across two floors arranged around an open courtyard make for a compact museum. Alongside changing exhibitions, works are shown from a collection of about 3,000 pieces, which the **pop-art artist Erró** (* 1932) – easily the most renowned contemporary Icelandic artist – bequeathed to the city in 1989.

❶ daily 1pm–5pm; admission 1650 ISK; www.listasafnreykjavikur.is

Museum Reykjavík 871

During construction in Aðalstræti in 2001 workers discovered archaeological finds, which turned out to be the remains of Reykjavík's **oldest house**. By testing volcanic ash remains, the long house could be dated to around 871, the time of the settlement. The wall remains were conserved and they are now on display in the museum in Aðalstræti 16. A multimedia exhibit also give a visual impression of what life on a farm was like during the time of the first settlers. The installations inform not only on the building and artefacts that were found there, they also let the former residents come alive as ghosts and go about their daily work.

i daily 10am–5pm, admission 1650 ISK, http://minjasafnreykjavikur.is

*Austurvöllur

The Austurvöllur seems more like a small park than one of the central squares of a capital. In nice weather, the grassy areas become a sunbathing lawn, and above everything, right in the middle on a high plinth stands **Jón Sigurðsson** (1811 – 1879), the 19th-century leader of the Icelandic independence movement and thus the father of the country's independence. The monument is a work by Einar Jónsson (1874 – 1954). Sigurðsson stands looking at the **Althingishús**, which he didn't actually see during his lifetime as it was only inaugurated in 1881, two years after his death. The **parliament building** is a simple, even modest affair with a grey basalt-block façade. Above the entrance, the coat-of-arms of the Danish king Christian IX can be seen, who at the time was Iceland's head of state. Before Iceland's parliament – the Althing – reconvened in 1845 in Reykjavík, it had sat exclusively in ▶Þingvellir, but had dissolved half a century earlier and slipped into complete obscurity. Up to moving into the new building, the **Menntaskólinn í Reykjavík**, old high school a few hundred metres further east at Bókhlöðustíg 7, served as the meeting place. Well into the 19th century, this was the only school in the country which would award a qualification for university entrance, which mostly led students to Copenhagen. Thus, many of the country's well-known personalities feature on the list of former pupils, amongst them two Nobel Prize winners. Born on the Faroe Islands, **Niels Finsen** (1860 – 1904) was awarded the Nobel Prize for Medicine in 1903 for his work on light therapy for tuberculosis patients, and **Halldór Laxness** (1902 – 1998) was awarded the Nobel Prize for Literature in 1955.

Between Althingishús and Menntaskólinn, the modest cathedral – the Dómkirkjan – occupies the southeastern corner of the Austurvöllur. It was built between 1788 and 1796 as the seat for the bishop of Iceland who had just moved from Skálholt to Reykjavík. At the time, the church didn't need to be big, as the town had fewer than 200 inhabitants. A real gem inside is the baptismal font, carved in 1839 from Carrara marble by **Bertel Thorvaldsen** (1770 – 1844) – »created in Rome and given to Iceland, his fatherland, in faith«, as a Latin inscription explains. Thorvaldsen, in his time one of the most important classical sculptors in Europe, worked in Rome for a long period and normally figures in the history of art as a Dane. Icelanders like to claim him as one of their own though, as his father came from the island. This is also the reason why a few more of his works can be seen in the city, amongst them a self-portrait from 1839 in the green spaces on the southern part of the Tjörnin, beyond the Skothúsvegur.

Dómkirkjan

Appearing bigger and more pompous than both parliament and cathedral, the Hotel Borg on the eastern side of the Austurvöllur is a house entirely inspired by Art Déco and built to designs by **Guðjón Samúelsson** (1887 – 1950). Since the day of its opening in 1930, the Borg has been Iceland's only real luxury hotel, with a long list of illustrious guests from the ranks of the aristocracy, politics and show business, including the Danish king Christian X, Marlene Dietrich and Kevin Costner.

Hotel Borg

TJÖRNIN – A PARADISE FOR BIRDS IN THE CITY CENTRE

Just a few steps south of the parliament and cathedral, visitors find themselves standing at the water's edge again: the Tjörnin city lake makes a natural boundary to the Old Town and forms an unusual **oasis of nature**: over 80 species of bird have been sighted here, nearly 50 of them regularly. In cold winters, when parts of the Tjörnin become an ice-skating rink, warm water is used to keep one piece on the Old Town side free of ice for the birds.

Oasis of nature

When the city fathers wanted to have a new **city hall** in the city centre, given the lack of other land to build on, their only choice was to pinch a corner of the Tjörnin. In 1992, the two-winged building with its striking, semi-circular roofs was put into service. The trademark feature is the southern façade looking onto the lake: mighty concrete

City hall

MARCO ⊕ POLO TIP

! *On the trail of elves* **Insider Tip**

Whilst the Icelanders have both feet firmly in the 21st century, they still have an enormous amount of trouble with gnomes, light-fairies, elves and trolls, who can get very annoyed when, for instance, roads are built through their invisible residences. Which is why in 1995 an elf school finally opened – the first and only one in the world! Since then, every Friday at 4pm historian Magnús Skarphédinsson has been initiating people, including tourists, into the universe of the elves (Álfaskólinn, Síðumúli 31, 108 Reykjavík, tel. 834 40 14, mhs@vortex.is).

pillars shelter a glass frontage reaching from the roof to the water level. Originally controversial because of its dimensions and building costs, the new town hall has long since become an accepted and central **part of the cityscape**. Inside, tourists find a municipal information office, rarely overrun with people, as well as a pretty and inexpensive cafeteria. There is also an impressive three dimensional model of Iceland with a scale of about 1 : 50 000.

On the eastern banks of the Tjörnin, a church clad in grey corrugated iron might catch the eye, but the museum right next to it is Listasafn Íslands, the ****National Gallery** of Iceland (Fríkirkjuvegur 7). Here, the architectural combination of a former ice storehouse – where blocks of ice sawed from the Tjörnin were kept cool for the summer – with a light-filled new construction works well. Changing exhibitions by national and international artists regularly fill the rooms, while in the summer months the museum fulfils its duties to visitors by showing selected works by Icelandic artists from the collection, always including the classical pieces of **landscape and nature painting** which dominated the art of the country up to the 1940s. A pioneer of Icelandic painting and the country's first full-time artist was **Ásgrimur Jónsson** (1876 – 1958), who studied in the early 20th century at the Royal Academy of Art in Copenhagen and had his first exhibition in his home country in 1903. Jónsson is well represented in the National Gallery.

● National Gallery of Iceland: Fríkirkjuvegur 7, Tues – Sun 10am – 5pm, Admission 1500 ISK, www.listasafn.is

LAUGAVEGUR AND BANKASTRÆTI

Forming an extension of the Austurstræti, the Laugavegur and its Bankastræti continuation represent the most important shopping streets in the city. Thanks to the geothermal springs under the cobbles providing under floor heating, they stay free of snow and ice even in the winter. This is where long-established jewellers, boutiques of international fashion chains and national designers, souvenir shops, book and music shops, restaurants and some **trendy hangouts** are clustered together.

Looking for art, crafts or simply a souvenir a little out of the ordinary? Where the Bankastræti becomes the Laugavegur, turn off onto the Skólavörðustígur leading up to the Hallgrímskirkja. On both sides there are many galleries and shops selling art, crafts and handicrafts, with souvenir hunters flocking in particular to the shop of the **Handknitting Association of Iceland** at Handprónasambandið, no. 19. Shoppers needing to take a breather during the »climb« should head for Reykjavík's oldest café at no. 3: the »Mokka Kaffi« is an institution, pervaded by a 1960s charm.

Arts and crafts

Art may be art but the risqué has appeal: during its first stint in Reykjavík the museum was one of the most popular in the country. It returned to Reykjavík after some years in Húsavik, during which time its collection was expanded to include its first human penis. The museum exhibits more than 100 penises from mammals, the largest being from whales. Along with originals, some of which are dried, some stuffed or preserved in alcohol, phallic articles of daily use and works of art are also on display and fore sale.

❶ Laugavegur 116, daily 11am–6pm, admission 1000 ISK

Moving from the Old Town via the Lækjargata to the Bankastræti, a complex of 19th-century houses catches the eye, one of them providing an appropriate setting for the **Restaurant Lækjarbrekka**, a culinary institution in Reykjavík. The conspicuous building with its jet black paint and gleaming white windows was built in 1832 as a private home for a Danish trader, but was converted and put to different uses several times. For some years a growing Reykjavík was provided from here with bread, rolls and cake by the bakery dynasty of Bernhöft, and today the whole area is still called Bernhöftstorf in memory of it. On fine days, the café tables sheltered from the wind on the small square between the houses are a popular pit stop with tourists.

At the corner of Lækjargata and Bankastræti, the Stjórnarráðshúsið functions as **the official residence**

MARCO❀POLO TIP

! *ÁTVR – Booze Central* ^Insider ^Tip

Legendary amongst tourists, they are not allowed to publicize themselves and their discreet exteriors are somewhat reminiscent of the chic of Soviet-bloc retail. Often visitors don't even realise they've reached their destination until they are standing more or less in front of them. These are the **sales outlets of the state-owned alcohol and tobacco monopoly ÁTVR**. Vínbúðin in Austurstræti 10 a is one of six liquor stores in Reykjavík and has an excellent selection. Visitors who appreciate the finest and more unusual tipples will be pleasantly surprised. (Mon–Fri 11am–6pm, Sat 11am–2pm.)

of the prime minister. The first residents to move in here in 1771 however were not highly regarded nor did they come here voluntarily: the building served as a prison until 1820, when a governor had it converted into an official residence. Since then it has always served this function for the most powerful in the country. The two statues in the front garden show **Hannes Hafstein**, who in 1904 became the first Minister for Iceland in the Danish cabinet to actually be Icelandic and reside in Reykjavík, and **Danish king Christian IX**, who in 1874 was the first Danish monarch ever to visit this part of his empire. With him he had a constitution for his subjects that promised them partial autonomy and paved the way for independence realized 70 years later.

Settlers monument

A few steps further north, from the Arnarhóll hill a belligerent-looking Ingólfur Arnarson, leaning on the dragon prow of his ship, is looking out for new shores. This monument to Iceland's first permanent settler, like the two outside the Stjórnarráðshúsið, was executed by Einar Jónsson.

**Safnahúsið cultural centre

Behind the monument to Ingólfur, the striking Þjoðmenningarhúsið building, also called Safnahúsið, catches the eye with its classical features (Hverfisgata 15). Built in the early 20th century to house various collections, for several years it sheltered nearly all its country's treasures – whether cultural or related to natural sciences – and then served for a long time as the National Library. The »books« exhibited here today are considered the most valuable art treasures in Iceland: the **originals of the medieval Saga manuscripts**.
➊ i Hverfisgata 15, daily 11am – 5pm; admission 700 ISK

National Theatre

The next house on Hverfisgata is the National Theatre, built in the late 1920s. The Art Déco influenced façade is a precursor of those basalt formations cast in concrete which **Guðjón Samúelsson** was to give full expression to on the Hallgrímskirkja.

The Living Art Museum

Visitors taking a stroll here should head back from the Hverfisgata onto the Laugavegur, to join one of the side streets, the Vatnsstígur. In late 2002 the Living Art Museum, **Nylistasafnið**, moved into its new premises here, often showing avant-garde exhibitions with works by the latest crop of Icelandic artists (Vatnsstígur 3; programme information online under: www.nylo.is).
➊ Vatnsstígur 3; Tue – Sun 12pm – 6pm, programme info at www.nylo.is

FROM TJÖRNIN TO THE HALLGRÍMSKIRKJA

Skóla-vörðuholt

Together with the Tjörnin to the west and the Laugavegur to the north, the hill of Skólavörðuholt towers above the historic city centre, with at its top the striking **Hallgrímskirkja**, the most conspicuous landmark in town. The rows of houses stretching up the hill above the lake are among the classier residential areas in Reykjavík. Many diplomatic representations – amongst them the British embassy at Laufásvegur 31 and the US embassy at no. 21 – can be found here, and Iceland's president has his official residence near the banks of the lake too.

Just beyond the National Gallery, visitors can discover art in a context that seems somewhat unusual at first glance: the well-known Hotel Holt (Bergstaðastræti 37). Seen from the outside, the hotel might display all the brutalist charm of prefab architecture, but inside it is a high-class hotel with equally classy cuisine, highly rated by gourmets. In its restaurant, bar, foyer and corridors, the Holt displays one of the best private art collections in the country, among them many landscape paintings and portrait sketches by Jóhannes S Kjarval. **Hotel Holt**

Between the National Gallery and the Hotel Holt, visitors pass the Volcano Show put together by nature filmmaker Villi Knudsen. This **institution of tourist entertainment** was set up by his father Ósvaldur. Over the past decades wherever a jet of lava has shot skywards in Iceland, Knudsen has quickly appeared with his camera, often circling the eruption site in a small plane. The mini cinema centre Red Rock at Hellusund 6a shows the constantly updated edits of the spectacular film material of volcanic eruptions. ***Volcano Show**
❶ showings up to 5 x daily, duration approx. 2 hrs; tel. 551 32 30

Visitors can't miss the Hallgrímskirkja, visible from all over the city and from far around. In 1986, after a good 40 years in construction, the church was finally consecrated. Reaching into the sky at the very top of the Skólavörðuhólt, the Hallgrímskirkja, with its striking profile and constantly blinking warning lights, is somewhat reminiscent of a space shuttle on its launch pad, even though Iceland's state architect **Guðjón Samúelsson** was thinking more of the basalt pillars of the volcanic regions when he drew up the plans. With its slim pillars, the light-filled interior draws on Gothic architecture, but as a modern interpretation rather than a copy. The central nave of the concrete church has extraordinary acoustics, a fitting theatre for the 5,275 pipes of the German-made 72-stop organ. In summer, there are lunchtime organ concerts on Thurs and Sat, as well as Sun evenings. The church's second attraction is the viewing platform in the nearly 75m/250-ft church tower, accessible by elevator (access: daily 10am – 6pm, in winter closed Mon). In front of the Hallgrímskirkja, look out for **Leifur Eiríksson**, the man who discovered America, cast in bronze on a granite plinth. Incidentally, created by the American sculptor A. S. Calder, the statue arrived in Iceland in 1930 as a pre- ***Hallgrímskirkja**

Insider Tip

Leifur Eriksson doesn't so much as glance at Hallgrimskirkja

sent from the US to celebrate 1,000 years since the foundation of the Althing.

❶ **Observation platform:** daily. 9am – 8pm, in the winter closed Mon, admission 400 ISK

Einar Jónsson Museum

Right next to the Hallgrímskirkja, an unusually severe-looking concrete building catches the eye too; this is the Listasafn Einars Jónssonar (Njarðargata), a museum and artists' residence designed by its long-term occupant Einar Jónsson (1874 – 1954), Iceland's first sculptor of note. The work was completed in 1923. Whilst Einar Jónsson portrayed several famous personalities, as shown by the statues in front of the Stjórnarráðshúsið and on the Austurvöllur, he only really achieved his breakthrough in 1901 with a sculpture of the outlaw Útlagar. Later, his work was increasingly informed by mythological and religious symbols; he felt very close to the Symbolists of his time. A good idea of Jónsson's own work can be gained in the **sculpture gardens** behind the museum.

❶ Njarðargata, June – mid-Sept Tues to Sun 2 – 5pm, mid-Sept. – May only Sat/Sun 2 – 5pm, closed Dec/Jan, admission 600 ISK; sculpture gardens always open, www.skulptur.is.

FROM TJÖRNIN INTO THE UNIVERSITY QUARTER

»Better classes«

In the first years of the 20th century, a row of villas was built for the »better classes« of the time above the western banks of the town pond. Today, these houses with their colourful corrugated iron façades along the Tjarnagata form a picturesque contrast to the Modernist grey concrete of the town hall. Running parallel a bit further up, the **Suðurgata** borders the old main cemetery of the city, not only the last resting place of many famous Icelanders, but also an idyllic spot with good views across the Tjörnin all the way to the Skólavörðuholt with the striking Hallgrímskirkja on top. At the roundabout, where the Suðurgata meets the Hringbraut, the city's most important east-west link, a despairing man looks over the traffic, a child on his arm, a lifeless woman across his shoulder, a dog at his feet: this is **Útlagar**, the sculpture by Einar Jónsson showing the outcast with his family after he had been declared an outlaw by the legal authorities of Old Iceland. Should he ever make it across the road, he will reach the extensive university quarter with the National Museum right opposite.

Þjóðminjasafnið Íslands, the National Museum (Suðurgata 41), registers all archaeological activities in the country, collects and preserves the finds and is responsible nationally for the restoration and preservation of nearly four dozen historic buildings, also for the many old grass sod farms and churches. The archive holds **tens of thousands of exhibits** from Viking times, the early settlements and later folk culture; however, only a part of it is on display in the museum. The collection is presented following the latest museum techniques, and a generously-sized café as well as a museum shop fill the ground floor.

**National Museum

● Suðurgata 41, May – 15 Sept daily 10am – 5pm, 16 Sept – April Tue – Sun 10am – 5pm, www.natmus.is.

The modern, bulky building on the other side of the Suðurgata is full of books – over a million volumes by now. Its fortress-like architecture has earned it the nickname of »**Book Castle**«. Opened in late 1994, the National Library (Þjóðarbókhladan) brought together under one roof the former state library and the university library.

National Library

Back on the other side of the Suðurgata lies the university's main building; dating from the late 1930s, it represents another major design by Guðjón Samúelsson. Today, some 6,000 students are enrolled in nine faculties at the Háskóli Íslands, formed in 1911 with the merger of the medicine, law and theological colleges.

Institute Árni Magnússon

The adjacent Árnagarður building houses the Institute Stofnun Árna Magnússonar, named after Árni Magnússon, who in the 17th century brought together most of the remaining **originals of the Icelandic sagas**, preserving them for posterity. Many of these are today in the possession of the Institute; a selection is exhibited in the Safnahúsið cultural centre.

Originals of the Icelandic sagas

Museum of Telecommuni-cations
Heading up the Sturlugata from the Árni Magnússon Institute to the Suðurgata, opposite the T-junction stands the former building of the »Reykjavík Radio« shipping broadcast station, called **Lofts-keytastöð**. For over half a century after its completion in 1918, it was from here that contact was maintained with Icelandic ships on the seas of the world. Today, its rooms house a display by the Fjarskip-tasafnið of the Icelandic Lands-síminn telephone company documenting telecommunications from its beginnings all the way into the mobile phone age. It is interesting to see how Iceland's geographic isolation was overcome: it was only in 1906 that a telegraph cable under the sea reached Seyðisfjörður in eastern Iceland from Scotland; after that, telephone and telegraph lines began to be put down in the country itself. By the 1960s, all populated areas were connected up. Today, Icelanders rank among the world's most dedicated users of all forms of modern communication; for example, no other country has a higher rate of mobile phones per capita.

? MARCO ◉ POLO INSIGHT

Wussten Sie schon

... that until 1986 the sparsely populated valleys of Iceland shared »communal lines«: all the farms in one valley were connected by one telephone cable, so that everybody was able to listen to the conversations of their neighbour.

❶ Tues, Thurs and Sun 11am–5pm, free admision.

IN REYKJAVÍK'S YOUNGER EAST

*Kjarvals-staðir
Still within walking distance of the city, nestling in the green spaces of the Miklatún lies the Kjarvalsstaðir (Flókagata) exhibition building, completed in 1973 as a further branch of the Listasafn Reykjavíkur Municipal Art Museum. The building is dedicated to **Jóhannes S Kjarval** (1885 – 1972), to this day Iceland's most prominent painter. Works from his oeuvre regularly fill one of the rooms. As Kjarval bequeathed his personal collection of paintings, drawings and sketches, as well as pieces from his artistic life – nearly 5,000 items – to the city of Reykjavík in 1968, the art museum is spoilt for choice. Kjarval lived in the capital from 1922 onwards, at least for the winters, while in the summer he would travel around Iceland looking for suitable subjects. The artist's fame and the admiration he inspires today still rest most of all on his images of the **people and landscapes of his native country**, which made him the painter of Iceland's nascent national identity in the first half of the 20th century.

❶ Flókagata, daily 10am–5pm, admission 1000 ISK,

Visitors driving eastpast the Kjarvalsstaðir on the major Miklabraut road linking west and east, will soon spot lying to the right the **Kringlan Shopping Center**, the centre of the so-called New City. Kringlan is one of those luxury malls that can be found in many large cities all over the world. Visitors who enjoy this kind of thing will find good shopping and eating opportunities here in around 140 shops and restaurants.

Luxury mall

In the east of Reykjavík, on the northern banks of the Elliðaár river above the small Arbæjarstífla dam, houses catch the eye that definitely don't match the modern architecture of the suburbs of Reykjavík: here grass sods, wooden planks tarred black and corrugated iron are the construction materials of choice. Today, nearly two dozen buildings from the 19th and early 20th centuries stand in the Árbæjarsafn open-air folk museum. Most were taken down from Reykjavík's Old Town and rebuilt again here; only the small grass sod church came from northern Iceland in 1959. It forms a pretty ensemble with the Árbær farmstead, built in several stages between 1880 and 1920 and the only building which has always stood on this site. A new exhibit on childhood and toys was opened in 2008. In many houses visitors can watch demonstrations of **traditional trades and old-fashioned household chores**, or shop like in grandmother's day in the store near the entrance, with all the employees here doing their jobs in traditional costumes. The museum café in the Dillonshusið serves home-baked goods and at weekends usually a sumptuous buffet with coffee, for which Icelanders also like to come to the museum.

**Árbæjar-safn

Historic household: open-air museum

Insider Tip

❶ June – Aug Tues – Fri 10am – 5pm, 1650 ISK, www.arbaejarsafn.is.

Another green oasis of relaxation and sport fills the Laugardalur. Its warm springs, the Þvottalaugarnar, once bubbled profusely and were used in the early days of Reykjavík as public washing places. It was also from here that in 1928 the first hot water flowed through a pipeline into town. A reminder of those times is the monument of the washerwoman by Ásmundur Sveinsson in the middle of the park. Four attractions come together in the Laugardalur: in the Grasagarður Reykjavíkur, the Botanic Gardens, some 4,000 species of plant grow, including all of Iceland's indigenous varieties. Families with children like to head next door for the Húsdyragardurinn petting zoo, containing all the mammals, wild or domesticated, that can be

Laugardalur sports and leisure park

Music from the North

It all started with Björk – at least, she was the first, along with her legendary band »Sugarcubes« and later as a solo artist to get noticed outside of her North Atlantic island. Her success made way for many musicians, all of whom have one thing in common: they try(ied) their luck in Reykjavík first.

Bands and Indie artists like **Sigur Rós, GusGus, Mammút, XXX Rottweiler** and **Ólafur Arnald**, which have long since been internationally established are only the peak of the unusually rich and diverse Icelandic music scene. Which, to be exact, is the same as the music scene in Reykjavík: anyone in Iceland who more or less knows how to hold an instrument correctly is attracted (at least in the summer) to the never sleeping capital, where he soon finds a few like-minded souls with whom he gets a band together. This is what makes the local music scene different from most of the others in the world: the music scene here is not divided up into different – in other places incompatible – scenes; here everyone plays with everyone and: it all works.

Unity in diversity

Whether rock or pop, hip-hop or punk, dance, trance or techno, classical or jazz: most Icelandic musicians don't make music for the drawer – that is, they leave it to someone else to classify their music in a certain style. Rather they often have several projects running at the same time, which to purist ears sound like complete opposites. They are not afraid to try something out either when they have the chance to collaborate with the most diverse kinds of musicians: Sigur Rós, for example, collaborate with a folk singer who puts Viking poems to music; organizers of a film music festival might organize a music festival with the same enthusiasm; even the public moves around without having blinkers on. A metal band sharing a concert with an electro project without splitting the audience down the middle – that probably only happens this naturally in Reykjavík. As small as the scene is, what with a national population of just about 320,000, that is how closely the musical »infrastructure« is meshed. This means that people help each other out – no matter if it's about a spontaneous concert in a record store, an improvised stage in a field, collaborating in a studio, a label functioning as a think tank like **Kitchen Motors** does, or about sales. Only the fewest bands can live off their music, but many of them dream of a career like Sigur

This side and left side: The whole world is a (sound) stage – this is especially true in Iceland

Rós, whose spherical soundscapes deeply-rooted in Icelandic culture made the quartet to the most successful Icelandic music export next to Björk.

At a glance

The **websites www.tonlist.is** and **www.icelandmusic.com** give a good overview over Reykjavík's music scene. The **music festival Iceland Airwaves**, which was first held in 1999 in a Reykjavík aeroplane hangar and where many international artists also perform, has become a classic. Buy tickets for this festival, which takes place in October, early: **www.icelandairwaves.is**. The film **Back Yard**, which is available on DVD gives an impression of the creative music scene in Reykjavíks; some of the country's best bands perform in the film.

found in Iceland, as well as the small **Fjölskyldugarðurinn family leisure park**, with all sorts of entertainment, rides and playing equipment for children. Slightly older children and teenagers prefer the Laugardalslaug, the largest open-air pool in town, featuring a huge slide, at the northern edge of the park, which also houses all the important sports facilities of Reykjavík, including Iceland's national stadium.

***Ásmundarsafn** A few metres west of the sports facilities, large sculptures grouped around an unusual building indicate the third branch of the Listasafn Reykjavíkur Municipal Art Museum, the Ásmundarsafn (Sigtún 5). What Jóhannes S Kjarval represents for painting, **Ásmundur Sveinsson** (1893 – 1982) represents for sculpture, and he also bequeathed the city of Reykjavík many of his works: a good 370 sculptures as well as the studio he planned and built himself in the 1940s with residence and exhibition hall – an extravagant building taking up forms of Arabic-Egyptian architecture. This is where nearly all the main works can be seen, at least as replicas, among them his famous sculptures of women from the 1930s, such as the Woman Churning Butter or the Water Carrier, but also some of his more abstract later works.

❶ Sigtún 5, May – Sept daily 10am – 4pm, Oct – April daily 1 – 4pm, admission 1650 ISK, www.artmuseum.is

Viðey Going north from Laugardalur it is a short walk to the Sundahöfn container port, where a boat leaves for Viðey Island from the pier several times a day. In the Middle Ages an important Augustinian monastery stood on the 1.7 sq km/0.6 sq-mile islet, while later important personalities resided on the island, among them »the father of Reykjavík« **Skúli Magnússon**, who is buried in the local church. Used as a restaurant today, the Villa Viðeyarstofa just above the island's pier was built for Magnússon in 1755 using designs by Nicolai Eigtved, most famous as the architect of the Amalienborg Palace royal residence in Copenhagen. In the cemetery next to the church, the writer **Gunnar Gunnarson** lies buried with his wife. Viðey has good hiking trails and paths for a leisurely

Weelcoming North Atlantic Insider Tip

Reykjavík can afford to heat the water of a small bay: **Ylströndin Nauthólsvík** is the name of the idyllic beach scene below the hot water tanks on Öskjuhlíð. The heaped up sand creates a real beach feeling, and while the sea hardly ever reaches temperatures of more than 12 °C/54°F, the water temperature in the bay doesn't sink much below 20 °C/68°F (at high tide maybe a bit cooler, at low tide warmer). A hot pot on the shore reaches a good 30 °C/86°F, another at the service center over 35 °C/95°F. (Mid-May – mid-Sept daily 10am – 8pm, free admission.)

The municipal art museum presents its collections in three places –
here in the Ásmundarsafn

stroll, and its nature is surprisingly undisturbed considering the proximity to the big city. In the western part a circular trail leads past secluded basalt pillars: this is a 1991 work of Land Art by Richard Serra called Afangar. Parts of Viðey are a bird conservation area, with access restricted during the breeding season. Further bird paradises can be found on the other islands off Reykjavík, small Akurey north of Seltjarnarnes and Lundey northeast of Viðey in particular, both with large populations of puffins. The birds can be found at their breeding grounds from May to July; after that they live on the open sea.

From October 9 to December 8 the Imagine Peace Tower on Viðey sends its beacon across the heavens, to be seen from far away. This monument to the British musician John Lennon was erected in 2007 by his widow Yoko Ono and it shines every year from Lennon's birthday to the anniversary of his death.

Imagine Peace Tower

The industrial area at the edge of the Sundahöfn is forever pushing further west, already stretching onto the headland of Laugarnes.

Museum Sigurjón Ólafsson

However, its western banks have managed to hang on to an artistic refuge: the Sigurjóns Ólafsson Safn (Laugarnestangi 70) honours the life and work of Sigurjón Ólafsson (1908 – 1982), an **exponent of spontaneous abstract sculpture**, well-known in Scandinavia mainly, but also in the US. Sigurjón was also one of the most important Icelandic portrait sculptors, often working with wood and other materials that he would find by the sea. It is no coincidence that the museum, which used to be his studio, is right on the water. Thanks to this location, the small museum café always offers great views, while the summer concerts, which are traditionally put on in the museum on Tuesday evenings, are a treat for both eyes and ears.

❶ Laugarnestangi 70, June – Aug Tues – Sun 1-5pm, otherwise Sat/Sun 2 – 5pm; closed Dec/Jan, admission 1000 ISK, www.lso.is

Höfði In one of his most famous works, Sigurjón Ólafsson in 1971 gave an abstract rendition of the pillars of the high seat that showed Ingólfur Arnarson the way into the Smoky Bay. The sculpture stands not far from the shore about halfway between Sundahöfn and the city centre right next to the Höfði, the house where guests of the Icelandic government are put up. This two-storey wooden house was built in 1909 for a French consul.

Change through rapprochement On 11 and 12 October 1986 Höfði suddenly found itself in the international spotlight when **Ronald Reagan, US President** at the time, and his Soviet counterpart, the **General Secretary of the Communist Party of the Soviet Union, Mikhail Gorbachev**, chose Reykjavík for their first summit, holding their talks here. What initially seemed like a failure, with hindsight marks the beginning of the end of the Cold War, thereby changing the world. It was here, amid the drizzling rain and stormy squalls that the ice between the two biggest world powers began to melt.

Sólfar The platform upon which the large, gleaming stainless steel sculpture Sólfar by **Jón Gunnar Árnasson** (1931 – 1989) looks ready to launch into the sky, has become a popular viewpoint on the coastal promenade. Even though the shape of the sculpture resembles a Viking boat, for the artist it represented more a spaceship for a voyage to the sun.

Laxness farmstead Outside Reykjavík, a little north of Mosfellsbær, the [36] turns off towards ▶Þingvellir. A few kilometres past the junction, in the Mosfellsdalur, the subsequent **Nobel Prize winner Halldór Laxness** spent his youth on the Laxness farm, nowadays a farm for riding holidays. Even though he had achieved fame and fortune, Laxness had the rather modest-looking Gljúfrasteinn residence built close by and lived there up to his death in 1998.

❶ **Museum,** daily 9am – 5pm, closed Mon

AROUND REYKJAVÍK

Kópavogur lies south of Reykjavík right along the city limits, so that the border can hardly be recognized. But the residents of Kópavogur still set great store in living in an independent city – not just any city, but the second-largest in Iceland. After all, Kópavogur has almost 30,000 residents – that's a lot on Iceland. So Reykjavík's neighbour city is also quite urban: Kópavogur has in »**Smáralind**« not only Iceland's largest shopping centre with cafés, restaurants, cinemas, galleries and around 80 shops. On the grounds of the centre stands **Smáratorg Tower**, Iceland's tallest building. At a height of more than 77m/250ft it is 3m/10ft taller than the Hallgrímskirkja in Reykjavík (Hagasmári 1, www.smaralind.is). Kòpavogur has another superlative as well: **Kopavógslaug**, one of Iceland's largest geothermally heated swimming pools (Borgarholtsbraut). But Reykjavík has passed its smaller neighbour on one point: the new concert hall Harpa puts the »**Salurinn**« concert hall in second place. But thanks to excellent acoustics it is still worth a visit (Hamraborg 6, www.salurinn.is). Near the concert hall there are two interesting museums: The museum **Gerðarsafn** has an extensive collection of works by Icelandic artists, like the sculptor Gerður Helgadóttir. And the **Natural History Museum** with its two collections, geological and zoological, focuses on the unique geological history of Iceland and on Iceland's fauna.

Gerðarsafn: Hamraborg 4, daily except for Mon 11am – 5pm, admission 500 ISK

Natural History Museum: Hamraborg 6a, Mon – Thu 10am – 7pm, Fri 11am – 5pm, Sat 1pm – 5pm, closed Sun

Kópavogur *(margin)*

> **!** MARCO POLO TIP
>
> *City of winter sports* — **Insider Tip**
>
> Within a radius of 25 km/15 miles around Reykjavik, there are three skiing areas to choose from: Skálafell at the eastern edge of the Esja Massif as well as Bláföll and Hamragil, both only a few kilometres off the Ring Road towards southern Iceland. When skiing is possible, buses link the BSÍ bus station (Vatnsmyrarvegur) with all three. For more information, contact Tourist Information.

Seltjarnarnes borders Reykjavík to the west and lies on an eponymous peninsula with the lighthouse **Grótta** at the extreme end; it is popular with fans of romantic sunsets.

Not far lies the stone house **Nesstofa**, which was built in the 18th century for Bjarni Pálsson, a pioneer in Iceland's health system. Today it houses a museum of medical history, which displays the country's first chemist shop as well as medical instruments from various periods.

Museum of Medical History: in the summer daily 1pm – 5pm

Seltjarnarnes *(margin)*

Pleasant Warmth from the Ground

On Öskjuhlid Hill the futuristic architectural work of art named »Perlan«, whichbegan operation in 1991, thrones over Reykjavík.   Six tanks are arranged around a glass dome; up to a few years ago the tanks held thermal water.

❶ daily from 10am, clsoing times vary, www.perlan.is

❶ Saga Museum
One of the tanks now houses a museum, whose initiators took it upon themselves to display the history of Iceland from the first settlement until the Reformation (April – Sept. daily 10am – 6pm, Oct. until March daily 12pm – 5pm admission: adults 2000 ISK, children 800 ISK, info: http://saga-museum.is).

❷ Hot water tanks
In the past each tank held four million litres (more than one million U.S. gallons) of clean thermal water at up to 85°C/185°F, which was used in the winter to heat (e.g. heating pedestrian walksways in the city).

Good view included

❸ Steel supports
Depending on the season cold or warm water circulates through the steel supports and keeps the temperature in the building constant. »Perlan« – »the pearl« – is what Icelanders proudly call this symbiosis of pragmatism and science.

❹ Restaurant »Perlan«
The revolving restaurant in the glass dome remains Iceland's number one gourmet temple.

Form and function are combined here to a practical total work of art

Sauðárkrókur

INFORMATION
Sauðárkrókur
Skagfirðingabraut 21
Tel. 455 61 61
www.northwest.is

Hólar
In the agricultural college
Tel. 455 63 00
www.holar.is

TRIPS
Boat trips to Drangey island
from Sauðárkrókur, Hofsós or Reykir
Tel. 8 21 00 90

Highland drives
From Varmahlíð via the [752] and the
[F 752] through the Vesturárdalur, access
to the Sprengisandur (only by jeep).
From Varmahlíð, driving west for
25km/15 miles the Kjölur Route turns
off the Ring Road. The first stretch of
the road is paved, and in favourable
conditions the whole road is negotiable
by normal saloon car.

LEISURE AND SPORTS
Rafting Insider Tip
The two glacier rivers Jökulsá Vestari
and Jökulsá Austari, with their source
south of Sauðárkrókur, lend themselves
superbly to rafting tours (Activity Tours,
Vegamot, Tel. 4 53 83 83).

WHERE TO EAT
Sauðárkrókur: Ólafshús ££
Aðalgata 15, tel. 453 64 54
It's hard to miss the blue house on the
main road. A restaurant with a long tradition, serving everything from pizza to
lobster.

Sauðárkrókur: Kaffi Krókur £/££
Aðalgata 16, tel. 453 62 99
The rival to the Ólafshús sits right across
the road. Good value in the daytime –
salads, pasta and soups – but markedly
more expensive in the evening. Live music at weekends.

ACCOMMODATION
Sauðárkrókur: Hótel Tindastóll £££
Lindargata 3
Tel. 453 50 02
Understatement is the trademark of the
Hótel Tindastóll in Sauðárkrókur. Only
from the outside however, as the »inner
qualities« are probably unrivalled in Iceland. The old timber-framed house,
where the first hotel in Iceland was
opened in 1884, has just ten double
rooms. They are all furnished in a different way, skilfully integrating the comforts of a high-end hotel without
destroying the antique-retro charm of
the house.

Sauðárkrókur: Hótel Mikligardur ££
Sæmundarhlíð
Tel. 4 53 68 80
www.mikligardur.is
Summer hotel in a boarding school with
65 comfortable rooms with shower. In a
quiet, central location.

Hólar £
Hjaltadal, Tel. 455 63 33
Holiday cottages and apartments, accommodation in the former school on
mattresses or in double rooms. Restaurant serving inexpensive snacks and
good Icelandic cuisine.

Minjahús
Sauðárkróks

The **heritage museum** shows all kinds of household items and musical instruments as well as an exhibition on Sauðárkrókur in the first half of the 20th century. Opening times: daily 2 – 6pm.

ⓘ i Aðalgata 16b, June – Aug daily 1pm – 9pm, admission 700 ISK

AROUND SAUÐÁRKRÓKUR

Drangey and
Málmey

In the fjord lie the islands of Drangey and Málmey, with the 180m/590-ft tuff rock of Drangey being the **emblem and landmark of the Skagafjörður**. The island used to be the residence of Grettir Ásmundarson (»Grettir the Strong«), the legendary Icelandic outlaw who was killed on Drangey in 1031. Today, in the early summer up to a million seabirds breed on the bird rock. For centuries, the island was a plentiful larder, where in one season up to 200,000 birds were caught and 24,000 eggs collected. For 50 years the **Earl of Drangey**, real name Jón Eiriksson, would collect eggs, while secured only by a rope, until he decided to take tourists onto the island on his boat and to tell them tales from his life. South of Drangey a single rock juts out of the water, called Kerlingin – »the Old Woman«. The rock is supposedly one of two trolls who led their cow across the fjord but were taken by surprise and petrified when the sun rose. The second troll, called Karlinn – »the Old Man« – and standing north of the island, was released from his tedious existence by an earthquake in 1755.

Reykir

Reykir is the last farmstead on the western shores of the bay, north of Sauðárkrókur at the foot of the Tindastóll mountain. Below the farm lies the flat **Reykjadiskur Peninsula**, where saga hero Grettir the Strong is said to have come ashore. A hot spring on the beach, south of the headland, bears the name of Grettislaug – »Grettir's Bath« – and has recently been recently restored as a place to bathe.

✳ GLAUMBÆR OPEN-AIR MUSEUM

Two to a bed

The buildings of this unique farmstead – 15km/9 miles south of Sauðárkrókur – were erected in the 18th and 19th centuries in the turf construction style. Along with its neighbouring church, Glaumbær is one of the most popular sights in Iceland. What is special about this farm is that all the furniture still dates from the 18th and 19th centuries too. The buildings of Glaumbær consist of thin slats of wood covered with thick layers of turf and roofed with thick sod for heat insulation. The frontages of the houses are clad with wood, pointing to the fact that the farm must have been a rich one. Because of their static qualities, turf houses could only be built relatively small, so the old Icelandic farms consisted of a **group of individual**

buildings, with those most often used linked by a central corridor. With a length of 20m/65ft, this corridor is unusually long in Glaumbær, linking nine individual houses. Two interior doors, in addition to the entrance door, protect the living rooms from the cold. Only the forge and the storage rooms have a separate entrance. The two guest rooms are located just past the entrance door, which is why it never really got properly warm there. Following on from the guest rooms, the kitchen also served as a smoking room for the **Hangikjöt** (smoked lamb meat), in addition to a few rooms used for storing provisions. Situated at the end of the corridor is the **baðstofa**, the largest room and living space of the farm where the farmer, his family and the labourers would work, eat and sleep. The baðstofa of Glaumbær has eleven beds, but as in those days there were often two to a bed, the farm was home to up to 22 people.

❶ Glaumbær: June–Sept daily 9am–6pm, admission 900 ISK

Standing in the cemetery of the neighbouring church is a small sculpture by Àsmundur Sveinsson showing Guðriður Þórbjarnardóttir with her son Snorri Þófinson, who was the first European to be born in America and the first American to die in Europe. Having in all likelihood had the first church in Glaumbær erected, he lies buried in the cemetery.

Sculpture by Àsmundur Sveinsson

There has been a simple country church in Víðimýri, a few kilometres south of Glaumbær, since as early as the 12th century, and many im-

Church of Víðimýri

Far away: a lone farm near Varmhalið, south of Sauðárkrókur

MARCO ⊕ POLO TIP

! *Icelandic horses for all* **Insider Tip**

Whether a short hack, day ride or an entire holiday on horseback, the area around Sauðárkrókur has a lot to offer horse lovers. For example, one option is to cross the highlands on the Kjölur Route in six days or, again in six days, ride to the Mývatn via the Sprengisandur highland track. When the sheep and horses are brought down from their summer pastures in September guests are welcome, and also in March to explore the wintry Iceland. An operator with lots of experience is **Hestasport Varmahlíð**, tel. 453 83 83, www. riding.is.

portant pastors, such as **Guðmundur Arason**, who later became bishop in Hólar, (1203 – 1237) have worked here. Today's church was erected in 1834 from driftwood from the coast of the Skagi peninsula and turf from the Víðimýri area. The church is one of the most beautiful and authentic examples of the traditional style of architecture; there are only six of this type of church left in Iceland. Most of the interior is original, with only the turf having been renewed in the meantime. The **altarpiece**, dating from 1616, was imported from Denmark. The small interior space is kept simple and almost entirely without decoration, so that even the beams and slats of the roof construction are visible. The narrow benches on the northern side used to be occupied by the women while the men had the southern side to themselves. The rich folk were allowed to sit at the front, while the poor had to sit at the back.

HÓLAR Í HJALTADALUR

Bishopric and educational centre

For seven centuries, little Hólar was the capital of northern Iceland, an **important bishopric and centre of education**. For a long time, wealth and power accumulated here, and by the first half of the 16th century every fourth farm in northern Iceland belonged to Hólar – over 350 in all. In addition, 36 bishops resided in Hólar, 23 of them Catholic and 13 Lutheran. Some of the best-known were Jón Ögmundsson (»the Holy«, 1106 – 1121), Guðmundur Arason (»the Good«, died after 1340), Jón Arason (1524 – 1550) and Guðmundur Þorláksson (1571 – 1627). Hólar – situated 25km/15 miles east of Sauðárkrókur – has been a bishop's see again since 1986.

Cathedral church and grass sod farm

The dominant building here is the cathedral; made of red sandstone and dedicated in 1763, today it has been restored to its original splendour. The protected grass sod building **Nýibær**, near the cathedral, dates from 1854 and was inhabited up to the mid-20th century. A marked one-hour history trail leads around the town; the historical background of the 14 stations en route is explained by a brochure available from the tourist office.

In the former stables of Hólar an exhibit explores the historical significance of the Icelandic farmers' most important helper, **Icelandic horses**.

Hólar

❶ June – mid Sept daily 10am – 6pm, mid Sept – Mai Mon – Thu 1pm – 4pm, admission 900 ISK

HOFSÓS

The small village of Hofsós on the eastern banks of the fjord extends on both sides of the Hofsá river and is one of the oldest trading places in the country. Due to the favourable position of the harbour, there was brisk trade here as early as the 16th century. Today, the community of Hofsós lives mainly off fishing and services, with the good museums bringing in tourism.

One of the oldest trading posts

The emigration centre of Hofsós, housed in several buildings in an attractive location on the water, illuminates the conditions in Iceland which led to a **mass emigration to America** (1870 to 1914). Visitors also learn a lot about the circumstances that the emigrants found in their new home country. Another role of the emigration centre is to support Americans of Icelandic heritage in tracing their ancestry.

Vestur-farasetrið

❶ Mid-June – early Sept daily 11am – 6pm, www.hofsos.is.

Grass sod farm Nýibær: well-protected against wind and weather

MARCO ⊕ POLO TIP

!

After a visit to the museum... Insider Tip

...the ideal place for a cup of coffee is the sunny terrace of the **Veitingastofan Sólvik**, right next to the Vesturfarasetrið, with a view across the sea. Inside, the blue wooden house is very snug and the little snacks, such as the fresh bread or the sweet waffles, are always tempting.

South of Hofsós, the estate of **Gröf** used to be one of the most important farms in the Skagafjörður area and is the birthplace of the poet, **Hallgrímur Pétursson**, who gave his name to the Hallgrímskirkja church in Reykjavík. Worth seeing is the small 17th-century grass sod church, which is one of the oldest churches in Iceland. The basalt columns on the beach south of Hofsós are also worth a short detour.

Seyðisfjörður

✳ L/M 4

Region: East Iceland
Population: 750

Visitors arriving by ship get their first impression of Iceland as they come into the Seyðisfjörður. They could not ask for a much more captivating introduction to the country, as the fjord presents itself in picture-book beauty with tiered layers of basalt and volcanic slag running up green slopes. Following a bend to the left, the town of Seyðisfjörður comes into view, with its colourful houses nestling beneath the peaks, which even in summer are still sprinkled with pockets of snow.

Charming start

On the day before the departure of the ferry, Seyðisfjörður is completely booked up and full of activity for a few hours after the arrival of the ship. But soon enough calm returns until the arrival of the next ferry, as most new arrivals head straight out, curious to see the rest of Iceland. In a way this is a shame, as it's worth spending a bit more time in Seyðisfjörður; the little town with the colourfully painted houses has a lot of charm.

Continuation worth seeing

Seyðisfjörður too owes its existence to the **herring boom** of the early 20th century, when Norwegian and Danish traders settled here. There are numerous houses still standing dating from this period, many of which, including the church, arrived as an assembly kit from Norway. This conspicuous light-blue church, where concerts are held in the summer on Wednesday evenings, used to be located further toward the outer end of the fjord, but after storm damage in 1922 it

Seyðisfjörður's »centre« with the blue church

Seyðisfjörður

INFORMATION
Austurvegur 42
Tel. 472 15 51, fax 472 13 15
www.sfk.is

FERRY TRANSPORT
The Norröna ferry runs all year round
from Seyðisfjörður via the Faroe Islands,
the Shetlands and Norway to Denmark.
In the summer arrival Thurs 7.30am, departure 10am.

EVENTS
From June to August visitors can take
advantage of the »Á Seyði« arts festival
with art exhibitions and concerts, while
the Norwegian Days run in mid-August.

WHERE TO EAT   Insider
Restaurant in Hótel Tip
Seyðisfjörður **££/£££**
Austurvegur 3, tel. 472 14 60
Although the pale blue house still carries
its old name of Hótel Snæfell in large
letters, it is impossible to miss. There is a
fish buffet on Wed and Sat.

Kaffi Lára **£/££**
Norðurgata 3, Tel. 4 72 17 03
Relaxed café in a former trading house

Café in the Hótel Aldan **££**
Norðurgata
Jón G Jónasson's old shop dating from
1920 now finds itself forming the reception area, café and restaurant of the Hotel Aldan. There is a lovely sun terrace,
although unfortunately right by the
road, and inside a touch of nostalgia.

WHERE TO STAY
Hótel Aldan **£££**
Oddagata 6
Tel. 472 12 77, www.hotelaldan.com
Faithfully restored 100-year-old Norwe-
gian wooden house, right in the centre
of town, with nine doubles.

Farfuglaheimili Hafaldan **£**
Ránargata 9, tel. 472 14 10
Cosy accommodation a few hundred
metres outside town in a former herring
station.

was rebuilt at its present location. The tourist office has a leaflet detailing the life story of nearly every house – good company for a stroll round the town.

Museum of Technology

The East Iceland Museum of Technology shows the history and development of telegraphy and medicine and is housed in the former residence of the Norwegian **Otte Wathne**, who played a major role in building up the local industry.

❶ Hafnargata 44, in the summer, daily 11am – 6pm

AROUND SEYÐISFJÖRÐUR

Good hiking opportunities

The area around Seyðisfjörður offers several opportunities for hikes, ranging from short trips to multi-day ventures. A simple **coastal walk** leads along the eastern side to Skálanes at the outlet of the fjord, 19km/12 miles away, where overnight accommodation can be found. East of Skálanes lies the **steep coast of Skálanesbjarg** with its bird colonies. Just past the end of the town, at Háubakkar on the western side of the fjord, the walk through the Vestdalur begins. The hike is relatively easy, but does ascend steeply up to the Vestdalsvatn (575m/1,890ft). In the past this path, leading on through the Gilsárdalur to the Lagarfljót lake, was an important postal and trading route (approx. 20km/12 miles). For longer tours, pick up a detailed hiking map from the tourist office.

Siglufjörður

✦ G 2

Region: Northwest Iceland
Population: 1300

Siglufjörður was discovered by the Norwegians – twice in fact! Around the year 900, the Vikings first came and settled here, and 1000 years later the Norwegians returned to transform this small village into the most important herring town in the world. A reminder of this is the award-winning herring museum.

It seems unlikely that anyone would have thought of settling on this unforgiving coast in the north of Iceland if it hadn't been for the huge shoals of herring at the beginning of the 20th century. The area is rough and inaccessible, offering practically no opportunities for agriculture. Even larger herds of sheep can't get much out of the steep, sparsely covered slopes. The wind is icy when blowing from the north, there is a lot of snow in the winter and transport links are

Herring Museum in Siglufjörður

tenuous. Thus, the next settlement, **Ólafsfjörður**, might only be 15 kilometres/9 miles away as the crow flies, but on the road, which has to make a sweeping detour inland, this turns into 60 kilometres/37 miles! A tunnel from Siglufjörður to Ólafsfjörður was opened in 2010.

When herring fishing started, the town was pervaded by a pioneering spirit, and Siglufjörður grew within 40 years from a small fishing village to the fifth-largest town in the country, with 3,000 inhabitants. Herring was salted and pickled in barrels at 23 catching stations, and whatever was not suitable for salting was turned into fish oil and flour in five boiling houses. Thus, Siglufjörður became one of the most important ports in the country, generating in its heyday around 20% of Icelandic exports. It must have been rather like the times of the great gold rush. The herring speculators came and went, some becoming rich, others losing everything. A few thousand seasonal workers ensured the town stayed lively. Good and bad herring summers alternated, with usually more good than bad. As the years went on, catching methods became more effective and yields higher and higher. Then all of a sudden, in 1969, the herring disappeared. The stocks had been over-fished, with dramatic consequences. Many factories had to close and many people left – the population fell by about half.

The herring boom

Siglufjörður

INFORMATION
In the Herring Museum
Tel. 467 16 04
www.sild.is

WHERE TO EAT
Bíó Café £
Aðalgata 30, Tel. 4 67 11 11
The only restaurant in town, centrally located and cosy.

WHERE TO STAY
Ólafsfjörður: Hótel Ólafsfjörður
££/£££
Bylgjubyggð 2
Tel. 466 24 00

www.brimnes.is
Situated right in the town centre, the hotel has comfortable en suite doubles with baths. Even more beautiful are the holiday cabins on the lake: completely furnished with one or two bedrooms, kitchen, bathroom – and their own boat outside the door.

Gistihúsið Hvanneyri £
Aðalgata 10
Tel. 4 67 15 06
www.hvanneyri.com
Guesthouse right in the town centre with 18 doubles and sleeping-bag accommodation.

Insider Tip

Today, the economic situation of the town seems to have stabilized. The largest fish boiling plant in the country produces fish flour and oil from capelin and herring, complemented by two shrimp cooperatives. The heydays of herring fishing are remembered by the »Herring Adventure Festival«, a major town celebration on the first weekend of August, with theatre, dance, music and, of course, the salting of herrings.

WHAT TO SEE IN SIGLUFJÖRÐUR

*Herring Museum

The Herring Museum (Síldarminjasafnið) is housed in the Roalds Barrack (Snorragate 15), which was built in 1907 and named after its builders Olav and Elias Roald from Ålesund in Norway, who had their herring salted in Siglufjörður for 20 years. The **Roald's Barracks** was one of the largest herring stations in Iceland, having four jetties and producing 30,000 barrels of herring per summer. The last herrings were salted here in 1968. The work was done on the ground floor, the office was on the first floor and the second floor was the living quarters for up to 50 seasonal workers. The award-winning museum has largely preserved the former partitioning of the barracks. The building next door houses a historical factory for fish flour and oil production. The dingy workshop gives a very realistic idea of the working conditions here. The third part of the herring museum, the **boat house**, is pretty new; housed in its own purpose-built building, it has many old fishing boats. The herring salting every Saturday at 3pm in front of the Roalds Barrack is another feature of this highly recommended museum.

❶ Snorragate 15, in summer daily 10am – 6pm, otherwise 1pm – 5pm, admission 1800 ISK, www.sild.is

While the area around Siglufjörður is ideal for hiking, there is not a lot of infrastructure in place; the tiny map given out by the tourist office is only suitable for initial orientation, and marked trails are the exception. One of the shorter tours runs up the gradual incline of the green **Hólsdalur**. At the end of the Hólsdalur, the Hólsskarð pass leads to the lonely Héðinsfjörður. It is possible to extend the circuit and return to Siglufjörður via another pass, the Hestskarð (min 2 days). Fairly easy in terms of orientation is the hike from the ski centre through the **Skarðalur** and via the 620m/just over 2,000-ft Siglufjarðarskarð pass to the [76] at Fljót (5 – 7 hrs).

Good hiking opportunities

✶✶ Snæfellsnes · Snæfellsjökull

✦ B/C 5

Region: West Iceland

On a clear day, the ice cap of the Snæfellsjökull can be made out from as far as Reykjavík, even though it is over 100km/60 miles away. Whether seen from afar or up close, it is difficult not to be captivated by the perfect glaciated cone of the Snæfellsjökull. Great literary figures such as Halldór Laxness and Jules Verne – whose »Journey to the Centre of the Earth« begins at the Snæfellsjökull – have been spellbound by the volcano at the far end of the Snæfellsnes peninsula, while mystics and ufologists have long suspected mysterious happenings here.

A FULL CIRCUIT

The highly rewarding route around the peninsula, with Borgarnes as the point of departure, is some 400km/250 miles long and offers a lot of typical Icelandic scenery: a sparsely populated southern coast, colourful towns with an Arctic character on the northern coast, sandy bays and steep shorelines, green meadows, lava fields practically bare of vegetation, and of course the high point, the snow-capped volcanic cone of the Snæfellsjökull. No wonder people have always been fasci-

✶✶Snæfells-jökull

nated by this spectacular landscape and that many sagas are set in this area. Halldór Laxness also chose this impressive backdrop for his novels Under the Glacier and World Light. Shrouded in myths and legends, the Snæfellsjökull is said to be a favourite landing place for UFOs, while some claim to sense a great energy emanating from the mountain, and count it among the strongest force fields on earth. To natural scientists, the 1,446m/4,744-ft Snæfellsjökull represents a **glacier-covered stratovolcano**, with at its summit a crater – one kilometre/0.6 miles in diameter whose steep walls plunge 200m/650-ft – which is open towards the west. In the last 10,000 years the volcano has erupted at least three times, the last time some 1,750 years ago. Despite being dormant for so long, the volcano is still not considered extinct. In 2001, 167 sq km/65 sq miles around the mountain were placed under protection as the Snæfellsjökull National Park. Among the highlights of the national park are the many fine lava formations and the spectacular coast, which may be explored on numerous hiking trails. Hellissandur has an information centre on the national park.

Information centre: Klettsbud 7, tel. 436 68 60, snaefellsjokull@ust.is

Snæfellsnes

INFORMATION
Stykkishólmur
Aðalgata 29 (Golf Club)
Tel. 4 33 81 20, www.stykkisholmur.is

Ólavsvik
Kirkjutun 2
Tel. 4 33 99 30
www.westiceland.is

FERRIES
In the summer, the Baldur car ferry runs twice daily (9am and 4pm) across the Breiðafjörður to the western fjords (from Stykkishólmur to Brjánslækur with a stop in Flatey). Booking essential (tel. 4 33 22 54) as only 20 cars fit onto the ferry (www.seatours.is).

LEISURE AND SPORTS
Whale watching in Stykkishólmur, Seatours, Smiðjustigur 3
Tel. 4 33 22 54
www.seatours.is

WHERE TO EAT
Restaurant in the Hótel Búðir £££/££££
On the southern coast
Accessible via the [574].
Tel. 435 67 00
The finest cuisine is celebrated in a hotel newly rebuilt following a fire, complemented by the beautiful location on the water with views of the Snæfellsjökull.

Stykkishólmur: Restaurant Fimm Fiskar ££/£££
Frúarstigur 1, tel. 4 36 16 00
As the sign with the five fishes at the door suggests, fish lovers will be very happy here.

Grundarfjörður: Krákan ££
Sæból 13 , tel. 4 38 69 99
The specialities of this somewhat hidden family restaurant are fish and lamb.

Stykkishólmur: Narfeyrarstofa ££
Aðalgata 3, tel. 438 11 19
www.narfeyrarstofa.is

This 100-year-old wooden house near the harbour is the very definition of cosiness. The café on the ground floor serves inexpensive dishes of the day, while in the evening the restaurant on the first floor offers good food, its enticing aromas wafting around outside the door – no shortage of garlic here.

Arnastapi: Restaurant and Bar Arnarbær £/££
Tel. 4 35 67 83
Picturesque restaurant in a house with a grass roof. Fresh fish, lamb and in summer on Sundays homemade cakes.

Fjöruhúsið £/££
Hellnar, Tel. 4 35 68 44, www.fjoruhusid.is
Tiny café in the harbour of Hellnar. On the wooden veranda enjoy the incomparable view of the cliffs and the sea as well as the excellent fish soup.

WHERE TO STAY
Grundarfjörður: Hótel Framnes ££
Nesvegur 6 – 8
Tel. 438 68 93, www.hotelframnes.is
A cosy retro ambience right next to the ocean. Good food, especially the homemade cakes. Various activities are organized by the hotel.

Ólafsvík: Hótel Ólafsvík ££
Tel. 436 16 50
https://www.facebook.com/Hringhotels-112698735441200/
18 well-equipped rooms with TV, 11 of which are en suite. With restaurant and swimming pool.

Stykkishólmur: _Insider Tip_ Farfuglaheimili Stykkishólmur £
Höfðagata 1
Tel. 438 10 95 or 8 61 25 17
50 beds, mostly in shared rooms. Guests

Homey atmosphere: restaurant and bar Arnarbær in Arnastapi

can use the house's own boat for bird-watching tours.

Grundarfjörður: Farfuglaheimili Grundarfjörður
Hlíðarvegur 15
Tel. 562 65 33
This old house right in the town centre has 21 beds, mostly in shared rooms.

Arnastapi: Ferðaþjónustan Snófell £
Tel. 435 67 83, www.snjofell.is
Rooms and sleeping-bag accommodation in an excellent spot between sea and volcano. The campsite also has a wonderful location, but is rather expensive considering the pretty basic facilities.

Eldborg   On the [54] from Borgarnes, just before the road leads across the Haffjarðará salmon river and turns off west to the Snæfellsnes peninsula, it runs through the lava field of **Eldborgarhraun**. Amidst the lava, the 112m/367-ft red »Fire Castle« (Eldborg) catches the eye, a classic lava ring which formed 5,000 to 8,000 years ago. The crater is best climbed from the southern side from the Snorrastaðir farm, and it is also possible to go around the crater rim.

Búðir   At the fork of the [54] to Ólafsvík and the [574] to the Snæfellsjökull is another lava flow worth seeing, the **Búðahraun**, which formed through the activities of the Búðaklettur crater. 88m/289ft high, the crater can be climbed via the historic Klettsgata path starting at the little church. The numerous lava cracks don't just host an unusual number of ferns – 130 different species of plant have been identified here. Under the lava flow lies the **Búðahellir** cave, about 40m/130ft long. The historic trading post of Búðir, inhabited since the time of the Settlement, is deserted today. The only remaining buildings are the small, black wooden church dating from 1848 and the hotel, rebuilt after a fire.

Arnarstapi   The small fishing village of Arnarstapi occupies an extremely scenic position on a green plateau between Snæfellsjökull and the steep coastline. To the east, the eye can see far across the sweeping bay of **Breiðavik** with its pretty sandy beach, while inland the conical 432m/1,417-ft Stapafell mountain looms into view. The picturesque harbour lies amidst a dramatic coast with imposing basalt cliffs, gnawed at by the waves for so long that now only stacks, arches and perforated rocks remain. This jagged coast extends west to the neighbouring village of Hellnar. In the summer, thousands of sea birds nest on the rocky ledges, including aggressive terns. Visible from afar, the main sight of Arnarstapi is the larger-than-life figure of Barður Snæfellsás made from lava rock.

Hellnar   A few kilometres further west a dead-end road leads to the neighbouring village of Hellnar, in a scenic seaside location. In the past, Hellnar was home to one of the largest fishing villages of the peninsula; today only a dozen people live in the tiny village, with its church in a picturesque cliff-top position. In recent times, Hellnar has turned into a **meeting place for mystics**, who use it as a base from which to search for the magic powers of the Snæfellsjökull.

Hikes between ocean and glacier   A 2.5km/1.5-mile waymarked trail leads from Arnarstapi along the coast to Hellnar. The reward at the end is the tiny **café in Fjöruhúsið**, awaiting its guests in a beautiful isolated position with a view of the cliffs. East of Arnarstapi, the [F 570] track branches off to the Snæfellsjökull and on to Ólafsvík. While the dirt road has steep gradients, in good conditions it is navigable by normal saloon car, while its spectacular views make it an outstanding hiking trail too. The highest point, the **Jökulháls Pass**, lies in the immediate vicinity of the glacier and is the starting point for two routes to the summit of the Snæfellsjökull.

On the way west from Hellnar several dead-end roads branch off the [574] towards the sea. One of them leads to the most southerly point of the peninsula, the lighthouse of Malarrif. Nearby, look out for the two striking rock pinnacles of **Lóndrangar**, where many sea birds breed. **Hellissandur** and Rif on the northern coast were major settlements as far back as 1700. The maritime museum of Hellissandur exhibits the Bliki, the oldest rowing boat in Iceland, which was built in 1826. Two reconstructed old fishing huts are also on show. The 412m/1350-ft **transmitter mast**, jutting up into the skies outside Hellisandur, was erected in 1963 and is the tallest structure in Western Europe, even beating the mast at Donington in the UK.

From Hellnar to Hellissandur

Fishing Museum: daily except Mon 9am – 12pm and 1pm – 6pm, Sat/Sun 1pm – 6pm

The rich fishing grounds off Ólafsvík were behind the establishment of a trading post here in the 17th century, which was also used by Danish merchants. Today the fishing fleet in the harbour is still at the economic heart of village life. The **Pakkhús**, a listed warehouse on the harbour

Ólafsvík

Formed by wind and weather: stone arch near Arnastapi on the southern coast of Snæfellsnes Peninsula

dating back to 1844, houses the tourist information and a maritime museum showing changing art exhibitions and fishing implements.
Pakkhús: in the summer daily 9am – 7pm

Grundar-fjörður
Due to the good natural harbour, trade and fishing flourished early in Grundarfjörður. At the start of the 19th century, many French fishermen came to the village, but they only stayed 60 years and took everything that would fit on a boat back to France with them. The links with France have not been cut completely though: for the past few years Grundarfjörður has had a twinning arrangement with Paimpol in Britanny. The symbol of this small and fairly inconspicuous village is the 436m/1,430-ft local mountain of **Kirkjufell** on a peninsula in the fjord. Climbing the distinctive mountain is fairly difficult, but taking a stroll around its base is rewarding and much easier. Climbing **Klakkur** (380m/1,247ft) to the northeast is well worthwhile for the beautiful views from the summit onto the Grundarfjörður. Allow around three hours to get to the top and back, with the path starting at the Suður Bár farm on the [576].

STYKKISHÓLMUR

Súgandisey
The Þórsnes Peninsula juts far out into the Breiðafjörður's world of little islands and skerries. Stykkishólmur, at its furthest point, is the fishing and trading centre of the region. Protected by the island of **Súgandisey**, the harbour was a busy trading post as early as the 16th century, and has always been the nerve centre of the town.

Norska Húsið
A beautiful view over Stykkishólmur with its harbour and colourful houses can be had from the plateau on top of Súgandisey Island, easily accessible via a causeway. Thanks to a few old, lovingly restored houses, the appearance of the town is fairly harmonious by Icelandic standards. The oldest two-storey building in Iceland, the Norska Húsið (Norwegian House), has been restored and is now used as a museum. It was built in 1832 by **Árni Thorlacius**, who in 1845 began making regular weather observations which were continued after his death. This made him the founder of the first weather station in Iceland. The Norwegian House hosts changing art exhibitions, the upper floor furnished as it would have been in Thorlacius' time, and the Galleri Lundi sells crafts.
❶ Hafnargata 5, June – Aug daily 11am – 5pm

Church
Stykkishólmur's modern church was consecrated in 1990. The striking white concrete building was designed by the architect **Jón Haraldsson** (1930 – 1989) and is often used for concerts, taking advantage of its excellent acoustics.

Lying south of Stykkishólmur, the mountain of **Helgafell** has been a   Helgafell
holy site since Saga times as the supposed burial place of the heroine
of the Laxdalssaga, Guðrún Ósvifurs-
dóttir. According to an old legend, anybody who climbs the mountain –
only 70m/230ft high – for the first
time is granted three wishes. However,
this requires climbing the mountain
without looking back or to either side,
and also without talking. Once on the
top of the hill, the wishes have to be
spoken facing east. If the wishes are
good ones and nobody overhears
them, they should be fulfilled. Those
who don't believe in this tradition can
at least enjoy the view. At the foot of

Futuristic: the church at Stykkishólmur

the Helgafell lies the farm of the same name, inhabited at the time of
the Settlement by the settler Þórólfur, as well as a small church.

Flatey, the largest of the roughly 3,000 islands in the Breiðafjörður,   Flatey
used to be a centre for the arts, mainly because of its **Augustinian
monastery**. Today, it is only inhabited in the summer. The quiet islet
is well worth a visit for its pretty wooden houses and diverse bird life.

Leave the peninsula at the north-eastern end and turn off onto the   Eiríksstaðir
[586] just before Búðardalur into Haukadalur Valley (not to be con-
fused with the valley with the same name in the south-west!) to get
to the **open-air museum** Eiríksstaðir. The seafarer and Viking chief
Erik the Red is supposed to have lived in a Viking long house like the
replica here. His son Leif Eriksson, the first European to set foot on
the American continent, was probably born here.
❶ June – September daily 9am – 6pm

★ # Sprengisandur

✦ G/H 4/5

Region: Highlands

**Depending on the points of departure and arrival, the Spreng-
isandur [F 26] is between 200 and 250km/125 and 155 miles
long, which makes it the longest of the Icelandic highland
tracks. While used since the settlement of the island as a link
between the north and the south of the country, it was always considered a difficult route due to its length and unpredictable weather.**

One of the most challenging highland routes

In 1933, a car first passed the Sprengisandur Route, although it took an entire week to do so. Now the route can be done in a day, but it still counts among the most challenging highlands tracks and, due to rivers without bridges, should only be attempted in an off-road vehicle. In some places orientation can be a bit tricky, but the biggest problem is the rivers with their constantly changing fords, which may swell considerably after rains or hot periods. The core of the Sprengisandur is the eponymous **highland desert between Hofsjökull and Vatnajökull**, with an average altitude of 750m/2,460ft and a length of some 70km/43 miles. Due to its barrenness and bleak landscapes, this desolate grey and rocky highland plateau is an impressive experience, while in bad weather its relentless dreariness can be

Sprengisandur

INFORMATION
Hrauneyjar Highland Center
Tel. 4 87 77 82, www.hrauneyjar.is

TOURS
Visitors who don't have a suitable four-wheel drive can still cross the Sprengisandur from Mývatn via Goðafoss, Nýidalur to Hrauneyjar and on to Landmannalaugar on Mon, Wed and Fri on the high-clearance buses (Tel. 5 80 54 00, www.re.is; departure 8.30am, arrival 6pm). For the return leg from Landmannalaugar to Mývatn, the buses run Tues, Thurs and Sun.

WHERE TO STAY
Nýidalur and Laugafell have simple sleeping-bag accommodation in the huts of the Icelandic Touring Association (www.fi.is/en). There is also the option of camping near the huts. Otherwise, all the places on the access roads have accommodation.

downright depressing. There are different access roads from the north to the Sprengisandur proper, the most difficult being via the [F 910], coming from the ▶Askja and joining the Sprengisandur at the **Tungnafellsjökull**. There are additional northern access roads from the Skagafjörður via the [F 752], which branches off the Ring Road at Varmahlíð, or from Eyjafjörður at ▶Akureyri via Hrafnagil and the [F 821]. The simplest way to get to the Sprengisandur from the north starts at the Goðafoss on the Ring Road.

Initially the [844], still well navigable here, follows the Bárðardalur before the highlands begin at the Mýri farm and the road becomes the [F 26] dirt road. A short and worthwhile detour leads to the **Al-deyarfoss**, surrounded by pretty basalt columns. Before reaching the Sprengisandur proper, there is the opportunity for another detour west to the Laugafell. Warm water bubbles to the surface here, transforming the otherwise barren highland desert into a small green oasis, and a hot pot looks inviting. On the way back to the main route [F 26], and on the Sprengisandur that follows, time and again there are spectacular views of the nearby glaciers of ▶Vatnajökull, Hofsjökull and Tungnafellsjökull. **Nýidalur**, which lies near the geographical centre of Iceland, marks roughly the halfway point of the highland crossing. The valley, at an altitude of around 800m/just over 2,600 feet, surprises with its astonishingly varied vegetation. This is a good place to take a longer stop for longer hikes to hot springs and the glacier tongues of the Tungnafellsjökull. The dirt road, in pretty bad condition, leads on south between the big glaciers, past the large lakes of Kvíslavatn, Þórisvatn and Hrauneyalón to the **Hrauneyjar highland service center**. Visitors with a bit more time on their hands should by all means take advantage of the detour from here via the [F 208] to ▶ Landmannalaugar.

The route

✶✶ Vatnajökull · Skaftafell
————————————— ✈ H/K 5-6
Region: Southeast Iceland

Meet the giant amongst the glaciers of Europe. With a surface area of around 8300 sq km/3200 sq miles it is 70 times bigger than the largest glacier in the Alps, the Aletsch Glacier, twice the size of the Malaspina Glacier in Alaska, and its ice is 1000m/3280-ft thick in places.

The Vatnajökull dominates and shapes the southeast of Iceland, in particular the stretch of coast between the Skeiðarársandur and the small town of ▶Höfn, an area which is the subject of this chapter. The

Europe's largest glacier

glacier's imposing ice caps, which even cover the **Hvannadals-hnúkur**, at 2,119m/6,952ft the highest mountain in Iceland, shape the landscape, and its lower reaches seem to creep frighteningly close to the settlements and Ring Road. The largest glacier in Europe dominates the region and its people through natural disasters too: glacier runs and volcanic eruptions underneath the ice cover have, in the past, regularly destroyed farms and arable land, roads and bridges.

Vatnajökull · Skaftafell

INFORMATION
Skaftafell National Park Visitor Centre
Fagurholsmyri, 2km/1.2 miles north of the Ring Road
Tel. 478 16 27
The information centre houses an exhibition on the glacier, sells hiking maps and souvenirs, and has a small supermarket and café. There is a large campsite here and daily bus connections from the visitor centre into the highlands and to Reykjavík.

GLACIER TOURS
Jeep, ski and snowmobile tours from the Jöklasel lodge (►p. 283).

WHERE TO STAY

Fosshotel Skaftafell ££/£££
Fagurholsmyri
Tel. 478 19 45
Unpretentious hotel standing by itself on the Ring Road, in the immediate vicinity of the national park. Friendly service, in good weather views of the glacier. Sleeping-bag accommodation also available.

Bölti £
To the west, above the campsite
Tel. 478 16 26
Guesthouse with cabins in beautiful location in national park territory. Doubles, sleeping-bag accommodation, cooking facilities.

Svinafell £
Oræfi
Tel. 478 17 65
Travellers finding the campsite at the visitor centre too full might prefer a quiet little meadow at Svinafell Farm a few kilometres further east. Another plus is the heated swimming pool right next door.

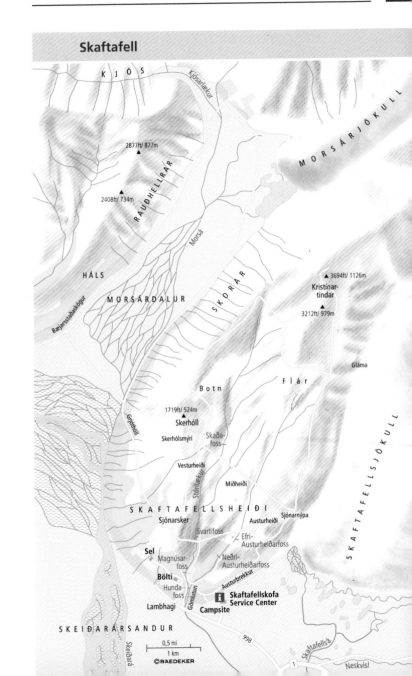

Skaftafell

K J Ó S

Kjósarlækur

2877ft/ 877m ▲

2408ft/ 734m ▲

R A U Ð H E L L R A R

Morsá

M O R S Á R J Ö K U L L

▲ 3694ft/ 1126m
Kristinar-
tindar
▲
3212ft/ 979m

H Á L S

M O R S Á R D A L U R

S K Ó R A R

Gláma

Bæjarstaðaskógur

B o t n

F l á r

1719ft/ 524m
▲
Skerhóll

Gríðhóll

Skerhólsmýri

Skaða-
foss

S K A F T A F E L L S J Ö K U L L

Vesturheiði

Stórilækur

Miðheiði

S K A F T A F E L L S H E I Ð I

Sjónarsker

Austurheiði

Sjónarnýpa

Svartifoss

Efri-
Austurheiðarfoss

Sel

Magnúsar-
foss

Neðri-
Austurheiðarfoss

Bölti

Hunda-
foss

Gömlutún

Austurbrekkur

ℹ️ Skaftafellskofa
Service Center

Campsite

Lambhagi

S K E I Ð A R Á R S A N D U R

Skeiðará

Gömlutún

0,5 mi

1 km

©BAEDEKER

998

Skaftafellsá

1

Neskvísl

THE SKEIÐARÁRSANDUR ALLUVIAL PLAIN

A land
shaped by
natural forces

Leaving the town of ►Kirkjubæjarklaustur (southwest of the Vatna-jökull) on the Ring Road going northeast, after some 30km/19 miles drivers will pass the farmstead of **Núpsstaður** (►p. 191), with its small 17th-century grass sod church, a listed monument. Núpsstaður is the last settlement before reaching the Skeiðarársandur alluvial plain, the piece of land which is most subjected to the elemental powers of the Vatnajökull: rivers of meltwater cross the sandur (glacial outwash plain) like countless veins, and glacier runs regularly flood the area.   Today, the bridges across the occasionally raging rivers Núpsvötn, Gýgjukvísl and Skeiðará withstand the flooding, whereas in the past they were repeatedly destroyed and reconstructed again. Small wonder given the mighty masses of water of the big **glacier runs**: in 1996, run-off quantities of up to 50,000 cubic metres per second were measured on their way to the sea. To put this into per-spective, the mightiest waterfall in Europe, the Rheinfall near Schaf-fhausen in Switzerland, reaches maximum quantities of 1100 cubic metres per second.

** SKAFTAFELL NATIONAL PARK

At the northeastern edge of the Skeiðarársandur, a cul-de-sac branch- **The first stop**
es off from the Ring Road to the campsite of Skaftafell National Park.
The **visitor centre** at the campsite should be the first point of contact,
both for visitors wanting to explore the national park on their own or
those looking to join a guided hiking tour – this is the place to get hiking maps, tips and recommendations for hikes, and the meeting point
for the two daily guided walks. There is also an interesting exhibition
on the origin of glaciers and volcanic eruptions.

Looking at the full extent of Skaftafell National Park (established in **A fraction of**
1967 and expanded twice since, now covering a surface area of 4,800 **the whole**
sq km/1,850 sq miles, today part of the Vatnajökull National Park), it
immediately becomes apparent that only a fraction of the protected
area, most of it covered by ice, can be explored on foot. This is the
part between the glacier tongues of **Skeiðarárjökull and Skaftafellsjökull**, which offers good access to ice-free hiking trails. Solitude is a rare commodity here though, as Skaftafell National Park is

one of the most popular sights in Iceland. The rule here is the same as everywhere: the longer and more strenuous the hike, the smaller the crowds.

Hikes As there are no roads in the national park – apart from the access road to the farms of Bölti and Hæðir – there is no other choice but to explore the charming landscape on foot. Apart from the one leading directly to the glacier tongue of the Skaftafellsjökull, all waymarked trails lead uphill at first from the campsite, and through a small, **idyllic birch forest**. Following the path northwest, it doesn't take long (about 45 mins from the campsite) to reach the Svartifoss, whose water plunges down over black basalt columns, which look like organ pipes. The trail running northeast leads to the viewpoints of **Sjónarnýpa** (45 mins from the campsite) and **Gláma** (2 hrs) above the glacier tongue of the Skaftafellsjökull, with views of the Öræfajökull volcano and the Hvannadalshnúkur on its northwestern rim. Continuing on this path, some 3.5 hours from the campsite hikers reach the **main summit of the Kristínartindar** (1,126m/3,694 ft). Although hard work, the ascent is manageable even for people with no great head for heights or experience in the high mountains. The tour, including an ascent of Kristínartindar and returning via the Skerhóll, the viewpoint of **Sjónarsker** and the Svartifoss (all in all 7 hrs walking time), is arguably the most beautiful in the national park. Be sure to get an early start, otherwise the Svartifoss is only reached in late afternoon when the light is fading. The wonderfully photogenic waterfall is then difficult to capture in all its glory. Another very long but recommended hike leads to the source of the Skeiðará glacier river.

> **! An icy experience** *Insider Tip*
>
> **MARCO ⊕ POLO TIP**
>
> Visitors not wanting to limit themselves to the ice-free zone of Skaftafell National Park should consider taking part in a **glacier tour**, in the most extreme case leading on to the summit of the Hvannadalshnúkur (information for interested guests at the visitor centre and/or from: **Icelandic Mountain Guides**, tel. 587 99 99). However, there is an easier way: where the dead-end road branches off the [1] towards the national park, look for a small airfield where sightseeing flights take off across the endless expanse of ice – an unforgettable experience (Atlansflug, tel. 8 99 25 32, www.atf.is)!

THROUGH THE ÖRÆFI TO THE JÖKULSÁRLON

»Wasteland« The year is 1362: the Hnappafellsjökull erupts, destroying at least 24 farmsteads and the surrounding agricultural land between the **Skeiðará** river to the west and the **Breiðamerkursandur** to the east. The local farmers lose their livelihoods. Subsequently, new farmsteads are established, but these are destroyed again by a second eruption in 1727. From that time on, the benighted land is called Öræfi – meaning something like a barren area, wasteland, desert – while the name of the destructive glacier volcano is changed from Hnappafellsjökull to **Öræfajökull**, »wasteland glacier«. Today, the area southeast of Skaftafell serves as a nesting ground for numerous species of bird, among them skuas, a type of predatory Arctic gull.

Offshore from the outwash plains of the mainland, the island peninsula of Ingólfshöfði offers ideal breeding conditions for numerous species of

bird. Being hardly separated from the mainland, Ingólfshöfði is more of a headland than an island proper and has only one building, a lighthouse. **Ingólfur Arnarson**, who began the permanent settlement of Iceland in the 9th century, supposedly spent his first winter on the island that bears his name. A monument commemorates his stay here. Anyone wanting to take a trip to Ingólfshöfði should contact the farmer of the Hofsnes estate where the [988] turns off the Ring Road. Einar Sigurðsson uses a tractor and hay wagon to lead visitors through the mud flats onto the island (tel. 899 64 88).
Excursion: Tel. 8 94 08 94, price 4000 ISK

The Ring Road heads northeast from here across the gravel plain of **Breiðamerkursandur**. Emerging unexpectedly to the left are the icebergs of the Jökulsárlón, looming majestically out of the water. Even though there are two more iceberg lakes in the immediate vicinity, Breiðárlón and Stemmulón, it is only the Jökulsárlón that attracts tourists. This is probably due to its position – right on the Ring Road between the glacier tongue of the **Breiðamerkurjökull** and the sea – and the convenient access to the lake: simply pull in at the parking area near the water's edge and enjoy the breathtaking views of the bizarrely shaped blocks of ice on the water with the glacier in the background. The bewitching beauty of the **glacier lagoon** works its magic whether on a clear day or in fog. Visitors wanting to get a close-up of the ice blocks can take part in a boat trip on the lake. However, as well as the icebergs, **seals** are also often visible here, making the Jökulsárlón in high season anything but a quiet place.
Boat trip: Tel. 4 78 21 22, www.glacierlagoon.com

*Jökulsárlón

At the southern edge of Vatnajökull, between Skaftafell National Park and Höfn: »glacier river lagoon« …

Jöklasel lodge

30km/19 miles northeast of the Jökulsárlón, the [F 985] track turns off the Ring Road to lead uphill to the **Jöklasel** lodge at the edge of the Vatnajökull. This route requires an off-road vehicle. In 1991 the mountain lodge with facilities and overnight accommodation was built at an altitude of 840m/2,750ft right on the edge of the glacier. It is a base for **jeep, ski and snowmobile** tours onto the endless ice, which can be booked on-site or by contacting Glacier Jeeps. Clients can be picked up on request at the junction of the [F 985] with the Ring Road and taken to the lodge. Otherwise it is possible to reach the lodge using the no. 15 and 17 buses of the Austurleið bus company from Skaftafell, Jökulsárlón, Smyrlabjörg or Höfn.

Tours: Glacier Jeeps, tel. 4 78 10 00, www.glacierjeeps.is
Reykjavík Excursions: Tel. 5 80 54 00, www.re.is

Vestmannaeyjar

✳ E 8

Region: South Iceland
Population: 4100

Two events brought the Westman Islands worldwide fame: the volcanic eruption of 1973, which nearly rendered the main island uninhabitable, and the 1998 arrival of the killer whale Keiko, protagonist of the »Free Willy« film. Otherwise, life on the archipelago is rather quiet, apart from the screeching of millions of sea birds nesting on the rocks off the southern coast of Iceland each summer.

... is what the name Jökulsárlón means. Iceland's deepest lake (248m/818ft) is also its largest lake.

The Westman Islands consist of 30 rocky crags, skerries and islands, scattered across 1,000 sq km/386 sq miles off the southern coast of Iceland. Only the largest island, Heimaey, is inhabited. To be precise, the rocks plunging dramatically into the sea are not exactly uninhabited either, as in the summer **millions of seabirds** nest there, and Heimaey is also home to far more birds than people. From a geological point of view, the islands are all recent, as there has been underwater volcanic activity off the southern coast of Iceland for hundreds of thousands of years, while the first islets only started surfacing some 10,000 years ago. Most of them were only formed around 5,000 years ago, following eruptions of the volcanic fissure which runs 30km/19 miles from southwest to northeast along the ocean floor.

Heimaey

Following an underground volcanic eruption that started in 1963 at a depth of 130m/425ft and continued until 1967, a new island soon emerged southwest of Heimaey. This new island was named after the Nordic fire giant Surtur, which according to the Edda comes from the south to set fire to the world. The islet grew continuously and by the end of the eruptions had reached a size of 2.8 sq km/just over one square mile. However, as fast as it had emerged from the sea, so the sea reclaimed it piece by piece, so that today **Surtsey** (UNESCO World Heritage site since 2008) is only about half its original size. The only people to be allowed onto the southernmost island of the archipelago are the scientists who have set up a research station here. Surtsey offers biologists the unique opportunity to research the establishment of plants on an entirely barren rock in the middle of the ocean.

The Nordic fire giant

Evacuating an entire island At 2 am on 23 January 1973, without any warning, a roughly 2km/1.2-mile long fissure opened at the **Helgafell**, sending enormous red fountains of lava into the night sky. Shortly afterwards a stream of incandescent lava began rolling inexorably towards the capital of the island. Luckily all the fishing boats had stayed in the harbour that night due to a storm, so evacuation could start immediately. Within a few hours, everybody had left the island. Over the following days, the whole of Heimaey was engulfed in black ash as the lava wall, up to 160m/525ft high, buried one house after another and threatened to make the entrance to the harbour impassable. As the **loss of the harbour** would have taken away the island's livelihood, there were frantic attempts to come up with plans to safeguard it. By using massive pumps, the hot lava flow was cooled down with cold seawater to the extent that it ground to a halt and the harbour was saved. When the eruptions came to an end in July, the island had grown by 2.2 sq km/over 0.8 sq miles, but some 400 houses, a third of the town, lay buried under the lava. Despite this, around 2,000 of the 5,300 evacuees returned to Heimaey that summer.

300 houses on Heimaey disappeared unter the lava after the breakout of the volcano

Vestmannaeyjar

INFORMATION
At the harbour, Básaskersbryggja
Tel. 481 35 55
www.vestmannaeyjar.is

GETTING THERE
The Herjólfur ferry runs daily between
Bakki on the southern coast of Iceland
and Heimaey, taking 30 minutes
Tel. 481 28 00, www.herjolfur.is

TOURS
Viking Tours offer sightseeing tours,
boat trips, bird and whale watching, as
well as deep-sea fishing. Suðurgerði 4,
Vestmannaeyjar, tel. 488 48 84, https://
vikingtours.is.

EVENTS
On the first weekend of July, there is a
feast in memory of the end of the volcanic eruptions. The biggest festival
takes place in early August: the Þjóðhátíð in the Herjólfsdalur commemorat-
ing the introduction of the 1874 constitution.

WHERE TO EAT
Restaurant Fjólan ££/£££
Vestmannabraut 28, Tel. 4 81 36 63
The restaurant on the ground floor of
Hotel Þórshamar is large and bright, but
not very comfortable. But the »catch of
the day« is fresh from boat to table.

Café Maria £
Skólavegur 5
Tel. 4 81 31 60
Restaurant, café and pub. The menu
ranges from sandwiches via pizzas all
the way to fish and meat dishes, including puffin.

The new ferry connection from Bakki
to Heimaey shortenes the trip of
almost three hours to about half an
hour

WHERE TO STAY
Hótel Eyjar ££
Bárustígur 2
Tel. 481 36 36
www.hoteleyjar.eyjar.is
Modern, comfortable and bright apart-
ment hotel.

Gistiheimilið Árný £
Illugagata 7
Tel. 481 20 82 www.arny.is
Relatively large guesthouse with 30
beds, plus sleeping-bag accommodation. Modern and pleasant furnishings,
kitchen facilities, and generally a welcoming atmosphere.

WHAT TO SEE ON HEIMAEY

Kirkjubæjar-
hraun

On the largest (13.4 sq km/just over 5 sq miles) and only inhabited Westman island, traces of the 1973 eruption are everywhere still. The huge dark lava wall of the Kirkjubæjarhraun looms directly behind the colourful corrugated-iron houses.

A view from above, the best being from the 221m/725-ft summit of the Eldfell, gives an idea of the extent of the 1973 eruption, which covered a sixth of the island with fresh lava. Right in the centre of the town, the **Landakirkja**, dating from 1778 and one of the three oldest stone churches in Iceland, catches the eye. Because of its compact size, Heimaey can be explored on foot in a day. For large stretches a path runs along the coast, giving excellent puffin watching opportunities. The southern cape of **Stórhöfði**, the most southerly inhabited point of Iceland, is occupied by a weather station and a lighthouse.

Volcanic film
show

The documentary describes the eruption of 1973. Further films show the clean-up operation and the fresh start, as well as the **emergence of Surtsey Island**.

❶ Vestmannabraut/Heiðarvegur, tel. 481 10 45. Summer showings daily at 11am, 3.30 and 9pm

Natural
history
museum/
Aquarium

The museum (Heiðarvegur 12) shows native fish, stuffed birds and a collection of rocks and minerals.

❶ Heiðarvegur 12, May to mid-Sept daily 11am – 5pm, otherwise Sat/Sun 3 – 5pm.

Regional
museum

The museum centre (Byggðasafn, Ráðhúströð) consists of the heritage museum, showing many interesting exhibits on life on the Westman Islands, and the art gallery, which display works by Icelandic artists. The **Jóhannes Kjarval Collection** is particularly extensive.

❶ May – mid-Sept daily 11am – 5pm, otherwise Sat, Sun 3 – 5pm.

> **?** *Did you know ...*
>
> **MARCO POLO INSIGHT**
>
> ... that the islands' name stems from **five Irish slaves** who around the time of the Settlement killed the stepbrother of first settler Ingólfur Arnarson and then fled from Vík to one of the islands off the coast? But the murders didn't go unpunished for long and the slaves were soon killed. Since then, the group of islands has been named after the »Westmen«, as the Irish were called at the time.

To celebrate the thousandth anniversary of the Christianization of Iceland, in the summer of 2000 a **stave church** was given as a present by the Norwegian government. The simple building is the only stave church in Iceland and has been reconstructed fol-

No Happy End for the Film Star

The orca whale Keiko, protagonist of the film Free Willy, arrived on Heimaey in 1998 amidst the blaze of media attention reserved for a film star. At Klettsviks Bay harbour everything was prepared for him. Would he remember that as a youngster he had already swum in Icelandic waters?

Following his arrival, Keiko was cossetted and pampered, fed delicacies, and his every breath documented. The goal of a whole team of researchers was to get him used to a life of freedom – a venture that had never been attempted before. Keiko was not exactly young anymore; when he arrived in Iceland, he had spent 20 years in tiny concrete basins and performed all kinds of tricks for his audiences. But Keiko found it hard to leave his full-board bay and to look after himself on the open seas. Endless training sessions and countless »Ocean Walks« finally convinced him of the attractions of a free life.

Without a Chance

Eventually he swam to Norway, but didn't manage to live there without humans either; he died – far too early really – of a lung infection in December 2003. This marked the tragic failure of an experiment that had cost the Free Willy foundation many millions of dollars. This film star found no happy ending; for him a life of freedom was not to be.

Leap into freedom like the dream factory Hollywood imagine(d) it

Life on the Westman Islands like on the main island Heimaey has long since settled down again

lowing the example of the old church of Haltdalen in Norway. Visitors might be interested to see the remains of the 16th-century English fortification **Skansinn**, which represents the oldest part of town, and the oldest house in Heimaey, Landlyst.

★ Vík í Mýrdal

★ F 8

Region: South Iceland
Population: 300

Petrified trolls in the water, a church in a picturesque location on a hill in front of volcanic rocks covered with greenery, some colourful corrugated-iron houses and a great beach set against the backdrop of the Mýrdalsjökull – Vík í Mýrdal is a village with magnificent scenery.

The southernmost village in Iceland, Vík í Mýrdal is the only settlement on the coast without a harbour. This makes it one of the very few places in Iceland that doesn't rely on fishing for its livelihood; here, it is down to trade, services and tourism to fill the coffers. The best example is the Factory Shop on the main road. Inside, travellers will find everything that could broadly be termed a souvenir, plus of course a lot of wool, whether balls of the stuff or ready-knitted Icelandic jumpers. Another trump card for Vík is its location, with the

Black sand beach Vík i Mýrdal

striking **Reynisfjall** mountain in the immediate vicinity and its bizarrely eroded volcanic hills covered by lush green carpets. The 700 sq km/270 sq-mile Mýrdalsjökull with its glacier tongues and outwash is not far away either. Whilst the glacier is spectacular to look at, below the ice slumbers the **Katla**, a mighty caldera with a diameter of 10km/6 miles. In reality, the Katla has been quiet for far too long already, as the volcano becomes active every 40 to 80 years – and the last time was in 1918! Its eruptions are feared, as they melt massive amounts of glacier ice, causing vast quantities of water to pour across the entire coast south of the glacier.

WHAT TO SEE IN VÍK Í MÝRDAL

From the Ring Road, it is only a short distance by foot to the beach – whose fine black sand stretches for miles – with its raging surf and views of the dramatic coastline. In the summer, on the beach and in the meadows behind, one of the largest Icelandic colonies of breeding Arctic terns create an incredible racket and spectacle. According to Islands Magazine, the beach at Vík ranks among the ten most beautiful in the world. Visible from the beach are the landmarks of the town, the **Reynisdrangar**. Protruding up to 66m/216ft from the water, the rock pinnacles at the foot of the Reynisfjall are unmistakable, even from afar. Supposedly these too are petrified trolls that tried to pull a three-masted ship onto land, but again didn't quite get the job done in time and were caught off guard by the sun. The Skessudrangur rock pinnacle is said to be the petrified troll woman, Langhamar,

*Beaches and trolls

VÍK Í MÝRDAL

INFORMATION
In the Museum Bryðebúð
Víkurbraut 28
Tel. 487 13 95

WHERE TO EAT
Halldórskaffi £/££
Bryðebúð,
Víkurbraut 28
Tel. 487 13 95
Inside the museum there is a cosy café, while outside a few tables stand in the sunshine. The menu offers snacks such as pizza, soup of the day, burgers, coffee and cake.

WHERE TO STAY
Hótel Edda ££/£££
Tel. 444 48 40
www.hoteledda.is
All 21 rooms en suite and with TV, in a pretty hillside location. Those who prefer something a bit different can rent six small double cabins right on the rock

wall; the screeching of the breeding birds comes free of charge. Restaurant and golf course nearby.

Hotel Lundi ££
Víkurbraut 26
Tel. 487 12 12
This new hotel next to the museum has ten comfortable doubles. The old Hotel Lundi is now a guesthouse with simple and good-value sleeping-bag accommodation.

Hotel Dyrhólaey ££
Brekkur (9km/5.5 miles west of Vík)
Tel. 487 13 33, www.dyrholaey.is
New guesthouse with 37 rooms, all en suite. Nice location with views across the bay; open all year round.

Farfuglaheimili Vík í Mýrdal £
Suðurvikurvegur 5, Tel. 4 87 11 06
300m/some 330 yds from the main road, just above the town, with 36 beds.

the pinnacle furthest away from the coast is the three-master, while the one nearest to the coast is Landdrangur, the giant accompanying the female troll.

The church of Vík The old church of Vík used to stand in Höfðabrekka, east of the town centre. Having been destroyed in 1924 by a storm it was not rebuilt at the same site, even though there had been a church there since the 12th century. The modern 1934 church lies on a hill above the houses, giving good views over the town.

Bryðebúð The Bryðebúð Museum is housed in Vík's first trading house. Although it was built in 1831 on the Westman Islands, Danish merchant Bryðe had it brought from the islands to Vík in 1895. The museum shows old photographs from the region and exhibitions on natural life. It also has information on the around 100 stranded ships that were shipwrecked off the coast over the course of the last century.
❶ Víkurbraut 28, in summer daily 10am–1pm and 2.30 – 5pm.

Basalt columns by Garðar near Vík í Myrdal

AROUND VÍK Í MÝRDAL

A few kilometres west on the Ring Road lies the turn to Garðar. The **Garðar** tarmacked road goes around the **Reynisfjall** mountain and finally ends at a seafront car park. The black sand and pebble beach here is definitely worth seeing: to the right the striking rock of Cape Dyrhólaey, to the left the Reynisfjall with numerous large caves and a frontage of vertical basalt pillars. On its sea-facing side, the Reynisfjall is so steep and smooth that even the sea birds, content with tiny ledges, find very few places for nesting. From the beach, the Reynisdrangar can be seen again; from this perspective it looks like one of the trolls is sunk up to his empty eye sockets beneath the water, and that the other can only manage to poke its forefinger out of the waves.

After circumnavigating the Dyrhólaós lagoon in a wide sweep on the ***Dyrhólaey** Ring Road, the [218] turns off towards the most southerly point of Iceland, Cape Dyrhólaey. The 120m/394-ft Dyrhólaey rock owes its name (»Island with the Hill Door«) to a large archway on the southern point, tall enough for small boats to pass through. From the lighthouse on the cape the view reaches across the sea arch to the Reynisfjall and the Reynisdrangar.

! MARCO ⊕ POLO TIP

Insider Tip

Tenting at the end of the world

One of the most beautiful campgrounds on Iceland is located at the end of the road to Þakgil. It may only be a grassy area on a valley floor but the green volcanic mountains around it are simply fantastic. A natural cave with candle lighting and a stove for heat serves as a commons room. A small waterfall nearby and, via steep meadows, the local mountain or Mýrdalsjökull are good hiking destinations. (Tel. 8934889, www.thakgil.is)

On the other side, the black **outwash of the Mýrdalsjökull** stretch to the horizon. Sea birds nest on the steep cliffs here, and it is particularly easy to see the dozens of puffins sitting on the ledges right underneath the cliff edge.

5km/3 miles east of Vík, the [214] turns off towards Þakgil and soon becomes a track, which is however passable by normal saloon car. The route leads through a **picture-book volcanic landscape** with bizarrely eroded volcanic rocks, often with a green cover, that could all be petrified trolls – after looking at them long and hard enough. The 14km/8.7-mile detour to the end of the road leads to a fairy-tale landscape at the foot of the Mýrdalsjökull.

Hjörleifshöfði In its isolated position, the striking 221m/725-ft island of tuff rock on the southwesterly part of the **Mýrdalssandur** can be seen from the Ring Road. It was formed in an interglacial period during an underwater eruption. Up to the 14th century, it was still surrounded by the sea, but afterwards cut off by alluvial sands from the glacier runs of the Katla. The rocky outcrop is named after Hjörleifur, the stepbrother of Ingólfur Arnarson, murdered by his slaves a year after arriving in Iceland. A track runs from the main road to the mountain, from where a hiking trail takes about an hour to reach the summit. It is also possible to circumnavigate the mountain on foot.

Vopnafjörður

⊹ L 3

Region: East Iceland
Population: 700

When the Danish king Haraldur Guttormsson was considering conquering Iceland, he sent north on a reconnaissance mission a sorcerer with the extraordinary gift of being able to turn himself into a whale. When the sorcerer wanted to land at Vopnafjörður, he was prevented from doing so by a dragon, thus thwarting the king of the Danes' plans for conquest. This is why Vopnafjörður's coat-of-arms bears a dragon.

Situated on the fjord of the same name, Vopnafjörður lies on the eastern bank of the Kolbeinstangi headland and served as an early trading post. A proper settlement was only established here in the late 19th century. The first settler was **Eyvindur Vopni**, who claimed the land here and built the Krossavík farm.

To both sides of the rather sprawling town, with its conspicuously colourful, well-cared for houses, lie fine wide sandy beaches. Kaupvangur, the house where trading goods were once stored, has since its renovation been used as a café, for tourist information and exhibitions.

WHAT TO SEE AROUND VOPNAFJÖRÐUR

The grass sod farm in the Hofsárdalur, southwest of Vopnafjörður, counts among the most beautiful and imposing in Iceland. For 500 years, up to 1966, the farmstead was inhabited by the same wealthy

Vopnafjörður

INFORMATION
Hafnarbyggd 4a
Tel. 473 13 31

WHERE TO STAY
Syðri Vík ££
Tel./fax 473 11 99

On a farm 8km/5 miles south of Vopnafjörður, two red, stand-alone holiday cottages with veranda are available for rent, one sleeping 5 people, the other 9. Fine views across the wide valley with green meadows and the fjord.

Island peace at Bustarfell, south of Vopnafjörður

family. As early as 1943, **Methúsalem Methúsalemsson** be-queathed the old buildings, some of which date back to the year 1770, to the state, on the condition that the six-gabled farmstead with 27 rooms be kept as a museum for posterity. With his extensive collection of old artefacts, Methúsalemsson laid the foundation for today's museum.

❶ **Bustarfell:** mid-June – mid-Aug daily 10am – 6pm

Hellisheiði From Vopnafjörður, the [917] leads initially along the eastern banks of the fjord, then leaves it to wind in hairpin bends up onto the barren high plain of Hellisheiði, lying at an altitude of 700m/2,300ft. While the gravel track is quite drivable, it does have a gradient of up to 14 % and no safety features. At the beginning it offers good views of the Vopnafjörður, and later onto the bay of Héraðsflói with the extensive river delta of the Jökulsá and the Lagarfljót, its large sedimentary tract visible far into the sea.

✱✱ Western Fjords

────────────────── ✦ A-D 1-4

Region: Western Fjords

Dozens of mighty fjords, framed by dark basalt mountains and gouged deeply by the glaciers of the last Ice Age, make the Westfjords a natural spectacle without equal. Here the solitude is almost boundless, as over the centuries the barren land and harsh climate have driven many to despair. On this westerly corner of Europe lies the Látrabjarg, the largest bird rock in the North Atlantic.

Iceland's hand Reaching out to sea like a many-fingered hand, the peninsula of the Western Fjords is only connected to the rest of Iceland by a narrow strip of land 10km/6 miles wide. Over 70 fjords, some large and wide, others narrow and long, pushing inland in a straight line or through tributaries, then again in a straight line, add up to a length of coastline of 2,100km/1,300 miles. The largest fjord, the **Ísafjarðardjúp**, practically divides the peninsula into two halves. Sitting proudly in the eastern half of the peninsula, the plateau glacier of Drangajökull can be seen far across the more northerly Westfjords. Since the melting of the ice cap of the Gláma plateau this is the only remaining glacier in the region. The coast at the foot of the **Drangajökull** is called Snæfjallas트rönd (»Snowy Mountain Coast«), as even in summer the snow fields here reach nearly down to the sea. Towering over the fjords are mighty table mountains with layers of basalt, ash and sediments, breaking off seawards with steep cliffs of up to 400m/over 1,300ft.

Western Fjords

INFORMATION
Ísafjörður
Aðalstræti 7
Tel. 4 50 80 60
www.westfjords.is

Hólmavík
In the community centre
Tel. 451 31 11

TOURS
The most comfortable way to experience the spectacular wilderness of Horn-strandir is on one of the organized tours from Ísafjörður. In the summer, a tour is available nearly every day, ranging from a short trip to Vigu Island to hikes lasting several days (for more information contact the Ísafjörður tourist office or check www.vesturferdir.is).

WHERE TO EAT
Hólmavík: Café Riis ££
Hafnarbraut 39
Tel. 451 35 67
Built in 1897 by the Danish merchant Richard Riis as a trading post, the green corrugated-iron house is the oldest in town. During the recent renovation a lot of care was taken to keep the original look. The use of wood contributes to the cosy feel; look out for the magic symbols decorating all the beams – and the good-value dish of the day.

Ísafjörður: Gamla Bakaríið £
Aðalstræti 24
Tel. 456 32 26
Small café with just a few tables inside and outside. Everything is homemade here, including the large selection of (cream) cakes and cookies.

Ísafjörður: Thai Koon £
Hafnarstræti 9-13
Tel. 456 01 23
The small Thai restaurant, a welcome respite from lamb and fish, closes at 9pm, the same time as the supermarket.

WHERE TO STAY *Insider Tip*
Reykjanes: Ferðaþjónustan Reykjanesi £/£££
Tel. 456 48 44
It takes some courage to want to convert a former school building, 17km/10 miles from the main road on a deserted penin-sula, into a hotel that supports its owner. The thermal spring bubbling out of the ground in Reykjanes that warms not just the hotel's hot pot, but also the seawater on the shore, could be the trump card that makes the project a success. Open all year round. With sauna, sleeping-bag accommodation, double rooms, petrol station, campsite and restaurant.

Ísafjörður: Hótel Ísafjörður £££
Silfurtorg 2
Tel. 456 41 11, www.hotelisafjordur.is
Modern 3-star hotel in the town centre. Fairly sober from the outside, but very comfortable inside.

Djúpavík: Hótel Djúpavík £/££
Tel. 451 40 37, www.djupavik.is
Arguably the most isolated hotel in Ice-land. Nice furnishings and good food.

Ísafjörður: Gamla Gistihúsið £/££
Mánagata 5
Tel. 456 41 46, www.gistihus.is
Small guesthouse with old-fashioned feel in a yellow corrugated-iron house with a red roof dating from 1897.

In part up to 400m/1300ft high, Látrabjarg in the West Fjords is the westernmost point of Europe

A hard life Today, only about 8,000 people live in the Western Fjords, a good third of them in and around **Ísafjörður**, while the entire eastern part, the coast of Hornstrandir, is completely devoid of people. Many abandoned farms bear witness to the difficulty of making a living and defying the loneliness out here in the Westfjords. The climate is even harder than in the rest of Iceland, with the wind, rain and fog taking its toll on the spirits. In the winter, snow more often than not makes the high plains impassable, and even in summer transport links are limited. Endless **gravel tracks** winding around every fjord arm, while the destination is only a few kilometres away as the crow flies, are part and parcel of any trip into the Western Fjords. Travellers who come prepared to accept this and with plenty of time on their hands will be sure to succumb to the fascination of a magnificent and wild primeval landscape, unlike any other in Europe.

WHAT TO SEE IN THE WESTERN FJORDS

A trip around A circumnavigation of the western fjords from Brjánslækur ferry port on the southern coast via Látrabjarg, Ísafjörður and Hólmavik up to the Hrútafjörður, covers some 600km/375 miles – without any major detours – and takes a lot of time because of the often serpentine gravel tracks.

As soon as the few cars have rolled off the Stykkishólmur ferry in Brjánslækur, absolute silence reigns again over the few buildings here. After only a few kilometres the Western Fjords begin to show their typical face with mighty mountains and many-fingered fjords. Going east, the [60] leads for just under 180km/112 miles along twelve narrow fjords to the **Gilsfjörður**, the slenderest point of the peninsula. The only places worth mentioning along the road that have some basic infrastructure and shopping options are Reykhólar and Króksfjarðarnes. Going west from Brjánslækur, the southern coast is no more densely populated; the landscape however is even more imposing. Rugged mountains, lonely sandy beaches, gently curving bays running for miles, bright dune landscapes, sand banks reaching into the fjords and a turquoise sea escort drivers to the westernmost point of Europe, the Látrabjarg. Along the way, at the **Patreksfjörður** near Hnjótur, is a privately operated aeronautical and folk museum. Up to his death, Egill Ólafsson collected all kinds of boats, aircraft parts and everyday items, including an old Russian Antonov biplane in good condition. The museum café is also well worth a visit.

Brjánslækur, Hnjótur

❶ **Museums:** in summer daily 10am – 6pm

The westernmost tip of Europe could not be more lonesome or spectacular. There is still a road up to the small lighthouse of Bjargtangi, and from the car park a path leads onto the cliffs and runs east along the edge for many miles. Látrabjarg is the largest bird rock in the North Atlantic, extending over 14km/nearly 9 miles, and reaching a height of up to 440m/1,440ft. On the rocky ledges of the vertical cliff nest an estimated **million seabirds** brood from May to July and create an almighty racket. Arranged on different levels are kittiwakes, razorbills, guillemots, Arctic terns and of course puffins, which are particularly easy to watch, as their breeding caves are situated at the very top near the edge. Off the coast near Bjargtangi lie the waters of Látraröst, one of the most feared shipping passages in Icelandic waters, where many ships have sunk over the years. Even if somebody were to survive the ship going down, getting them to safety over the rock face would be practically impossible.

**Látrabjarg

With their wide, deserted sandy beaches and towering mountain backdrops, the two major bays of Breiðavík and Látravík, on the way to the Látrabjarg, are among the most beautiful in Iceland. Unfortunately, the water is so cold here that even in bright sunshine hardly anyone dares to dip more than their feet into the sea.

Breiðavík, Látravík

Patreksfjörður, with its 700 inhabitants one of the largest settlements in the Western Fjords, owes its title to the Irish settlers naming it after Saint Patrick. Only with the construction of fishing huts in the late 19th century did the core of a town develop on two small peninsulas.

Patreksfjörður

! *Hot pots off the beaten track* Insider Tip

The tiny village of Tálknafjörður is not really enough to warrant the detour off the main road, but visitors looking for a soak in lonely hot pots should make the effort. After about 3km/1.9 miles' drive on the [617], look out for a path branching off to the right; just above the road await three hot pots of different temperatures.

While the high mountains in the background provide a **spectacular setting**, it stays pretty gloomy in winter, as the sun takes a long time to make it across the mountain range. Also, on several occasions avalanches have tumbled down above the town.

With 200 inhabitants, **Bíldudalur** on the Arnarfjörður has been a fishing and trading post since the 16th century. Some old trading houses from that time are still standing today. A worthwhile detour from Bíldudalur runs along the western shores of the Arnarfjörður along the bumpy [619] to the point of the headland at Selárdalur. In addition to the pretty, sandy beaches along the way, the main attractions in **Selárdalur** are the derelict artists' houses and the concrete sculptures by the farmer and self-taught artist Samúel Jónsson (1884 – 1969).

From Bíldudalur, the road winds its way along the fjord and then crosses the high plain of Dyjandisheiði, passing the 100m/330ft-high waterfall of **Dynjandi**. The best views of the **highest waterfall in the Westfjords** can be had from the small car park at its foot, which also makes a good campsite. Past the waterfall, the road returns to the fjord and soon crosses another high plain, the Hrafnseyrarheiði, before reaching Þingeyri, the oldest trading post of the region on the southern side of the Dýrafjörður. Here stands one of the oldest warehouses in Iceland, the Pakkhús, dating from the mid-18th century. A mountain with good views here is the Sandafell, 367m/1204ft high. The jeep track leading onto its summit also serves as a hiking path. 20km/12 miles past Þingeyri, the [624] turns off the main road. At Núpur, it's well worth a visit to the ornamental gardens of **Skrúður**. Laid out some 100 years ago by the pastor Sigtryggur Guðlaugsson, they are now, after a chequered history, in the possession of the town of Ísafjörður, which maintains them as a flowering treasure.

At Dynjandi Falls, the highest waterfall in the Western Fjords

ÍSAFJÖRÐUR

A spectacular sight

From a bird's eye view, Ísafjörður, which used to be called Eyrarhreppur, offers a spectacular sight, as many parts of the town lie on a sandbank reaching far out into the Skutulsfjörður. The surroundings are also worth seeing: behind the town the steep Eyrarfjall rock wall, over 700m/2,300ft high, and to the north the Ísafjarðardjúp, the largest of the Western Fjords.

Town of the Norwegians and Danes

Traders settled on the headland as early as 1569, and the place soon became the most important goods terminal of the Western Fjords. Around the mid-18th century, when huge quantities of cod were caught, dried and salted here, Ísafjörður became wealthy. During that time, Danish and Norwegian traders had grand houses built for themselves, some of which are still standing. At first glance Ísafjörður seems little different from the other towns, although the houses are maybe a bit more colourful. A closer inspection however reveals a **surprising architectural variety**, with all the building styles of the past 250 years represented in a very small area and, it seems, in a completely haphazard way. There are Danish merchants' houses in the Aðalstræti, the Faktorshúsið built by Norwegians, residences clad with colourful corrugated iron, the concrete buildings typical of Iceland, but also modern aluminium façades, all blended into an extremely varied townscape.

Maritime museum

The interesting regional and maritime museum is situated in the historic centre of **Neðstikaupstaðurs**, where the oldest house in Iceland, the Tjöruhúsið (1734) is resisting the ravages of time until today. It is a listed building, along with a few other contemporaneous houses in the neighbourhood.

● Mid-May – mid-Sept daily 10am – 5pm, admission 550 ISK

Vigur and Æðey

The two largest and still inhabited islands in the Ísafjarðardjúp are known for their diverse bird life and were important territorial possessions in early times. In the summer there are boat trips to Vigur, site of one of the few windmills in Iceland.

Bolungarvik

North of Ísafjörður lies the fishing village Bolungarvík. A visit to the fishing settlement **Ósvör** at the eastern end of town, which was converted into am open-air museum, is worthwhile. Go back in time in the grass-covered fishermen's huts to when rowboats were used for fishing. A walk to the bright orange lighthouse **Óshólaviti** from 1937 is also worthwhile. An affordable meal is available at »Einarshusið« (Hafnargata 41) in Bolungarvík; there is a seaman's pub in the basement.

Open-air museum: in summer daily 10am – 5pm, admission 700 ISK

South-east of Ísafjörður, in Súðavík, the Arctic fox centre has an ex- **Arctic fox**
hibit on the biology and history of the Arctic fox. The centre is in **centre**
Evardalur House in Súðavík. There is also a small café here, as well as
a souvenir shop and free internet access for visitors.

❶ in summer daily 10am – 16m, 1200 ISK, www.arcticfoxcenter.com

✳ STRANDIR

The Strandir coast on the western shore of Húnaflói Bay and the adjacent **Hornstrandir** nature reserve to the north count amongst the
loneliest and wildest landscapes in Iceland. Steeply sloping mountains on the coast as well as narrow bays and valleys at the end of the
fjords – which are relatively short with the exception of the Steingrímsfjörður and Reykjafjörður – characterize a landscape that bears

**The open-air museum Ósvör gives a good impression of the difficult
working life of Icelandic fishermen**

!

A warm bath in the North Atlantic   Insider Tip

Just before the [643] runs out at Fell, an unbelievable sight unfolds before the eyes: the Krossnes open-air swimming pool beckons for a warm swim in no-man's-land, a few metres from the ice-cold waters of the North Atlantic. Strange but true!

clear traces of the Ice Age. While this region was inhabited from the Settlement up to the mid-20th century, today the seabirds have the mighty cliffs entirely to themselves, and the **Arctic fox** can roam the interior without being disturbed. This vast, secluded area is popular with experienced wilderness hikers. There are a good number of hiking trails, most of them leading along the coast, but expeditions in Strandir require careful planning. The weather is unpredictable even in summer, with fog, rain and snow always a possibility and nowhere to take shelter or to stock up on food. Hikers should take tents and provisions for the entire tour. For large stretches there is not even a mobile phone signal for emergencies. Another problem is transport, particularly since the **boat service from Ísafjörður to Hornstrandir** was stopped; now the organized trips from Ísafjörður are about all there is. Overland there are two roads passing near the interesting hiking areas: the [635] at the eastern shores of the Ísafjarðardjúp and the [643] running up to a few kilometres past Gjögur on the western bank of Húnaflói Bay.

Hólmavík The settlement on the Steingrímsfjörður fjord, for the past 100 years or so a trading post and now the administrative centre of the region, is a good base for exploring the Strandir coast. In Hólmavík, also suffering from a declining population, look for the Icelandic Museum of Sorcery and Witchcraft, which gives a very visual account of the Icelandic **witch-hunt** of the 17th century, as well as covering more recent magic and folklore.

❶ **Museum:** June – mid-Aug daily 10am – 6pm, admission 680 ISK

Drangsnes This village on the northern shores of the Steingrímsfjörður, which was established in the 1930s, owes its name to a rock off the coast, which according to legend is supposed to be yet another **petrified troll**. In the summer boat tours run from here to Grímsey Island, with its puffin colony (for more information, contact the Bær III farm, tel. 451 32 41).

The former fishing village at the end of the Reykjafjörður was once a busy centre of herring fishing and fish processing. However, when the herring disappeared, Djúpavík's fortunes took a nosedive too. Today the place is virtually deserted in winter, with just a few tourists coming to stay in the local hotel in the summertime. Similarly, **Gjögur**, a few kilometres further north, was once a bustling community known for its shark fishing. A few more kilometres past the now abandoned village and the road ends; the only way to go further north from here is by boat or on foot.

*Djúpavík

** **Þingvellir**

⟡ D 6

Region: West Iceland

On the one hand, Þingvellir National Park protects a piece of Icelandic heritage – the historical assembly place of the world's oldest parliament – on the other a geological singularity: nowhere else in the world is the drifting apart of two continental plates as evident as here.

Located 40km/25 miles northeast of the Icelandic capital of Reykjavík, the Þingvellir National Park surrounds the northern tip of Þingvallavatn Lake. Measuring some 50 sq km/nearly 20 sq miles, the national park is the oldest in the country, established in 1928 following the American model. It is intended to not only preserve for the future a place of extraordinary importance to the Icelandic people, but also to make it accessible. Thus, the park features a modern **Edutainment Center**, tarmacked roads, a dense network of hiking trails, large camping areas, a hotel, a cafeteria and a few summer houses.

Good tourist infrastructure

THE VALLEY BETWEEN THE CONTINENTS

The core of the national park is a depression above the tectonic fault, which marks the rift zone of the American and Eurasian continental plates. This depression is bounded to the west and east by large fault fissures. The **Almannagjá** (All Men's Gorge) on the American side, more famous due to its historical importance, is easily accessible, but the less-known **Hrafnagjá** (Ravens' Gorge) on the European side is also easily visible from the roads to the east of the national park. The Almannagjá stretches over 7km/4.3 miles from the slopes of the Ármannsfell to the north right up to the Þingvallavatn, and the Hrafnagjá is not much shorter. The continental drift is noticeable in two measurable movements: every year, the Almannagjá and Hrafnagjá drift apart by some 8mm/0.2in (sometimes more), while

Two plates and a valley

Assembly of Free Men

Historic Þingvellir, the assembly field, lies in the west of Þingvellir National Park (UNESCO World Heritage site) at the foot of the Almannagjá. It was here in 930 that the free men of Iceland first convened for the Althing, the national assembly, which Iceland's modern day parliament claims to be directly descended from.

Until 1798, the **Althing** convened once a year at midsummer for a 14-day session in Þingvellir. Rapidly, the Althing developed into a complex system of legislative and judicial instruments for the young independent state. To be exact, Althing stands for the full assembly of free men, a body that played a role in the original Icelandic Free State, but then gave up its authority, along with the country's independence, in 1262. In the long run, the **Lögrétta** law committee turned out to be the more important and lasting body. Even after the king in Copenhagen had become an absolutist ruler in 1622, it still convened for 176 years in Þingvellir as a **judi**-

cial organ. Initially in the Lögrétta, the country's rich and powerful, the goðar and the bishops, were amongst their own. In the last years of the historical Althing, the circle of members was reduced to a handful of legal men who were effectively only able to proclaim law following Danish royal laws that had been decreed in far away Copenhagen.

Historic Milestones

Þingvellir is linked to many important dates in Icelandic history: this is where the decisions were taken to introduce Christianity in the year 1000, to establish a bishopric in Skálholt in 1056 and then a rival

Þingvellir National Park, UNESCO World Heritage site since 2004

one in Hólar in 1109. It was here in 1097 that the young but already influential church succeeded in introducing, for its own benefit, a tithe as the first tax in the country. Here, the Icelanders pledged allegiance to the Norwegian king in 1262, sealing the fate of their own nation. It was also here in 1271 that for the first time a **code of law**, no longer submitted by the Althing but by a legal commission under the aegis of the Norwegian king, was put to the vote. 1271 was also the last time that the old laws of the land were recited orally in front of the assembly.

Stronghold of National Identity

In the centuries under colonial rule the assemblies at Þingvellir proved themselves to be a stronghold of the Icelanders' national identity. Even when the nation no longer had any political clout, it was at least still able to make **appeals to the king**. Moreover, the Althing as an assembly had developed an important social function, becoming a mixture of public fair, market place, centre of trade, job exchange, national marriage market and a place for families to meet and catch up on news and gossip. According to Iceland's great cultural historian Sigurður Nordal, the assemblies in Þingvellir moulded the people of the island into an Icelandic nation. Also the fact that no dialects developed, even in the most remote parts of the country, is said to be due to the linguistic diffusion during the annual meetings in Þingvellir. Only when land subsidence in 1789 made a part of the old assembly place disappear into the Þingvallavatn did Þingvellir lose support. In 1798, the Althing moved to Reykjavík. With the last link to the old free state severed, it was completely abolished two years later – but against all

expectations, not for long. Intellectuals inspired by a romantic nationalism soon organized informal meetings in Þingvellir which harked back to the old Althing assemblies. By doing so, they hoped to keep alive a sense of **national identity**. Through the 19th century Iceland gradually gained more autonomy in a piecemeal fashion, and in 1845 the Althing convened again. Conservative forces within the independence movement would have preferred to see their parliament at historic Þingvellir, but the modernizers insisted on Reykjavík. Þingvellir however became the stage for major events moving the nation. It was here that the Icelanders celebrated 1000 years of the settlement of their country in 1874 and 1100 years in 1974. In 1944, the new republic was proclaimed on the Lögberg in front of 30,000 people, and in 1994 its 50th anniversary was marked with the biggest party that the country had ever seen. The traffic jam created that day by visitors coming into town for the occasion stretched from Þingvellir all the way back to Reykjavík city centre. Pope John Paul II had not been quite able to match these numbers when he celebrated an open-air Mass in front of a few hundred faithful during his visit to Iceland 5 years before.

Modest Remains

The original parliamentarians used natural features as far as possible. A small elevation served as the speakers platform, and when the legislative speaker recited laws, a rock wall provided the necessary acoustics. The course of the Öxará river was diverted to plunge into the Almannagjá Gorge, and to this day flows right past the original place where the assembly convened. In later years, a deep basin in the river was used for the **execution of divine judgements**: supposed female adulterers in particular were thrown into the ice-cold water with its dangerous current – drowning was seen as a sign of guilt.

With Þingvellir, history has created a place that for Icelanders has major national significance, but that features no historical buildings in the way visitors might expect to see elsewhere. The only physical reminders of the past are inconspicuous remains of the foundations of the so-called »búðir«, more flat earthen walls than groundworks. These simple huts made from stone and grass sod served delegations and also traders, as accommodation or sales booths. Only from the 17th century onwards were there assembly huts used for instance as a venue for the Lögrétta to convene. Most of the known foundations date from the last two centuries of the Althing convening in Þingvellir. Only two have been dated by archaeologists to the period of the first free state between the 10th and 13th centuries, for instance the Biskupshólar on the eastern banks of the Öxará below the small church; this was the residence of Iceland's bishops during the assemblies. The few buildings shaping the image of Þingvellir today may be among the most photographed in Iceland, but they are younger.

the bottom of the depression between them sinks on average half a centimetre/0.2 inches annually, and in extreme cases, such as during the **1789 earthquake**, by as much as half a metre/one and a half feet in ten days. Today, this ground lies a good 40m/130ft below the surrounding land, having been level with it until round 9000 years ago according to geologists.

Topped with thick vegetation, lava some 10,000 years old covers the low-lying terrain. In this protected location it is not only mosses – as well as the obligatory birch and willow shrubs – that thrive, but also a colourful spread of **wild flowers and berries**. And towards the end of the summer, the flora seems to want to show that North America is not only geologically close: this is the time when Þingvellir National Park seems to imitate the splendid colours of the fall foliage.

Protected plants flourish

Other than a national park manager, who doubles up as the pastor of Þingvellir church, nobody lives permanently in the park. It never gets too lonely though, as the holiday cottages around the Þingvallavatn lake are used in all seasons, and each year the national park sees around half a million visitors. It's a must-see for tourists from all over the world, an obligatory part of the protocol for guests of state, and the Icelanders love it too as one of the most popular destinations for a day trip in their own country.

Visitor magnet

WHAT TO SEE IN ÞINGVELLIR

Right next to the crossroads of the [36], [52] and [362], where the access road to the Þingvellir proper turns off the main road, the **information centre of the national park** reveals itself to be a mixture of information office, kiosk, cafeteria and reception for the campsites. Of the latter there are several around the information centre, as well as on the shore of the lake east of the historic Althing site. Opened in the summer of 2002 on the plateau above the Almannagjá, the **Edutainment Center with interactive multimedia technology** documents the history, natural history and geology of the national park and its historic sites, and tries to explain the most spectacular phenomena here. The centre may be reached either from the Althing site on foot through the Almannagjá, or by car from the access road via the [36] to the Hakið viewpoint.

Information and Edutainment Center

❶ April – Oct daily 9am – 4pm, free admission

Coming from Reykjavík, it makes sense to stop first at the Edutainment Center and to get an overview from the Hakið viewpoint right next to it. Visitors stand on the edge of the fault fissure of Alman-

Fascinating views from the Hakið

Þingvellir

INFORMATION
Þingvellir service centre
Tel. 482 26 60, www.thingvellir.is

WHERE TO EAT/STAY

Icelandair Hotel Hengill ££
Nesjavollum, Selfoss
Tel. 4 44 40 00
New hotel on Mount Hengill with 22
modern rooms, about 18km/10mi from
Þingvellir, near Lake Þingvallavatn. Most
of the rooms have a spectacular view of
the mountain panorama, but some also
of the nearby geothermal power station
Nesjavellir.

Camping £
Camping is only allowed in two places in
the national park: near Leirar (four
campgrounds: Fagrabrekka, Syðri-Leirar,
Hvanna brekka and Nyrðri-Leirar) and in
Vatnskot near the lake.

---

nagjá, looking down onto the historic sites of Þingvellir, to the right
the **Þingvallavatn** lake, ahead the wide depression of the Þingval-
lahraun lava field, thick with vegetation, and towards the north the
mountains on the edge of the highlands, with the eye-catching, near-
perfect shield volcano of Skjaldbreiður.

*Almannagjá
From the viewpoint a path leads through the Almannagjá down to the
assembly field proper. According to legend, the name – Almannagjá
translates as **All Men's Gorge** – derives from the fact that all the participants at the first Althing fitted into the gorge. Thus, the fascination
exerted by the gorge is founded in a historical event, although it is the
geology that first catches the eye. The trail through the Almannagjá
leads past the Lögberg, the »law rock«, which is marked by a flagpole.
This spot has been chosen even though historians are not quite sure
whether it is really the place where, at the time of the free state, the
speaker fulfilled his task by proclaiming from memory the country's
entire code of law to those gathered. From the Lögberg, paths lead
down to the plains along the river Öxará.

Öxará, the
sculpted river
Staying on the path through the Almannagjá, a bridge soon crosses
the Öxará. At the time of the original free state, the river had already
been artificially rerouted into the gorge in order to provide a better
supply of water for the assemblies; the natural river bed ran further
north. From the bridge, below lies the deep basin in the watercourse
that was used as the Drekkingarhylur, or **drowning pool**, mainly for
female adulterers – a reminder of Þingvellir's darker side. Further
north there is a good path, with steps to aid the ascent, leading up to
the waterfall of Öxaráfoss, where the Öxará plunges down into the
Almannagjá.

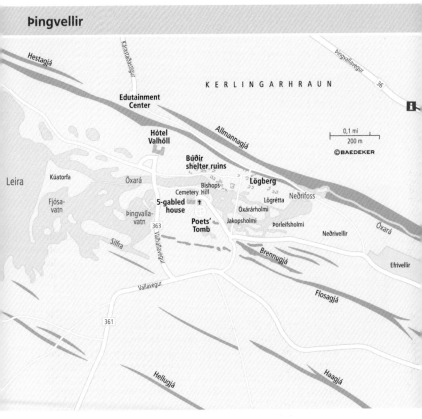

Þingvellir

Hestagjá

Kárastaðastígur

KERLINGARHRAUN

Þingvallavegur 36

Edutainment Center

Hótel Valhöll

Allmannagjá

0,1 mi
200 m
©BAEDEKER

Búðir shelter ruins

Kúatorfa

Öxará

Bishops Hill

Lögberg

Leira

Cemetery Hill

Lögrétta

Neðrifoss

Fjósa-vatn

5-gabled house

Öxarárholmi

Þingvalla-vatn

Poets' Tomb

Jakopsholmi

Þorleifsholmi

Neðrivellir

363

Silfra

Vallhallarvegur

Brennugjá

Öxará

Efrivellir

Vallavegur

Flosagjá

361

Hellugjá

Haagjá

Below the bridge the water gushes onto the plain of Þingvellir, where the Öxará broadens and becomes more sedate. On the eastern banks the few buildings at this historic place can't fail to catch the eye: the small church (Þingvallakirkja) and the striking **five-gabled house**. While the current church was consecrated in 1859, there was a church here as far back as the early 11th century and it was customary to hold the Althing's assemblies here in bad weather. The pulpit and two of the bells are significantly older than the church itself, while the third bell is younger. This is **Iceland's Liberty Bell**, cast to ring in independence in 1944. Þingvallabær, the building with the five gables, was constructed in stages for two great anniversaries celebrated in Þingvellir: one part in 1930 for the 1000th anniversary of the Althing, and the rest in 1974 for the celebration marking 1,100 years of Iceland's settlement. The house

Þingvallakirkja, Þingvalla-bær, Skjáldareifur

serves as official accommodation for the manager of the national park and also as guesthouse for members of the government. Skjáldareifur, the shield-shaped area behind the church, was laid out in 1939 as a memorial garden for important personalities of the Icelandic independence movement, but only the bones of two 19th century poets whose verse supported their nation's freedom – **Jónas Hallgrímur** (1807 – 1845) and **Einar Benediktsson** (1846 – 1940) – were laid to rest here. Hence the alternative name for the area of **Poets' Tombs**.

Flosagjá and Nikulásargjá This historic assembly field ends only a few metres behind the church and Þingvallabær at the expanding fissures of Flosagjá and Nikulásargjá, up to 25m/82ft deep. These chasms are a further indication that the **continental plates** are drifting apart. The stillness of the water in the fissures is deceptive; with a temperature remaining at a more or less constant 4°C/39°F all year round, it flows slowly in the direction of Þingvallavatn, using subterranean connections where the fissures are not visible on the surface. For decades, the southern continuation of the Nikulásargjá has had its own name: Peningagjá, the »money gorge«. In 1907, a bridge was put across it, and soon tourists started to throw coins into the water. As is customary in these circumstances, a wish is made, and it is said that those who keep their eye on the coin they have thrown all the way to the bottom should see their wish granted.

> **?** MARCO POLO INSIGHT
>
> *Did you know..?*
>
> ... that due to its steep gradient, the runoff of the Þingvallavatn, the Sog river, flows at high speed – making it look like some invisible force is sucking the water out of the lake. In fact, the name **Sog** can be derived from the Old West Nordic word for »suck«.

ÞINGVALLAVATN – CLEAR, DEEP AND FULL OF FISH

Iceland's largest natural lake Iceland's largest natural lake, the Þingvallavatn, measures just under 84 sq km/32 sq miles, and at its deepest point of 114m/374ft even reaches below sea level. Sandey and the second island, Nesjaey, are easily recognizable as former **volcano cones**. Like the plain of Þingvellir the lake was formed by the area above the rift zone of the continental plates subsiding. Deep down, the Þingvallavatn must have abundant sources, as the inflows, of which the Öxará is the largest, are nowhere near enough to feed into the lake the 100 to 115 cubic metres/26–30,000 US gal of water per second that leave it at its southern point by way of the Sog river.

The water conditions in the Þingvallavatn are favourable to some species of fish. This is the only place in the world for instance where four varieties of the Arctic char coexist in one body of water. These trout-like relatives of the salmon love deep, rocky lakes and are coveted in turn by anglers, being considered a delicacy. One of them, the **murta**, has not been discovered anywhere else in the world outside the Þingvallavatn, which doesn't stop it from being tinned and sold as the lake speciality in the shop of Þingvellir's information centre, among other places.

Local fish

Fed by hot steam from numerous boreholes in the valley and on the mountain slopes, the geothermal energy plant in the Nesjavellir, southwest of the Þingvallavatn, produces hot water and electricity, and makes for a rather odd combination of fascinating **high-tech architecture** and spectacular panoramic views of nature. A visitor centre has information on the plant and its technology.

*Nesjavellir

ⓘ June – Aug Mon – Sun 9am – 6pm, Sept – May by appointment, tel. 480 24 08, www.or.is

* Þjórsárdalur

✳ E/F 6/7

Region: South Iceland

The valley of the Þjórsá river has many aspects, with meadows and fields in the southwest giving way to a harsher, more barren landscape further northeast. While the Þjórsá west of the Búrfell is unspoilt, hydroelectric plants dominate the northeastern region.

The Þjórsárdalur proper is a tightly bounded valley north of the Þjórsá level with the Búrfell mountain. However, the name is also given to the landscape along the Þjórsá, accessible via the [32], the Þjórsárdalsvegur, and broadly covers the rural community of **Gnúpverjahreppur** too. Approaching from the southwest and turning off the [30] into this area between the villages of Brautarholt and Fluðir, the first few kilometres travel through good agricultural land with lush hay meadows, greenhouses and cultivated fields.

Tightly bounded valley

The more the journey continues northwest, the harsher, more barren and lonely the area becomes, with large parts of the soil covered in lava ash. Up to the level of the striking **Búrfell** mountain, the [32] more or less follows the northwestern banks of the Þjórsá. The course of the river, from its source at the watershed between northern and southern Iceland – in the middle of the ▶Spengisandur highlands

Harsh, barren land

Þjórsárdalur

INFORMATION
Félagsheimilið Árnes
Árnes, 801 Selfoss
Tel. 486 60 44
Around the Árnes community centre, a few kilometres past the spot where the [32] turns off the [30], next to the tourist information visitors will find a restaurant, guesthouse, youth hostel, campsite and swimming pool. Further tourist information can be had from the Hrauneyjar Highlands Center.

WHERE TO EAT
Restaurant Árnes ££
Tel. 486 60 48
Large restaurant in the community centre with an attractive terrace. Good home-cooked food at relatively affordable prices.

WHERE TO STAY
Steinsholt ££
801 Selfoss (on the [326]
4km/2.5 miles from the [32])
Tel. 486 60 69
www.steinsholt.is
Cosy little guesthouse with five rooms. Hot pot for guests and many options for riding trips into the surrounding area.

Farfuglaheimili Árnes £
Gnúpverjahreppi
801 Selfoss
Tel. 486 60 48
www.hihostels.is
Youth hostel with 26 beds, mainly in double rooms. Nearby there is a swimming pool with hot pots and a restaurant.

route – to its mouth, at 230km/143 miles is longer than any other river in Iceland. The stream is visible everywhere from the road south of the Búrfell; it seems to be allowed to meander through the landscape unhindered, with many branches and offshoots. North of the Búrfell however, the Þjórsá and its tributaries show their other, more industrialized face.

ENERGY PRODUCTION ON THE ÞJÓRSÁ

Enormous power potential Over a distance of less than 50km/31 miles as the crow flies, tremendous volumes of water, with their source at the Hofsjökull and Vatnajökull, cascade downhill from a good 570 metres/1,870ft in height – the water level of the **Þórisvatn** – to a level barely above 120 metres/394ft on the Þjórsá south of Búrfell. When the snow thaws and the early summer sun turns up the heat on the two glaciers to the right and left of the Sprengisandur, up to 42,000 cubic metres/ over 11 million US gal of water per minute take this route. The latent **energy potential** here is consequently used for energy production, while the landscape is adapted to the requirements of technology: reservoirs, dams and interconnecting canals ensure that the water flows consistently all year round and is always able to provide sufficient power to the turbines of five power plants. All this was put into place from 1969 onwards, showing that even a highly prized green energy like hydroelectric power makes its demands on nature.

Lying at the foot of the Búrfell is the oldest and most southerly of the five power plants which currently make the river system of the Þjórsá Iceland's biggest source of power. The actual power plants are mainly built into the mountains and, compared to the dams and barriers, the artificial watercourses and lakes, the substations and power lines, are relatively inconspicuous. Still, humans have transformed a landscape previously untouched and practically uninhabited. Depending on the point of view, while critics would say the landscape has been ruined, others are fascinated by the particular **aesthetics of this combination of technology and nature**. The main consumers of the power are a few energy-intensive industrial companies, such as the aluminium factories of Straumsvík and on the Hvalfjörður.

A source of power

Striving for a positive image, the Landsvirkjun energy company regularly opens its power plants to visitors, puts a lot of money into reforestation projects around its facilities and has a tradition of commissioning contemporary artists to put »Construction Art« on its buildings. Thus, the 90m/295-ft long **Hávaðatröllið concrete relief** by Sigurjón Ólafsson adorns a façade of the Búrfellsvirkjun, and a few kilometres upriver, a sculpture made of 17 steel plates, completed in 2000, throws shadows that vary with the course of the sun onto the concrete walls of the Sultartangavirkjun power plant. Intended to symbolize energy waves, this work by the multimedia artist **Sigurdur Árni Sigurdsson** (* 1963) is called Sun Wave.

Art and power

The two main tributaries of the Þjórsá, the Tungnaá and the Kaldakvísl, have been altered perhaps even more. As a result the Þórisvatn – the most important reservoir of the whole system – has expanded from its original 70 sq km/27 sq miles to an artificial 90 sq km/35 sq miles, making it Iceland's largest inland body of water. Three power plants – Hrauneyarfossvirkjun, Sigölduvirkjun and Vatnsfellsvirkjun – lie close to each other near the point where the two rivers flow into the Þjórsá, operating since 2001 as **peak load power plants** which always operate when demand for power is particularly high. The Hrauneyarfossvirkjun, with its control centre for all three facilities, also has a visitor and information centre which in the summer is often used for art exhibitions.

Tungnaá and Kaldakvísl

ⓘ **Visitor information centre:** in the summer daily 1 – 5pm, with guided tours available

WHAT TO SEE ALONG THE ÞJÓRSÁ

The Hekla – volcano from a distance

On a clear day, the views across the Þjórsá of the 1,491m/4,892-ft ▶Hekla volcano, shrouded in legends, turn the drive on the [32] into a truly spectacular sightseeing trip. As beautiful as the Hekla may appear in such conditions, it can also be very unfriendly; **Iceland's most active fire mountain** (last eruption spring 2000) has repeatedly wreaked destruction on the Þjórsárdalur and indeed large parts of the whole country with ash rain and lava bombs, the worst example being in 1104.

Gaukshöfði

Where the mountains nearly push the road into the Þjórsá, the rocky ledge of Gaukshöfði juts out like a headland. While the main road below between its foot and the river was given a new route, the old road leads high up to a **viewpoint** – the steep detour is well marked, but not tarmacked. From the car park on the pass it's just a short scramble onto the summit of the Gaukshöfði. The reward for the effort is a wonderful view of the Hekla and the Búrfell, only half its height, as well as the Þjórsá way down below, which cannot be viewed anywhere else in its full expanse. Soon afterwards the landscape opens up towards the north; this is where the real Þjórsárdalur begins. With its mountain backdrop, shaped by **vulcanism**, it is a beautiful if less well-known landscape, its charms attracting more Icelandic than foreign visitors. The two farms at the entrance are given over to tourism – horse riding tours, campsite, summer houses – and are the only ones in the whole valley to have continually defied the vagaries of the Hekla. Some twenty others have been located by archaeologists further inland of the Þjórsárdalur since the late 1930s, many of them buried under ash. They were known about through medieval manuscripts telling of farms in the region which were still fertile at the time. Devastated by eruptions of the Hekla on a regular basis from 1104 onwards, the Þjórsárdalur was a **barren wasteland** for a long time, before massive reforestation in the 20th century once more gave it some touches of green.

!

MARCO POLO TIP

Healing from Hekla **Insider Tip**

Insider all know it: while Hekla is feared as the gateway to hell and sometimes brings trouble, it also brings about good things. Every time the volcano erupts a fine mineralized ash rains down, which is known as »**Havnejordit lava**« and which is used by homoeopaths around the world to heal bone and periosteum infections as well as osteophytes, painful finger and toe joint infections and especially to treat heel spurs. **Hekla lava** also has cosmetic uses, for example in organic exfoliating scrubs. Hekla lava is a recognized homoeopathic substance that is available without prescription.

It only takes a minor detour off the [32] heading south to visit the Hjálparfoss in front of the backdrop of the Búrfell. Hundreds of **basalt columns** in interesting shapes form a cauldron into which the Fossá plunges through a crevice. Before the edge of the fall, a basalt island divides the river into two arms.

Hjálparfoss

The access road to the Þjóðveldisbær leads on further to the Búrfells-virkjun, the **power plant on the Búrfell**. Its water is taken from the Þjórsá a good 5km/3 miles northeast and channelled into a reservoir, eventually shooting through subterranean tunnels onto the turbines, while the old river bed winds its way around the 669m/2,195-ft mountain. In the power plant's visitor centre the technology is explained using a model.

Búrfells-virkjun

❶ **Visitor's centre:** June – Aug Mon – Fri 1 to 5pm, Sat/Sun to 6pm

The Gjárfoss in the Rauðá could be the smaller, slimmer brother of the Hjálparfoss, as they are both framed by basalt pillars and split by a basalt nose right on the crest line. The Gjárfoss plunges into the Gjáin Gorge east of Stöng. To get there from the excavated farmstead either take the jeep track on the eastern banks of the Rauða or keep your feet dry following its western banks for some 10 to 15 minutes. The track leads to a viewpoint above the gorge. Gjáin is a small **green paradise**, a garden created by nature with the most varied water features and lava sculptures. In many places small brooks spring from the walls of the gorge, fringed by the most diverse wild flowers and sturdy angelica plants. The Gjárfoss is not the only waterfall here, but it's the most photogenic. The view of it is better from the path on the western banks of the Rauða than from the viewpoint on the eastern banks.

*Gjáin

The Fossá (foss = waterfall) does not only do full justice to its name at the Hjálparfoss but also forms Iceland's second-highest waterfall, the Háifoss. The **»High Fall«** – the clue is in the name – plunges 122m/400ft down into the narrow Fossárdalur, with its walls showing a distinct cross-section of the various layers of lava. The Háifoss can be reached from Stöng in a 2 to 3-hour hike through difficult terrain, or by four-wheel drive via a gravel track running alongside a power line which turns west off the [32] shortly before the Sultartanga power plant.

*Háifoss

Despite all the reshaping by human hand, the Þjórsá still has a few waterfalls even in its industrialized part. The star amongst them is Dynkur, a good 15km/9 miles north of the Hrauneyarfoss power plant. Here, the Þjórsá splits into many rivulets and plunges down 38m/125ft over several tiers into the **Gljúfurleit** Canyon. The best source of information on the current access route (by jeep only) is the Hrauneyjar Highland Center.

Dynkur

Everyday Life in the 11th Century

In 1104 an eruption of the volcano Hekla buried the estate Þjóðveldisbær. The foundations of the estate farm Stöng have been excavated. Stöng is a milestone in architectural development from the pure rural house of Viking times, which had only one large room, called a skáli, to a complex of several rooms with different functions. The original was reconstructed a few miles from Stöng and as the museum farm Þjóðveldisbær it gives insight into Iceland's everyday life in the 11th century.

❶ June–Aug. 10am – 6pm, Admission: 600 ISK, www.thjodveldisbaer.is

❶ Entrance
The low entrance leads to a foyer with a closed storeroom in the opposite corner.

❷ Toilet
The toilet is quite large by modern standards. But in the saga period it was anything but private as its »business« was done communally.

❸ Hall
A wooden wall separated the foyer from the skáli, the hall, where most of everyday life took place. A long fire burned constantly in the middle of the room; it was also used for cooking. Broad earthen benches along the wood-panelled long walls served as seating during the day and as beds at night.

❹ Room
The room on the west side appears for the first time in Stöng – in later centuries it became the most important room in icelandic farms, the stofa, the parlour. Women used them daily for spinning and weaving.

❺ Dairy kitchen
Skyr, a kind of Icelandic yoghurt, was made in the dairy kitchen and milk was also stored there. It can be clearly seen that some of the barrels were set into the ground.

Þjóðveldisbær historic farmstead

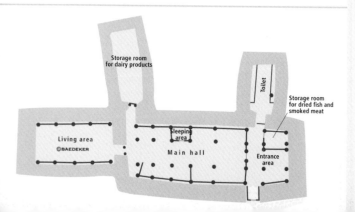

Þórshöfn · Langanes

INFORMATION
At Þórshöfn's public pool
Tel. 468 15 15

EVENTS
From mid-May to 10 June, in keeping
with an old tradition, the eggs on the
bird rocks are collected by abseiling.
Courageous visitors are welcome to take
part!

ACCOMMODATION
Þórshöfn: Hótel Jórvik £
Langanesvegi 31, tel. 468 14 00
jorvik@netfang.com
Colourful concrete building in Þórshöfn

high above the sea. This is more of a private house offering sleeping-bag accommodation than a hotel.

Þórshöfn: Lyngholt £
Lauganesvegur 12
Tel. 897 50 64, www.lyngholt.is
Well-kept wooden house on the main
street in the village, with modern rooms
and a light-filled breakfast room.

Langanes: Ytra-Lón £
Tel./fax 468 12 42
Youth hostel in an old restored farm-
house with 16 rooms, run by a Dutch-
Icelandic family. Good fishing and hiking.

normal saloon car will find it heavy going and soon be unable to go
any further. **Ytra Lón** is a good base for walks through this deserted
landscape, for instance onto the 266m/873-ft mountain viewpoint
of Heiðarfjall. Before the summit, a path branches off to lead along
the east coast to the abandoned settlement of Skálar (approx
32km/20 miles). Those who don't want to go all the way to the
point of the duck's beak, should turn north in Skálar and follow the
coast on a rough track to the deserted **Skóruvík farmstead** and on
to the Skoruvíkurbjarg bird rock, reaching – after some 40km/25
miles – the point of departure at Ytra Lón.

** Þórsmörk

‑✦‑ F 7

Region: South Iceland

**»Green Oasis«, »A Paradise between Glaciers« – Þórsmörk
seems to be begging for rhapsodic descriptions. Protected by
its position in the rain shadow of the Eyjafjallajökull and the
Mýrdalsjökull, which provide an imposing backdrop, the valley with its lush meadows and small birch forest has been
protected under a conservation order since 1921. The micro
climate promotes plant growth, making the flora among the
most varied in the country.**

HARD TO ACCESS

Thunder god
Thor's forest

About 20km/12 miles east of Hvolsvöllur, just past the new Markar-fljót bridge, the track [249/F 249] to Þórsmörk turns off the Ring Road. It is probably just as well – for the sake of the rather fragile plant life – that the influx of visitors is controlled somewhat by the only drivable link to the outside world being a difficult four-wheel drive track [F 249]. For it is here that Thor, god of thunder, has placed several fords before his paradisiacal forest – Þórsmörk meaning **Thor's forest**. The last one in particular, through the Krossá glacier river, is considered unpredictable and dangerous, and even all-terrain buses sometimes struggle here. With the right vehicle though the track offers a lot of variety.

HIKES IN ÞÓRSMÖRK

Krossár-jökull

The area from Þórsmörk up to the surrounding glaciers is crossed by paths of varying degrees of difficulty. The paths on both sides of the Krossá to its source at the **Krossárjökull**, a valley glacier of the Mýrd-alsjökull, are popular because they are long but have few climbs. Don't be shocked on reaching it: as with so many glacier tongues in southern Iceland, it is more reminiscent of a slag heap than a mountain made of ice. While the ice melts, the ash and other deposits brought onto the glacier by volcanic eruptions or storms do not.

Valahnúkur

The hill of Valahnúkur due west of the FÍ mountain hut in the Lan-gidalur can be managed even by less experienced hikers in just under an hour. They are rewarded by one of the most spectacular vistas in the whole country: the **green of the forests and meadows**, the ancient gravel beds of the glacier rivers – with the mountain hut and the cars parked there appearing as spots of colour – and the majestic glaciers as backdrop, provide a five-star photo opportunity.

Stakkholtsgjá

Insights instead of views can be had at the southern bank of the Krossá, with a walk into the Stakkholtsgjá Gorge. With its steep walls, a good 100m/330 ft high, and a small waterfall at the end of a side gully, this is another popular destination for a short hike. However, visitors should take the precaution of checking locally for options of how to traverse the **Krossá**, as every spring, when the snows melt, it makes a new bed for itself.

Trekking via
Þórsmörk

Þórsmörk is also the start and end point of the Laugavegur trek from ▶Landmannalaugar, as well as of the challenging mountain tour via the **Fimmvörðuháls** to Skógar. The latter route leads near the Básar hut some 900m/2,950ft up the 1,116m/3,661ft pass between Eyjafjal-

Þórsmörk

INFORMATION
In the huts

GETTING THERE
Highland buses run once or twice daily from Reykjavík via Hella and Hvolsvöllur to Þórsmörk. Day trips with about 3.5 hours' stopoff or overnight stays are on offer. Travellers with cars unsuitable for the track to Þórsmörk may park in Hvolsvöllur at the Hlíðarendi service station and take the bus from there. The bus runs to a fixed schedule in Þórsmörk, linking all three huts as well as the Stakkholtsgjá (see below); the round trip takes 1.5 hours. Timetables are available online:
www.bsi.is and www.austurleid.is

Þórsmörk, the green »paradise between the glaciers«

ACCOMMODATION
Skagfjörðsskáli £
Reservations through Ferðafélag Íslands:
tel. 568 25 33, www.fi.is
Simple mountain hut in the Langidalur with a small shop and campsite. Information available in the summer from the hut keeper.

Básar £
Booking through Útivist
Laugavegur 178
Tel. 562 10 00
Two huts near the Krossá, run by Útivist,

sleeping 60 or 20 people respectively, with a hut keeper in the summer. Busy, but with a friendly atmosphere, plus there is a campsite. Booking essential.

Húsadalur £
Bookings under:
Tel. 545 17 17, www.thorsmork.is
Simple hut and campsite, run by Austurleið.

Stóta Mörk III £
Tel. 487 89 03
Rooms and apartment on the farm, 24km/15 miles from Hvollsvöllur on the [248]/[249].

lajökull and Mýrdalsjökull. Up here extreme weather conditions such as ice and snow can occur even in summer.

There is a visitor's centre on the farm Þorvaldseyri at the foot of Eyjafjallajökull with information on the spectacular eruption in spring 2010 and its consequences. **Þorvaldseyri**

Visitor's centre: June – Aug daily 9am – 6pm, otherwise 11am – 4pm, Dec – Feb only by appointment, tel. 4 87 57 57, www.icelanderupts.is

PRACTICAL INFORMATION

What's the best way to get to Iceland? Which documents are necessary, which currency is used and where can you find information on the island? How do you say »thank you« in Icelandic? Find all the answers here, preferably before departure!

Arrival · Before the Journey

By air   Year-round air links with Iceland from Britain, the US, Canada, and major European hubs are provided by **Icelandair**. Icelandair flies from London Heathrow, as well as Manchester and Glasgow, from Boston, New York JFK, Minneapolis/St Paul, Orlando, Toronto-Pearson and Halifax, to Keflavík near Reykjavík. Apart from the traditional flight tickets, the airline often offers attractive excursion, family and group fares. Particularly good-value offers become available in the low season. Budget carrier Iceland Express links London Stansted (twice daily), and European cities such as Alicante, Berlin, Copenhagen and Warsaw with Keflavík, adding more services and cities in peak season. Charter company JetX Airlines operates seasonal flights from Montreal. Flight time from England is three hours, and five-and-a-half hours from the east coast of the United States. Visitors from Ireland, Australia, New Zealand and South Africa usually use London as a gateway.

Airport bus   Keflavík international airport and Reykjavík are linked by an airport bus, the journey taking about 45 min. The bus makes two stops

AIRLINES
Icelandair in Iceland
Hotel Loftleiðir
IS-101 Reykjavík
Tel. 50 50 757
www.icelandair.is

Icelandair in the United Kingdom
Adam House, 2nd Floor – 1 Fitzroy
Square
London W1T 5HE
Tel. 0207 874 10 00, fax 0207 387 57 11
www.icelandair.co.uk

Icelandair in North America
5950 Symphony Woods Rd – Suite 410
Columbia, MD 21044
Tel. 1 800 223 5500,
Fax 1 410 715 35 47
www.icelandair.com
www.icelandair.ca

Icelandair in Australia
Level 7 – 189 Kent Street
Sydney, NSW 2000
Tel. 02 9087 0244
www.icelandair.com

Iceland Express
Efstaland 26 IS-108 Reykjavík
Tel. 55 00 600, 01 27 966 52 20 (UK),
03 54 550 06 00 (international)
www.icelandexpress.com

FERRIES
Smyril Line Iceland
Stangarhýl 1
IS-110 Reykjavík
Tel. 570 86 00
www.smyril-line.com

Smyril Line UK
Tel. 84 70 420 12 67
www.smyriline.co.uk

(Hafnarfjörður and Garðabær) before its final stop at the BSI bus terminal in the middle of Reykjavik. Tickets are available in the airport
and at the exits. The bus leaves 40 minutes after a flight arrives. With
a »Flybus plus« ticket you can be brought right to one of more than
50 hotels on a smaller bus. A one-way ticket for the airport bus costs
€13, a one-way Flybus ticket is about €17. By taxi, the drive from Keflavík to Reykjavik is around €90. Internal flights depart from Reykjavík city airport.

Travellers crossing from Scandinavia can take advantage of the year- By boat
round weekly ferry link established in 2004 between Hirtshals in
Denmark and Seyðisfjörður in East Iceland. The passenger and car
ferry of the **Smyril Line**, the **Norröna** sets sail from Hirtshals in the
summer on Tuesday evening at 9pm and, after 36 hours with a stop
in Tórshavn on the Faroe Islands, it reaches the east Icelandic port of
Seyðisfjörður at 7.30am on Thursday morning. The return trip starts
on Thursday at 10am and goes via Tórshavn to Hirtshals, where the
ship arrives on Saturday at 12.30pm.

ENTRY AND EXIT REQUIREMENTS

To enter Iceland, visitors from the United Kingdom, Ireland, the US, Entry
Canada, Australia and New Zealand do not require a visa, only a requirements
passport valid for three months after the planned date for leaving the
country. Visitors from South Africa
need to apply to the Royal Danish
Embassy in Pretoria. Any other visa
enquiries are also handled by the re-
spective Royal Danish Embassies,
not by the embassies of Iceland. In
the UK, however, the Icelandic embassy is the point of call for any tour-
ism-related enquiries, as there is no
tourist board office. Duty-free import limits are 1 l of spirits and 1 l of
wine, or 1 l of spirits and 6 l of beer,
or 3 l of wine, plus 200 cigarettes or
250 g of other tobacco products. The
legal age for alcohol is 20, and for tobacco products 18. Only 3kg/6.6lb of
foodstuff per person may be brought
into Iceland, with the import of eggs
and dairy produce completely pro-

> **! Don't forget!** *Insider Tip*
>
> **MARCO POLO TIP**
>
> Children must have their own tra-
> vel documents when travelling
> abroad – entries into their pa-
> rents' passports are no longer va-
> lid. The type of required docu-
> ment – child's passport, adult
> passport or personal identity card
> – depends on the child's age. In
> any case apply for the document
> in good time before you start
> your trip. Children without a valid
> passport will not be allowed to
> enter the country. This new law
> applies for trips to EU countries as
> well.

hibited. Meat, poultry and sausages are only allowed in tinned form.
Bringing pets into the country is more or less impossible, as entry

regulations for live animals are very strict. The veterinary authorities usually demand that the animal be put into quarantine for several months. Travelling with **fishing and riding gear** is also subject to restrictions, as its geographical isolation makes Iceland particularly vulnerable to contagious diseases. Icelandic animals are not vaccinated, thus have no protection against pathogens brought into the country from abroad. Therefore used saddlery may not be imported at all, and used riding and fishing gear has to travel accompanied by paperwork proving proper disinfection.

Reentry into EU countries: All personal possessions brought into Iceland are duty free. Souvenirs with a total value of €430 (adults) or €175 (children and teens under 15 years). Also duty free: for people older than 15 years 500 g coffee or 200 g instant coffee and 100 g tea or 40 g tea extract, 50 g perfume and 0.25 l eau de toilette as well as for people older than 17 1 l spirits with more than 22 vol.-% alcohol or 2 l spirits with less than 22 vol.-% alcohol or 2 l sparkling wine and 2 l wine as well as 200 cigarettes or 100 cigarillos or 50 cigars or 250 g tobacco.

Electricity

220 Volt   Electricity supply is 220 Volt, 50Hz. British three-pin plugs and US flat two-pin plugs will require an adapter to fit the power points.

Emergencies

Fire service, ambulance and police	*Breakdown service*
Tel. 112	F.I.B., tel. 5 112 112

Etiquette and Customs

Blame it on the weather   Even though in daily life Icelanders tend to act with Scandinavian reserve, sometimes visitors might feel that their hosts are the »Italians of the North«. Most are past masters in improvisation,c and **punctuality** is not their strong point either. Thus, it is the rule rather than the exception that jobs only get done after a major last-minute effort. A large part of the problem could be the weather – not the inclement variety as one might think, instead it's the short, unexpected periods of good weather that play havoc with schedules. These brief windows of opportunity must be taken full advantage of, being far too valuable not to arrange a picnic with friends or play a round of golf. Who knows when the sun will shine again, meaning any overtime will have to wait for the next shower of rain.

At first glance, many Icelanders might seem a bit surly and taciturn, but once the ice is broken, visitors will be surprised by their **warmth and hospitality**. Even at times when the service might not be less than ideal, keep calm; loud criticism doesn't help much with the proud Icelanders. Try to appreciate that in this country which is so sparsely populated, every tiny village offers travellers accommodation and help. Often the petrol station attendant or the cashier at the supermarket also manage the tourist information centre, or the school kid, whose boarding school bed you are sleeping in, serves breakfast too. The tourist season is short, far too short to warrant keeping the infrastructure going all year round. So it's all a matter of improvisation!

Keep calm!

One of the best ways of meeting Icelanders are the hot tubs, available not only at every swimming pool, but also in the most remote places. Hot tubs take on the function of pubs, which are rare here. Sitting there up to the neck in relaxing warm water, even the Icelandic reserve melts. Don't be surprised if the person sharing the tub uses the familiar form of address; and when Icelanders ask for your name they always mean the first name. This is nothing to do with a lack of respect, but with different **linguistic habits**. So forget titles and formal terms of address, in Iceland everyone is on first-name terms. Visitors lucky enough to be invited into a home should take off their shoes before entering the house. Incidentally, the same is true for swimming pools and youth hostels, where there is usually a sign up to that effect. Be prepared also to **write in the guest book**, and don't forget to give the hosts a few words of thanks for their hospitality at the end of a visit. A sure way to **put your foot in it** is to discuss whaling with Icelanders, assuming you are against it, as are the great majority of people in most other countries. This is a topic where most Icelanders display a good deal of **stubbornness** and usually refuse to be swayed by even the best arguments. Visitors should also take into account the Icelanders' extremely strong national identity, pride in their cultural heritage and sense of independence.

Bath instead of pub

Consumption of alcohol (including beer) is allowed from the age of 20 in Iceland; smoking however from the age of 18. In restaurants, cafés etc. and public buildings smoking is not allowed. Alcoholic drinks are only sold in state-owned shops; tobacco products are not allowed to be displayed.

Alcohol and smoking

Health

Health centres – joint practices grouping together various doctors and specialists – or hospitals can be found in practically all Iceland's larger towns. In an emergency call the national **emergency number 112**. Medicines are only available in pharmacies (apóteks), which can be found in every town and have the usual opening hours. Some pharmacies stay open at night.

The **quality of tap water** is good everywhere, while the water from streams and rivers is also usually drinkable. Be careful however in thermal areas, where the water may taste and smell of sulphur.

Highlands

Iceland adventure

Crossing the Icelandic highlands is still something of an adventure, as nowhere else in Europe has such vast **untamed wildernesses**. There are good reasons why nobody ever settled here for long. Regardless of the mode of transport, whether on foot, by mountain bike, on horseback or by car, a highland crossing should be planned well in advance. The only exceptions are the organized tours which give a good overview of this primeval landscape.

The most important tracks

The two most important tracks connecting the north with the south are the Kjölur Route and the Sprengisandur. Of these two, the Kjölur is the easier option, and in favourable conditions is even manageable for **vehicles without four-wheel drive**. The Sprengisandur is more challenging and definitely requires a four-wheel drive. Apart from these two main road links there are several other shorter highland tracks and connecting link roads. As a general rule drivers should never leave the tracks, as the soil and vegetation are extremely sensitive, with car tyres leaving imprints that, like wounds on the landscape, won't heal for years.

Geared up for the highlands

MARCO ⊕ POLO TIP

The Icelandic road authority issues a weekly overview map detailing the state of the highland tracks (www.vegagerdin.is). The state television's teletext service contains information on pages 483 to 485. Call tel. 1777 daily from 8am to 4pm to receive information on the state of the roads.

PLANNING

When planning a drive into the highlands one thing should be borne in mind: up to the end of June, and sometimes even later, visitors should be prepared for the highland tracks to be closed still where rivers or mud have made

APPROXIMATE OPENING TIMES
OF THE HIGHLAND TRACKS
Skaftártunga – Eldgjá
from 8 June

Kaldalsvegur (F 550)
from 15 June

Kjölur (F 35)
from 15 June

Sigalda – Landmannalaugar
from 17 June

Landmannaleið (F 225)
from 19 June

Askja (F 88)
from 20 June

Laki Fissure (F 206)
from 20 June

Landmannalaugar – Eldgjá
from 28 June

Sprengisandur (F 26)
from 1 July

Southern Route (F 210, »Behind the mountains«)
from 5 July

Eyjafjörður Highlands (F 82)
from 9 July

them completely impassable. Once these tracks are opened to traffic, most are only manageable by jeep. Some of them should really only be attempted in convoy with at least two vehicles.

It is essential for drivers to familiarize themselves with the planned route before departure. Petrol stations are sources of information too. Good maps and a **compass** are essential equipment during a tour through the highlands. — **Maps**

Rivers and streams without bridges require maximum concentration, as the points where **glacier rivers** ford the road can change quickly. Solo travellers should take their time and only cross glacier river fords once another vehicle comes into sight. Due to the lower water level, a river crossing is easier in the morning than in the evening. — **Fords**

Sufficient provisions, water and petrol have to be brought along – there is hardly any opportunity to stock up or fill the tank along the way. — **Provisions**

Apart from (very few) lodges, camping is the only **accommodation** en route. — **Tents**

The weather being unpredictable, visitors should be prepared for strong winds, rain and snow showers. The weather forecast issued by the Meteorological Office in English also contains the **highland weather**. — **Meteorological Office**

Information

TOURIST INFORMATION
IN THE UK
Brochure request line
POSTCODE
Tel. 020 7 636 96 60
www.visiticeland.com

TOURIST INFORMATION
IN THE US
Icelandic Tourist Board
655 Third Avenue
New York N.Y. 10017
Tel. 212 885 97 00 Fax 212 885 97 10
www.icelandtouristboard.com

TOURIST INFORMATION
IN ICELAND
Reykjavík
Promote Iceland, Borgartún 35
IS-105 Reykjavík
Tel. 35 45 11 40 00
www.visiticeland.com

Visit Reykjavík
Aðalstræti 2
IS-101 Reykjavík
Tel. 590 15 50
www.visitreykjavik.is

Keflavík/Reykjanes Peninsula
Tourist Information Center
Leifur Eiríksson Airport
IS-235 Keflavík
Tel. 425 03 30
www.reykjanes.is
Tourist Information Center
Kjarninn – Hafnargata 57
IS-230 Keflavík
Tel. 421 67 77
www.reykjanes.is

South Iceland/Hveragerði
Tourist Information Center
Sunnumörk 2 – 4
IS-810 Hveragerði
Tel. 483 46 01
www.south.is

West Iceland
Tourist Information Center
Brúartorg
IS-310 Borgarnes
Tel. 437 22 14
www.west.is

Western fjords
Tourist Information Center
Aðalstræti 7
IS-400 Ísafjörður
Tel. 456 80 60
www.westfjords.is

North Iceland
North Iceland Marketing
Hafnarstræti 82
IS-600 Akureyri
Tel. 550 07 20
www.northiceland.is

East Iceland/Höfn
Tourist Information Center Nýheimar
IS-780 Höfn
Tel. 478 15 00
www.east.is

East Iceland
East Iceland Information Center
Kaupvagur 6
IS-700 Egilsstaðir
Tel. 471 23 20
www.east.is

EMBASSIES AND CONSULATES

British Embassy Reykjavík
Laufásvegur 31 | IS-101 Reykjavík
(postal address: PO Box 460
121 Reykjavík)
Tel. 550 51 00
https://www.gov.uk/world/organisations/
british-embassy-reykjavik

Honorary Vice-Consulate Akureyri
Central Hospital
(Fjordungssjukrahusid a Akureyri v/
Eyrarlandsveg)
IS-602 Akureyri
(postal address: PO Box 380,
IS-602 Akureyri)
Tel. 436 01 02

Irish Honorary Consulate
Laufásvegur 31
IS-210 Gardabaer
Tel. 554 23 55
davidcsh@islandia.is

Irish diplomatic representation via Irish Embassy, Denmark
Ostbanegade 21
2100 Copenhagen
Tel. 550 51 00
irlemb_dk@yahoo.com

American Embassy Reykjavík
Laufásvegur 21
IS-101 Reykjavík
Tel. 562 91 00
https://is.usembassy.gov/

Embassy of Canada Reykjavík
Túngata 14
IS-101 Reykjavík
Tel. 562 91 00
rkjvk@international.gc.ca

Australian diplomatic representation via Australian Embassy, Denmark
Dampfaergevej 26, 2nd floor
2100 Copenhagen
Tel. 70 26 36 76
www.denmark.embassy.gov.au

Australia/New Zealand diplomatic representation (via PR of China)
Landmark Tower 1, # 802
8 Dongsanhuan Bei Lu
100004 Beijing
Tel. 10 65 90 77 95/6
www.iceland.org/cn

Embassy of Iceland UK
2a Hans Street
London SW1X 0JE
Tel. 020 72 59 39 99
www.iceland.org/uk

Icelandic Consulate in Ireland
Cavendish House
Smithfield Dublin
Tel. 01 87 29 299

Embassy of Iceland in the US
1156 15th Street, NW, Suite 1200
Washington DC 20005-1704
Tel. 202 265 66 53
www.iceland.org/us

Consulate General of Iceland in New York
800 3rd Avenue, 36th floor
New York, NY 10022
Tel. 212 593 27 00
www.iceland.org/us

Embassy of Iceland in Canada
Constitution Square 360
Albert Street, Suite 710
Ottawa, Ontario K1R 7X7

Tel. 613 482 19 44
www.iceland.org/ca

Consulate of Iceland in Australia
16 Birriga Road, Bellevue Hill
Sydney 2000, NSW
Tel. 2 936 57 345
Iceland@bigpond.net.au

Consul of Iceland in Auckland,
New Zealand
Eric Francis Barratt
c/o Sanford Ltd, 22 Jellicoe Street
Auckland
Tel. 9 379 47 20
www.sanford.co.nz

Consul of Iceland in Nelson, New
Zealand
Sigurgeir Pétursson
5 Noel Jones Drive, Atawahi Nelson
Tel. 3 545 29 44
geiri@xtra.co.nz

ICELAND ON THE NET
www.visiticeland.com
Website of the Icelandic Tourist Board in
several languages

www.icelandair.com
Alongside extensive flight details the site
also contains a lot of practical information on Iceland.

www.geysir.com
Private Icelandic information service

www.iceland.org
Background information on Iceland

www.iww.is
General information on Iceland

www.travelnet.is
Practical information on Iceland

www.exploreiceland.net
Information on Iceland and its activities

www.visitreykjavik.is
www.reykjanes.is
Information on the capital and the
southwest

www.whatson.is
Events, restaurants, hotels and background information on Reykjavík

www.south.is
Information on South Iceland

www.west.is
Information on West Iceland

www.northwest.is
Information on Northwest Iceland

www.east.is
Information on East Iceland

www.south.is
Information on South Iceland

www.vedur.is/english
Weather forecasts from the Icelandic
Meteorological Institute

www.norvol.hi.is
Information on volcanism

www.icelandreview.com
Online version of Iceland Review magazine

Language

The official language is Icelandic, a Germanic-Nordic language which, due to the country's isolated position, has remained more or less the same since the island's settlement by Norwegian immigrants, unlike the other northern European languages which have changed much over the course of the centuries. **Linguistic identity** is an important part of Icelandic culture, which tries to avoid overloading the language with foreign words. Instead, modern concepts that aren't available in the Old Icelandic vocabulary are formed by paraphrasing. Thus, the word »tölva« (computer) was put together from the words »tala« (number) and »völva« (clairvoyant). The Icelandic alphabet has the special characters þ, ð, and æ, but the letters c, q, w and z are missing. Apart from that, the vowels a, e, i, o, u and y occur with and without accents, resulting in differing pronunciations. Icelandic pronunciation is relatively difficult, and few tourists master it straight away. Luckily many Icelanders speak English well, so there are few problems with communication.

Official language

Icelandic language guide

Pronunciation

a	as in 'art', but before ng or nk like 'ow', before gi like 'I'
á	like 'ow'
e	like an open e
é	as in 'share'
ý, í	as in 'it'
ó	as in 'no'
u	as in German 'über'
ú	as in 'zoo'
au	approx. as in 'purr'
æ	as in 'I'
ei	as in 'pray'
ð	like the voiced 'th'
f	at the beginning of a word and before k, s and t like f, otherwise like a v
r	rolled
v	like v
þ	like the unvoiced 'th'

Basic words

yes	já
no	nei
please	gjörðu svo vel
thanks	takk
Good morning/Good day	Góðan dag
Good evening	Gott kvöld
Good night	Góða nótt
Good bye	Vertu sæll/vertu sæl
Excuse me	Afsakið
I don't speak Icelandic	Ég tala ekki íslensku
I don't understand	Ég skil ekki
Do you speak English?	Talar þú ensku?
How much is it?	Hvað kostar þetta?
Can you help me?	Getur þú hjálpað mér?
Where is ...?	Hvar er ...?
I need	Mig vantar
I'd like	Ég ætla að fá

Accommodation

Do you have a room?	Er laust herbergi?
breakfast	morgunmatur
dinner	kvöldmatur
double room	tveggja manna herbergi
guesthouse	gistiheimili
hotel	hótel
lunch	hádegismatur
room	herbergi
shower	sturta
single room	eins manns herbergi
sleeping bag	sumarhús
youth hostel	farfuglaheimili

Food and drink

beer	bjór/öl
low-alcohol beer	Pilsner
butter	smjör
cheese	ostur
dried fish	harðfiskur
Icelandic quark (low-fat curd cheese)	skyr
milk	mjólk
restaurant	veitingastaður
sandwich	samloka
shark	hákarl

smoked lamb

tourist menu

white/red wine

hangikjöt

sumarréttir

hvít-/rauðvín

On the road

arrival/departure

bank

blind road

bus station

city bus

drive carefully

ferry

garage

harbour/port

hillside

hospital

information

mortal danger

one-way street

open-air pool

overland bus

petrol station

plane

police

post

round-trip

street, path

taxi

telephone

ticket

timetable

to the left/right

koma/brottför

banki

blindhæð

umferðarmiðstöð

strætó

akið varlega

ferja

verkstæði

höfn

brekka

sjúkrahús

upplýsingar

lífshætta

einstefna

sundlaug

rúta

bensínstöð

flugvél

lögregla

póstur

fram og tilbaka

gata, braut, vegur

leigubíll

sími

miði

ferðaáætlun

til vinstri/hœgri

Geographical terms

east

west

north

south

mountain

mountain range

bay

cave

farm

fjord/fjords

austur

vestur

norður

suður

fjall

fjöll

vik

hellir

bær

fjörður/firðir

forest	skógur/mörk
glacial outwash plain	sandur
glacier	jökull
gravel plain	melur
hot spring	hver
island	ey/eyja
lake	vatn
lava field	hraun
plain	völlur
pond	tjörn
river	á
river bank	bakki
sandbank	eyri
small island	hólmi, hólmur
valley	dalur
warm spring	laug
waterfall	foss

Weather

The weather is good	veðrið er gott/fínt/ágætt
calm	logn
cloudy	skýað
fog	þoka
rain	rigning
storm	stormur/rok
sunny	bjart
sunshine	sólskín
weather forecast	veðurspá
wind direction	átt
wind speed	vindstígur

Days of the week

Monday	mánudagur
Tuesday	þriðjudagur
Wednesday	miðvikdagur
Thursday	fimmtudagur
Friday	föstudagur
Saturday	laugardagur
Sunday	sunnudagur

Numbers

0	núll
1	einn, eitt
2	tveir

3	þrir
4	fjórir
5	fimm
6	sex
7	sjö
8	átta
9	níu
10	tíu
11	ellefu
12	tólf
13	þrettán
14	fjórtán
15	fimmtán
16	sextán
17	sautján
18	átján
19	nítján
20	tuttugu
30	þrjátíu
40	fjörutíu
50	fimmtíu
60	sextíu
70	sjötíu
80	áttatíu
90	níutíu
100	hundrað
1000	þúsund

Media

Newspapers

For a quick check on the weather forecast, take a look at one of the three national daily newspapers (Morgunblaðið, DV or Dagur Tíminn); English-language newspapers are available, at least in the summer and with the usual delays, at some larger newsstands. The English-language magazine **Iceland Review** is published four times a year and is well worth getting for its excellent photographs and features on many aspects of Icelandic life (www.icelandreview.com).

Radio

A round-up of the news in English is broadcast on the public-service **radio** from 1 June to 1 September Mon – Fri at 7.31am on 92.4 and 93.5 FM. The BBC broadcasts on 90.9 FM. Foreign films on Icelandic **television** and in cinemas are shown in the original version with subtitles. Many hotels also have satellite TV receiving English-language programmes.

Midnight Sun

Light summer nights
Due to its position just below the Arctic Circle, summer nights in the whole of Iceland are light-filled and short. In the north, it's even possible to see the midnight sun. To be precise, it is not really the midnight sun, as the Icelanders take liberties with their time zone. Iceland runs on Greenwich Mean Time all year round, even though the island really lies one or two time zones further west.

As a result, at midsummer (21 June) the sun can be seen until after midnight in Akureyri, but then disappears for a short time below the horizon. Visitors who want to see the real midnight sun have to take a trip to Grímsey Island, situated exactly on the Arctic Circle around 100km/62 miles north of Akureyri.

In the winter, the days are extremely short; in December and January, the sun only appears for 3.5 to 4.5 hours. Due to the shifted time zone, at this time of year the sun only comes up around midday. By early March however, the days have over ten hours and by early May as much as 17 hours.

Money

Currency
The unit of currency is the **Icelandic krona** (króna, ISK). Coins in circulation have values of 1, 5, 10, 50 and 100 krónur. All coins show Iceland's four guardian spirits on the front and sea animals on the back. The National Bank of Iceland issues notes of 500, 1,000, 2,000 and 5,000 krónur.

? MARCO ⊕ POLO INSIGHT

Exchange rates

£1 = 192.7 ISK; US$1 = 118.6 ISK; €1 = 153.6 ISK; CAN$1 = 107.1 ISK; AUS$1 = 107; ISK ZAR1 = 10.75 ISK.

Up-to-date exchange rates online: www.oanda.com

The rate of exchange in Iceland is more favourable than elsewhere. The airport and all banks have ATMs where money can be withdrawn using a bank card. **»Hraðbanki«** is the Icelandic word for ATM.

Paying by credit card (Visa and Mastercard) is no problem in Iceland, while American Express cards are less readily accepted. With the value of the currency falling amidst the country's near-bankruptcy in the credit crisis of 2008, the notoriously expensive destination has seen its prices go down – good news for tourists.

National Parks

Iceland's three national parks count amongst the most beautiful and most popular natural landscapes on the island and offer many opportunities for hiking tours.

With an area of almost 13,000 km² (5000 sq mi) Vatnajökull National Park in the south-east is not only the largest national park in Iceland, but also in all of Europe. It was established in 2008 and includes Vatnajökull Glacier (8100 sq km/3100 sq mi), Skaftafell National Park and Jökulsárgljúfur National Park as well as bordering regions.

Vatnajökull

At 25km/15.5 miles long, 0.5km/0.3 of a mile wide and over 100m/328ft deep, the Jökulsá Canyon in the northeast of the island is one of the most impressive erosion gorges in Iceland. Jökulsárgljúfur National Park (120 sq km/46 sq miles) was established in 1973. A particularly spectacular view of the gorge can be had between the **Dettifoss** and the Syðra Þórunnarfjall. The hiking trail from the Dettifoss to the campsite at Ásbyrgi runs along wide stretches of the gorge. Alongside the gorge, the Dettifoss and some other waterfalls are worth seeing. The best access routes to the area are the [F 862] west of the **Jökulsá á Fjöllum** and the [864] east of the valley. Information can be picked up in Ásbyrgi.

Jökulsárgljúfur

Skaftafell National Park (4,800 sq km/1,850 sq miles) was established as early as 1967 and has been extended several times since then. It stretches from the Grímsvötn amidst the **Vatnajökull** in the north, to the Skeiðararjökull or Skaftafellsjökull in the south. The mountain ridge of the Skaftafellsheiði forms the core of the national park. A pretty view of the Skaftafellsjökull can be had from the Gláma mountain viewpoint at 600m/1,968ft high. Its position right on the ring road and the large campsite make access to the national park easier.

Skaftafell

The relatively small Snæfellsjökull lies at the top of the **Snæfellsnes Peninsula** in the west of Iceland. The national park (167 sq km/65 sq miles) was established in 2001 to protect the lava formations, the spectacular coast and traces of old settlements. The Snæfellsjökull, a volcanic cone that is glaciered over but still active, is considered the king of Icelandic mountains. There are many hiking trails in the national park, of which some are waymarked. Information can be picked up in the Hellissandur post office.

Snæfellsjökull

Established in 1930, Þingvellir National Park is the oldest in the country, comprising 50 sq km/19 sq miles. The park's proximity to the capital Reykjavík (50km/31 miles to the east) and its historic sig-

Þingvellir

nificance make it one of the most-visited tourist destinations in Iceland. The particular interest of the area lies in its numerous tectonic fissures and faults, which give an **insight into the geology of the island**. The information centre is located at the junction of the [36], [52] and [361], near the campsite, and has information on the national park, as well as maps with marked hiking trails and sights.

Personal Safety

Minimal crime rate

Iceland is one of the world's safest destinations. Whilst the crime rate is rising in the capital Reykjavík, compared to most Western countries it remains very low. In the countryside there is **hardly any crime**. Women travelling on their own should experience no problems in Iceland. However, while many Icelanders don't lock their cars or houses, tourists travelling with cars packed to the brim should exercise a modicum of caution in order to avoid unpleasant surprises.

Post · Telecommunications

Post offices, postage

Post offices can be found in every larger community and are usually open Mon – Fri from 8.30am – 4.30pm. Sending letters (up to 50 g) and postcards within Iceland costs ISK 130, letters and postcards to Britain and other European countries ISK 175.

Phone boxes

Iceland is not exactly littered with phone boxes; post offices and petrol stations offer the best chance of finding one. All phones offer direct dialling within Iceland and abroad, and most are **card and coin-operated**, with credit card phones less common. Phone cards to the value of ISK 500 and 1000 are available from post offices. Calling within Iceland requires dialling the 7-digit number; there are no local dialling codes.

DIALLING CODES
From Iceland ...
... to Britain: 00 44
... to the US/Canada: 00 1
... to Australia: 00 61
... to New Zealand: 00 64

... to South Africa: 00 27
The zero of the following local dialling code is dropped.

Calling Iceland
00 354 (followed by the 7-digit number)

Mobile phones automatically dial into the roaming partner in Iceland. A prepaid card bought locally could be cheaper. The Icelandic word for mobile phone is »Farsími«, literally »distance wire«.   Mobile phones

Prices

Living costs in Iceland are substantially higher than most visitors will be used to. Alcoholic beverages in particular are very expensive.

Time

Iceland is on **Greenwich Mean Time** (GMT) all year round.

?

MARCO ⊕ POLO INSIGHT

What does it cost?

Double room (comfortable)
   from 13,000 ISK
Hostel (bunk bed) from 2300 ISK
1 l petrol ca. 250 ISK
Main dish from 2000 ISK
Glass of beer from 900 ISK
Cup of coffee 140 ISK
Rental car (1 week)
   from 75 000 ISK

Toilets

There are toilets at all larger tourist sights and most petrol stations and they are especially clean. Many restaurants allow people who are not guests to use the sanitary facilities.

Tour Operators

A number of tour operators feature an extensive Iceland programme, ranging from Fly and Drive via hiking, cycling and horseback riding holidays to tailor-made tours.

Icelandic Travel (UK)
Whitehall House, Nenthead Alston,
Cumbria, CA9 3PS
Tel. 01 434 38 14 40

Tel. 1 866 423 72 42/
508 825 92 92
Fax 508 825 99 33
www.icelandsagatravel.com

Iceland Saga Travel (US)
3 Freedom Square
Nantucket, MA 02554

Exodus UK
Grange Mills, Weir Road
London, SW12 0NE

Tel. 02 08 675 55
www.exodus.co.uk

The Nordic Company (US)
5930 Seminole Center Court Suite C
Madison, Wisconsin 53711
Tel. 888 806 72 26, fax 608 288 80 71
www.nordicco.com

*The Great Canadian Travel
Company (Canada/US)*
158 Fort St Winnipeg, MB, R3C 1C9
Tel. 1 866 949 01 29
333 N. Michigan Avenue Suite 711
Chicago, IL 60801
Tel. 888 806 72 26
Fax 608 288 80 71
www.iceland-experience.com

Nordic Travel (Australia)
Suite 4B, 600 Military Road
Mosman (Sydney), NSW 2088

Tel. 02 99 68 17 83
Fax 02 99 68 19 24

Wild Earth Travel (NZ)
538 Montreal Street
PO Box 7218, Christchurch
Tel. 3 365 13 55
Fax 3 365 13 00
www.wildearth-travel.com

Isafold Travel Ltd.
Sudurhraun 2 B I
S-210 Gardabar
Tel. 544 88 66, fax 544 88 69
www.isafoldtravel.is

Iceland Total/Icelandair
Skúturogar 13A
104 Reykjavík
Tel. 585 43 78, fax 28 38 72
www.icelandair.com

Transport

BY AIR

Close net-
work of
routes

Iceland boasts a fairly comprehensive network of domestic flight routes. Particularly popular are the flights from Reykjavík to Akureyri and to the Westman Islands. **Domestic flights** depart in Reykjavík from the city airport. The main routes are served several times a day by the two largest companies, Air Iceland and Íslandsflug. All in all the following destinations are served: Akureyri, Egilsstadir, Ísafjörður, Hornafjörður, Bíldudalur, Gjögur, Sauðárkrókur, Vopnafjörður, Grímsey and Heimaey. A one-way ticket from Reykjavík to Akureyri starts at €60. Visitors wanting to fly more often should get an **Air Iceland Pass** with four, five or six coupons. Within its 30-day validity, any destination served by Air Iceland can be booked. The Air Iceland Pass is available at any branch of the airline outside Iceland. Also on offer is the »Fly As You Please« Pass, valid for twelve days and for any number of flights on all domestic Air Iceland routes. Several smaller companies such as Mýflug offer charter and sightseeing flights which, on a clear day, give great views of the island's glaciers and volcanoes. For more information, contact the airlines (▶ p. 345).

BY FERRY

The **Baldur** ferry takes passengers and cars from Stykkishólmur via Flatey to Brjánslækur, considerably shortening travel times to the Westfjords (www.saeferdir.is). The **Herjólfur** ferry (www.herjolfur.is) runs from the new harbour by Bakki on the southern coast, and takes passengers and cars on to the Westman Islands.

Shortened route

BY BUS

Scheduled coaches can take visitors to nearly every town and village in Iceland. In summer, even the **highland routes** are served by buses suited to uneven terrain. Tickets are available from the bus driver or the bus station. The buses are in principle only obliged to take a limited number of bikes (often max 5).

To almost all towns

Several bus companies, which travel along the Ring Road and several side roads, have joined together to form »Reykjavík Excursions«. They offer »bus passes«, flat-rate tickets that can be used all summer to travel various bus routed inexpensively and without much organizing. The »Beautiful South Tour Pass«, for example, Landmannalaugar or Skaftafell National Park can be visited while touring southern Iceland. It costs about €110 per person. The »Beautiful South Pass« is valid for these and additional routes in either direction. It is valid optionally for three, five, seven, nine or eleven days, and it costs between €120 and €300. Bus passes are also offered by Sterna Bus Company: the »Full Circle Pass«, for example, allows you to travel the entire Ring Road around Iceland, optionally including the Westfjords. There are also passes for Snæfellsnes National Park, West Iceland and the Westfjords, for eastern Iceland and for the »Goldenen Ring«. Prices run between around €50 for the »Goldenen Ring« and €311 for the complete Ring Road round trip including the Westfjords; the trip can be interrupted as often as desired within the period of validity. All bus passes area available at the bus terminals in Reykjavík and Akureyri. Further information: www.re.is, www.sterna.is.

Reykjavik Excursions

BY CAR

With a length of just under 1,400km/870 miles, the ring road forms Iceland's most important lifeline and is the centrepiece of the overall

State of the roads

road network, which covers more than 10,000km/6,200 miles. With a lot of financial expenditure and years of hard work, the ring road has become a near-complete and quite easily negotiable tarmacked route. The gravel sections become shorter year on year, meaning that these days drivers can use any car to go round the island. Drivers leaving the ring road, however, can expect substantially more **gravel stretches, corrugated-iron tracks and potholes**. These slow travellers down substantially, jarring the passengers and leaving their mark on the car at the end of the holiday. Where the gravel cover is loose, stones thrown up by oncoming and overtaking cars are always a risk to the paintwork and the windscreen. Due to the required river crossings, the highland tracks – with the exception of the Kjölur and Kaldidalur – are only suitable for four-wheel-drive vehicles. In the winter, the main roads are the first to be cleared of snow, while the minor roads can take a bit longer to be passable again.

Road-numbering
The quality of the roads may be gauged more or less by their numbering. The ring road deservedly bears the number 1, the other main transit roads can be recognized by their two-digit numbers. The quality of the three-digit roads is worse, whilst roads marked by an »F« or paths without a number are usually only passable by four-wheel drive.

Petrol/Gas stations
The ring road boasts a comprehensive network of petrol stations, while filling-up early is recommended. In Reykjavík and in towns with more than 800 inhabitants, at least one petrol station stays open till 11.30pm. In smaller towns shorter opening hours are quite common. Self-service petrol pumps allow payment by notes or credit cards outside opening hours. There are no opportunities for filling-up in the highlands, only emergency petrol pumps such as the one in Hveravellir, which should not be factored into the planning. Therefore it's best to fill up in good time and consider bringing spare cans. A breakdown service is provided by the Icelandic Automobile Association »Félag Íslenskra Bifreiðaeigenda« (▶ p. 345).

Traffic regulations
The speed limit in built-up areas is 30mph/50km/h, on gravel tracks 50mph/80km/h and on tarmacked roads 55mph/90km/h. Off-road driving is prohibited. Headlights have to be switched on even in the daytime, and seat belts must be worn by everyone, including those in the back seat. **The permitted blood alcohol level is 0.0!** Penalties for traffic violations are higher than most visitors will be used to. Even the slightest violations get high fines on the spot. If alcohol is involved your driver's licence may be withdrawn for a longer period. Traffic signs warn of danger spots, but most don't explicitly ask drivers to reduce speed. Do bring relevant car insurance documentation; car insurers issue a Green Card proving that drivers are insured to drive in Iceland. If an accident happens, be sure to notify the police.

AIRLINES
Air Iceland
Reykjavík Airport
Tel. 570 30 30
www.airiceland.is

Mýflug
Reykjahlíð Airport
Tel. 464 44 00
www.myflug.is

FERRIES
Seatours/Ferry Baldur
Smiðjustígur 3
340 Stykkishólmur
Tel. 438 14 50
www.saeferdir.is

Herjólfur
Básaskersbryggja 900
Vestmannaeyjar
Tel. 481 28 00
www.herjolfur.is

TRAVELLING BY CAR
Breakdown service
Félag Íslenskra Bifreiðaeigenda
Borgartúni 33, 105 Reykjavík
Tel. 414 99 99
www.fib.is
Breakdown service: tel. 5 112 112.
Mon – Fri 8.15am – 4.30pm. Outside
these times: VAKA breakdown service,
tel. 567 67 00

*Information on the current state of
the roads*
Tel. 17 77 (daily 8am – 4pm) or at
www.vegagerdin.is

CAR RENTAL
ICELAND car rental
Blikavöllur 3
235 Keflavík Airport
Tel. 4 15 25 00
www.icelandcarrental.is

Avis
Knarrarvogur 2,104 Reykjavík
Tel. 5 91 40 00
www.avis.is

Budget Car Rental
Malarhöfði 2
110 Reykjavík
Tel. 567 83 00
www.budget.is

Hertz
Kevlavík Airport
Tel. 5 22 44 00
www.hertz.is

Rás Car Rental
Kevlavík Airport
Tel. 5 65 38 00
www.rascar.com

Visitors unfortunate enough to have accidents involving sheep or
horses have to pay compensation.

Foreign diesel vehicles no longer have to pay a fixed diesel tax. This   **Diesel tax**
has been added to the price per litre at the diesel fuel pump. Payment
is due when leaving the country; what counts is the amount of time
between the arrival of the ferry and the verifiable departure of the
boat according to the ticket. For further information, email the customs office (tollstjori@tollur.is) or go to www.tollur.is.

Car rental Hire cars can be rented from various Icelandic and international companies through travel agents, airlines, at airports and numerous other places. The choice ranges from small cars all the way to four-wheel drives. Prices however are significantly higher than most visitors might expect. A small car costs around €120 per day and around €600 per week. **Four-wheel drive vehicles** will set the budget back by on average €300 per day and €2000 per week. Booking a hire car together with the flight can get you significant discounts. The minimum driving age is 20, and for jeeps usually 23 to 25. The driving licence must have been held for one or two years, and a credit card is required for security. Highland tracks may only be attempted by jeep, which means that during high season it is a good idea to reserve four-wheel drives early.

Travellers with Disabilities

Good contact A useful contact is the **Sjálfsbjörg Disabled Association** (Hátúni 12, 105 Reykjavík, tel. 550 03 00, www.sjalfsbjorg.is). All airlines are geared up for wheelchair users, as are many hotels, restaurants and supermarkets. More problematic are older public buildings, scheduled buses and off-the-beaten-track destinations in the highlands. Bearers of the identity card for the disabled **Disabled Person** receive many discounts, for example, in admission fees.

When to Go

The Iceland low-pressure area The first thing many people think about when it comes to Icelandic weather is the Icelandic low-pressure area that brings Europe bad weather. These low-pressure areas can form all year round when, south of Greenland and near Iceland, the continental American **cold air mass meets the Gulf Stream**. Statistically it rains about every other day in Iceland; however, thanks to the fact that the wind is usually blowing these are often only showers, and they seldom turn into the kind of rain that carries on relentlessly for days. And another bit of good news: the months with least rain are the main travel months of May, June and July; only August can be a bit wetter. The south sees a fair bit more rain as the prevailing **southern and western winds** bring a lot of moisture from the sea, depositing it at the mountains and glaciers. Thus, the average precipitation on the southern coast registers as much as 3,000mm/118 inches per year, while the highlands north of the Vatnajökull only receive 400mm/16 inches annually. If the wind is coming from the north however, which is more unusual, it is probably raining in the northern part of the island.

The rule of thumb is: if the weather is good in the south, it will be raining in the north and vice versa.

Rule of thumb

The island location creates a mostly quite steady climate, at least in the coastal regions of Iceland. Winters are generally mild, with average temperatures around 0 °C/32°F in Reykjavík and around -2 °C/28°F in Akureyri. In summer, average temperatures hover around 10 °C/50°F, while daily highs of 20–25 °C/68–77°F in June, July and August are a definite possibility. In the highlands, temperatures in the winter sink far below zero and even in summer it is perceptibly colder than on the coast. At higher altitudes, snow may stay on the ground up to June, and snow showers may occur even in summer.

Water/air-temperatures

As a general rule, the weather changes faster and more violently than most visitors might be accustomed to. With longer tours in particular, always be prepared for bad weather and cold winds. Considering the northerly position of Iceland **near the Arctic Circle**, temperatures are very pleasant here thanks to the Gulf Stream, as this gigantic warm-water heating system provides much friendlier temperatures than in Siberia or Alaska, which lie on a comparable latitude. However, even the Gulf Stream doesn't manage to warm the sea to a bearable swimming temperature; even in the summer, don't expect anything much above 10 °C/50°F.

Change of weather: quicker and stronger

The best months for visiting are June, July and August, although June may still be problematic for crossing the highlands. During these three months all the tourist facilities are open, while for the rest of the year the choice is much more limited. The long days in summer allow more or less round-the-clock open-air activities. In September, the sheep being driven down from their mountain pastures and the resplendent autumn colours are two high points before the country goes into hibernation: ferries stop running, buses run far less frequently, the highland tracks are impassable, and even the ring road can be blocked at short notice.

Three months of high season

Outside the **main travelling months** generally only very few tourists come to Iceland, even though airlines and hotels advertise special offers.

Discounts

The low season offers the more independent traveller interesting options such as dog sleighing or ski tours. Even in summer, clothes should be able to withstand any kind of weather – including wind, rain and cold. Visitors should also bring a pair of sturdy walking shoes.

Tips for individualists travellers

Index

List of Maps and Illustrations

Photo Credits

Publisher's Information

2nd Edition 2019
Worldwide Distribution: Marco Polo Travel Publishing Ltd
Pinewood, Chineham Business Park
Crockford Lane, Chineham
Basingstoke, Hampshire RG24 8AL,
United Kingdom.

Photos, illlustrations, maps:
126 photos, 21 maps and and illustrations, one large map
Text:
Dr. Christian Nowak, Hans Klüche, Odin Hug, Andrea Mecke, Robert Fischer
Editing:
Kathleen Becker, Rainer Eisenschmid
Translation: Kathleen Becker, Barbara Schmidt-Runkel
Cartography:
Christoph Gallus, Hohberg; Franz Huber, Munich; MAIRDUMONT Ostfildern (city map)
3D illustrations:
jangled nerves, Stuttgart
Infographics:
Golden Section Graphics GmbH, Berlin
Design:
independent Medien-Design, Munich

Editor-in-chief:
Rainer Eisenschmid, Mairdumont Ostfildern

Printed in China

Despite all of our authors' thorough research, errors can creep in. The publishers do not accept any liability for thi Whether you want to praise, alert us to errors or give us a personal tip Please contact us by email or post:

MARCO POLO Travel Publishing Ltd
Pinewood, Chineham Business Park
Crockford Lane, Chineham
Basingstoke, Hampshire RG24 8AL
United Kingdom
Email: sales@marcopolouk.com

MIX
Paper from responsible sources
FSC
www.fsc.org
FSC® C124385

MARCO POLO

HANDBOOKS

ANDALUCÍA

BALI

BARCELONA

BERLIN

BUDAPEST

DRESDEN

DUBAI

FLORENCE

FLORIDA

GRAN CANARIA

ICELAND

IRELAND

LONDON

MADEIRA

NEW YORK

NEW ZEALAND

NORWAY

PARIS

PRAGUE

ROME

SRI LANKA

TUSCANY

VENICE

VIETNAM

www.marco-polo.com

Iceland Curiosities

Quite a few things in Iceland are different from other places. And some of it is pretty strange. Here is a small selection:

►Heated Sidewalks
Everywhere in Iceland there are heated swimming pools, hot springs, hot pots, water parks and even heated beaches where swimming is a pleasure all year round. That may not be special. But did you ever think that Reykjavík has heated sidewalks?

►Yes, we have bananas
Iceland's hot houses make the northernmost banana plantation in the world possible.

►More sheep than people
On the whole island there are more sheep than people. To be precise, in Iceland there are almost twice as many sheep as people.

►Literature records
Iceland has the largest per capita number of Nobel laureates for literature in the world: 1 for every 318,000 people!

►What's a penis doing in a museum?!
Since 2011 the Phallological Museum in Reykjavík has one from the species homo sapiens on exhibit.

►Free fallin'
On Heimaey Island birds fall from the sky in fall. How come? Puffins are excellent divers and swimmers but their wings are too short to fly with them. They young ones especially might take a fall then.

►The book of first names
For Icelanders first names are more important than last names. So the Icelandic last name is formed by adding –son to the father's first name for boys, and –dóttir to the father's first name for girls. Even in the telephone book Icelanders are listed by first names, which can make searching for someone a bit time- consuming.